Adobe®
Photoshop® 7.0

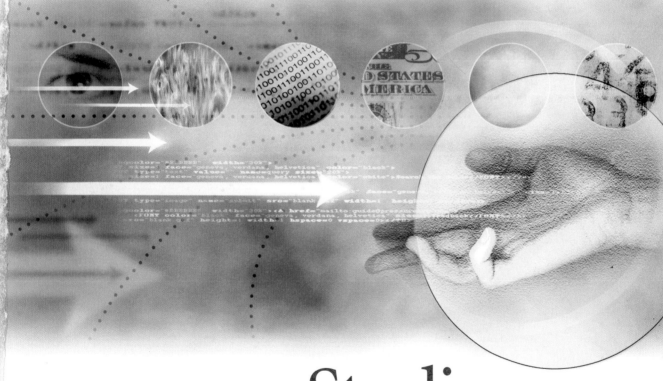

Studio
Techniques

Ben Willmore

Adobe Photoshop 7.0 Studio Techniques

Ben Willmore

Copyright © 2002 by Ben Willmore

This Adobe Press book is published by Peachpit Press. For information on Adobe Press books, contact:

Peachpit Press
1249 Eighth Street
Berkeley, CA 94710
(510) 524-2178
Fax: (510) 524-2221
http://www.peachpit.com

To report errors, please send a note to errata@peachpit.com
Peachpit Press is a division of Pearson Education

For the latest on Adobe Press books, go to http://www.adobe.com/adobepress

Editor: Serena Herr
Production Coordinator: Kate Reber
Contributing Editor: Regina Cleveland
Technical Editors: Victor Gavenda, Conrad Chavez
Copy Editor: Brenda Benner
Compositor: Maureen Forys, Happenstance Type-O-Rama
Indexer: Karin Arrigoni
Cover design: Mimi Heft
Cover illustration: Alicia Buelow

Notice of Rights

All rights reserved. No part of this book may be reproduced or transmitted in any form by any means, electronic, mechanical, photocopying, recording, or otherwise, without the prior written permission of the publisher. For information on getting permission for reprints and excerpts, contact permissions@peachpit.com.

Notice of Liability

The information in this book is distributed on an "As Is" basis, without warranty. While every precaution has been taken in the preparation of the book, neither the authors nor Peachpit Press shall have any liability to any person or entity with respect to any loss or damage caused or alleged to be caused directly or indirectly by the instructions contained in this book or by the computer software and hardware products described in it.

Trademarks

Throughout this book trademarked names are used. Rather than put a trademark symbol in every occurrence of a trademarked name, we state we are using the names only in an editorial fashion and to the benefit of the trademark owner with no intention of infringement of the trademark. Photoshop, Illustrator, GoLive, ImageReady, Acrobat, Streamline, and After Effects are all trademarks of Adobe Systems, Inc.

ISBN 0-321-11563-5

9 8 7 6 5 4 3 2

Printed and bound in the United States of America

Contents

Introduction   xi

Part I Working Foundations

Chapter 1   Tool and Palette Primer   3
 Preparing Your Workspace   4
 Working with Screen Modes   10
 A Quick Tour of the Tools   13
 Navigating Your Document   15
 Picking Colors   18
 Basic Editing Tools   26
 Closing Thoughts   52
 Ben's Techno-babble Decoder Ring   52
 Keyboard Shortcuts   54

Chapter 2   Selection Primer   57
 What Is a Selection?   58
 Basic Selection Tools   60
 Refining a Selection   72
 The Select Menu   74
 Quick Mask Mode   85
 Closing Thoughts   91
 Ben's Techno-babble Decoder Ring   91
 Keyboard Shortcuts   92

Chapter 3   Layers Primer   95
 How Do Layers Work?   96
 Meeting the Layers   97
 Leapin' Layers! More Tools and Toys   106
 Done Playing Around?   121
 Closing Thoughts   122
 Ben's Techno-babble Decoder Ring   123
 Keyboard Shortcuts   123

Part II Production Essentials

Chapter 4   Resolution Solutions   129
 Understanding Pixel Size   130
 Printing   131
 Closing Thoughts   147
 Ben's Techno-babble Decoder Ring   147

Chapter 5	Line Art Scanning	149
	Avoiding the Jaggies	152
	Straightening the Image	154
	Improving Definition	154
	Converting to Line Art	155
	Minimizing File Size	161
	Converting to Bitmap	161
	Closing Thoughts	162
	Ben's Techno-babble Decoder Ring	163

Chapter 6	Optimizing Grayscale Images	165
	Levels Is the Solution	167
	The Histogram Gives You Feedback	173
	Setting Up Your Images for Final Output	174
	A Quick Levels Recap	179
	Postadjustment Analysis	180
	Sharpening	182
	Closing Thoughts	185
	Ben's Techno-babble Decoder Ring	187
	Keyboard Shortcuts	187

Chapter 7	Understanding Curves	189
	With Power Comes Complexity	192
	Take Curves for a Test Drive	200
	Input and Output Numbers	211
	Closing Thoughts	215
	Ben's Techno-babble Decoder Ring	215
	Keyboard Shortcuts	216

Chapter 8	Color Management	217
	Implementing Color Management	223
	Color Management in Action	239
	Closing Thoughts	245
	Ben's Techno-babble Decoder Ring	246

Chapter 9	Color Correction	247
	Use Gray to Fix Color?!?	249
	Professional Color Correction	252
	Refine the Result	262
	Closing Thoughts	264
	Ben's Techno-babble Decoder Ring	264

Chapter 10	Channels	267
	Channels Are Worth the Pain!	268
	Three Varieties of Channels	270

Navigating the Channels Palette   272
Understanding Color Channels   273
Understanding Spot Channels   280
Understanding Alpha Channels   287
Use Extract to Select Complex Objects   295
Closing Thoughts   302
Ben's Techno-babble Decoder Ring   302
Keyboard Shortcuts   304

Part III Creative Explorations

Chapter 11 Shadows   309
How to Think About Shadows   310
Four Shadow Types   311
RGB Versus CMYK   325
Closing Thoughts   326
Keyboard Shortcuts   326

Chapter 12 Collage   327
Four Ways to Blend   328
Grouping Layers   332
Blending Sliders   336
Layer Masks   343
Vector Masks   359
Closing Thoughts   367
Keyboard Shortcuts   368

Chapter 13 Enhancement   373
The Battalion of Blending Modes   375
Liquify   413
Closing Thoughts   416
Ben's Techno-babble Decoder Ring   417
Keyboard Shortcuts   418

Chapter 14 Retouching   423
Patch Tool   425
Healing Brush Tool   428
Clone Stamp Tool   431
The Dodge and Burn Tools   440
The Sponge Tool   447
The Sharpen and Blur Tools   447
Closing Thoughts   450
Ben's Techno-babble Decoder Ring   451
Keyboard Shortcuts   451

Chapter 15 Type and Background Effects   455

No More Jaggy Text   456

Entering Text   457

Editing Text   458

Type Layers   470

Layer Styles   471

The Styles Palette   475

Backgrounds & Textures   476

Repeating Patterns   480

Closing Thoughts   485

Ben's Techno-babble Decoder Ring   485

Part IV Web Graphics

Chapter 16 Interface Design   489

Consistent Design Principles   491

Creating Interface Elements   500

Sophisticated Designs Start with Simple Shapes   506

Closing Thoughts   511

Ben's Techno-babble Decoder Ring   511

Chapter 17 Slicing and Rollovers   513

The Slice Tool   516

The Image Map Tools   523

Creating Rollovers   524

Saving Your Image with Slices   530

Closing Thoughts   531

Ben's Techno-babble Decoder Ring   531

Chapter 18 Animation   533

Simple Animations   535

Text Warping   538

Other Text Transformations   538

Rollover Animations   541

Closing Thoughts   541

Ben's Techno-babble Decoder Ring   541

Chapter 19 Optimization   543

JPEG Compression   544

GIF Compression   546

Optimize in Photoshop or ImageReady?   547

Closing Thoughts   560

Ben's Techno-babble Decoder Ring   561

Index   563

Dedication:

To my father, Nate (N8 for short), who taught me that technology doesn't always have to be complicated.

About the Author

Ben Willmore is the founder of Digital Mastery, a Boulder, Colorado-based training and consulting firm that specializes in electronic publishing. Ben has always been known to be a little nutty about all things technical, even as a child. Not long after he traded in his tricycle for training wheels, he started building cameras out of do-it-yourself kits. In 1981, at the tender age of 14, he made his official debut into computer nerd-dom when he attended CompuCamp. That's where he discovered his first two loves, computers and graphic design, and where he learned how to use a graphics tablet to produce art on an Apple][computer— three full years before the Macintosh said its first, "Hello."

Not surprisingly, he went on to become a graphic designer. In those days that meant knowing all about such primitive things as typesetting, keylining and stat cameras. When the first tools of electronic publishing started showing up, Ben began his trend as an aggressive early adopter of new technologies. While most people in the business were holding back in a wait-and-see attitude, Ben was charging ahead and embracing the new tools like long-lost friends. His first serious push into the new arena was when he converted his college's daily newspaper from traditional techniques to electronic tools in the late '80s.

Ben became known as someone who likes to push his tools to the limit, causing man y printing companies and service bureaus to ask "How'd you do that?" His obsession with the nuts and bolts of electronic publishing turned him into an unwitting one-man customer support center for all his friends and coworkers. It was this, he discovered that was his third love—helping others truly understand graphics software. And so he decided to go out on his own and teach his favorite program (Photoshop) full time.

In 1994, he created what has become the hugely successful seminar, Photoshop Mastery (aka Master Photoshop in 3 Days). Since then he has taught over 12,000 Photoshop users, and travels all over the country presenting his seminars and speaking at publishing events such as Photoshop World. He is an alpha and beta tester for Adobe Photoshop and writes a monthly column for *Photoshop User Magazine*. Ben can be reached at willmore@digitalmastery.com.

Much Obliged!

Even though my name appears on the cover of this book, as with all collaborative efforts, this would not have been possible without the help of the following people:

Regina "GNR's" Cleveland, the Queen here at Digital Mastery, who (as usual) burned gallons of midnight oil to help get this book out the door. To her credit she only had crabby outbursts only when I was truly difficult. She's recovered, but I'm still in the doghouse with her eight-year-old daughter, who thinks that Photoshop is part of the Evil Empire because it makes Mommy miss bedtime stories.

Marjorie Baer (executive editor), for making it through two books with me, and for not giving up on me when I extended a few deadlines.

Serena Herr, for being a cheerleader when I made my deadlines, and for using the velvet glove when I didn't.

Kate Reber and Maureen Forys, for being so focused and graceful under pressure, and for keeping track of the millions of bits and bytes of information that go into making a book.

Chris Murphy and Jeff Tranberry for helping out with the color management and animation chapters.

Chris Klimek, who is always ready to jump on an airplane at a moment's notice to help me out.

Conrad Chavez, for his ability to pick up the pieces at the last moment, and for going through the technical content with a fine-tooth comb, and splitting hairs when necessary.

Susan Walton, for putting her trust in me when I was a first-time author.

Matt Wagner and Vivian Glyck, for helping make my writing more rewarding.

Jay Nelson, who has helped me in more ways than I can imagine or remember. He's an amazing guy who always comes through in a pinch, and seems to be most happy whenever he's lending someone a hand.

Jerry Kennelly at Stockbyte and Stephanie Robey at PhotoSpin, whose generous contributions of stock imagery made it possible for us to include a bunch of great practice images on the CD at the back of the book.

Andy Katz, for keeping things lively with his maniacal laugh, and for his stunning imagery.

My brother Nik, who was always at the ready with as much constructive criticism as I could handle, when others would simply say "Oh, that's nice."

Scott Kelby, Jim Workman, and the rest of the gang at NAPP (National Association of Photoshop Professionals), who have made my life as a Photoshop hack more enjoyable than I thought possible.

To all the gifted artists and organizations who contributed images to this book. Your illuminating work transformed our bare pages into things of elegance, sparkle, and humor.

Don Barnett	Chris Klimek
Howard Berman	Andy Katz
David Bishop	Nick Koudis
Robert Bowen	Gregg Lauer
Steve Bronstein	Kear/Stevens Creative
Alicia Buelow	Gregg Lauer
Skip Caplan	Mercedes- Benz USA
Jimmy Chen	Plamen Petkov
Tom Nick Cocotos	James Rothwell
Jim DiVitale	Michael Slack
Factmonster.com	Bronson Smith
Diane Fenster	Sony Electronics Inc.
Andy Katz	Gordon Studer
Lewis Kemper	Sony Electronics, Inc.

And finally, I thank all the people who have attended my seminars over the past eight years. You've given me a limitless supply of inspiration and feedback and have allowed me to follow my passion for knowledge and understanding.

Foreword

Learning to use Adobe Photoshop is similar to learning to play an electric guitar; with a little instruction and a little practice, you can create some very pleasant art. Or, if you're really motivated, you can lock yourself in a closet with it for 12 years and emerge playing some amazing "chops." Most of us fall somewhere in between, and all of us have more to learn.

But the thing is, while few people are frightened by a guitar, many people find Photoshop intimidating. That's what is so great about Ben Willmore, the author of this book: he takes away your fear.

For the past several years, Ben has traveled across the United States, presenting his unique Photoshop seminar. Unique, because it focuses on real-world jobs done every day by Photoshop users, and unique because Ben explains concepts and techniques in a way that everyone in the room can understand. Ben's examples are based on his professional production experience, so everything he teaches helps you create images that successfully reproduce on paper or the web.

I attended his seminar and was especially impressed by his ability to avoid technical jargon, and by his uncanny knack for answering questions before they're asked. Ben is a rare teacher; even advanced users are satisfied, and rank beginners never feel lost. Like all great teachers, Ben uses metaphors, relating new ideas to concepts you're already comfortable with. In the pages of this book, you'll see Photoshop's most esoteric concepts clearly explained, while its major features are masterfully positioned into a framework of "how do I accomplish the task at hand?"

We each have different uses for Photoshop, and we each have different ways of learning. Fortunately for our increasingly overtaxed brains, less than half of Photoshop's features are used to accomplish most real-world tasks. And more fortunately for us, Ben Willmore has written this book.

Enjoy the time you share with Ben and Photoshop. I'm sure you'll find it a rare pleasure.

—Jay J. Nelson
Editor
Design Tools Monthly
www.design-tools.com

I
Introduction

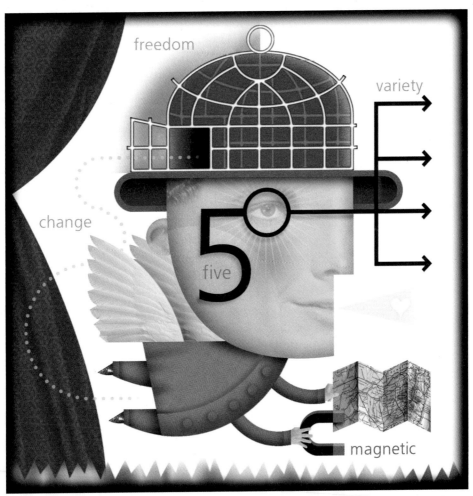

Courtesy of Gordon Studer, www.gordonstuder.com

Introduction

Ben Willmore, founder, Digital Mastery

*My mission is to help you graduate from 'I'm just going through the motions,' to 'At last, I **really** understand Photoshop.'*

Why *This* Book?

Well, I asked the same question when I set out on this project. I found myself at Barnes & Noble staring at a daunting abundance of Photoshop books, and I discovered that there were more special-effect "cookbooks" and technical tomes than I'd ever care to read. The problem was that none of the "cookbooks" gave enough detail to really let me feel like I understood the program (I just blindly followed the listed steps), and all of the technical books seemed to want to turn me into a slide rule–toting nerd (talking about terms like rasters, vectors, and bit-depth settings). That's when I decided that there was a void just begging to be filled. And that void is the primary reason that most people aren't truly comfortable with Photoshop. They either got the 1, 2, 3 steps (but no real understanding), or they got so many technical terms that it made Photoshop impossible to grasp.

So how is this book different? My approach is to use the same language that you use in everyday life to explain everything from the simplest feature to the most advanced techniques. I acquired this approach as a result of teaching tens of thousands of people in hundreds of seminars and hands-on workshops. I'll still provide a fair share of step-by-step techniques, and we will delve into some rather advanced features, but through it all I'll use metaphors and stories that will make everything easy to understand and digest. Because often the difference between a confident Photoshop master and a struggling amateur is how much they truly understand the way Photoshop works behind the scenes.

With that in mind, my mission is to help you graduate from "I'm just going through the motions" to "At last,

I *really* understand Photoshop." Once you've made that leap, you will experience an incredible ripple effect. Your efficiency will skyrocket. Your costs will go down. Your creative genius will come out of the closet like gang-busters, and your clients (or boss) will be thrilled. But what's most important to me is that through learning how to master Photoshop, you'll find the passion and energy that come from knowing you're really good at something.

Will I Understand It?

First and foremost, I hate technical mumbo jumbo! If words like raster, gamma, absolute colorimetric, bitmapped, clipping paths, algorithms, dither, and anti-aliasing drive you crazy, you better believe that they drive me even crazier. I see no reason that those terms can't be done away with and be replaced by plain English. I'll do whatever it takes to communicate a concept to you, with-out relying on ten-syllable words or terms that sound like they came from the inside of an engineer's head. And for those of you who have to deal with those technicians, you'll learn how to translate their techno-babble into English in my "Techno-babble Decoder Ring" at the end of most chapters.

Does It Start at My Level?

In terms of skill level, this book is written in such a way that if you are generally comfortable with your computer, you should be able to fully comprehend the information, no matter how advanced the topic. I've made the assump-tion that you've either installed Photoshop or that you're using the *Photoshop User Guide* to figure out how to do that. (There's no reason to duplicate that kind of information here.) And if you're an advanced user, don't worry. Just because the book is very understandable doesn't mean that we won't get into the real meat of Photoshop.

Mac or Windows?

From a functionality standpoint, Photoshop is pretty close to identical on Mac and Windows platforms. Anything you can do on one platform, you can do on the other. But those darn keyboards are different. You can put your worries aside, because *both* Mac and Windows keyboard commands are integrated right into the text. Because I'd get dizzy if I had to switch between the two for every screen shot, I just picked one platform and ran with it. And I just happened to choose Mac OS X.

What's on the CD?

To make it as easy as possible for you to follow along with my examples, I've provided a boatload of practice images for you to play with. You'll find these on the shiny disc that is hiding inside the back cover, in a folder called Practice Images. You'll find even more images to play with in a folder called Stockbyte. Stockbyte was kind enough to provide many of the images provided in this book, and if you haven't seen their stuff before, it is definitely worth a look.

What About the Web Site?

It's really hard for me to call this book done and send it off to press because once I've finished writing, I feel like I'm struck mute until the next version of Photoshop ships. Well, I've found a way to keep the dialogue going. Every day that I play with Photoshop, I come up with new ideas, and rather than hold those ideas back, I thought it would be great to share them with you through a companion Web site at www.digitalmastery.com/companionsite. There's no password needed and you'll find all this for free! Go ahead and visit the companion Web site, where you will find hundreds of free tips, my magazine article archives, and a bunch of other resources.

Then I'm sure you'll have a few questions while you read the book, so don't be afraid to send them my way at questions@digitalmastery.com. I read every one of them, but there aren't enough hours in the day to answer each person individually. But each week, I pick about a dozen readers' questions and answer them as part of my free Photoshop Questions of the Week. You can sign up for this service at www.digitalmastery.com/questions.

I also bet you'll also end up with a few problem images where a simple question can't accurately describe the problem. Well, that's when you might want to consider sending it to me at problems@digitalmastery.com (please keep images under 200 Kbytes and include a description of the problem). This is the emergency room for disaster images where I put on my surgical mask and tackle the image problems I feel will benefit my readers. The solutions come through future magazine articles and tutorials on my Web site.

Also, if you'd like to get some new ideas each week, sign up for my free Photoshop Tip of the Week by pointing your browser to www.digitalmastery.com/tips. I'll send you 6–12 tips every Monday morning.

Finally, if you'd like to get beyond the pages of this book and the free resources of the companion site, be sure to check out my seminars, videos, and other products at www.digitalmastery.com.

Where Can I Find the New Stuff?

If you've owned a previous edition of this book or just want to jump right into the new features of Photoshop 7.0, this is the place to start. Instead of wading through the whole book, looking for what's new, I've compiled a mini guide to what's new and improved both in this revision to my book and in Photoshop 7.0 in general.

Chapter 1 Tool and Palette Primer

Workspace Presets let you automate different palette layouts for different tasks. (Page 9)

The completely revamped Brushes and Brushes Presets palettes have dozens of new options that were nowhere to be found in previous versions, including new tip shapes, scattering, shape dynamic, texture, and color options. And while you're in this chapter, check out the nifty new dual-tip brush. (Page 31)

New Tool Presets let you customize your tools to your specific needs. (Page 48)

You'll love the awesome new File Browser, which introduces a whole new level of versatility when it comes to managing your files in Photoshop. (Page 49)

Chapter 3 Layers Primer

The new Delete Hidden Layers and Delete Linked Layers commands make working in the Layers palette easier than ever. (Page 121)

Chapter 4 Resolution Solutions

The concepts behind resolution have not changed in Photoshop 7.0, but resolution is such a critical issue that I've completely rewritten this chapter in an attempt to make it easier for you to understand.

Chapter 7 Understanding Curves

Newly developed techniques in this chapter show you how to work in Lab mode to prevent color shifts (Page 203) and how to use a histogram to help determine which areas of an image can be safely adjusted with Curves (Page 207).

Chapter 8 Color Management

Most books seem to make the process of achieving consistent color among scanner, monitor, and printer harder than Chinese calculus. Well, I don't think color management has to be that difficult. In this new chapter, I'll walk you through what's needed to get accurate color and help you to understand the process while bringing things down to a level anyone understand.

Chapter 9 Color Correction

This chapter was revised to make the entire process of professional color correction much easier and includes the new Auto Color feature, which attempts to automate the process. (Page 258)

Chapter 10 Channels

Learn how to master the Edge Cleanup and Smart Highlighting options in the Extract command. (Page 300)

Chapter 13 Enhancement

Say "Hi" to the newest blending modes on the block: Vivid Light, Pin Light, Linear Light, Linear Burn, and Linear Dodge. (Pages 385, 391, 394–396, and 398)

I've also included dozens of new techniques and ideas for using the existing blending modes.

The new Turbulence tool in the Liquify dialog box creates a truly ghoulish effect that should serve you well at Halloween. Also added to the Liquify dialog box are the much needed zoom in and zoom out icons. (Page 413)

Chapter 14 Retouching

Open your arms to welcome the new Patch and Healing Brush tools—which just might be the answer to your retouching prayers. (Page 425)

Chapter 15 Type and Background

Can you spell "Hallelujah"? Photoshop fiinally has a spelling checker and a find-and-replace feature. For those of us who are spelling impaired, these new additions wiil be a lifesaver. (Page 469)

Photoshop's Character palette has a number of improvements that make it more versatile and easy to use.

I've completely rewritten the chapter to include all new type effect and background texture techniques.

Photoshop's new Pattern Maker lets you create a repeating image based on the current image.

Chapter 17 Slices and Rollovers

I'll show you the completely revamped Rollovers palette, the new Selected State feature, the new Hide Auto Slices button and the Propagate Frame 1 Changes option.

Chapter 18 Animation

Get my new techniques on how to create animations that get around the limitations of tweening, filters, and the Liquify command.

Chapter 19 Optimization

The new dithered transparency feature is great for soft-edged shadows that will be placed over multicolored backgrounds on a Web page. (Page 555)

Have you ever sliced an image and wondered why you ended up with such a jumble of new files? I'll explain why slicing creates new files and exactly what you can expect after optimizing a sliced image. (Page 560)

Are You Ready to Get Started?

So, enough blabbing, let's get on with your personal Photoshop "transformation." I'll make it as easy on you as I possibly can, but just remember the words of my favorite character, Miracle Max, from the movie *The Princess Bride:* "You rush a miracle, man, you get rotten miracles."

PART I

Working Foundations

Courtesy of Gregg Lauer, www.gregglauer.com

1

Tool and Palette Primer

©Don Barnett, Nekton Inc., www.donbarnett.com

Out of clutter, find simplicity.

–Albert Einstein

NEW IN 7

We'll explore Photoshop 7.0's awesome new Brushes, palettes, Workspace, and Tool Presets as well as the File Browser.

Tool and Palette Primer

Opening Photoshop for the first time and seeing all the tools and palettes competing for space on your screen can be a dizzying experience. You might find yourself thinking, "That's great, but they forgot to leave room in there for me to work!" Some of the more fortunate Photoshoppers get to have a second monitor, just to hold all their palettes. The rest of us make do and find ways to keep our screens neat and tidy. You'll discover that finding places to put your tools and palettes is almost as important as knowing how to use them. This chapter is all about effectively managing your workspace and getting acquainted with the oodles of gadgets and gizmos found in the tools and palettes.

Preparing Your Workspace

Before we get into functionality, we'll talk about how to control the prodigious profusion of palettes. But first, a word of advice: No matter how many times you feel like nuking a palette when it's in your way, no matter how many times your screen turns into a blinding jumble of annoying little boxes, just remember that you can organize the clutter into an elegant arrangement in just a few seconds.

Controlling Those Palettes

The first order of business is to get you enough space to work effectively with your images. We'll accomplish this by organizing the palettes so that they don't obstruct your view of your document. I don't think you'll like the default position of the palettes—that is, unless you use a 36-inch screen. The palettes take up too much valuable screen real estate (**Figure 1.1**).

Collapsing the Palettes

One way to maximize your workspace is to collapse the palettes when you're not using them and move them to the bottom of your screen. To collapse a palette, double-click any of the name tabs at the top of the palette. To reposition a palette, click the little gray bar at the top of the palette and then drag it toward the bottom of your screen. When you move a palette close to the bottom of the screen, it should snap into place (**Figure 1.2**).

NOTES

To force a palette to snap to the edge of your screen, press the Shift key as you reposition the palette.

Figure 1.1 Photoshop's palettes take up a large portion of the screen. (multiple images © 2002 Stockbyte, www.stockbyte.com)

Figure 1.2 Stowing palettes at the bottom of the screen.

NOTES

If you click on the Zoom tool and then turn on the Ignore Palettes button in the Options bar, Photoshop will ignore your palettes whether or not they're close to the right edge of your screen.

One thing you need to make sure of when repositioning your palettes is that you don't place any palettes too close to the right edge of your screen. This edge, affectionately known as palette alley, can cause you great pains when you zoom in on your images (**Figure 1.3**). Here's why: If you have a palette too close to the right edge of your screen and you press Command-+ (Macintosh) or Ctrl-+ (Windows), Photoshop can't resize the document window to the width of your screen. Instead, it leaves palette alley open and doesn't allow the document window to intrude into this space. This means your efforts to reposition the palettes in order to save space were futile.

If you need access to any of these palettes, double-click the palette's name tab and the palette will instantly pop open (**Figure 1.4**). When you're done using the palette, just double-click its name tab to collapse it again.

If you turn off the Save Palette Locations checkbox in the File > Preferences > General dialog box, each time you launch Photoshop, the palettes will be at their default locations.

Regrouping the Palettes

Another way to maximize your screen real estate is to change the way your palettes are grouped. For example, if your most frequently used palettes are the Color and

Figure 1.3 Palette alley stays clear whenever a palette is close to the right edge of your screen.

History palettes, you can put them in one group so that you have one palette open at any given time instead of two. To regroup the palettes, drag the name tab of the palette you want to move (in this case, Color) on top of the palette grouping you want to move the palette into (in this case, History). You can then remove any palettes you don't want in this grouping by dragging the name tab of that palette onto an open area of the screen (**Figure 1.5**).

NOTES

If you really mess things up and your screen gets to looking like an Escher print, you can easily set all the palettes back to their default locations. To do this, choose Window > Workspace > Reset Palette Locations.

Figure 1.4 To collapse or expand a palette, double-click the name tab.

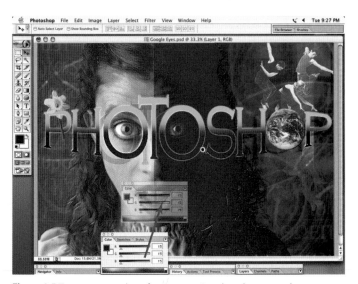

Figure 1.5 To separate a palette from a grouping, drag the name tab to an open area of your screen.

If a gray surround isn't your taste, just change the foreground color and then grab the Paint Bucket tool and Shift-click in the gray area to change it. Not too many people know this trick, so you can use it to mess with your coworkers' minds. Just set the color to an irritating color such as fluorescent green.

The Palette Well

If you have a screen that can display more than 800 pixels in its width, then you'll have another special place to store your palettes—the Palette well. If you look in the Options bar at the top of your screen, you should notice a dark gray area on the far right. That's a special spot where you can drag the name of a few palettes to store them until they're needed. Then, when you'd like to have access to one of those palettes, just click on the name of the palette, and it will drop down from the Palette well (**Figure 1.6**). After you're done using a palette, just click anywhere outside of the palette and it should collapse itself back into the Palette well.

Figure 1.6 To temporarily expand a palette, click on the name of a palette in the Palette well.

Stacking Palettes

You can stack palettes one on top of another, and if you move the top palette (by dragging the gray bar at the top of the palette), the palettes that are stacked will move together. To stack two palettes, drag the name tab of one palette to the middle of another palette and then drag down until you see a black rectangle appear across the bottom of the palette you are dragging onto. You can drag to the top or bottom of a palette depending on how you'd like the palettes to be stacked. I like to stack the Character and Paragraph palettes together so I can keep all the type settings in one convenient area (**Figure 1.7**). After you have two palettes stacked together, you can drag other palettes into the grouping so that the top palette might be a group of three and the bottom a single palette.

If, after moving and regrouping your palettes, you find that a palette appears to be missing, don't panic. You can always find it in the Window menu. This menu lists all the palettes that are available (**Figure 1.8**).

Workspace Presets

You might find that different palette layouts work better for different tasks. For instance, when retouching an image, you might find that you like to have the Brushes palette extend all the way down the right side of your screen and have most of the other palettes hidden away. Later, when you start to paint, you might prefer to have the Color, Swatches and Brushes palettes along the right side of your screen. Well, this is just fine in Photoshop 7, which allows you to save workspace presets that will remember exactly

NOTES

You can also move a palette into the palette well by choosing Dock to Palette Well from the side menu of the palette.

Figure 1.8 The Window menu

Figure 1.7 You can stack two palettes by dragging the name of one palette to the top or bottom of another.

Figure 1.9 The Window > Workspace menu.

where all your palettes were at the time you saved the preset. To save a preset, choose Window > Workspace > Save Workspace. Then to switch between different saved workspaces, just choose the name of the workspace you desire from the bottom of the Window > Workspace menu (**Figure 1.9**). This feature is great for people who have to share a computer with others because each user can have a different arrangement of palettes saved as a workspace and different users can quickly swap between those workspaces.

Working with Screen Modes

Even with the palettes conveniently stowed at the bottom of your screen, your image still doesn't use all of the screen space available. You can use the three screen mode icons at the bottom of the Tools palette to easily solve this problem.

Standard Screen Mode

The first icon, Standard Screen Mode, is the default mode (**Figure 1.10**). You're probably used to working with this one. In this mode, the name of your document is at the top of the document window, and the scroll bars are on the side and bottom of that window.

Figure 1.10 The first screen mode is Photoshop's default.

Full Screen Mode with Menu Bar

The second icon, Full Screen Mode With Menu Bar, lets the image flow all the way across your screen and slip right under the palettes (**Figure 1.11**). If you click this icon, the scroll bars will disappear, so you'll have to use the Hand tool to navigate around your document. But that's okay, because you can hold down the spacebar at any time to temporarily use the Hand tool. If you zoom out of a document so that it doesn't take up the entire screen, Photoshop will fill the area around the image with gray.

Figure 1.11 The second screen mode allows you to use the entire screen.

Full Screen Mode

The third screen mode icon, Full Screen Mode, is my favorite. In this mode, Photoshop turns off even the menu bar! Now your image can take over the entire screen (**Figure 1.12**). You can still use many of the menu commands, as long as you know their keyboard equivalents. If you zoom out while in this mode, Photoshop will fill the area around your image with black (I don't know how to change that one). I use this mode whenever I show images to clients. If you don't let them know you're in Photoshop, they might think you are in a cheap little slide-show program, and won't ask you to make changes on the spot.

NOTES

When using Full Screen mode, you can type Shift-F to toggle the menu bar on and off.

To temporarily use the Zoom tool—that is, to use the Zoom tool without deselecting the active tool—hold down Command-space-bar (Macintosh) or Ctrl-spacebar (Windows).

However, you won't be able to fool anyone if all those palettes are still on your screen. Just press Tab and they'll all disappear (**Figure 1.13**). Don't worry, you can get them back just as quickly by pressing Tab again.

Figure 1.12 The third screen mode uses the full screen and removes the menu bar.

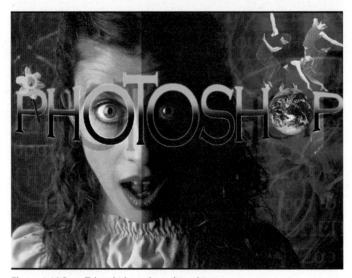

Figure 1.13 Press Tab to hide or show the palettes.

Screen Mode Shortcuts

I use the different screen modes every single day, but it's not very often that I actually click those three little toolbox icons. Instead, I use keyboard commands. Just press the F key on your keyboard to cycle through the different screen modes. You can even type F-F-Tab while an image is opening; that way, when it's done loading, Photoshop will switch to the third screen mode and rid your screen of all the palettes!

Now that you have your screen under control, we can start to explore some of the tools and palettes.

A Quick Tour of the Tools

There are more than 40 tools available in the Tools palette. Describing all of them in detail would take up a huge chunk of this chapter (which you probably don't have the patience for), so for now we'll take a look at the ones that you absolutely can't live without. Don't worry about missing out on anything—as you work your way through the book, you'll get acquainted with the rest of the tools. In the meantime, I'll introduce you to some tool names so that when I mention one, you'll know what to look for (**Figures 1.14** and **1.15**).

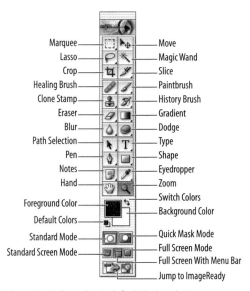

Figure 1.14 Photoshop's default Tools palette.

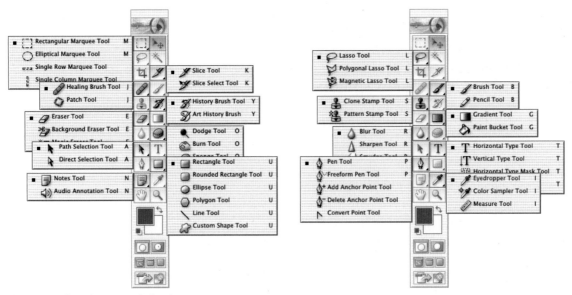

Figure 1.15 Photoshop's arsenal of tools.

The Options Bar

Most of the tools have settings associated with them. To access these settings, take a peek at the Options bar that extends across the top of your screen.

You'll be able to change the various settings more quickly if you know exactly how to navigate the Options bar. For example, each of the painting and retouching tools has a percentage setting near the right side of the bar. There are quite a few ways to change this number. One is to highlight the number and then type a new one. You can also click the number and then use the up arrow and down arrow keys on your keyboard (hold down the Shift key to change the number by increments of 10). You can also click the arrow to the right of the number and drag across the slider that appears. All of these options will work with any numeric entry in a palette (not just the Options bar), but there is a special method for changing the percentage setting for your painting tools. If none of the text fields in the Options bar is active for editing, then you can just type a number (not in a field, just type). If you type 1, you'll end up with 10 percent, 23 will give you 23 percent, 0 will give you 100 percent, and so forth.

If there's more than one setting that lets you enter a number, press Return or Enter to highlight the first one, then tab your way through the others. Once a number is highlighted, you can change it by pressing the up arrow and down arrow keys or by typing a new number.

Navigating Your Document

Most of us struggle with monitors that are not large enough to view an entire document (except, of course, the more privileged Photoshoppers who have monitors that are practically as large as drive-in movie screens). To deal with this ever-present limitation, you must train yourself to be a quick and nimble navigator. Photoshop offers you a huge array of choices, and, as usual, you'll need to weed through them to find your favorite method. In this section, we'll cover the palettes and tools you need to maximize the speed with which you get around your document.

The Navigator Palette

If you do a lot of detail work where you need to zoom in on your image as if you're wearing glasses as thick as Coke bottles, you should love the Navigator palette (**Figure 1.16**). The Navigator palette floats above your document and allows you to quickly move around and zoom in and out of your image. A little red box indicates which area of the image you're currently viewing. By dragging this box around the miniature image of your document that appears in the Navigator palette, you can change which area you're viewing in the main image window. You can also just click outside the red box and the box will center itself on your cursor.

Figure 1.16 The Navigator palette.

There are a number of ways to zoom in on your document by using this palette. Use the mountain icons to zoom in or out at preset increments (50%, 66.67%, 100%, 200%, and so on), or grab the slider between them to zoom to any level. You can change the number in the lower-left corner of the palette to zoom to an exact percentage. However, my favorite method is to drag across the image while holding down the Command key (Macintosh), or the Ctrl key (Windows), to zoom into a specific area.

NOTES

If you don't like the color of the little red box, or if there's so much red in your image that the box becomes difficult to see, you can change the box color by choosing Palette Options from the side menu of the palette.

Hand Tool

The Hand tool is definitely the most basic tool in Photoshop. By clicking and dragging with the Hand tool, you can scroll around the image. This tool is—excuse the pun—handy for scrolling around images that are too large to fit on your screen and for moving without the scroll bars. Since this tool is used so often, Adobe created a special way to get to it. While working with most of Photoshop's tools, if you press the spacebar, you will temporarily activate the Hand tool. When you release the spacebar, you'll be back to the tool you were using previously.

Zoom Tool

Whenever you click on your image by using the Zoom tool, you zoom in on the image to a preset level (just like the mountain icons in the Navigator palette). I almost never use the tool in this way because it takes too long to get where I want to be. Instead, I usually click and drag across the area I want to enlarge, and Photoshop immediately zooms me into that specific area.

In addition to zooming in, you also have options for quickly zooming out. Double-click the Hand tool icon in the Tools palette to fit the entire image on screen. You can also double-click the Zoom tool icon in the Tools palette to view your image at 100% magnification. (This will show you how large your image will appear when viewed in a Web browser or in any program designed for multimedia. It is not an indication of how large it will be when printed.) Option-clicking (Macintosh) or Alt-clicking (Windows) with the Zoom tool zooms you out at preset levels. Clicking on Photoshop 7.0's new Zoom Out icon in the Options bar (**Figure 1.17**) will allow you to zoom out without having to hold a key on your keyboard. When the Zoom Out icon is chosen, holding down Option (Mac) or Alt (Windows) will cause you to zoom in on the image.

Figure 1.17 Photoshop 7.0's new zoom in and zoom out icons.

View Menu

If you're going to be doing a bunch of detail work in which you need to zoom in really close on your image, you might want to create two views of the same document

(**Figures 1.18** and **1.19**). That way, you can have one of the views at 100% magnification to give you an overall view of your image, and you can set the second one to 500% magnification, for instance, to see all the fine details. To create a second view, choose View > New View. This will create a second window that looks like a separate document, but it's really just another view of the same document. You can make your edits in either window and both of them will show you the result of your manipulations.

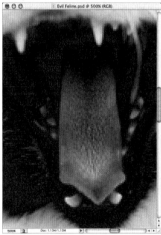

Figure 1.18 100% magnification.
(© 2002 Stockbyte, www.stockbyte.com)

Figure 1.19 500% magnification.

From the View menu, you can also select from the Zoom In, Zoom Out, Fit On Screen, and Actual Pixels options. As you'll probably notice, each of these actions can also be accomplished by using the Zoom and Hand tools. The reason they're also listed under the View menu is to allow you to quickly use them with keyboard commands. Here are the View menu options:

▶ **Zoom In/Zoom Out**—Same as clicking with the Zoom tool. Uses the easy-to-remember keyboard shortcut Command-+ (Macintosh) or Ctrl-+ (Windows) to zoom in and Command-– (Macintosh) or Ctrl-– (Windows) to zoom out. Those are plus signs and minus signs, in case that's not completely clear.

NOTES

The Print Size option rarely reflects how large your image will print. It assumes that your screen is using pixels that are .014 inches square (or 72 ppi). When the Mac was released back in 1984, it had a built-in screen that used pixels of that size. Now, there are so many kinds of monitors that there is no standard. If you really want to see how large an image will print, choose View > Show Rulers. You can set the ruler measurement system (inches, points, picas) by choosing Edit > Preferences > Units & Rulers. The keyboard command to show the rulers is Command-R (Macintosh) or Ctrl-R (Windows); to hide the rulers press the same shortcut again. Then choose View > Print Size and hold a real ruler up to your screen to see how far off it is from reality.

▶ **Fit On Screen**—Same as double-clicking the Hand tool. Uses the shortcut Command-0 (Macintosh) or Ctrl-0 (Windows). That's a zero, not the letter O.

▶ **Actual Pixels**—Same as double-clicking the Zoom tool. Uses the shortcut Option-Command-0 (Macintosh) or Alt-Ctrl-0 (Windows). Again, that's zero, not the letter O.

▶ **Print Size**—Allows you to preview how large or small your image will appear when it's printed.

Just when you thought there couldn't possibly be any more ways to zoom in and out of your document, Adobe threw in just one more method for good measure. You can change the percentage that appears in the lower-left corner of your document window; just drag across it and enter a new percentage.

There are indeed many ways to zoom around in Photoshop. Now all you have to do is test out all the options, decide which one you prefer, and ignore the rest.

Picking Colors

My father's Webster's dictionary—a 1940 model that's over half a foot thick—devoted four entire pages to describing one word: *color*. These pages are filled with lush descriptions of hue, tint, shade, saturation, vividness, brilliance, and much, much more. It's no wonder that choosing colors can be such a formidable task. Do you want Cobalt Blue or Persian Blue? Nile Green or Emerald? Carmine or Vermilion? Fortunately, Photoshop has done an excellent job of providing the tools you need to find the colors you want. Of course, each tool has advantages and disadvantages. You just have to play around with them and decide which one you prefer.

Foreground and Background Colors

The two square overlapping boxes that appear toward the bottom of your Tools palette are the foreground and background colors (**Figure 1.20**). The top box is the foreground color; it determines which color will be used when you use any of the painting tools. To change the foreground

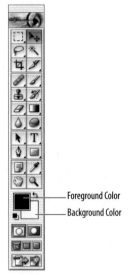

Foreground Color

Background Color

Figure 1.20 Foreground and background colors.

color, click it once (this will bring up a standard Color Picker). The bottom box is the background color; it's used when you're erasing the background image or when you increase the size of your document by using Image > Canvas Size. When you use the Gradient tool with default settings, your gradient will start with the foreground color and end with the background color. You can swap the foreground and background colors by clicking the small curved arrows next to them in the Tools palette. You can also reset the colors to their default settings (black/white) by clicking the small squares in the lower-left corner of that same area.

Color Picker Dialog Box

The Color Picker dialog box is available in many areas of Photoshop. The easiest way to get to it is to click your foreground or background color. There are many choices in this dialog box because there are many different ways to define a color. In this section, we'll cover all the various ways you can choose a color. I'll start off by showing you how to preview the color you're selecting.

Previewing a Color

While you're choosing a color, you can glance at the two color swatches to the right of the vertical gradient to compare the color you've chosen (the top swatch) to the color you had previously (the bottom swatch).

Be sure to watch for the out-of-gamut warning, which is indicated by a small triangle that appears next to these color swatches (**Figure 1.21**). This triangle warns you that the color you have chosen is not reproducible in CMYK mode, which means that it cannot be printed without shifting to a slightly different color. Fortunately, Photoshop provides you with a preview of what the color would have to shift to in order to be printable. You can find this preview in the small color swatch that appears directly below the triangle icon, and you can select this printable color by clicking the color swatch. Or, you can have Photoshop show you what all the colors would look like when printed by choosing View > Proof Colors while the Color Picker

NOTES

CMYK colors are meant to be printed (which involves ink), whereas RGB colors (which involve light) are meant for multimedia. Due to impurities in CMYK inks, you can't accurately reproduce every color you see on your screen.

Figure 1.21 The warning triangle indicates a color that is not reproducible in CMYK mode. The cube symbol indicates that a color is not a Web-safe color and might appear dithered in a Web browser.

The Proof Colors command is only accurate when you have the proper settings specified in the View > Proof Setup menu.

If your method for picking white is to drag to the upper-left corner of the color field, be sure to drag beyond the edge of the square; otherwise, you might not end up with a true white. Instead, you'll get a muddy-looking white or a light shade of gray.

dialog box is open. That will change the look of every color that appears in the picker, but you will still have to click that little triangle symbol, because that's just a preview—it doesn't actually change the colors you're choosing.

Choosing Web-safe Colors

In Part Four of this book, you'll learn all about Web graphics, but for now, let's take a look at just one Web-related feature in the Color Picker dialog box. There is a set of special colors, known as Web-safe colors, that are used for large areas of solid color. By using a Web-safe color, you will prevent those areas from becoming dithered (that is, simulated by using a pattern of two solid colors; for example, adding a pattern of red dots to a yellow area to create orange). So, if you are choosing a color that will be used in a large area on a Web page, look for the Color Cube symbol (**Figure 1.21**). Web-safe colors are also known as colors that are within the color cube—that's why Adobe used a cube symbol for this feature. When you click the cube symbol, the color you have chosen will shift a little to become a Web-safe color.

Selecting with the Color Field

Usually, the simplest method for choosing a color is to eyeball it. In the Color Picker dialog box, you can click in the vertical gradient to select the general color you want to use. Then click and drag around the large square area at the left to choose a shade of that color.

Selecting by Hue, Saturation, and Brightness

You can also change what appears in the vertical gradient by clicking any of the radio buttons on the right side of the dialog box (**Figures 1.22** to **1.24**). In this dialog box, H = Hue, S = Saturation, and B = Brightness. You can use the numbers at the right of the dialog box to describe the color you've chosen. (This can be a big help when you're describing a color to someone on the phone). So, if you know the exact color you need, just type its exact numbers into that area.

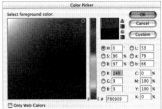

Figure 1.22 Hue.

Figure 1.23 Saturation.

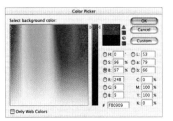

Figure 1.24 Brightness.

Selecting Custom Colors

If you want to pick your colors from a swatch book (PAN-TONE, TruMatch, and so on), click the Custom button. This will bring up the Custom Color Picker (**Figure 1.25**). Choose the swatch book you want to use from the pop-up menu at the top of the dialog box, then scroll through the list to find the color you desire. You can also type in numbers to select a specific color (I know, there isn't the usual text field to enter them in, but just start typing), but make sure you type really fast. I'm not sure why it works this way, but this part of Photoshop gets impatient with slow typists. For example, if you slowly type the number 356, Photoshop might jump to a color number starting with 3 and then go to one that starts with 5. This is sort of annoying, but it shouldn't pose a problem as long as you type the number quickly. (You can purchase swatch books at an art supply store.)

Color Palette

You can think of the Color palette as a simplified version of the Color Picker dialog box. Just as with the Color Picker, you can pick colors by typing in numbers. However, you first need to choose the type of numbers you want to use from the side menu (**Figure 1.26**).

There's one special option that's not available in the Color Picker dialog box and can only be used in the Color palette. Web Color Sliders will allow you to choose colors that are made from red, green, and blue light, but it will also force the sliders to snap to the tick marks that appear along the slider bars. Those tick marks indicate Web-safe

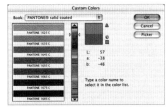

Figure 1.25 The Custom Color Picker.

WARNING

Although the Custom Color Picker is great for users printing with CMYK inks, it's not so hot for those using true spot colors (metallic, fluorescent, and other colors that cannot be reproduced using CMYK inks). If you're going to be using true spot colors, see Chapter 10, "Channels."

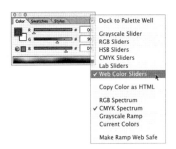

Figure 1.26 Choosing the slider type from the palette's menu.

NOTES

The Copy Color As HTML choice in the side menu of the Color palette will allow you to paste the currently chosen color into an HTML editor. The HTML code that is used to create a Web page uses a special method to define colors that is known as Hexadecimal, and that's what is copied when you choose this option.

You can change the gradient bar at the bottom of the Color palette by clicking it while holding down the Shift key. This will cycle between the settings available from the side menu. You can also Control-click (Macintosh) or Right-click (Windows) on the gradient bar to access the same settings that are available from the side menu.

colors and makes this choice especially useful for creating Web graphics (**Figure 1.27**).

You can also pick colors by clicking the color bar at the bottom of the palette (use Option-click on the Macintosh or Alt-click in Windows to change your background color). You can change the appearance of the color bar by choosing a color-range option near the bottom of the side menu of the palette (**Figure 1.28**). Here are the options:

▶ **RGB Spectrum**—Displays all the colors that are usable in RGB mode. Use this setting for multimedia and the Web.

▶ **CMYK Spectrum**—Shows all the colors that are usable in CMYK mode. Use this setting for images that will be reproduced on a printing press.

▶ **Grayscale Ramp**—Shows shades of gray from black to white. Use this setting any time you need shades of gray that do not contain a hint of color (also known as neutral grays).

▶ **Current Colors**—Displays a gradient using your foreground and background colors.

▶ **Make Ramp Web Safe**—Shows only the colors that are Web safe from the above choices.

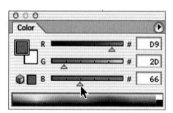

Figure 1.27 When you choose Web Color Sliders, the sliders will snap to the tick marks on the slider bars that indicate where Web-safe colors are located.

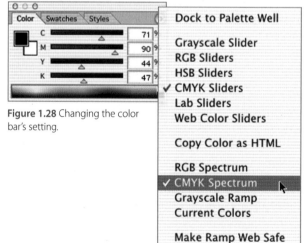

Figure 1.28 Changing the color bar's setting.

Eyedropper Tool

In addition to using the Color Picker and Color palette to select colors, you can use the Eyedropper tool. One advantage to the Eyedropper is that you can grab colors from any open Photoshop file. After selecting the Eyedropper, you can click any part of your image and bingo!—you've got a new foreground color. You can also Option-click (Macintosh) or Alt-click (Windows) to change your background color. You don't have to click within the document you're currently editing; you can click any open image.

You can also change the Sample Size setting in the Options bar to choose how it looks at, or samples, the area you click (**Figures 1.29** to **1.32**). Here are your options:

▶ **Point Sample**—Picks up the exact color of the pixel you click.

▶ **3-by-3 Average**—Averages the area around your cursor using an area that's three pixels wide and three pixels tall.

▶ **5-by-5 Average**—Works the same way as 3-by-3 Average, but with a larger area.

In many cases, you'll find it helpful to use one of the Average settings. They prevent you from accidentally picking up an odd-colored speck in the area from which you're grabbing, thereby ensuring that you don't select a color that isn't representative of the area you're choosing.

NOTES

With Photoshop 7.0's Eyedropper tool, you can click within a document and then drag to any area of your screen to choose a color. That means you can pick up a color from the menu bar, or any other area of your screen. I use this all the time to pick colors from my web browser.

Figure 1.29 The Sample Size option determines the area the Eyedropper tool will average when you're choosing a color.

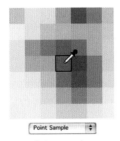

Figure 1.30 Point sample.

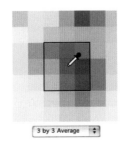

Figure 1.31 3-by-3 Average.

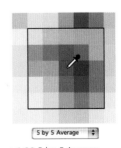

Figure 1.32 5-by-5 Average.

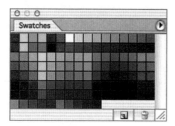

Figure 1.33 The Swatches palette using Small Thumbnail view.

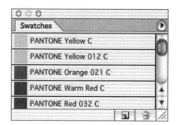

Figure 1.34 The Swatches palette using Small List view.

Figure 1.35 The dialog box for saving swatches.

Swatches Palette

The Swatches palette is designed to store colors that you can use again and again. You can choose how you'd like to view the swatches by choosing either Small Thumbnail (**Figure 1.33**) or Small List (**Figure 1.34**) from the side menu of the Swatches palette. To paint with one of the colors stored in the Swatches palette, move your cursor over a swatch and click the mouse button. Your foreground color will change to the color you clicked. To change your background color, hold Command (Macintosh) or Ctrl (Windows) while clicking any swatch.

To store your current foreground color in this palette, just click in the open space below the swatches. Photoshop will prompt you to name the color and then will add that color to the bottom of the palette. If there is no open space, resize the palette by dragging its lower-right corner. You can also click the New Swatch icon (it looks like a sheet of paper with the corner turned up) at the bottom of the Swatches palette. That will add a new swatch without asking for a name (hold Option on the Macintosh or Alt in Windows to be prompted for a name).

You can also remove a color from the Swatches palette by Option-clicking (Macintosh) or Alt-clicking (Windows) on the swatch. To reset the swatches to their default settings, choose Reset Swatches from the side menu of the palette.

If you'd like to change the order of the swatches, choose Edit > Preset Manager, then choose Swatches from the pop-up menu at the top of the dialog box and click and drag to move the swatches around.

After you've stored the colors you want, you can choose Save Swatches from the Swatches palette's side menu. This will bring up a standard Save dialog box to allow you to assign a name to your personal set of swatches (**Figure 1.35**). After saving a set of swatches, you can reload them by choosing Replace Swatches from the side menu.

Photoshop comes with a bunch of preset swatch files you can load into the Swatches palette. These files are stored in the Color Swatches folder in your Presets folder, which resides in your Photoshop application folder. If you save your swatches file into this folder, it will show up along with other preset swatch files at the bottom of the side menu in the Swatches palette (**Figure 1.36**). When you choose one of those presets, Photoshop will prompt you with a dialog box that has two options (**Figure 1.37**). Append will add the swatches you are loading to the bottom of the swatches that are already there; OK will replace the current swatches with what you are loading. If you'd like to avoid this dialog box altogether, you can hold the Option key (Macintosh) or Alt key (Windows) when you choose one of the presets from the side menu, and Photoshop will replace the swatches automatically.

Info Palette

Although you can't actually choose a color by using the Info palette, you'll find it helpful for measuring the colors that already reside in your document. The top part of the Info palette measures the color that appears below your cursor.

You can change the measurement method used by the Info palette by clicking the tiny eyedropper icons within the palette (**Figure 1.38**). RGB is usually used for multimedia purposes; CMYK for publishing. Total Ink adds together the C, M, Y, and K numbers to indicate how much ink coverage will be used to reproduce the area under your cursor.

You can set up the Info palette to keep track of different areas of your image, so you can see what's happening when you make adjustments. You can do this by clicking your image using the Color Sampler tool. This will deposit a little crosshair on the area you click and will also add another readout to the Info palette (**Figure 1.39**). You can add up to four of these "samples" to your image. Then when you are adjusting the image using any of the choices under the Image > Adjust menu, the Info palette readouts will change into two readouts for each Color Sampler (**Figure 1.40**). The left number indicates what the color was before the adjustment; the right number indicates what the color will be after the adjustment. You can even add a color sample

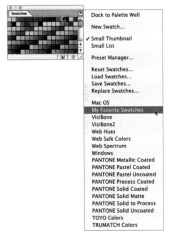

Figure 1.36 Preset swatch files are listed at the bottom of the menu.

Figure 1.37 The Replace Swatches dialog box

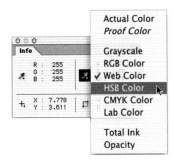

Figure 1.38 Changing how the Info palette measures color.

to your image while an adjustment dialog box is active by holding the Shift key and clicking on the image (the Color Sampler tool does not need to be active to do this).

Figure 1.39 Color samples and Info palette readouts.

Figure 1.40 Info palette readouts while an adjustment dialog box is in use.

To remove a sample, hold the Option key (Macintosh) or Alt key (Windows), and click on the sample, or just drag it off the screen. Or, if you'd like to remove all the color samples, click the Clear button in the Options bar (it's available only when the Color Sampler tool is active). Occasionally you may want to hide the sample points when you're working on your image; you can do this by choosing Hide Color Samples from the side menu of the Info palette. We'll use these samples when you read about color correction in Chapter 9, "Color Correction."

Basic Editing Tools

As with the majority of Photoshop's features, you'll find there's more than meets the eye with the editing tools. For now, we'll cover their most obvious applications, but as you make your way through the rest of the book, keep in mind that these deceivingly simple tools can perform some remarkable tricks. For example, the painting and gradient tools can be used for more than just painting and adding color—they can also be used for making intricate selections, compositing photos, and creating cool fade-outs. You can use them to create an infinite number of dazzling effects.

Painting

In Photoshop 7.0, you have two choices for painting; the Paintbrush tool or the Pencil tool. The only difference between the two is that the Paintbrush always delivers a soft-edged stroke, whereas the Pencil tool always has a hard edge (**Figures 1.41** to **1.42**).

NOTES

All painting tools use the current foreground color when you're painting on the image, so before you begin painting, make sure the active foreground color is the one you want.

To quickly change the Opacity setting of a painting tool, use the number keys on your keyboard (1 = 10%, 3 = 30%, 65 = 65%, and so on).

Figure 1.41 Paint stroke created with the Paintbrush tool.

Figure 1.42 Paint stroke created with the Pencil tool.

You can change the softness of the Paintbrush by choosing different brushes from the Brushes palette. When the Pencil tool is active, all brushes will have a hard edge.

Opacity

If you lower the Opacity setting of the Paintbrush tool, you can paint across the image without worrying about overlapping your paint strokes (**Figure 1.43**). As long as you don't release the mouse button, the areas that you paint over multiple times won't get a second coat of paint.

If you're not familiar with the concept of opaque versus transparent, take a look at **Figures 1.44** and **1.45**.

Figure 1.43 A continuous stroke using the Paintbrush tool.

Figure 1.44 Opaque (left) versus transparent (right). (© 2002 Stockbyte, www.stockbyte.com)

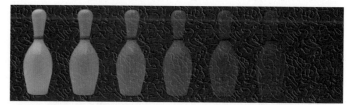

Figure 1.45 Varying opacity. (© 2002 Stockbyte, www.stockbyte.com)

Flow

Using the Flow setting is a different story. When you paint over an area multiple times, this setting causes another coat of paint to appear each time you drag the tool across the area (**Figure 1.46**). The Opacity setting determines the maximum opacity you'll be able to achieve after painting back and forth with the Flow setting set below 100%. The Pencil tool doesn't use the Flow setting and therefore will deliver the desired opacity setting in a single pass.

Now let's take a look at the options available to you when using the painting tools.

Blending Mode

The Mode pop-up menu in the Options bar is known as the blending mode menu. We'll be covering all the options under this menu in Chapter 13, "Enhancement," so right now I'll just explain a few basic uses (**Figures 1.47 to 1.49**). If you would like to change the basic color of an object, you can set the blending mode to Hue. If you're using a soft-edged brush, you can set the blending mode to Dissolve to force the edges of your brush to dissolve out. That's all for now; we'll explore the rest of this menu in Chapter 13.

Figure 1.46 Paint stroke using the Flow setting.

NOTES

In Chapter 12 you'll learn about layer masks, which will allow you to do all the things that the Eraser tools does, but the changes will not be permanent. With a layer mask, you'd be able to bring deleted areas back even after you've saved and closed the file.

Figure 1.47 Normal.(© 2002 Stockbyte, www.stockbyte.com)

Figure 1.48 Hue.

Figure 1.49 Dissolve.

Eraser Tool

If you use the Eraser tool while you're working on a background image (we'll talk about the background in Chapter 3, "Layers Primer"), it acts like one of the normal painting tools—except that it paints with the background color instead of the foreground color. It even lets you choose which type of painting tool it should mimic by allowing you to select an option from the pop-up menu in the Options bar (**Figure 1.51**).

However, when you use the Eraser tool on a non-background layer, it really erases the area. If you lower the opacity setting, it makes an area appear partially transparent. Bear in that mind that the same does not apply to the background image. You cannot "erase" the background.

Background Eraser Tool

Hiding under the normal Eraser tool is a special version known as the Background Eraser. Click and hold on the Eraser tool until you see a drop-down menu—the Background Eraser is the middle tool shown in that menu. When you move your cursor over an image, you'll notice that the Background Eraser gives you a round brush with a crosshair in the middle (**Figure 1.52**). When you click on the image, it will look at the color that is under the crosshair and delete it from within the circular cursor (**Figure 1.53**). It will even convert a Background layer into a normal layer so that it's able to delete areas.

NOTES

To draw straight lines, Shift-click in multiple areas of your image; Photoshop will connect the dots (**Figure 1.50**). You can also hold down the Shift key when painting to constrain the angle to a 45% increment.

Figure 1.50 Shift-click to create straight lines.

Figure 1.51 Choosing Eraser tool behavior.

NOTES

Adobe InDesign 2.0 can directly import Photoshop format images and transparent areas will remain transparent. That's not the case with most electronic publishing applications. If you want a transparent background that will still be transparent in other programs (for instance, if you're preparing an image for use in QuarkXPress), be sure to check out Chapter 12, where we'll talk about clipping paths.

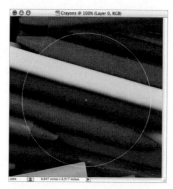

Figure 1.52 The Background Eraser will present you with a round cursor with a crosshair in the middle. (© 2002 Stockbyte, www.stockbyte.com)

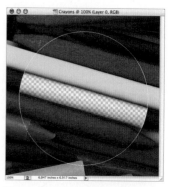

Figure 1.53 The Background Eraser erases (from within the circular cursor) the color that's under the crosshair.

If you look up at the Options bar, you'll notice a lot of choices affecting how the Background Eraser will look at your image:

▶ **Tolerance**—determines the range of colors that will be erased, based on the color that appears under the crosshair (high settings erase a large range of colors; low settings erase a narrow range of colors).

▶ **Protect Foreground Color check box**—protects colors in the image that are similar to the current foreground color.

▶ **Sampling pop-up menu**—determines how often Photoshop will look at the color under the crosshair and therefore which colors will be deleted. Continuous keeps a constant watch; Once only looks at the moment you click the mouse button; and Background swatch uses the current background color instead of looking at the image to determine what should be erased.

▶ **Limits pop-up menu**—changes what the Background Eraser is capable of erasing. Discontiguous allows the Background Eraser to jump across areas that shouldn't be deleted to erase areas that don't touch the crosshair (**Figure 1.54**). Contiguous limits what can be erased to areas that actually touch the crosshair (**Figure 1.55**). Find Edges uses the Contiguous option, but will try to maintain crisp edges instead of allowing the edges to become partially transparent (**Figure 1.56**).

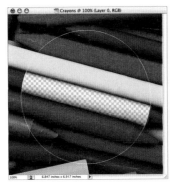

Figure 1.54 The Background Eraser using the Discontiguous option.

Figure 1.55 The Background Eraser using the Contiguous option.

Figure 1.56 The Background Eraser using the Find Edges option.

Brush Presets Palette

The Brushes palette has been completely revamped in Photoshop 7.0. There are dozens of new options that were nowhere to be found in previous versions. Let's look at how Photoshop deals with brushes in general, then we'll start to explore how to create your own custom brushes. When a painting or retouching tool is active, you'll see the currently active brush shown in the Options bar. If you click on that preview, the Brush Presets drop-down palette will appear (**Figure 1.57**). All of the painting and retouching tools available in the Tools palette use the Brush Presets palette to determine their brush size. Each individual tool remembers the last brush size you used with it, and will return to that same size the next time you select the tool. In other words, the brush size you choose doesn't stay consistent when you switch among the tools.

You can change the active brush by clicking once on any brush that's available in the Brush Preset palette (double-clicking will choose a brush and then hide the brushes palette). Each brush has a number below it, which indicates how many pixels wide the brush is.

For even more fun, keep an eye on the brush in the Options bar and then press the < or > key on your keyboard (without holding Shift). You can use these keys to cycle through all the brushes shown in the Brush Presets palette.

NOTES

Use the bracket keys (] [) to change the diameter of your brush, or hold Shift and use the brackets to change the hardness of your brush.

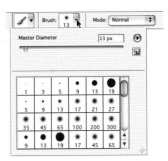

Figure 1.57 The Brush Presets palette.

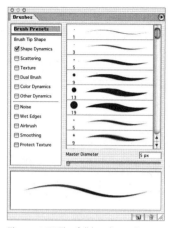

Figure 1.58 The full brushes palette.

Brushes Palette

There are two versions of Photoshop's Brushes palette, each found in a different location in Photoshop. The one we've been talking about so far is the Brush Presets palette. When using that version (the "lite" edition), all you can do is switch between pre-made brushes. If you'd rather change the characteristics of a brush, then you'll need to abandon that palette and work with the full Brushes palette by choosing Window > Brushes (**Figure 1.58**). In this version of the palette (the "I'll take that with everything" edition), you can still access the "Brush presets" by clicking on the words 'brush presets' in the upper-left of the palette. But you can do a heck of a lot more if you click on the choices that appear across the left side of the palette. When you do that, be sure to click on the *words* that describe the feature you'd like to change, not the check boxes. Clicking on the check boxes just lets you turn a feature on or off, and you won't see the options for that feature within the palette… to do that, you must click on the *name*, not the check box. By clicking on each of those choices, you'll find that there are well over thirty settings that you can apply to a brush. When I first saw them, it felt like I was going to need to go back to college to learn how to use everything. But then I looked a little closer and noticed that the settings aren't that hard to deal with and that if you combine a bunch of the features, then you can create some pretty awesome brush effects.

There's one thing you'll need to think about before you start experimenting with all of Photoshop's new settings. There are two types of brushes you can work with: round brushes, and sampled brushes. A round brush is the just what you'd expect … it's round. It's the way most brushes were created in previous versions of Photoshop. The second type of brush you can use is one that's based on a picture (known as a sampled brush) (**Figure 1.59**).

In order to work with a round brush, you must first select a round brush from the Brush Presets. To work with a Sampled Brush, either choose a non-round brush from the presets, or select an area that you'd like to convert into a brush from the active document and then choose

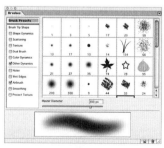

Figure 1.59 The left side of these brush presets are all round brushes, while the right side contains only sampled brushes.

Edit > Define Brush. Once you've chosen the type of brush you'd like to work with, you're ready to start experimenting with all the brush settings.

Brush Tip Shape

These settings determine the overall look of your brush. A paint stroke is made from multiple paint daubs. That is, Photoshop simply fills the shape of your brush with the current foreground color, moves over a distance and then fills that shape again (**Figure 1.60**). The Brush Tip Shape settings determine what the paint daubs will look like and how much space there will be between them.

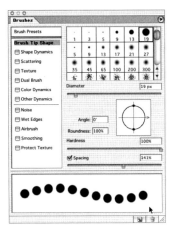

Figure 1.60 The Brush Tip Shape options.

▶ **Diameter**—Determines the size of the brush (**Figure 1.61**). You can use a setting between 1 and 2500 pixels. The Use Sample Size button will appear anytime you're using a Sampled Brush that has been made larger or smaller than its original size. When you click the Use Sample Size button, Photoshop will reset the Diameter setting to the original size of the sampled brush, therefore delivering the highest quality. When you reduce the size of a Sampled brush, it won't degrade the quality of the image much at all. Increasing the size of a sampled brush will cause the brush shape to have a less crisp appearance (**Figure 1.62**).

▶ **Hardness**—Determines how quickly the edge fades out. Default brushes are either 100% soft or 0% soft (**Figure 1.63**). This option is only available with round brushes.

▶ **Roundness**—Compresses a brush in one dimension. When using round brushes, changes to the Roundness setting will result in an oval shaped brush (**Figure 1.64**). When working with a sampled brush, this setting will compress the brush horizontally (**Figure 1.65**).

▶ **Angle**—Rotates oval and sampled brushes but has no effect on round ones (**Figure 1.66**).

▶ **Spacing**—Determines the distance between the paint daubs that make up a brush stroke (**Figure 1.67**). Turning spacing off will cause Photoshop to adjust the spacing setting based on how fast you move the mouse while painting (**Figure 1.68**).

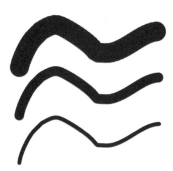

Figure 1.61 Diameter from top to bottom: 100 pixels, 50 pixels, 20 pixels.

Figure 1.62 Left: Sampled brush at actual size. Right: Sampled brush scaled to be much larger than sampled size.

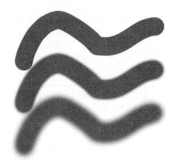

Figure 1.63 Hardness from top to bottom: 100, 50, 20.

Figure 1.64 Roundness from top to bottom: 100, 50, 20.

Figure 1.65 Roundness from top to bottom: 100, 50, 20.

Figure 1.66 Angle from top to bottom: 0, 45, 90.

Figure 1.67 Spacing settings from top to bottom: 25%, 75%, 120%.

Figure 1.68 Turning spacing off varies the spacing setting based on the speed at which you paint.

The rest of the choices that are available on the left side of the Brushes palette allow you to change how the brush tip shape is applied to your image. You'll find that there are three basic concepts that are used over and over with the brush options. Let's first take a look at these three concepts, so you won't have to listen to me repeat myself when we get to the actual settings involved. Jitter settings will allow a particular option (like size or opacity) to vary across a paint stroke (**Figure 1.69**). The higher the Jitter setting, the more the setting will vary. You will also find a setting called Minimum, which determines the range the Jitter setting can use to vary a setting (**Figure 1.70**). If the Minimum option is set to 10%, then the Jitter control will be able to vary a setting between the amount specified in the Brush Tip Shape panel or Options bar and the amount you specified in the Minimum setting (10% means 10% of the setting that's specified in the Brush Tip Shape or Options Bar). The third setting you'll find is called Control and it determines when Photoshop should vary a setting using Jitter. When it's set to Off, the Jitter command will apply all the time. Fade will cause the variance to slowly fade out in a particular number of brush applications. If you set Fade to 20, then Photoshop will start with whatever setting is specified in the Brush Tip Shape area, or Options bar, and then lower the setting over the next 20 paint daubs where it will end up with the amount specified in the Minimum setting (**Figure 1.71**). Setting the Control pop-up menu to any of the bottom three choices (Pen Pressure, Pen Tilt and Stylus Wheel) will cause the variance to be determined by the input of a graphics tablet.

NOTES

Instead of entering values for the Angle and Roundness settings, you can modify the diagram in the middle-right corner of the dialog box. Drag one of the two small circles to change the roundness setting; drag the tip of the arrow to change the angle.

Lower the Spacing setting when using large hard-edged brushes to prevent rough edges.

Figure 1.69 Jitter settings from top to bottom: 20, 50, 100.

Figure 1.70 Minimum settings from top to bottom: 1, 30, 75.

Figure 1.71 Fade settings from top to bottom: 20, 75, 130.

Shape Dynamics

These settings will change the shape of the brush you have chosen. In essence, they allow you to vary the same settings that you specified in the Brush Tip Shape section of the Brushes Palette (**Figures 1.72** through **1.74**).

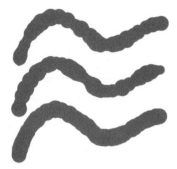

Figure 1.72 Shape Dynamics Size Jitter settings from top to bottom: 100, 50, 20. The higher the setting, the more variation in the blobs.

Figure 1.73 Angle Jitter settings from top to bottom: 100, 50, 20. The higher the setting, the more variation in the angle of the leaves.

Figure 1.74 Roundness Jitter settings from top to bottom: 100, 50, 20. This rotates the leaves on an axis parallel to the brush stroke.

Scattering

The Scatter setting will cause Photoshop to vary the position of the paint daubs that make up a stroke (**Figure 1.75**). The Count setting allows you to vary how many paint daubs are applied within the spacing interval that you specified in the Brush Tip Shape area of the Brushes palette (**Figure 1.76**).

Texture

The texture settings allow you to vary the opacity of your brush based on a texture that you specify (**Figure 1.77**). The Depth Jitter setting allows Photoshop to apply the texture in varying amounts (the Texture Each Tip setting must be turned on in order to use the Depth Jitter setting, **Figure 1.78**). If you find that the texture isn't changing the look of your brush, then experiment with the Mode pop-up menu until you get the result you are looking for.

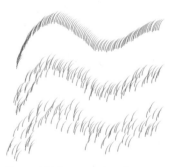

Figure 1.75 Scatter settings from top to bottom: 20, 100, 200.

Figure 1.76 Count settings from top to bottom: 1, 3, 7.

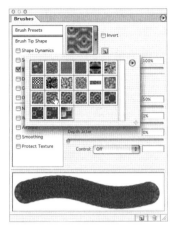

Figure 1.77 The Texture settings.

Figure 1.78 Depth Jitter settings from top to bottom: 100, 50, 20

Figure 1.79 Three examples of dual brushes.

Dual Brush

This option allows you to create a brush stroke that's made with two brushes at once. Paint will only show up where the two brush shapes would overlap each other (**Figure 1.79**). This is a nice way to create sponge effects. You simply choose a normal, round brush in the Brush Tip Shape area of the brushes palette, and then choose a textured brush in the Dual Brush area. If you find that the brushes aren't combining the way you'd like them to, then experiment with the Mode pop-up menu until you get the results you desire.

Color Dynamics

These settings allow you to vary the color of your brush across the brush stroke. The Foreground/Background setting allows Photoshop to vary the brush color between the two colors being used as foreground and background colors (**Figure 1.80**). The Hue setting allows Photoshop to change the basic color of the brush to random colors. The higher the setting, the more it will deviate from your foreground color (**Figure 1.81**). The Saturation setting varies the vividness of the color that you are painting with … or at least that's what it supposed to do. I find that it will vary both the saturation and brightness of the brush (**Figure 1.82**). The Brightness setting allows Photoshop to randomly darken the

Figure 1.80 Foreground/Background using red and blue settings from top to bottom: 100, 50, 20

Figure 1.81 Hue settings from top to bottom: 100, 50, 20.

color you are painting with (**Figure 1.83**). The Purity setting lets you change the saturation of the color you are painting with. A setting of zero makes no change, while negative settings lower the saturation and positive settings increase it (**Figure 1.84**).

Figure 1.82 Saturation settings from top to bottom: 100, 50, 20.

Figure 1.83 Brightness settings from top to bottom: 100, 50, 20.

Figure 1.84 Purity settings from top to bottom: +50, 0, -50.

Other Dynamics

The Opacity and Flow settings allow you to vary the settings that appear in the Options bar for the painting tool that is currently in use (**Figures 1.85** and **1.86**). When you use these controls, Photoshop will vary the Opacity and Flow settings across a brush stroke, but will never exceed the settings specified in the Options bar.

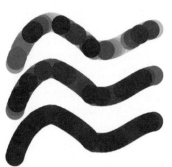

Figure 1.85 Opacity settings from top to bottom: 100, 50, 20.

Figure 1.86 Flow settings from top to bottom: 100, 50, 20.

The Rest of the Brush Settings

Now let's look at the settings that are found at the bottom of the left side of the Brushes palette. The Noise setting will add a noisy look to soft-edged brushes (**Figure 1.87**). The Wet Edges setting will cause the center of your brush to become 60% opaque and will apply more and more paint as it gets towards the edge of your brush (**Figure 1.88**). The Airbrush setting just toggles the Airbrush icon that appears in the Options bar on or off. It works in concert with the Opacity and Flow settings found in the Options bar. The Opacity setting always determines the maximum amount that you'll be able to see through your brush stroke. The Flow setting determines how quickly you will end up with the opacity that you specified. When Flow is set to 100%, you will achieve the opacity amount specified in the options bar on each paint stroke. Lower flow settings cause Photoshop to apply a lower opacity while you paint, but will allow you to overlap your brush strokes to build up to the opacity setting that's specified in the Options bar. The Airbrush setting comes into play when the Flow setting is below 100%. It causes paint to build up when you stop moving your cursor just as it would if you held a can of spray paint in one position (**Figure 1.89**).

Saving Brushes

Once you have changed the settings of a brush, you have in essence created a new brush that is no longer related to the original one that you chose in the Brushes palette. But the changed brush won't show up in the Brushes palette unless you resave it by choosing New Brush from the side menu of the Brushes palette. Once you have created a collection of brushes you like, you can choose Save Brushes from the side menu of the palette to save the currently loaded brushes into a file. If you ever need to get back to a saved set of brushes, choose Replace Brushes from the same menu. You can also choose Reset Brushes to get the brushes back to the default settings.

NOTES

Preset brushes are located in the Brushes folder within the Presets folder in your Photoshop program folder. If you want your own brushes to show up in the Brushes drop-down palette, you'll need to store them in the same location.

Figure 1.87 A brush stroke with Noise applied.

Figure 1.88 The effect of the Wet Edges setting.

Figure 1.89 The Airbrush option causes more paint to apply wherever you pause when painting.

Preset Brushes

Photoshop comes with a variety of preset brushes. You can load these sets by choosing either Replace Brushes or choosing a specific name that appears at the bottom of the Brushes palette side menu. (**Figures 1.90** to **1.93**).

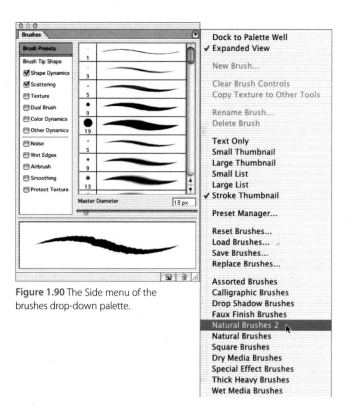

Figure 1.90 The Side menu of the brushes drop-down palette.

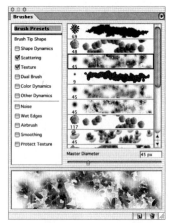

Figure 1.91 Special Effect brushes.

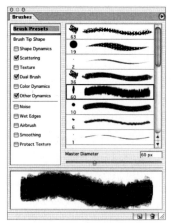

Figure 1.92 Dry Media brushes.

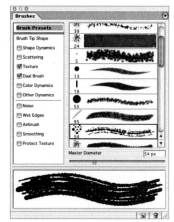

Figure 1.93 Wet Media brushes.

Paint Bucket Tool

Use the Paint Bucket tool to fill areas with the foreground color. Each time you click on the image, Photoshop will fill areas that contain colors similar to the one you clicked. You can specify how sensitive the tool should be by changing its Tolerance setting (**Figures 1.94** to **1.96**). Higher Tolerance settings will fill a wider range of colors.

Figure 1.94 The Paint Bucket Options bar.

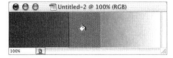

Figure 1.95 Tolerance: 32.

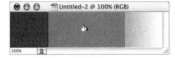

Figure 1.96 Tolerance: 75.

Shape Tools

The Shape tools are great for creating simple geometric shapes (**Figure 1.97**). These tools are much more powerful than what you'd expect at first glance. We'll look at the basics here, and then expand on them in later chapters.

Figure 1.97 Press and hold one of the Geometric Shape tools to see a full list of the tools available.

Before you dive into the Shape tools, you need to think about what kind of result you want to achieve, because you have three ways of using these tools, each of which will lead you to a different outcome. You'll find the trio of choices in the far left of the Options bar (**Figure 1.98**). The first (leftmost) choice will create a special layer that's new to Photoshop. It's known as a Shape layer and it has some very special qualities:

Figure 1.98 These three icons determine how the shape will be applied.

▸ It will have crisp edges when printed on a PostScript printer (even if the pixels that make up the image are large enough to cause the rest of the image to appear jagged).

▸ You can scale it (up or down) without degrading its quality. This makes it ideal for creating button bars on Web sites where the client might decide to add more text to a button, which would require a larger button.

Vector Masks were known as Layer Clipping Paths in previous versions of Photoshop.

To straighten a crooked document, first drag with the Measure tool along a line which should be horizontal or vertical; then choose Image > Rotate Canvas > Arbitrary and click OK. Photoshop calculates the exact angle needed to rotate the image.

To rotate a layer to a specific angle, first use the Measure tool to specify the angle you'd like to use, then choose Edit > Transform > Rotate. Photoshop enters the angle of the line you drew into the Options bar and rotates the active layer that amount.

▶ You can add to or take away from it using the other Shape tools.

▶ It can be filled with a solid color, a gradient, pattern, or adjustment.

The second choice in the Options bar will deliver a path that will show up in the Paths palette. This can be useful when creating a Vector Mask, as we'll discuss in Chapter 12. The third choice in the Options bar will fill an area on the currently active layer using the current foreground color. I mainly use the Shape layer option because it seems to give me the most flexibility.

Once you've decided what type of result you want, you can click and drag across an image to create a shape. If you'd like to have a little more control over the end result, you can click on the small triangle that appears to the right of the Shape tools in the Options bar. That will present you with options that are specific to the particular shape you are creating.

You can quickly create interesting effects by choosing a style from the drop-down menu (small triangle) next to the Layer Style preview image in the Options bar. A layer style is a collection of settings that can radically transform the look of a layer by adding dimension, shadows, and other effects to the layer. You can also apply a layer style to any layer (it doesn't have to be one that was created using a Shape tool) by opening the Styles palette and clicking on one of the styles listed (**Figure 1.99**). We'll talk more about layer styles in Chapter 15.

Measure Tool

The Measure tool allows you to measure the distance between two points or the angle of any area of the image, which can be helpful when you want to rotate or resize objects precisely. In order to see the angle and distance measurements, you must have the Info palette open. As you drag with the Measure tool, the Info palette indicates the angle (A) and length (D, for Distance) of the line you're creating (**Figure 1.100**). You can change the measurement system used to measure distance by clicking the small cross in the lower-left corner of the Info palette. After creating a line, you can click directly on the line and drag it to different positions. You can also click and drag one end of the line to change the angle or distance.

If you want to resize an image so that it fits perfectly between two objects, you can measure the distance between them with this tool and then choose Image > Image Size to scale the image to that exact width.

You can also use the Measure tool to determine the angle between two straight lines. If you Option-drag (Macintosh) or Alt-drag (Windows) the end of the line, you can pull out a second line and move it to any angle you desire. Now the angle (A) number in the Info palette displays the angle between those two lines.

Gradient Tool

At first, you might not see any reasons to get excited about using the Gradient tool. However, after we cover Layers (Chapter 3), Channels (Chapter 10), and collage techniques (Chapter 12), you should find that the Gradient tool is not only worth getting excited about, it's downright indispensable. I want to make sure you know how to edit and apply gradients before we get to those chapters, so let's give it a shot.

First let's look at how to apply gradients to an image. To apply a gradient, simply click and drag across an image using the Gradient tool. You'll get different results depending on which type of gradient you've chosen in the Options bar (**Figure 1.101**).

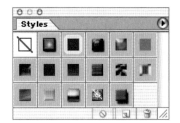

Figure 1.99 The Layer Styles palette

Figure 1.100 The Info palette indicates the angle of the Measure tool. (© 2002 Stockbyte, www.stockbyte.com)

Unless you select an area before applying a gradient, the gradient will fill the entire image.

Figure 1.101 The Gradient options bar.

You can press Enter to show or hide the preset gradients without accessing the Options bar.

Here's an explanation of the gradient settings (**Figures 1.102** to **1.106**):

▶ **Linear**—Applies the gradient across the length of the line you make. If the line does not extend all the way across the image, Photoshop fills the rest of the image with solid colors (the colors you started and ended the gradient with).

▶ **Radial**—Creates a gradient that starts in the center of a circle and radiates to the outer edge. The point where you first click determines the center of the circle; where you let go of the mouse button determines the outer edge of the circle. All areas outside this circle will be filled with a solid color (the color that the gradient ends with).

▶ **Angle**—Sweeps around a circle like a radar screen. Your first click determines the center of the sweep, then you drag to determine the starting angle.

▶ **Reflected**—Creates an effect similar to applying a linear gradient twice, back to back.

▶ **Diamond**—Similar to a radial gradient except that it radiates out from the center of a square.

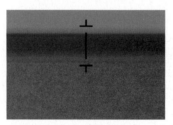

Figure 1.102 Linear gradient

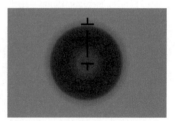

Figure 1.103 Radial gradient.

Figure 1.104 Angle gradient.

Figure 1.105 Reflected gradient.

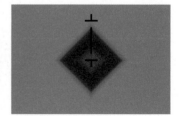

Figure 1.106 Diamond gradient.

Gradient Colors

You can choose from different preset color combinations by clicking on the small triangle that appears next to the gradient preview in the Options bar (**Figure 1.107**). You can also reverse the direction of the gradient by turning on the Reverse check box in the Options bar. Then, if you have a gradient that usually starts with blue and ends with red, it would instead start with red and end with blue (**Figures 1.108** and **1.109**). Some of the preset gradients will contain transparent areas. To disable transparency in a gradient, turn off the Transparency check box.

Figure 1.107 The Linear Gradient Options bar.

Figure 1.108 Reverse "off."

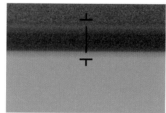

Figure 1.109 Reverse "on."

Figure 1.110 Dither "off."

Dithered Gradients

When you print an image that contains a gradient, you'll sometimes notice banding across the gradient (also known as stair-stepping or posterization). To minimize this, be sure to turn on the Dither check box in the Options bar. This will add noise to the gradient in an attempt to prevent banding. You won't be able to see the effect of the Dither check box onscreen; it just makes the gradient look better when it's printed (**Figures 1.110** and **1.111**). If you find that you still see banding when you print the gradient, you can add some additional noise by choosing Filter > Noise > Add Noise (use a setting of 3 or less for most images).

Figure 1.111 Dither "on."

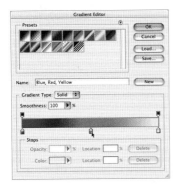

Figure 1.112 Click just below the gradient preview to add colors to the gradient.

Custom Gradients

The Gradient drop-down menu might not always contain the exact type of gradient you need. When that's the case, click directly on the gradient preview in the Options bar to create your own custom gradient. The Gradient Editor dialog box that appears has so many options that it can sometimes feel overwhelming, but if you take it one step at a time, you shouldn't run into any problems (**Figure 1.112**).

The list at the top of the dialog box shows you all the gradients that usually appear in the Options bar. Click any one of them, and you'll be able to preview it at the bottom of the dialog box. Once you have chosen the gradient you want to edit, you can modify it by changing the gradient bar (or you can click New to make a copy and proceed from there). To add additional colors (up to a maximum of 32), click just below any part of the bar. This adds a color swatch to the bar and changes the colors that appear in the gradient.

You have three choices of what to put into your new color swatches. You'll find these choices on the drop-down menu to the right of the Color swatch at the bottom left of the dialog box. The Foreground and Background choices don't just grab your foreground or background colors at the time you create the gradient, as you might expect. Instead, they look at the foreground and background colors when you apply the gradient. Therefore, each time you apply the gradient, you can get a different result by changing the foreground and background colors. If you don't want the gradient to contain your foreground or background colors, then choose User Color from the same menu and click on the Color swatch to access the Color Picker.

After you have added a swatch of color to the gradient bar, you can reposition it by dragging it from left to right, or by changing the number in the Location box below. I like to click the Location number and then use the up arrow and down arrow keys on my keyboard to slide the color swatch around. A little diamond shape, known as the midpoint, will appear between each of the color swatches; it indicates where the two colors will be mixed equally.

Transparent Gradients

You can also make areas of a gradient partially transparent by clicking just above the gradient preview. In this area, you cannot change the color of a gradient; you can only make the gradient more or less transparent. You can add and move the transparency swatches just as you would the color swatches below. Transparent areas are represented by the checkerboard pattern (**Figure 1.113**).

Notes Tool

When you use the Notes tool (which looks a bit like a Post-it note), you can click and drag on your image to create a text box in which you can then type a note (**Figure 1.114**). Once you're done typing, you can close the note by clicking the tiny box in its upper left corner (Macintosh) or in its upper right corner (Windows) and all you'll see is a tiny icon that indicates there is a note in that spot. Then, when you want to read the note, just double-click on that icon and the note will expand. Each note can have a different color and author, which you specify in the Options bar. If you find the notes to be distracting, then you are welcome to choose View > Show > Annotations to hide the notes.

Hidden under the Notes tool is another tool that allows you to record audio annotations. You'll have to have the proper hardware (a microphone, etc.) to get this feature to work. With the audio annotation, you simply click on your image, and a Record dialog box will appear (**Figure 1.115**). Click the Record button and then start talking. Once you're done, click the Stop button and you're all set. Now anytime someone double-clicks that audio annotation, they will hear your notes. That's pretty slick, but be careful, because audio annotations can really increase the file size of an image.

If you no longer need to keep the annotations you've created and you'd like to reduce your file size, you can click the Clear All button in the Options bar (the Annotations tool must be active for this button to be available).

You can remove a color swatch or a transparency swatch by simply dragging it away from the gradient bar.

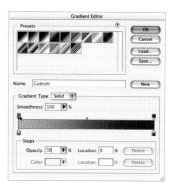

Figure 1.113 Editing the transparency of a gradient.

Figure 1.114 A text annotation. (© 2002 Stockbyte, www.stockbyte.com)

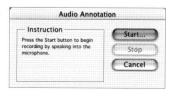

Figure 1.115 The Audio Annotation record dialog box.

PDF Annotations

What's really special about annotations is that you can save them (along with the image, of course) in a PDF file. You can give that file to anyone; they can read the annotations and see the image without having to use Photoshop. All they need is a free program called Acrobat Reader (available at www.adobe.com). Or, if they have the full version of Acrobat, they can add their own annotations to the PDF file. Then you can import them into the original Photoshop file by choosing File > Import > Annotations. This allows you to save an image in a universal file format, send it out for review to as many people as you like, and get back comments that you can re-import into the original high-resolution Photoshop file. It's a great way to communicate with clients.

Tool Presets

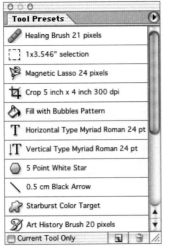

Figure 1.116 The Tool Presets palette.

Figure 1.117 The Include Color check box.

With Photoshop 7, Adobe has added the ability to save tool presets. You can access the presets in two ways: click on the tool icon that appears on the left side of the Options bar, or choose Window > Tool Presets (**Figure 1.116**). To save a preset, click on the new preset icon at the bottom of the Tool Presets palette (it looks like a piece of paper with the corner turned down). You'll also find the same icon in the upper-right area of the drop-down palette that you can access from the Options bar. When you save a preset, Photoshop remembers all the settings that were specified in the Options bar and the Brushes palette (if you're using a painting or retouching tool) and if you check the Include Color check box (**Figure 1.117**), then it will even remember your foreground and background colors. Once you've saved a preset, you can get back to those settings at any time by clicking on the name of the preset from the Tool Presets palette.

There are two ways of working with the Tool Presets palette. The first is to use it as a replacement for Photoshop's main Tools palette. After all, when you click on a preset, Photoshop will switch to the referenced tool and load up the setting you saved, so you could completely replace the main Tools palette with the presets. The only problem with that is that it can get rather crowded once

you have four or five settings saved for each tool. I prefer
to select tools using the normal Tools palette, and then
to streamline the tool in the Tool Presets palette, I choose
Show Current Tool Presets so that I only see presets that
relate to the tool I have active. I also usually close the
palette and access it by clicking on the tool icon that
appears at the left end of the Options bar. That way I
reduce my screen clutter and can still quickly access the
presets with a click or two of my mouse.

File Browser

If there's one feature that I use the most in Photoshop 7.0,
it's got to be the new File Browser. I've almost completely
replaced the standard File > Open command and now I
just type Shift-Command-O (Mac), or Shift-Ctrl-O (Windows)
and up pops the wonderful new file browser (**Figure 1.118**).
The upper left of the dialog box presents a hierarchical
view of your hard drive, where you can click the arrow
next to each folder to view its contents. Once you've got
it pointed to the proper location on your hard drive, then
Photoshop will present you with thumbnail images for the
files in that folder (click the tiny left/right arrow icon at
the bottom of the window to hide the left panes of the
browser). You can control the size of the thumbnails by
changing the settings that appear in the right-most menu
that appears at the bottom of the browser. Smaller thumbnails will allow you to see more images at once, while
larger thumbnails will allow you to see more detail in each
thumbnail image. If an image is sideways, then click the
rotate icon in the lower right of the browser window to
rotate the thumbnail Clockwise (hold Option on a Mac,
Alt in Windows to rotate counter-clockwise) and let Photoshop know that you'd like to rotate the actual image when
it's opened in Photoshop. When you click on a file within
the right pane of the browser, a preview image will appear
just below the folder list that appears in the upper left. If
the preview isn't big enough for you, then click and drag
on the borders of the different panes of the browser to
make more room. Below the preview will be information
about that particular image, including its size and resolution. If you find an image that you simply don't need

anymore, then click on it and then press Delete (Mac), or Backspace (Windows) to delete the file from your hard drive.

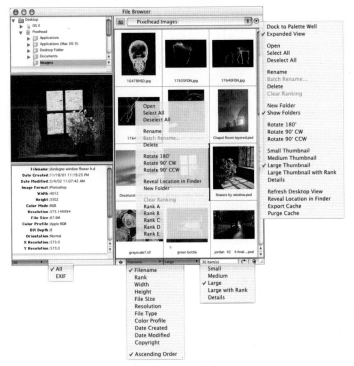

Figure 1.118 Photoshop 7.0's File Browser.

Sorting the Thumbnails

You can control the sorting order of the files by clicking the middle pop-up menu that appears at the bottom of the dialog box. I really like that you can sort the files by file size and resolution. That makes it easy to find the images that can be used at a large size very quickly. You can even rank each file on an A–F scale by Control-clicking (Mac), or right-clicking (Windows) on one of the thumbnail images. That way you can sort through a folder of images, marking the great images an A, the OK images a B and the ones that should be trashed an F, and then you can view them based on the rating you assigned. You can even move a file on your hard drive by dragging it to one of the folder icons that appears in the upper left. If you'd rather make a duplicate, then hold Option (Mac), or Alt (Windows) to drag a copy.

Double-click on any image that appears in the right side of the File Browser to open it within Photoshop. You can Command-click (Mac), or Ctrl-click (Windows) to select multiple files, or Shift-click to select a range of files.

Renaming Files

You can quickly rename a file by clicking on its name and typing a new one. You can even press Tab to go to the next file in the list and rename it as well. That makes it very easy to rename an entire folder of images. If you'd like to do that even faster, then make sure you don't have any files highlighted in the browser and choose Batch Rename from the side menu of the dialog box (**Figure 1.119**). This is where you can have Photoshop automatically rename an entire folder's worth of images. This is great for when you get images off a digital camera where you get odd file names like 09864-01.JPG. Just use Batch Rename and specify the naming convention you'd like to use by changing the pop-up menus that appear in the Batch Rename dialog box. I usually set the first field to something like "Ben's Vacation," set the second field to 3 Digital Serial Number and then set the third one to "extension." That way all the images end up being named "Ben's Vacation 00X.jpg" where the X would be a unique number for each image.

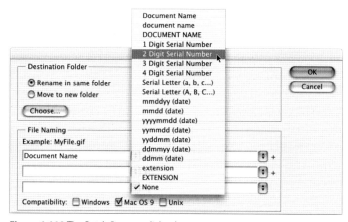

Figure 1.119 The Batch Rename dialog box.

Closing Thoughts

If you've made it through this entire chapter, you've just passed through Photoshop's welcoming committee of tools and palettes. By now your screen should look neat and tidy and you should be able to zoom in and out and scroll around your image with ease. You should also have a nodding acquaintance with a good number of the tools and palettes—at least be familiar enough with them to know which ones you want to get more friendly with later.

Don't panic if some of this still seems like a blur. It will all begin to take shape once you spend some more time with the program. After a few intense Photoshop sessions, the things you learned in this chapter will become second nature to you. If any of the tools are completely new to you, you should probably play around with them before you move on to the next chapter.

But for now, let's get into the first installment of Ben's Techno-babble Decoder Ring. And just for the fun of it, I'll throw in some keyboard commands that can really speed up your work.

Ben's Techno-babble Decoder Ring

Anti-aliasing: Smoothing the edge of an otherwise hard-edged object by adding partially transparent pixels. These pixels help to blend the edge of the object into the surrounding image, making it harder to see the edge of the pixels.

Posterization: The process of breaking up a smooth transition into visible steps of solid color. This is often called stair-stepping, or banding, when referring to a gradient.

Dither: Simulate color by using a pattern of two solid colors (for example, adding a pattern of red dots to a yellow area to create orange). This term also refers to adding a pattern of noise to a sharp transition to make the edge less noticeable.

Noise: A pattern of dots that resembles the static that appears on some televisions when no station is tuned in.

This pattern is often used to break up crisp transitions between two colors by replacing a straight-line transition with one that has more of a random edge.

RGB: A model for creating color using red, green, and blue (RGB) light. You are able to see color because your eye contains cones in its retina that are sensitive to red, green, and blue. Scanners capture information by measuring how much RGB light is reflected off the original image. Computer monitors display information by shining RGB light into your eyes. All the colors you have ever seen with your eyes have been made from a combination of red, green, and blue light. It really is an RGB world out there.

CMYK: A model for reproducing RGB colors using cyan, magenta, yellow, and black inks. (Black is abbreviated "K" for Key.) Any time you print an image you will be using CMYK inks. Ideally, cyan ink would absorb only red light, magenta ink would absorb only green light, and yellow ink would absorb only blue light; you could therefore reproduce an RGB image by absorbing the light falling on a sheet of paper instead of creating the light directly. But due to impurities in these inks, CMYK inks (also known as process color) cannot reproduce all the colors that can be created using RGB light.

HSB: A method of manipulating RGB or CMYK colors by separating the color into components of hue, saturation, and brightness. Hue is the pure form of the color (red is the pure form of pink, maroon, and candy-apple red). Saturation is the intensity or vibrancy of the color (pink is a not very saturated red; candy-apple red is a very saturated red). Brightness is how bright or dark a color appears (pink is a bright, just not vibrant, tint of red; maroon is a dark shade of red). So, when talking about the hue of a color, you are not describing how bright and vibrant (saturated) the color appears. When talking about saturation of a color, you do not reveal its basic color (hue), or how bright or dark it appears (brightness). When talking about the brightness of a color, you are not describing the basic color (hue) or how vibrant it appears (saturation).

Lab: A scientific method of describing colors by separating them into three components called Lightness, A, and B. The Lightness component describes how bright or dark a color appears. The "A" component describes colors ranging from red to green. The "B" component describes colors ranging from blue to yellow. Lab color is the internal color model used in Photoshop for converting between different color modes (RGB to CMYK, etc.).

Keyboard Shortcuts

FUNCTION	MACINTOSH	WINDOWS
Zoom in	Command-+ (plus sign)	Ctrl-+
Zoom out	Command-– (minus sign)	Ctrl-–
Fit on Screen	Command-0	Ctrl-0
Temporarily use Zoom tool	Command-spacebar	Ctrl-spacebar
Zoom out by clicking	Option-Command-spacebar	Alt-Ctrl-spacebar
Show/Hide palettes	Tab	Tab
Cycle through screen modes	F	F
Hide or show menu bar when in full screen mode	Shift-F	Shift-F
Temporarily use Hand tool	Spacebar	Spacebar
Show/Hide rulers	Command-R	Ctrl-R
Select previous brush	, (comma)	, (comma)
Select next brush	. (period)	. (period)
Select first brush	Shift-, (<)	Shift-, (<)
Select last brush	Shift-. (>)	Shift-. (>)
Hand tool	H	H
Paintbrush tool	B	B
Eraser tool	E	E
Airbrush option	Option-Shift-P	Alt-Shift-P
Pencil tool	N	N
Reset Foreground/Background Colors	D	D
Exchange Foreground/Background Colors	X	X

Courtesy of Michael Slack, www.slackart.com

Courtesy of Michael Slack, www.slackart.com

Selection Primer

Courtesy of Tom Nick Cocotos, www.cocotos.com

I choose a block of marble and chop off whatever I don't need.

—François-Auguste Rodin,
when asked how he managed
to make his remarkable statues

Selection Primer

You've got to love the selection tools. I like to think of them as the chisels of Photoshop. With names such as Lasso, Magic Wand, Feather, and Transform, you get a sense that these aren't just everyday tools—they're the fine instruments of a digital sculptor. Selection tools can do so much more than just draw outlines: they can help you dig down into the guts of an image and perform wondrous transformations. What's more, you don't have to be a wizard to know how to use them. Selection tools take a little getting used to, but once you're familiar with them, they can help you tremendously.

Whatever you do, don't skip this chapter, because the selection tools are central to your success in Photoshop. They allow you to isolate areas of your image and define precisely where a filter, painting tool, or adjustment will change the image. Also, selections are not specific to a particular layer (we'll talk about layers in Chapter 3, "Layers Primer"). Instead, they're attached to the entire document. That means you can freely switch among the different layers without losing a selection. After you've mastered the basics, you'll be ready to jump into more advanced selections in Chapter 10, "Channels."

What Is a Selection?

Before you can edit an image, you must first select the area with which you want to work. People who paint cars for a living make "selections" very much like the ones used in Photoshop. If you've ever seen a car being painted, you know that painters carefully place masking tape and paper over the areas they don't want to paint (such as the windows, tires, door handles, and so on). That way, they can freely spray-paint the entire car, knowing that the taped areas are protected from "overspray." At its most basic level, a selection in Photoshop works much the same way. Actually, it works much better, because with one selection, you have a choice—you can paint the car and leave the masked areas untouched, or you can paint the masked areas and leave the car untouched.

When you select an area by using one of Photoshop's selection tools (Marquee, Lasso, Magic Wand, and so on), the border of the selection looks a lot like marching ants. Once you've made a selection, you can move, copy, paint, or apply numerous special effects to the selected area (**Figures 2.1** and **2.2**).

Figure 2.3 Normal selections have hard edges. (© 2002 Stockbyte, www.stockbyte.com)

Figure 2.1 When no selection is present, you can edit the entire image. (© 2002 Stockbyte, www.stockbyte.com)

Figure 2.2 When a selection is present, you can change only the selected area.

There are two types of selections in Photoshop: a normal selection and a feathered selection (**Figures 2.3** and **2.4**). A normal selection has a hard edge. That is, when you paint or apply a filter to an image, you can easily see where the effect stops and starts. On the other hand, feathered selections slowly fade out at their edges. This allows filters to seamlessly blend into an image without producing noticeable edges. An accurate selection makes all the difference when you're enhancing an image in Photoshop. To see just how important it can be, take a look at **Figures 2.5** to **2.7**.

Figure 2.4 Feathered selections have soft edges.

Figure 2.5 The original image. (© 1998 Photodisc)

Figure 2.6 An unprofessional selection.

Figure 2.7 A professional selection.

Basic Selection Tools

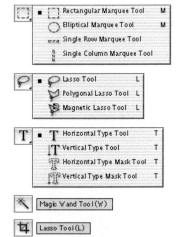

Figure 2.8 The basic selection tools.

The Marquee, Lasso, Magic Wand, and Type Mask tools (**Figure 2.8**) are the essential ingredients in your selection toolkit, and they're the ones you'll be using the most in your everyday work. It's a good indication that you've come to master these tools when you find yourself trying to use them in other software programs where they don't exist. When using other programs, I sometimes find myself muttering, "Why can't I just lasso this thing?"

The Marquee tool is the most basic of all the selection tools, and we'll cover it first. However, don't let this tool's simplicity fool you—it can perform a surprising number of tasks, so there's quite a bit to learn about it. If you hold your mouse button down while your cursor is over the Marquee tool icon, you'll get a variety of choices in a pop-up menu. We'll cover these choices one at a time, and I'll throw in some tricks along the way.

Rectangular Marquee Tool

The Rectangular Marquee tool is the first choice listed in the Marquee pop-up menu. It can select only rectangular shapes. With it, you create a rectangle by clicking and dragging across your document. The first click creates one corner, and the point at which you release the mouse button denotes the opposite corner (**Figure 2.9**). To start in the center and drag to an outer edge, instead of going corner to corner, press Option (Macintosh) or Alt (Windows) after you have started to drag (**Figure 2.10**). If you want to create a square, just hold down the Shift key after you start to drag. You can even combine the Option (Mac) or Alt (Windows) and Shift keys to create a square selection by dragging from the center to an outer edge.

WARNING

If you press any combination of the Option (Mac) or Alt (Windows) and Shift keys before you begin a selection, they might not perform as you expect, because these keys are also used to manipulate existing selections.

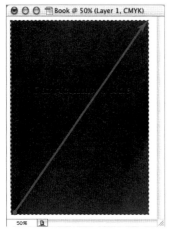

Figure 2.9 A corner-to-corner selection. (© 2002 Stockbyte, www.stockbyte.com)

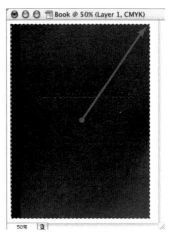

Figure 2.10 A center-to-edge selection.

Figure 2.11 Original selection is misaligned. (© 2002 Stockbyte, www.stockbyte.com)

To discard the areas that appear outside the selection border, choose Image > Crop.

If you hold down the spacebar and drag around your screen while you're making a selection (but don't release the mouse button), you'll move the selection instead of changing its shape. This can be a real lifesaver. If you botch up the start of a selection, this enables you to reposition it without having to start over. After you have moved the selection into the correct position, just let go of the spacebar to continue editing the selection. After you've finished making the selection, you no longer need to hold the spacebar to move it. To move a selection after it's created, select the Marquee tool and then click and drag from within the selection outline (**Figures 2.11** and **2.12**).

Elliptical Marquee Tool

The second choice under the Marquee pop-up menu is the Elliptical Marquee tool. This tool works in the same way as the rectangular version, except it creates an ellipse (**Figure 2.13**). And it's a little bit trickier to define its size because you have to work from the "corner" of the ellipse, which doesn't really exist. (What were they thinking when they came up with this idea?) Actually, I find it much easier to choose View > Show Rulers and then drag out a few guides (you can get them by dragging from the rulers)

Figure 2.12 Use the spacebar to reposition a selection while creating it.

Figure 2.13 The Elliptical Marquee tool in action (from center to edge). (© 2002 Stockbyte, www.stockbyte.com)

and let the "corners" snap to them. Either that, or hold the spacebar to reposition the selection before you release the mouse button, just as I mentioned with the Rectangular Marquee tool.

Now let's look at the choices in the Marquee Options bar (**Figure 2.14**). When you click on any of the Marquee

Figure 2.14 The Marquee Options bar.

tools, their options will automatically be available in the Options bar at the top of your screen. The following list describes the options you'll find in this palette:

▶ **Feather.** Allows you to fade out the edge between selected and unselected areas. I usually leave this option turned off, because I might forget that a Feather setting had been typed in previously. This one little setting might mess up an otherwise great selection. Instead, I find it much easier to make a selection and then press Option-Command-D on the Mac or Alt-Ctrl-D in Windows (or just choose Select > Feather).

▶ **Anti-aliased.** This checkbox determines whether a one-pixel-wide border on the edge of a selection will blend with the image surrounding it. This provides nice, smooth transitions, and helps prevent areas from looking jagged. I recommend that you leave this checkbox on at all times, unless, of course, you have a great need for jaggies (sometimes they're preferred for multimedia applications).

▶ **Style menu.** Controls the shape and size of the next selection made. When the Style pop-up menu is set to Normal, your selections are not restricted in size or shape (other than their having to be rectangles or ellipses). After changing this menu to Fixed Aspect Ratio, you'll be confronted with Width and Height settings (**Figure 2.15**). By changing the numbers in these areas, you can constrain the shape of the next selection to the ratio between the Width and Height settings. For example, if you change Width to 2 and leave Height at 1, your selections will always be twice as wide as they are tall. This can be useful when you need to find out how much of an image needs to be cropped when printing it as an 8 by 10, for example.

Figure 2.15 The Fixed Aspect Ratio option.

I use the Fixed Size option (**Figure 2.16**) much more often than the Fixed Aspect Ratio option. Fixed Size lets you type in an exact width and height; that way, anytime you click using either the Rectangular or Elliptical Marquee tool, you'll get a selection exactly that size. What's more, if you didn't get it in exactly the right spot, you can just drag the selection around the screen before releasing the mouse button. For instance, Macintosh OS 9 desktop icons are always 32 pixels wide and 32 pixels tall, so I use these numbers when selecting something I want to use as an icon. When entering a Width or Height setting, you can specify a measurement system by adding a few letters after the number you enter; otherwise Photoshop will default to the measurement system used for the rulers.

Figure 2.16 The Fixed Size option.

Single Row and Single Column Marquee Tools

The third and fourth choices under the Marquee tool pop-up menu are the Single Row and Single Column Marquee tools. These tools are limited in that they select only a one-pixel-wide row or one-pixel-tall column. To be honest, I rarely use them (maybe once or twice a year). However, they have gotten me out of few tight spots, such as when I had to clean up a few stray pixels from in between palettes when taking screen shots for this book.

NOTES

If the cropping rectangle extends beyond the edge of your screen, the extended areas will be filled with the current background color (if you have a background image) or transparent (filled with a checkerboard pattern) if you don't have a background image.

To match the size of another open document, click that document to make it active for editing and then click the Front Image button in the Options bar. This will enter the Width, Height, and Resolution settings of that document into the Options bar. Now you can use the Crop tool on any open document, and the result will match the size of the original document. When you're rotating the cropping rectangle, the Info palette will indicate the exact angle you're using.

To specify a width and height for cropping your image, add the following letters to select the measurement system:
- ▶ px = pixels
- ▶ in = inches
- ▶ cm = centimeters
- ▶ pt = points
- ▶ pica = picas

If you don't want to resize the image when you crop it, be sure the Width, Height, and Resolution fields are empty in the Options bar before you create a cropping rectangle.

Crop Tool

Two spaces below the Marquee tool, you'll find the Crop tool. While the Crop tool doesn't produce a selection, it does allow you to isolate a certain area of your image. Using this tool, you can crop an image as well as resize and rotate it at the same time (**Figures 2.17** and **2.18**).

Figure 2.17 The original image. (© 2002 Stockbyte, www.stockbyte.com)

Figure 2.18 The original image cropped and rotated.

When you click and drag over an image with the Crop tool selected, a dashed rectangle appears. When the Shield Cropped Area checkbox is turned on, the area outside the cropping rectangle will be covered with the color indicated in the Options bar and might appear to be partially transparent, depending on the Opacity setting (**Figure 2.19**). You can drag any one of the hollow squares on the edge of the rectangle to change its size. Also, you can hold down the Shift key while dragging a corner to maintain the width-to-height proportions of the rectangle. Anything beyond the edge of the rectangle is discarded when the image is cropped (if you haven't turned on the Hide option).

To rotate the image, you can move your cursor just beyond one of the corner points and drag (look for an icon that looks like a curve with arrows on each end). You can also drag the crosshair in the center of the rectangle to change the point from which the rectangle will be rotated. To complete the cropping, press Return or Enter (or double-click within the cropping rectangle). Press Esc to cancel. If you're working on a layer (instead of the background) and the Delete option is chosen in the Options bar, then all information that appears outside the cropping rectangle will be discarded. If the Hide option is chosen, then the area outside the cropping rectangle will not be discarded but will instead remain as image data that extends beyond the bounds of the visible image. This option is very useful when you are creating animations in ImageReady and you'd like part of the image to start outside the image area. We'll explore animation in Chapter 18.

Occasionally, you'll need to crop and resize an image at the same time. Maybe you need three images to be the exact same size, or perhaps you need your image to be a specific width. You can do this by specifying the exact Width, Height, and Resolution settings you desire before you create a cropping rectangle. Once you've created a cropping rectangle on your image, you'll notice that different options appear in the Options bar (**Figure 2.20**). By typing in both a Width and a Height setting, you constrain the shape of the rectangle that you draw. I occasionally leave one of these values empty so that I can still create any rectangular shape.

Figure 2.19 The cropping rectangle. (© 2002 Stockbyte, www.stockbyte.com)

Figure 2.20 The Options bar after a cropping rectangle is added to the image.

When the Perspective Crop choice in the Options bar is turned on (it becomes available once you've created a cropping rectangle), you will be able to move each corner of the cropping rectangle independently. This allows you to align the four corners with lines that would be level in real life but may appear in perspective in a photograph (**Figure 2.21**). Once you have all four corners in place, you can press Return or Enter to crop the image and correct the perspective of the image in one step (**Figure 2.22**).

Figure 2.21 Getting the corners to line up with level lines. (© 2002 Stockbyte, www.stockbyte.com)

Figure 2.22 Result of applying a perspective crop.

You don't have to crop the image while you are correcting its perspective. Once you have the corners in the correct location to establish the perspective of the image, move the side handles—or Option-drag (Mac)/Alt-drag (Windows) the corner handles—until the area you'd like to keep is within the cropping rectangle, and then press Enter (**Figures 2.23** and **2.24**).

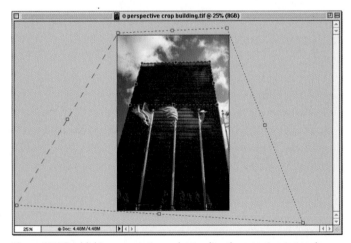

Figure 2.23 Establishing perspective and extending the cropping rectangle.

Figure 2.24 Result of correcting perspective.

Lasso Tool

The Lasso tool is the most versatile of the basic selection tools. By holding down the mouse button, you can use the Lasso to trace around the edge of an irregularly shaped object (**Figure 2.25**). When you release the button, the area will be selected. Be sure to create a closed shape by finishing the selection exactly where you started it; otherwise, Photoshop will complete the selection for you by adding a straight line between the beginning and end of the selection.

Sometimes you'll need to add a few straight segments in the middle of a freeform shape. You can do this by holding down Option (Mac) or Alt (Windows) and then releasing the mouse button (but not the Option or Alt key). Now, each time you click your mouse, Photoshop will connect the clicks with straight lines (**Figure 2.26**). To go back to creating a freeform shape, just start dragging and then release the Option key (Mac) or Alt key (Windows).

NOTES

You can zoom in on your document to get a more precise view by typing Command-+ (Mac) or Ctrl-+ (Windows). You don't even have to let go of the mouse button—just press this key combination as you're dragging.

I suggest you zoom in on your image to make sure you're creating an accurate selection. If you can't see the entire image, you can hold the spacebar to access the Hand tool. You can do this without ever releasing the mouse button, which means you can alternate between scrolling and selecting until you've got the whole object.

Figure 2.25 The Lasso tool in action. (© 2002 Stockbyte, www.stockbyte.com)

Figure 2.26 Using the Option or Alt key while clicking to create straight-line segments. (© 2002 Stockbyte, www.stockbyte.com)

Figure 2.27 The Polygonal Lasso tool in action. (© 2002 Stockbyte, www.stockbyte.com)

Polygonal Lasso Tool

You can use the Polygonal Lasso tool whenever you need to make a selection that consists mainly of straight lines. Using this tool, you just click multiple areas of the image, and Photoshop connects the dots for you (**Figure 2.27**). If you need to create a freeform selection, hold down Option (Mac) or Alt (Windows) and drag. To finish a selection, you can either click where the selection began or double-click when you add the final point.

Magnetic Lasso Tool

Whereas the Lasso and Polygonal Lasso tools are relatively straightforward, the Magnetic Lasso tool has a bunch of neat tricks up its sleeve. This tool can be a huge timesaver in that it allows you to trace around the edge of an object without having to be overly precise. You don't have to break a sweat making all of those tiny, painstaking movements with your mouse. Instead, you can make big sloppy selections, and the Magnetic Lasso will do the fine-tuning for you. What's more, if it doesn't do a great job in certain areas, you can hold down Option (Mac) or Alt (Windows) to use the freeform Lasso tool. However, before using the Magnetic Lasso tool, you'll want to change its settings in the Options bar (**Figures 2.28** to **2.30**). Let's take a look at these settings:

Figure 2.28 The Magnetic Lasso Options bar.

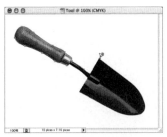

Figure 2.29 A Magetic Lasso selection with a frequency setting of 5. (© 2002 Stockbyte, www.stockbyte.com)

Figure 2.30 A Frequency setting of 99.

▶ **Edge Contrast.** I think this setting is the most important of the bunch. It determines how much contrast there must be between the object and the background for Photoshop to select the object. If the object you're attempting to select has well-defined edges, you should use a high setting (**Figure 2.31**). You can also use a large Lasso tool width. On the other hand, if the edges are not well defined, you should use a low setting and try to be very precise when dragging (**Figure 2.32**).

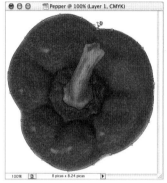

Figure 2.31 High edge contrast (20%). (© 2002 Stockbyte, www.stockbyte.com)

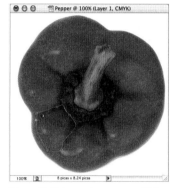

Figure 2.32 Low edge contrast (7%).

If the Magnetic Lasso tool is not behaving itself, you can temporarily switch to the freeform Lasso tool by holding down Option (Mac) or Alt (Windows) as you drag. You can also periodically click to manually add anchor points to the selection edge. If you want to use the Polygonal Lasso tool, hold down Option (Mac) or Alt (Windows) and click in multiple areas of the image (instead of dragging). If you don't like the shape of the selection, you can press the Delete key to remove the last anchor point. (Pressing Delete multiple times deletes multiple points.) Once you have a satisfactory shape, finish the selection by pressing Return or Enter or by double-clicking. Remember, if you don't create a closed shape, Photoshop will finish it for you with a straight-line segment.

Figure 2.33 A simple click of the Magic Wand tool can select a solid area of color with ease. (© 2002 Stockbyte, www.stockbyte.com)

NOTES

To quickly change the Tolerance setting, press Enter and then type the desired number and press Enter again. I know it sounds weird, but try it—it works!

If you really get used to the features available with the Magnetic Lasso tool, you'll be able to create most of your basic selections with this tool alone. This will take some time, and you'll sometimes have to supplement its use by holding down Option (Mac) or Alt (Windows) to access the other Lasso tools for areas the magnetic one has trouble selecting. And if it ever gets completely out of hand, you can always press the Escape key to abort your selection and then start from scratch again.

Magic Wand Tool

The Magic Wand tool is great for selecting solid (or almost solid) colored areas, because it selects areas based on color—or shades of gray in grayscale mode—as shown in **Figure 2.33**. This is helpful when you want to change the color of an area or remove a simple background.

You'll probably find it easier to understand how this works if you start by thinking about grayscale images, because they're less complex than color images. Grayscale images can contain up to 256 shades of gray. When you click one of these shades with the Magic Wand tool, it will select any shades that are within the Tolerance specified in the Options bar. For instance, if you click shade 128 (Photoshop numbers the shades from 0 to 255) and the Tolerance is set to 10, you'll get a selection of shades that are 10 shades darker and 10 shades brighter than the one you clicked (**Figures 2.34** to **2.36**). When the Contiguous checkbox is turned on, the only shades that will be selected are those within an area that touches the spot you clicked—Photoshop can't jump across areas that are not within the tolerance.

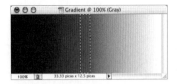

Figure 2.34 Tolerance: 10

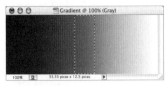

Figure 2.35 Tolerance: 20

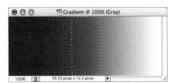

Figure 2.36 Tolerance: 30.

Just in case you're not comfortable thinking in the 0-to-255 numbering system and would rather think about percentages, I've included the conversion table at right. Otherwise, you can make this conversion by multiplying any percentage by 2.55 (1% in the 0-to-255 numbering system). Remember, the Magic Wand tool will select twice as much as the number you type in.

Color images are a little more complex. They're made from three components: red, green, and blue (that is, when you're working in RGB mode). The Magic Wand tool will analyze all the components (known as channels) in your file to determine which areas to select. For example, if you click a color made up of the components 32 red, 120 green, 212 blue (these numbers can be found in the Info palette) and you use a Tolerance setting of 10, Photoshop will look for colors between 22 and 42 in the red channel, 110 and 130 in the green channel, and 202 and 222 in the blue channel. The only colors that will be selected are ones that fall within all three ranges. Doesn't that sound complicated? Well, I have to confess, I don't usually think about the numbers, because they're something of a pain. Instead, I just experiment with the setting until I get a good result. Now, doesn't that sound a lot easier than dealing with all those numbers? If you really want to understand all about the color channels, take a look at Chapter 10, "Channels."

PERCENTAGE CONVERSIONS	
Percentage	Tolerance Setting
0%	0
10%	26
20%	51
30%	77
40%	102
50%	128
60%	153
70%	179
80%	204
90%	230
100%	255

Type Tool

You can use Photoshop's Type tool to create a selection by choosing the Type Mask tool, which is hanging out with the normal Type tool in the Tool palette (**Figure 2.37**). When you use that tool, Photoshop will show you a preview of the selection (with a red overlay on the image, as shown in **Figure 2.38**) while you are editing the text, and then it will deliver a selection when you press Enter. We'll cover the options of this tool in Chapter 15, "Type and Background Effects."

Figure 2.38 The selection will be previewed using a red overlay on the nonselected areas.

Figure 2.37 The Type Mask tool.

Refining a Selection

Selecting complex objects in Photoshop usually requires multiple selection tools. To combine these selection tools, you'll need to either use a few controls in the Options bar (**Figure 2.39**) or learn a few keyboard commands that will allow you to add, subtract, or intersect a selection.

Figure 2.39 These four choices in the Options bar allow you to create, add, subtract, or intersect a selection.

Adding to a Selection

To add to an existing selection, either click on the second icon on the far left of the Options bar (it looks like two little boxes overlapping each other) or hold down the Shift key when you start making the new selection. You must press the key *before* you start the selection; you can release it as soon as you've clicked the mouse button (**Figures 2.40 to 2.42**). If you press it too late, the original selection will be lost. Let's say, for example, you would like to select multiple round objects. One way would be to use the Elliptical Marquee tool multiple times while holding down the Shift key. But you might find it easier to use the choice available in the Options bar because then you don't have to remember to keep any keys held down.

Figure 2.40 The original selection. (© 2002 Stockbyte, www.stockbyte.com)

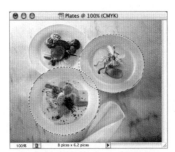

Figure 2.41 Adding to the selection.

Figure 2.42 The end result.

Removing Part of a Selection

To remove areas from an existing selection, either click on the third icon on the far left of the Options bar (it looks like one little box stacked on top of another) or hold down Option (Mac) or Alt (Windows) when you begin making the selection. If, for example, you want to create a half circle, you could start with an Elliptical Marquee tool selection and then switch over to the Rectangular Marquee tool and drag while holding down Option (Mac) or Alt (Windows) to remove half of the circle (**Figures 2.43** to **2.45**).

Clicking while holding down the Option (Mac) or Alt (Windows) key is particularly helpful when you're using the Magic Wand tool to remove areas of a selection (**Figures 2.46** and **2.47**). With each click of the Magic Wand tool, you can use a different Tolerance setting.

Figure 2.43 The original selection. (© 2002 PhotoDisc)

Figure 2.44 Subtracting a second selection.

Figure 2.45 The end result.

Figure 2.46 The original selection.

Figure 2.47 Option-clicking (Mac) or Alt-clicking (Windows) with the Magic Wand tool.

Intersecting a Selection

To end up with only the overlapped portions of two selections, click on the fourth icon on the far left of the Options bar (it looks like two squares intersecting, with the overlap area colored in), or hold down Shift-Option (Mac) or Shift-Alt (Windows) while editing an existing selection. Sometimes I use the Magic Wand tool to select the background of an image and then choose Select > Inverse to get the object (or objects) of the selected image (**Figure 2.48**). However, when there are multiple objects in the image, as there are in **Figures 2.49** and **2.50,** I often have to restrict the selection to a specific area by dragging with the Lasso tool while holding down Shift-Option (Mac) or Shift-Alt (Windows).

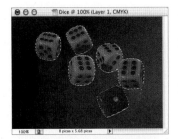

Figure 2.48 Applying the Magic Wand tool to the background and then choosing Select > Inverse. (© 2002 Stockbyte, www.stockbyte.com)

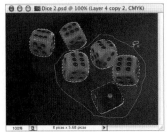

Figure 2.49 Dragging with Lasso tool while holding down Shift-Option (Mac) or Shift-Alt (Windows).

Figure 2.50 The end result.

The Select Menu

The Select menu offers you many choices that supplement the basic selection tools. Learning these features is well worth your time because they'll help you save heaps of it in your everyday work. We'll look at these features in the same order they appear in the menu; then, later in this chapter, I'll show you how to replace many of these commands with an alternative that allows you to think visually instead of numerically.

Select All

Select > All selects the entire document. This can be useful when you need to trim off any part of an image that extends beyond the edge of the document (**Figure 2.51**). You can crop out those areas by choosing Select > All and then Image > Crop (**Figure 2.52**). Also, if you need to copy an entire image, you'll need to select everything, because without a selection, the Copy command will be grayed out.

Figure 2.51 An example of areas that extend beyond the document's bounds (these areas are not usually visible). (© 2002 Stockbyte, www.stockbyte.com)

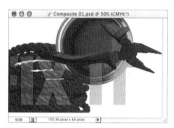

Figure 2.52 Layers repositioned after the image has been cropped.

Deselect/Reselect

If you're done using a selection and would like to work on the entire image, choose Select > Deselect. If you don't have a selection, you can work on the entire image. Now, if you need to use the last active selection (and there isn't a selection on your screen), you can choose Select > Reselect. This is great when you need to use the same selection over and over again. I use these two commands all the time. However, I usually opt for the keyboard commands: Command-D (Mac) or Ctrl-D (Windows) for Deselect, Shift-Command-D (Mac) or Shift-Ctrl-D (Windows) for Reselect.

Inverse

As you might expect, the Inverse command selects the exact opposite of what you originally selected. If, for example, you have the background of an image selected, after choosing Select > Inverse, you'll have the subject of the image selected instead (**Figures 2.53** and **2.54**). I use this command constantly, especially with the Magic Wand tool. Sometimes it's just easier to select the areas that you don't want and then choose Select > Inverse to select what you really want to isolate. Sound backwards? It is, but it works great.

Figure 2.53 A Magic Wand tool selection. (© 2002 Stockbyte, www.stockbyte.com)

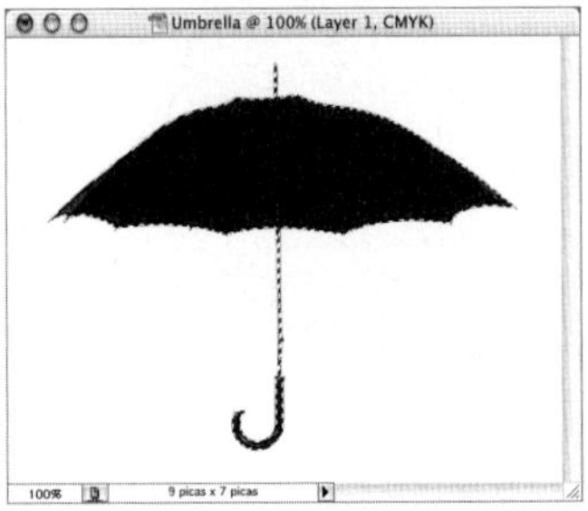

Figure 2.54 The selection after using the Select > Inverse command.

Color Range

You can think of the Select > Color Range command as the Magic Wand tool on steroids. With Color Range, you can click multiple areas and then change the Fuzziness setting (how's that for a technical term?) to increase or reduce the range of colors that will be selected (**Figures 2.55** and **2.56**).

As you click and play with the Fuzziness control, you'll see a preview of the selection in the middle of the Color Range dialog box. Areas that appear white are the areas that will be selected. The Selection and Image radio buttons allow you to switch between the selection preview and the main image. (I never actually use these two controls because I find it easier to switch to the image view at any time by just holding down Command on the Mac or Ctrl in Windows.) You can also see a preview of the selection within the main image window by changing the Selection Preview pop-up menu to Grayscale, Black or White Matte, or Quick Mask (**Figures 2.57** to **2.59**).

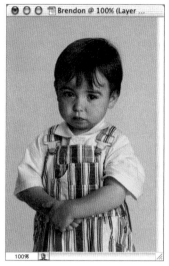

Figure 2.55 The original image.
(© 2002 Stockbyte, www.stockbyte.com)

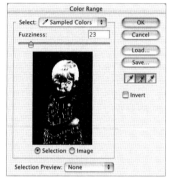

Figure 2.56 The same image in the Color Range dialog box after clicking on multiple areas within his hair.

Figure 2.57 Choosing Grayscale will display the same preview that appears in the Color Range dialog box.

Figure 2.58 Choosing Black Matte or White Matte will fill the unselected areas with black or white.

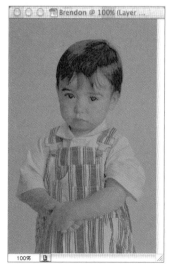

Figure 2.59 Choosing Quick Mask uses the settings in the Quick Mask dialog box to create a preview of the image.

Figure 2.60 An example of a single click with a high Fuzziness setting.

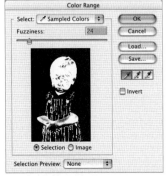

Figure 2.61 An example of five clicks with a low Fuzziness setting.

The Eyedropper tool on the right side of the dialog box allows you to add and subtract colors from the selection. Using the Eyedropper with the plus symbol next to it is really helpful, because it allows you to click the image multiple times. With each click, you tell Photoshop which colors you want it to search for. A low Fuzziness setting with many clicks usually produces the best results (**Figures 2.60** and **2.61**).

The selections you get from the Color Range command are not ordinary selections, in that they usually contain areas that are not completely selected. For instance, if you're trying to select the red areas in an image and there happens be a flesh tone in the same image, the fleshy areas will most likely become partially selected. If you then adjust the image, the red will be completely adjusted, and the flesh tones will shift only a little bit.

If a selection is already present when you choose Select > Color Range, the command will analyze the colors only within the selected area. This means you can run the command multiple times to isolate smaller and smaller areas. If you want to have the Color Range command added to the current selection, be sure to hold down the Shift key when choosing Select > Color Range.

Feather

Unlike the Feather option in the selection tools, this version affects only the selection that's currently active and has no effect on future selections. You can't reduce the amount of feathering with this command once it's applied. Therefore, if you apply it once with a setting of 10 and then try it again on the same selection using a setting of 5, it will simply increase the amount again. It's just like blurring an image—each time you blur the image, it becomes more and more blurry.

I prefer using this command instead of entering Feather settings directly into the tool's Options bar (where they affect all "new" selections). If you enter these values directly, you might not remember that the setting is turned on days later, when you spend hours trying to select an intricate object. By leaving the tools set at 0, you can quickly press Option-Command-D (Mac) or Alt-Ctrl-D (Windows) to bring up the Feather dialog box and enter a number to feather the selection. Because this affects only the current selection, it can't mess up any future ones (**Figures 2.62** and **2.63**).

Figure 2.62 A coin pasted with a normal selection. (© 2002 Stockbyte, www.stockbyte.com)

Figure 2.63 A coin copied using a feathered selection and then pasted into this document.

The problem with the Feather command is that there is no way to tell if a selection is feathered by just looking at the marching ants. Not only that, but most people think the marching ants indicate where the edge of a selection is, and that's simply not the case with a feathered selection. If you take a look at **Figure 2.64**, you'll find that the marching ants actually indicate where a feathered selection is halfway faded out.

Modify

The features in this little menu have helped get me out of many sticky situations. At first glance, it might not be obvious why you would ever use them, but I guarantee they'll come in very handy as you continue through the book. Here's a list of the commands found under the Select > Modify menu, as well as descriptions of what they do:

▶ **Border.** Selects a border of pixels centered on the current selection. If you use a setting of 10, the selection will be five pixels inside the selection and five pixels outside the selection. You can use this to remove pesky

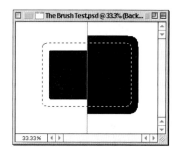

Figure 2.64 The left half of this split image shows where the selection would start to fade out and blend with the underlying image. The right half shows where the selection would stop affecting the image. Notice that the marching ants show up halfway between those two areas.

halos that appear when you copy an object from a light background and paste it onto a darker background (**Figures 2.65** and **2.66**).

▶ **Smooth.** Attempts to round off any sharp corners in a selection (**Figure 2.67**). This can be especially useful when you want to create a rounded-corner rectangle. It can also produce an interesting effect after you've used the Type Mask tool (**Figures 2.68** and **2.69**).

▶ **Expand.** Enlarges the current selection while attempting to maintain its shape (**Figure 2.70**). This command works well with smooth, freeform selections, but it's not my first choice for straight-edged selections because it usually slices off the corners.

▶ **Contract.** Reduces the size of the current selection while attempting to maintain its shape (**Figure 2.71**). The highest setting available is 16. If you need to use a higher setting, just use the command more than once.

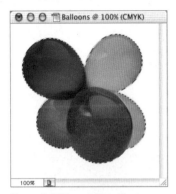

Figure 2.65 The original selection. (© 2002 Stockbyte, www.stockbyte.com)

Figure 2.66 A 10-pixel border.

Figure 2.68 The original selection.

Figure 2.70 Expand 12 pixels.

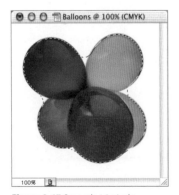

Figure 2.67 Smooth 16 pixels.

Figure 2.69 After applying a Smooth setting of 6.

Figure 2.71 Contract 12 pixels.

Grow

The Select > Grow command will search for colors that are similar to an area that has already been selected (**Figures 2.72** and **2.73**). In effect, it will spread your selection in every direction—but only into areas that are similar in color. It cannot jump across areas that are not similar to the ones selected. The Grow command uses the Tolerance setting that's specified in the Magic Wand Options bar to determine the range of colors it will look for.

Figure 2.72 The original selection. (©2002 PhotoSpin, www.photospin.com)

Similar

The Select > Similar command works just like the Grow command except that it looks over the entire document for similar colors (**Figures 2.74** and **2.75**). Unlike the Grow command, the colors that Similar selects don't have to touch the previous selection. This can be very useful when you've selected one object out of a group of the same colored objects. For example, if you have a herd of gray elephants standing in front of a lush green jungle, you can select the first elephant and then use Select > Similar to get the rest of the herd (provided, of course, that they're all a similar shade of gray). The same works for a field of flowers, and so on.

Figure 2.73 The selection after Select > Grow is used.

Transform Selection

After making a selection, you can scale, rotate, or distort it by choosing Select > Transform Selection. This command places handles around the image. By pulling on the handles and using a series of keyboard commands, you can

Figure 2.74 The original selection.

Figure 2.75 The selection after Select > Similar is used.

distort the selection as much as you like. Let's take a look at the neat stuff you can do with Transform Selection:

▶ **Scale.** To scale a selection, pull on any of the handles. Pulling on a corner handle will change both the width and height at the same time. (Hold the Shift key to retain the proportions of the original selection.) Pulling on the side handles will change either the width of the selection or its height, but not both. This can be a great help when working with elliptical selections because it lets you pull on the edges of the selection instead of its so-called corners (**Figures 2.76** and **2.77**).

Figure 2.76 The original selection. (© 2002 Stockbyte, www.stockbyte.com)

Figure 2.77 After choosing Select > Transform to scale the selection.

▶ **Rotate.** To rotate the image, move your cursor a little bit beyond one of the corner points; the cursor should change into an arc with arrows on each end. You can control where the center point of the rotation will be by moving the crosshair that appears in the center of the selection (**Figures 2.78** to **2.80**).

▶ **Distort.** To distort the shape of the selection, hold down the Command (Mac) or Ctrl (Windows) key and then drag one of the corner points. Using this technique, you can pull each corner independently (**Figures 2.81** to **2.83**).

▶ You can also distort a selection so that it resembles the shape of a road vanishing into the distance. You do this by dragging one of the corners while holding down Shift-Option-Command on the Mac or Shift-Alt-Ctrl in Windows (**Figures 2.84** to **2.86**).

▶ To move two diagonal corners at the same time, hold down Option-Command on the Mac or Alt-Ctrl in Windows while dragging one of the corner handles (**Figures 2.87** and **2.88**).

▶ Finalize your distortions by pressing Enter (or by double-clicking inside the selection). Cancel them by pressing Esc.

NOTES

If you forget the keyboard commands that are required to distort a selection, you can instead choose Select > Transform Selection and then Control-click (Mac) or right-click (Windows) to choose the type of distortion you want to perform (**Figure 2.89**).

Figure 2.78 The original selection. (© 2002 Stockbyte, www.stockbyte.com)

Figure 2.79 Rotating and scaling the selection.

Figure 2.80 The end result.

Figure 2.81 The original selection. (© 2002 Stockbyte, www.stockbyte.com)

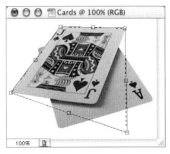

Figure 2.82 Dragging a corner while holding down Command (Mac) or Ctrl (Windows).

Figure 2.83 The selection after all four corners have been dragged.

Figure 2.84 The original selection.
(© 2002 PhotoDisc)

Figure 2.85 Dragging a corner while holding down Shift-Option-Command (Mac) or Shift-Alt-Ctrl (Windows).

Figure 2.86 The end result.

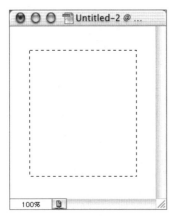

Figure 2.87 The original selection.

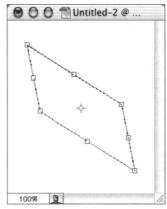

Figure 2.88 Dragging a corner handle while holding down Option-Command (Mac) or Alt-Ctrl (Windows).

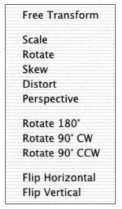

Figure 2.89 The menu that appears as a result of Control-clicking (Mac) or right-clicking (Windows) while you're transforming a selection.

Load Selection and Save Selection

If you've spent hours perfecting a selection and think you might need to use it again in the future, you can apply the Select > Save Selection command (**Figure 2.90**). This stores the selection as an alpha channel (you can think of channels as stored selections). Don't worry, you don't need to know anything about channels to use these commands—all you have to do is supply a name for the selection. If you want to find out more about channels, you can check out Chapter 10.

These saved selections remain in your document until you manually remove them using the Channels palette (see Chapter 10 to find out how to delete a channel). They won't be saved on your hard drive until you actually save the entire file. Only the Photoshop (.psd) or TIFF (.tif) file formats support saved selections.

Figure 2.90 The Save Selection dialog box.

Figure 2.91 The Load Selection dialog box.

When you want to retrieve the saved selection, choose Select > Load Selection and pick the name of the selection from the Channel pop-up menu (**Figure 2.91**). When you use this command, it's just like re-creating the selection with the original selection tool you used, only a whole lot faster.

Quick Mask Mode

Remember when we were talking about the marching ants and how they can't accurately show you what a feathered selection looks like? Well, Quick Mask mode can show you what a feathered selection *really* looks like and can also help create basic selections. The quick-mask icon is located directly below the foreground and background colors in your Tools palette (**Figure 2.92**). When the left icon is turned on, you are in Standard mode, which means you create selections using the normal selection tools, and they will show up as the familiar marching ants. The right icon enables Quick Mask mode, and that's where selections will show up as a translucent color overlay.

To see how it works, first make a selection using the Marquee tool, and then turn on Quick Mask mode by clicking on the right icon under the foreground and background colors (or just type Q to do the same thing). In

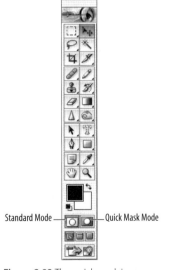

Standard Mode — Quick Mask Mode

Figure 2.92 The quick-mask icons.

Quick Mask mode, the selected area should look normal and all the nonselected areas should be covered with a translucent color (**Figure 2.93** and **2.94**).

Figure 2.93 A selection shown in Standard mode. (© 2002 Stockbyte, www.stockbyte.com)

Figure 2.94 The same selection shown in Quick Mask mode.

Now that you're in Quick Mask mode, you no longer need to use selection tools to modify a selection. Instead, you use standard painting tools and paint with black to take away from the selection, or white to add to it. When you're done modifying the selection, switch back to Standard mode and you'll be back to marching ants (**Figures 2.95** and **2.96**).

Figure 2.95 A selection modified in Quick Mask mode.

Figure 2.96 End result after switching back to Standard mode.

Now let's see what feathered selections look like in Quick Mask mode. Make another selection using the Marquee tool. Next, choose Select > Feather with a setting of 10, and then switch to Quick Mask mode and take a look (**Figures 2.97** and **2.98**). Feathered selections appear with blurry edges in Quick Mask mode. This happens because partially transparent areas (that is, ones that are more transparent than the rest of the mask) indicate areas that are partially selected (50% transparent means 50% selected).

The confusing part about this process is that when you look at the marching ants that appear after you switch back to Standard mode, they only show you where the selection is at least 50% selected. That isn't a very accurate picture of what it really looks like (**Figure 2.99**). But in Quick Mask mode, you can see exactly what is happening on its edge. So, if you want to create a feathered selection in Quick Mask mode, just choose a soft-edged brush to paint with. Or, if you already have a shape defined, then choose Filter > Blur > Gaussian Blur, which will give you the same result of feathering but will show you a visual preview of the edge.

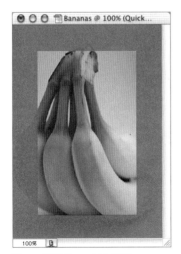

Figure 2.97 Normal. (© 2002 Stockbyte, www.stockbyte.com)

Figure 2.98 Feathered.

Figure 2.99 The marching ants show up where an area is at least 50% selected.

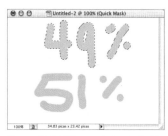

Figure 2.100 When painting in Quick Mask mode, only the areas that contain less than 50% gray will be visible when the selection is viewed as marching ants.

Figure 2.101 When you paint with shades brighter than 50% gray, a warning will appear when you go back to Standard mode.

Figure 2.102 Applying the Ripple filter in Quick Mask mode.

Shades of Gray

Try this out. Turn on Quick Mask mode—you don't need a selection to begin with. Type D to reset the foreground color to black, and then Option-Delete (Mac) or Alt-Backspace (Windows) to fill the Quick Mask. Now paint within the Quick Mask with 20% gray (you can use the Color Picker palette to choose grays). Then turn off Quick Mask mode and paint in the selected area with bright red. Now choose Select > Deselect, lower the opacity of the painting tool to 80%, and paint with bright red. Your reds should look exactly the same. That's how Photoshop makes a selection fade out—simply by lowering the opacity of the tool you are using. This can sometimes be confusing, though, because the marching ants show up only where an image is at least 50% selected. So, try this one on for size. Turn on Quick Mask mode and paint with 49% gray, and then paint in another area with 51% gray. Then go back to Standard mode and paint across the area. Only the areas that are at least 50% gray show up as marching ants, but the other areas are still selected, even though the marching ants don't show up in those areas (**Figure 2.100**). Try turning on Quick Mask mode and then paint with 55% gray. Now go back to Standard mode and you'll even get a warning message, pictured in **Figure 2.101**.

We really haven't done anything fancy yet, so let's try something fun. To start with, you have to remember that when you work in Quick Mask mode, Photoshop treats the selection as if it is a grayscale image that you can paint on. That means you can use any tool that is available when working on grayscale images. So select an area using the Marquee tool, turn on Quick Mask mode, choose Filter > Distort > Ripple, and mess with the settings until you've created something that looks a little kooky (**Figure 2.102**). Finally, go back to Standard mode and see what you've got. You can create infinite varieties of fascinating selections with this simple technique.

You can also convert a logo or sketch into a selection using Quick Mask mode. All you need to do is copy the image, turn on Quick Mask mode, choose Edit > Paste and then choose Image > Adjustments > Invert (**Figure 2.103**). If the logo was in color, then you might end up with shades of gray (which will look like shades of red in Quick Mask mode), and in that case, you'll need to choose Image > Adjustments > Levels and pull in the upper-right and upper-left sliders until the image is pure black and pure white. Once everything looks right, then turn off Quick Mask mode and you'll have your selection.

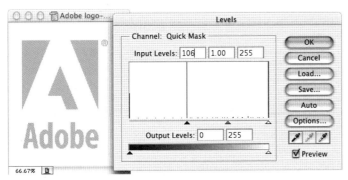

Figure 2.103 Adjusting a logo using the Levels dialog box.

Now let's figure out how to "unfeather" a selection using Quick Mask mode (**Figure 2.104**). Remember, a feathered edge looks like a blurry edge in Quick Mask mode. All you have to do to remove that blurry look is to then choose Image > Adjustments > Threshold. This will give the mask a very crisp, and therefore unfeathered, edge.

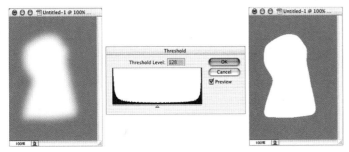

Figure 2.104 Unfeathering a selection using Threshold. Left: Original image. Center: Threshold setting used. Right: Result of applying Threshold.

Selections in Quick Mask Mode

You can even use a selection to isolate a particular area of the Quick Mask, as shown in **Figure 2.105**. A selection in Quick Mask mode can help you create a selection that is only feathered on one side. To accomplish this, turn on Quick Mask mode, type D to reset the foreground color, and then type Option-Delete (Mac) or Alt-Backspace (Windows) to fill the Quick Mask. Next, choose the Marquee tool and select an area. Now use the Gradient tool set to Black, White and create a gradient within the selected area. Once you're done, switch off Quick Mask mode. Now to see exactly how this selection will affect the image, choose Image > Adjustments > Levels and attempt to lighten that area by dragging the lower-left slider.

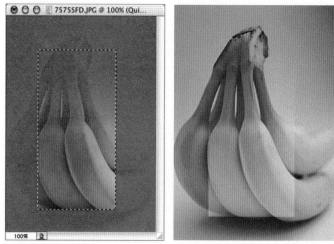

Figure 2.105 Using a selection in Quick Mask mode to restrict which areas can be edited.

Color

Photoshop also allows you to switch *where* the color shows up. You can specify whether you want the selected or un-selected areas to show up. To change this setting, double-click on the quick-mask icon and change the Color

Indicates setting (**Figures 2.106** and **2.107**). Photoshop uses the term Masked Areas to describe areas that are not selected.

The Opacity setting determines how much you will be able to see through the Quick Mask.

Closing Thoughts

After a few practice rounds with the various tools we covered in this chapter, you should be selecting like a pro. We'll go over more advanced methods of creating selections in Chapter 10, "Channels." But until then, it really is worth your while to build up your selection skills because you will be using them every day in Photoshop. And now it's time for another dose of Ben's Techno-babble Decoder Ring.

Ben's Techno-babble Decoder Ring

Big data: Any area of a layer that extends outside the physical dimensions of the document.

Cropping: The process of reducing the dimensions of an image by removing unneeded space from the edge of the document. Also used to remove big data.

Feather: The process of converting a hard-edged selection into one that blends into the underlying image as you move closer to its edge.

Marching ants: Term used to describe the edge of a selection. Used because the edges appear as very small moving specks (similar to ants).

Marquee: Like the rectangular marquees (signs) used at movie theaters to display the movies that are currently showing. In Photoshop, the Marquee tool is used to create rectangular (or elliptical) selections, and the resulting marching ants even resemble the flashing lights that used to be found surrounding movie marquees.

Figure 2.106 Changing the Color Indicates setting changes where the color overlay appears.

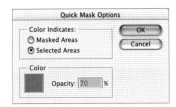

Figure 2.107 Quick Mask Options settings used.

Keyboard Shortcuts

Function	Macintosh	Windows
Select All	Command-A	Ctrl-A
Deselect	Command-D	Ctrl-D
Reselect	Shift-Command-D	Shift-Ctrl-D
Select Inverse	Shift-Command-I	Shift-Ctrl-I
Feather	Option-Command-D	Alt-Ctrl-D
Marquee Tool	M	M
Lasso Tool	L	L
Fill Selection	Shift-Delete	Shift-Backspace
Magic Wand Tool	W	W
Fill with Foreground	Option-Delete	Alt-Backspace
Fill with Background	Command-Delete	Ctrl-Backspace

Courtesy of Tom Nick Cocotos, www.cocotos.com

Courtesy of Tom Nick Cocotos, www.cocotos.com

3
Layers Primer

Courtesy of Tom Nick Cocotos, www.cocotos.com

The first rule to tinkering is to save all the parts.

—Paul Ehrlich

NEW IN 7

Adobe has added just a few new features to the Layers palette in 7.0. In this chapter we'll look at the new Delete Hidden Layers and Delete Linked Layers commands.

Layers Primer

Our capacity to take things for granted seems to have no bounds. How often do you sit back and think, "Wow, life has really changed since the days when Smith Corona ruled and an Apple was just something you ate for lunch"? Probably seldom. However, if you think about it, you'll realize that colossal changes have taken place. We attained a unique kind of digital freedom when we evolved from the primordial ooze of manual typewriters, stat cameras, and typesetters. For graphic artists, this change has been nothing short of revolutionary.

In its own way, Photoshop's introduction of the Layers palette has had an equally profound impact on the graphic arts community. Before the Layers palette, we were forced to be very precise and final in our thoughts, because having to redo the work was incredibly time-consuming. The Layers palette released us from the shackles of single-layer images and gave us the ability to really let loose and explore our creative ideas.

How Do Layers Work?

Figure 3.1 Layers isolate different parts of the image.

At first glance, layers might seem complex, but the idea behind them is rather simple. You isolate different parts of your image onto independent layers (**Figure 3.1**). These layers act as if they are separate documents stacked one on top of the other. By putting each image on its own layer, you can freely change your document's look and layout without committing to the changes. If you paint, apply a filter, or make an adjustment, it affects only the layer on which you're working. If you get into a snarl over a particularly troublesome layer, you can throw it away and start over. The rest of your document will remain untouched.

You can make the layers relate to each other in interesting ways, such as by poking holes in them to reveal an underlying image. I'll show you some great techniques using this concept in Chapter 13, "Enhancement."

But first, you need to pick up on the basics—the foundations—of layers. If you've used layers for a while, you might find some of this chapter a bit too basic. On the other hand, you might find some juicy new tidbits.

Meeting the Layers

Before we jump in and start creating a bunch of layers, you should get familiar with their place of residence: the Layers palette (**Figure 3.2**). You're going to be spending a lot of time with this palette, so take a moment now to get on friendly terms with it. It's not terribly complicated, and after you've used it a few times, you should know it like the back of your hand.

As you make your way through this chapter, you'll learn about the Layers palette and the fundamental tasks associated with it. Also, I'll throw in a few layer styles just for the heck of it. Now, assuming that you've done your part and introduced yourself to the Layers palette, let's get on with the business of creating and manipulating layers in Photoshop.

Creating Layers

Photoshop will automatically create the majority of layers for you. A new layer is added anytime you copy and paste an image or drag a layer between documents (we'll talk about this later in the chapter). If you're starting from scratch, however, you can click the new-layer icon at the bottom of the Layers palette to create a new, empty layer.

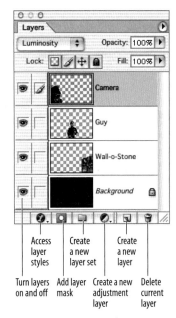

Figure 3.2 The Layers palette.

Figure 3.3 A new layer.

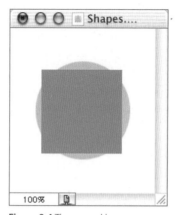

Figure 3.4 The second layer.

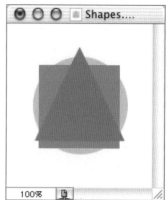

Figure 3.5 The third layer.

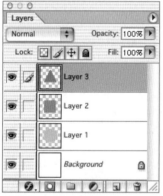

Figure 3.6 The Layers palette view.

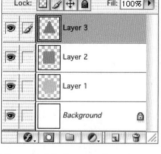

NOTES

To create a triangle, use the Polygon Shape tool and set the Sides setting to 3 in the Options bar.

I often create a new layer before using any of the painting tools or the Gradient tool. Because these tools apply changes directly to the active layer, the changes are difficult to modify once they've been applied. I like working with a safety net, so before using these tools, I create a new layer where I can easily edit the changes without disturbing the underlying image.

Give it a try: Create a new document and then use the Layers palette to create a new layer. Pick a bright color to paint with and then use one of the shape tools (using the rightmost setting of the three available in the upper left of the Options bar) to draw a big circle (**Figure 3.3**). Now create another layer, and draw a square on it, using a different color (**Figure 3.4**). Finally, create a third layer, and draw a triangle on it (**Figure 3.5**). You can use this simple document you've just created to try out the concepts in the following sections that describe the features of the Layers palette (**Figure 3.6**).

Active Layer

You can edit only one layer at a time. Remember, Photoshop thinks of the layers as if they were separate documents. The layer you're currently working on is highlighted in the Layers palette. You should also see a little paintbrush icon next to it—that's just another indication that the layer is active for editing. To change the active layer, just click the name of another layer. Only one layer can be active at a time.

Stacking Order

You can change the stacking order of the layers by dragging the name of one layer above or below the name of another layer in the Layers palette. The topmost layers can often obstruct your view of the underlying images. You can change this by reordering the layers so that small images are near the top of the stack and the larger ones are near the bottom (**Figures 3.7 to 3.10**).

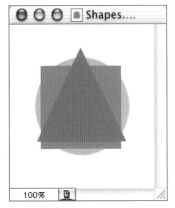

Figure 3.7 The original image.

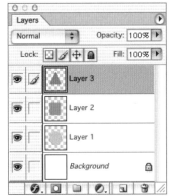

Figure 3.8 The original Layers palette.

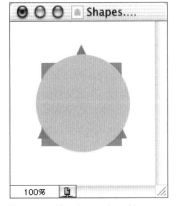

Figure 3.9 The changed stacking order.

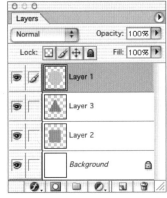

Figure 3.10 The revised Layers palette.

Background Image

Photoshop will not permit you to drag a layer below the background, because it doesn't think of the background as a layer. If you liken the layers to the individual pages in a pad of tracing paper, you could think of the pad's cardboard backing as the background layer. The background is always opaque and cannot be moved. In some circumstances, though, you might want to delete the background. For example, when you output images to videotape, they can't be overlaid onto video if the background layer is present.

However, most of the time, keeping the background or not is just a personal preference. You don't have to have

NOTES

If your document doesn't have a background (because you accidentally deleted or renamed the background), you can convert one of the existing layers into a background by choosing Layer > New > Layer from Background. Just changing the layer's name back to "Background" will not do the job.

In previous versions of Photoshop, you had to press Option (Mac), or Alt (Windows) and double-click on a layer to change its name (the Background layer could be changed without holding a key). The naming was done in a dialog box instead of happening directly in the Layers palette.

You can change the checkerboard's appearance by choosing Edit > Preferences > Transparency & Gamut. You can even change it to solid white by changing the Grid Size setting to none.

a background in your document. If you want to convert the background into a normal layer, just change its name (the background image must be named "Background"; otherwise, it becomes a normal layer). To change the name of a layer, double-click the layer's name in the Layers palette and then type a new name.

The Eyeballs: What They See Is What You Get

The eyeballs in the Layers palette aren't just cute; they determine which layers will be visible in your document as well as which ones will print. The eyeballs turn on and off in a toggle effect when you click them: Now you see them, now you don't.

If you turn off all the eyeballs in the Layers palette, Photoshop will fill your screen with a checkerboard. This checkerboard indicates that there's nothing visible in the document. (If Photoshop filled your screen with white instead, you might assume that there was a layer visible that was filled with white.) You can think of the checkerboard as the areas of the document that are transparent. When you view a single layer, the checkerboard indicates the transparent areas of that layer. As you turn on the other layers in the document, the checkerboard is replaced with the information contained on those layers. When multiple layers are visible, the checkerboard indicates where the underlying image will not be obstructed by the elements on the visible layers (**Figures 3.11** to **3.14**).

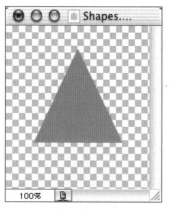

Figure 3.11 The checkerboard indicates a transparent area.

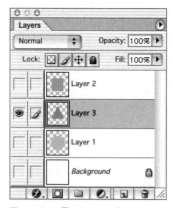

Figure 3.12 The Layers palette view.

Figure 3.13 As more layers become visible, the transparent areas become smaller.

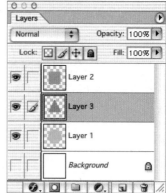

Figure 3.14 The Layers palette view.

Opacity

The Opacity setting at the top of the Layers palette controls the opacity of the active layer. When this setting is lowered, the entire layer becomes partially transparent (transparent is the exact opposite of opaque). If you want to lower the opacity in a specific area instead of the entire layer, you can lower the opacity of the Eraser tool and then brush across the area of the layer you want to become more transparent—that is, unless the background is active. If you use the Eraser tool on the background, it will simply paint with your background color instead of truly deleting areas (remember, the background is always opaque).

Try this: Open the document you created earlier in this chapter. Create a new layer and then use any painting tool to brush across the layer. Now, lower the Opacity setting in the Layers palette to 70% (**Figures 3.15** to **3.17**).

Now let's compare this effect with what happens when you lower the Opacity setting of the Paintbrush tool. Create another new layer; however, this time leave the layer's Opacity setting at 100%. Now choose the Paintbrush tool, change the tool's Opacity setting to 70% (in the Options bar), and then brush across the layer (just don't overlap the paint you created earlier). The paint should look exactly the same as the paint that appears in the other layer (**Figures 3.18** and **3.19**).

NOTES

To quickly turn off all the eyeballs in the Layers palette and view only the layer you're interested in, simply Option-click (Mac) or Alt-click (Windows) one of the eyeball icons. You can turn all the eyeball icons back on by Option-clicking (Mac) or Alt-clicking (Windows) the same eyeball a second time.

To quickly change the opacity of a layer, switch to the Move tool (typing V will switch you to the Move tool) and then use the number keys on your keyboard (1=10%, 3=30%, 56=56%, and so on).

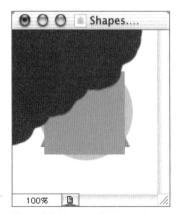

Figure 3.15 Layer at 100% opacity.

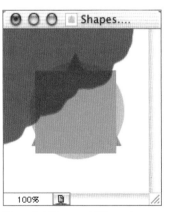

Figure 3.16 Layer at 70% opacity.

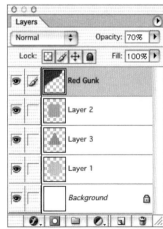

Figure 3.17 Lowering the opacity of a layer affects the entire layer.

NOTES

You can figure out the exact opacity of an area by Option-clicking (Mac) or Alt-clicking (Windows) its eyeball icon and then opening the Info palette. Click the eyedropper in the Info palette, and choose Opacity; you'll get a separate readout that indicates how opaque the area is below your cursor.

You'll be using the Move tool a lot. Because of this, Adobe has provided a quick way to temporarily switch to the Move tool: Just hold down Command (Mac) or Ctrl (Windows). As long as that key is held down, you're using the Move tool (even though it isn't highlighted in the Tools palette).

You can use the arrow keys (up arrow, down arrow, and so on) to nudge a layer one pixel at a time. Use Shift with the arrow keys to nudge a layer 10 pixels at a time.

Figure 3.18 The Paintbrush Options view.

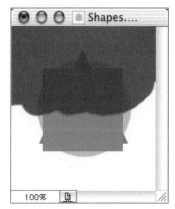

Figure 3.19 Painting with a 70% Opacity setting.

Finally, create one more new layer, and paint across it with the tool's Opacity setting at 100%. Now, brush across an area with the Eraser tool using an Opacity setting of 30% (**Figures 3.20** and **3.21**).

Figure 3.20 The Eraser Options view.

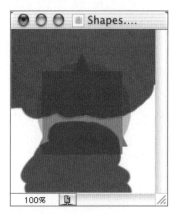

Figure 3.21 Using the Eraser tool with a low Opacity setting will also make areas of a layer transparent.

All of these options do the same thing to your image. You just have to think a bit: Do you want to apply the Opacity setting to the entire layer? If so, use the Layers palette's Opacity setting. Do you want to apply the Opacity setting to only part of the layer? If so, use the Opacity setting in the tool's Options bar. Do you want to change the opacity of an area you've already painted across? If so, use the Eraser tool with an Opacity setting.

Photoshop always (well, almost always) offers you more than one way of doing things. It reminds me of my favorite hardware store, McGuckins. It's the kind of place that takes your breath away—it has everything! If you just want a screwdriver, you'll probably find an entire aisle full of screwdrivers, each one designed for a specific use. Photoshop has the same approach; you just have to play around with it to figure out which tool best suits your needs.

Moving Layers

If you want to move everything that's on a particular layer, first make that layer active by clicking its name; then use the Move tool to drag it around the screen (**Figure 3.22**). If you drag the layer onto another document window, Photoshop will copy the layer into that document. If you want to move just a small area of the layer, you can make a selection and then drag from within the selected area using the Move tool.

Trimming the Fat

If you use the Move tool to reposition a layer, and a portion of the layer starts to extend beyond the edge of your document, Photoshop will remember the information beyond the edge (**Figure 3.23**). Therefore, if you move the layer away from the edge, Photoshop is able to bring back the information that was not visible. You can save a lot of memory by getting Photoshop to clip off all the information beyond the edge of the document (**Figure 3.24**).

NOTES

If you've made a portion of a layer partially transparent with the Eraser or Paint tool set to a low opacity, you can attempt to bring a layer back to 100% opacity by duplicating it multiple times. Keep in mind that it might take quite a few duplicates to get the layer back to full opacity. Once the image is completely opaque, just merge all the duplicate layers together.

When I need to precisely position a layer, I usually lower the Opacity setting just enough so I can see the underlying layers. You can do this quickly by using the number keys on your keyboard (0 to 9) when using the Move tool. After positioning the layer, just press 0 to bring the layer back to 100% opacity.

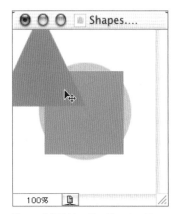

Figure 3.22 Using the Move tool to reposition a layer.

WARNING

Use the "trim the fat" technique only if you're absolutely sure you won't need the information beyond the edge of the document, because you cannot get it back once you've cropped it (that is, without resorting to the History palette).

The default setting in the Crop tool is to delete the areas that extend beyond the edge of your image. You can prevent it from deleting those areas by clicking the Hide setting in the Crop tool Options bar (it will be available only in files that contain layers). That will cause Photoshop to reduce the size of the image based on the cropping rectangle you specify, but it will retain the information that extends beyond the edge of the image. This setting can be useful when you'd like to create an animation in Adobe ImageReady and you'd like an object to start offscreen.

Here's a little trick for trimming off that fat (or big data, as Adobe calls it). Just choose Select > All and then choose Image > Crop—no more wasted memory.

Figure 3.23 The original image. (© 2002 Stockbyte, www.stockbyte.com)

Figure 3.24 After the image is cropped.

Copying Between Documents

When you use the Move tool, you can do more than just drag a layer around the document on which you're working. You can also drag a layer on top of another document (**Figure 3.25**). This copies the entire layer into the second document. The copied layer will be positioned directly above the active layer. This is similar to copying and pasting, but it takes up a lot less memory because Photoshop doesn't store the image on the clipboard. You can achieve the same result by dragging the name of a layer from the Layers palette onto another document window.

When you drag layers between documents, occasionally an image will appear as if it has not only been copied, but also scaled at the same time. That's not what's really happening. Instead, you're viewing the two images at different magnifications (**Figure 3.26**). Look at the tops of the documents; if the percentages do not match, the image size will appear to change when you drag the image between the documents. If you view both images with the same magnification, this won't happen. It doesn't change how large the image is; it simply gives you a preview of how large it will look. It's just like putting your hand under a magnifying glass. Your hand looks larger, but when you pull your hand out, it looks normal again.

NOTES

When dragging between documents, Photoshop will position the layer based on where your cursor was when you clicked the image and where you released the mouse button in the second document. To center the image, hold down the Shift key when dragging to another document.

Figure 3.25 To copy between documents, use the Move tool to drag from the image window, or drag the name of the layer in the Layers palette. (© 2002 Stockbyte, www.stockbyte.com)

Figure 3.26 Images viewed at different magnifications.

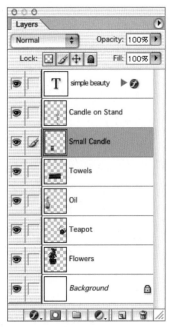

Figure 3.27 The Layers palette view.

Figure 3.28 Transforming a layer.

Duplicating Layers

If you have a picture of Elvis, and you want to make Elvis twins, just drag the name of the layer onto the new-layer icon at the bottom of the Layers palette. This icon has two purposes: It will duplicate a layer if you drag one on top of it, or it will create a new empty layer if you just click it.

Deleting Layers

If you've created a document that looks a little cluttered, you can delete a layer by dragging its name onto the trash icon at the bottom of the Layers palette. Or, if you have a long distance to drag to get your layer in the trash, try Option-clicking (Mac) or Alt-clicking (Windows) the trash icon instead (the Option or Alt key prevents a warning dialog box from appearing). However, this icon does not work like the trash on a Mac or the recycle bin in Windows. Once you put something in it, you can't get it back (that is, without resorting to the History palette).

Leapin' Layers! More Tools and Toys

Photoshop packs a large array of layer-manipulation controls. These controls allow you to go way beyond just creating, duplicating, and deleting layers. You'll be able to distort, adjust, and add wild effects after you wade through all these options.

Transforming Layers

To rotate, scale, or distort a layer, choose one of the options in the Edit > Transform menu; then pull the handles to distort the image. This will distort the current layer as well as any layers linked to it (**Figures 3.27** and **3.28**). When you like the way your image looks, press the Enter key to commit to the change (press Esc to abort). If you want to know more about the transformation controls, see Chapter 2, "Selection Primer."

Linking Layers

If you need to move or transform more than one layer at a time, just click to the left of one of the preview thumbnails in the Layers palette. When you do, a link (chain) symbol will appear (**Figure 3.29**). This indicates that the active layer is now linked to all the layers that have the link symbol next to them. When you use the Move tool or choose Edit > Transform, the current layer and all the layers linked to it will change. This feature doesn't allow you to do anything other than move or transform layers (for example, you can't apply a filter to multiple layers).

When layers are linked, you can choose one of the options from the Layer > Align Linked menu or the Move tool Options bar to change their position relative to each other. For example, you can align the top edges of the linked layers, or you can center them horizontally.

Locking Up

The icons at the top of the Layers palette allow you to lock the transparency, image, and position of an individual layer (**Figure 3.30**). Once a layer has been locked, changes that can be performed on that layer are limited.

Lock Transparency

The Lock Transparency icon (which looks like a checkerboard) at the top of the Layers palette gets in my way most often (because I forget it's turned on). Lock Transparency prevents you from changing the transparency of areas. Each layer has its own Lock Transparency setting. Therefore, if you turn on the Lock Transparency checkbox for one layer and then switch to another layer, the Layers palette will display the setting for the second layer, which might be different from the first one.

Try using the Eraser tool when Lock Transparency is turned on—it will mess with your mind! Because the Eraser tool usually makes areas transparent (by completely deleting them), it will start painting instead when Lock Transparency is turned on. It will fill with the current background color any areas you drag over. However, if you paint across an area that's

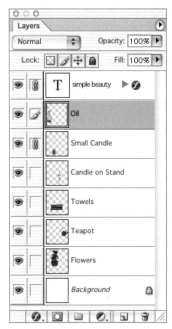

Figure 3.29 The chain icon indicates linked layers.

NOTES

When dragging linked layers between documents, be sure to drag from the image window instead of the Layers palette; otherwise, only one layer will be moved.

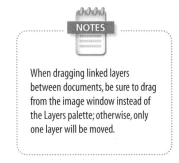

Figure 3.30 The Lock checkboxes.

transparent, it doesn't change the image at all (because the transparent areas are being preserved). You can see how it can get in your way if you forget you turned it on.

Try this: Open a photo, and delete areas around it using the Eraser tool. To accomplish this, you'll have to change the name of the background first (you can't poke a hole in the background, but you can on a layer); then make sure Lock Transparency is turned off. Otherwise, you can't make areas transparent. Now use the Eraser tool to remove the areas that surround the subject of the photo, then choose Filter > Blur > Gaussian Blur and use a really high setting. You'll notice that the edge of the image fades out and blends with the transparent areas surrounding it (**Figure 3.31**). Now, choose Edit > Undo and try doing the same thing with the Lock Transparency option turned on (**Figure 3.32**). Notice that the edge cannot fade out because Photoshop will not change the transparency with this option turned on.

Figure 3.31 Lock Transparency is off.   **Figure 3.32** Lock Transparency is on.

Here is another example: Create a new layer, and scribble across it with any painting tool, making sure the Lock Transparency option is turned off. Next, drag across the image with the Gradient tool. The gradient should fill the entire screen (**Figure 3.33**). Now, choose Edit > Undo, and try doing the same thing with the Lock Transparency option turned on (**Figure 3.34**). Because Photoshop can't change the transparency of the layer, it cannot fill the transparent areas and therefore is limited to changing the areas that are opaque to begin with.

NOTES

Lock Transparency (also called Lock Transparent Pixels) was known as Preserve Transparency in previous versions of Photoshop.

Figure 3.33 Lock Transparency is off.

Figure 3.34 Lock Transparency is on.

When you're trying to use any of the techniques in this book, be sure to keep an eye on that little Lock Transparency checkbox. If it's turned on when you don't want it to be, it might ruin the entire effect you're trying to achieve. Therefore, unless I specifically tell you to turn it on, you should assume that it should be left off (that's the default setting). If I ever tell you to turn it on, I'll let you know when to turn it back off again so that you don't get messed up when trying to reproduce a technique from this book. Now, turn off that pesky (but useful) setting, and let's continue exploring Photoshop.

Lock Image

The lock-image icon (which looks like a paintbrush) at the top of the Layers palette prevents you from changing the pixels that make up a layer. That means you won't be able to paint, erase, apply an adjustment or filter, or do anything else that would change the look of that layer. Just as with Lock Transparency, each layer has its own Lock Image setting. I use this feature after I've finished color-correcting and retouching a layer so I don't accidentally change it later on.

Lock Position

The lock-position icon (which looks like the Move tool) at the top of the Layers palette prevents you from moving the active layer. I check this feature to prevent someone else from accidentally moving an element that I've taken great care to position correctly.

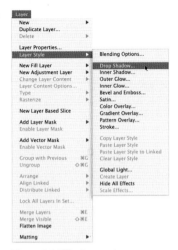

Figure 3.35 The Layer > Layer Style menu.

Lock All

The lock-all icon (which looks like a padlock) at the top of the Layers palette locks the transparency, image, and position of the current layer.

Layer Styles

A bunch of really neat options are available under the Layer > Layer Style menu (**Figure 3.35**). You'll find the same options under the Layer Style pop-up menu at the bottom of the Layers palette (it's the leftmost icon). To experiment with these options, first create a new, empty layer, and paint on it with any of the painting tools. Then apply one of the effects found in the Layer > Layer Style menu: Drop Shadow, Inner Shadow, Inner Glow, Outer Glow, Bevel and Emboss, etc. (**Figures 3.36** to **3.38**). You can use the default settings for now. After applying an effect, use the Eraser tool to remove some of the paint on that layer. Did you notice that the layer effect updates to reflect the changes you make to the layer? You can even lower the Fill setting at the top of the Layers palette to keep the effects at full strength while you make the rest of the image on that layer disappear. Layer styles create in one simple step the same results that would usually require multiple layers and a lot of memory.

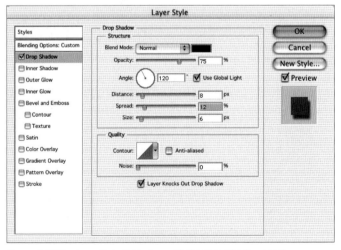

Figure 3.36 The Layer Style dialog box with the Drop Shadow panel.

Figure 3.37 The original image.

Figure 3.38 Drop Shadow style is shown in the middle of the document.

In fact, you can choose Layer > Layer Style > Create Layer to have Photoshop create the layers that would usually be needed to create the effect. For example, you might want to choose Create Layers when you're going to give your file to someone who is using an older version of Photoshop. (Photoshop 5.5 supports some, but not all, of the styles in Photoshop 6.0 and 7.0.) Let's take a look at what different layer styles do to your image (**Figures 3.39** to **3.42**). You can even lower the Fill setting at the top of Photoshop 7.0's Layers palette to reduce the opacity of the layer contents, while keeping the Layer Style at full strength (**see Figure 3.42a**).

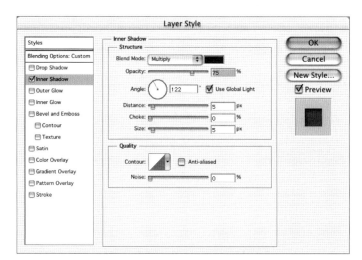

Figure 3.39 The Layer Style dialog box with the Inner Shadow panel

Figure 3.40 Inner Shadow style is shown in the middle of the document.

Figure 3.41 Outer Glow style is shown in the middle of the document.

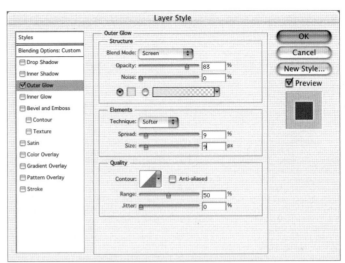

Figure 3.42 The Layer Style dialog box with the Outer Glow panel.

Figure 3.42a A result of lowering the fill opacity to 0.

NOTES

In previous versions of Photoshop, you had to press Option (Mac), or Alt (Windows) and double-click on a layer to find the Fill Opacity setting.

Adjustment Layers

When you choose an option available in the Image > Adjustments menu, it affects only the layer that's currently active. (Remember, Photoshop treats each layer as if it were a separate document.) However, there's a special type of layer that will allow you to apply these adjustments to multiple layers. This is known as an *adjustment layer.*

To create an adjustment layer, choose Layer > New Adjustment Layer, or choose the type of adjustment you'd like from the Adjustment Layer pop-up menu at the bottom of the Layers palette (it looks like a circle filled with half black and half white). After you choose which type of adjustment you want to use (we'll discuss adjustment settings in the Production Essentials section of this book), the changes will modify all the layers that are underneath the adjustment layer. You can move the adjustment layer up or down in the layers stack to affect more or fewer layers.

These changes are not permanent; at any time you can simply turn off the eyeball icon on the adjustment layer and the image will return to normal. You can also lessen the effect of the adjustment layer by lowering its Opacity setting. To change the adjustment settings, simply double-click the Adjustment Layer icon on the left side of the adjustment layer (**Figures 3.43** to **3.47**).

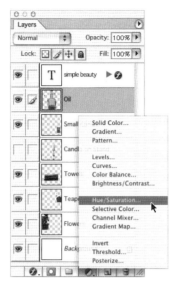

Figure 3.43 The Adjustment Layer pop-up menu.

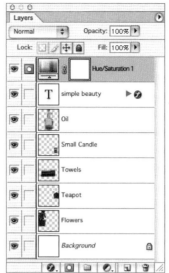

Figure 3.44 The Hue/Saturation adjustment layer at the top of the Layers palette.

Figure 3.45 Hue/Saturation affects all layers.

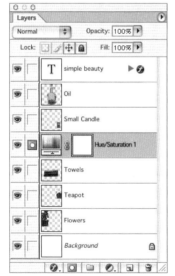

Figure 3.46 Changing the stacking order of the Hue/Saturation adjustment layer.

Figure 3.47 The adjustment layer applies to all layers below it but not to the layers above it.

Fill Layers

The options in the Layer > New Fill Layer menu allow you to add solid color, gradient, and pattern content to a layer. This is especially useful when combined with Vector Mask as described in Chapter 12. If you don't want a fill layer to fill your entire document, then make a selection before creating one. After a fill layer has been created, you can reset your foreground and background colors to black/white by pressing D. Then you can use the Eraser tool to hide the area and the Paintbrush tool to make areas visible again.

Solid Color Layer

Choosing Layer > New Fill Layer > Solid Color will bring up a color picker where you can specify the color that will be used for the solid color layer. After you've created one of these layers, you can double-click the leftmost thumbnail of the layer in the Layers palette to edit the color.

Gradient Layer

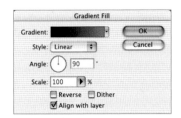

Choosing Layer > New Fill Layer > Gradient will ask you to name the layer and then it will create a new layer that contains a gradient (**Figure 3.48**). The gradient is always editable by double-clicking the leftmost thumbnail in the Layers palette. If the "Align with layer" checkbox is turned on, then the start and end points of the gradient are determined by the contents of the layer instead of the document's overall size.

Figure 3.48 The Gradient Fill dialog box.

Pattern Layer

Choosing Layer > New Fill Layer > Pattern allows you to create a new layer that contains a repeating pattern (**Figure 3.49**). I like to use this type of layer to add a brushed-aluminum look to a background. Then, if I ever decide to change the pattern, it's as simple as double-clicking the thumbnail in the Layers palette and choosing New Pattern from the drop-down menu.

Figure 3.49 The Pattern Fill dialog box.

The Blending Mode Menu

The Blending Mode menu at the top left of the Layers palette is immensely useful. It allows the information on one layer to blend with the underlying image in interesting and useful ways. Using this menu, you can quickly change the color of objects, colorize grayscale images, add reflections to metallic objects, and much more. This is an advanced feature, so you'll have to wait until you get to Chapter 13 to find out more about it.

Automatic Selections

To select everything on a particular layer, just Command-click (Mac) or Ctrl-click (Windows) the name of the layer. You can hold down the Shift key to add to a selection that already exists, or use the Option key (Mac) or Alt key (Windows) to take away from the current selection (**Figures 3.50** to **3.53**).

Figure 3.50 Command-click (Mac) or Ctrl-click (Windows) a layer to select all the objects on that layer.

Figure 3.51 The result of Command-clicking (Mac) or Ctrl-clicking (Windows).

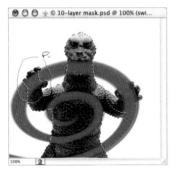

Figure 3.51 Refining the selection with the Lasso tool, while holding down Option (Mac), or Alt (Windows) to take away from the selection.

Figure 3.53 The result of copying the selected area of Godzilla and pasting it on a layer above the swirl (look at his neck).

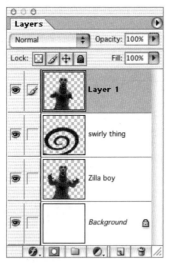

Figure 3.54 Result of using Layer > New Layer Via Copy and moving the new layer over the swirly layer.

Via Copy

The Layers menu offers you a wide variety of options for copying, merging, and manipulating layers. Let's look at one of these choices. If you select an area of your image and then choose Layer > New Layer Via Copy, the area you've selected will be copied from the layer you were working on and moved to a brand-new layer in the same position (**Figure 3.54**). This is particularly handy when you want to move just a portion of a layer so that you can place it on top of another layer.

All Layers

When you're editing on a layer, some of the editing tools might not work the way you expect them to. This happens because most of the tools act as if each layer is a separate document—they ignore all layers except the active one. That is, unless the tool has the All Layers checkbox turned on in the Options bar of the tool you're using. This checkbox allows the tools to act as if all the layers have been combined into one layer (**Figures 3.55** to **3.57**).

Figure 3.55 Using the Paint Bucket tool to add color with the All Layers option turned off.

Figure 3.56 Using the Paint Bucket tool with All Layers turned on.

Figure 3.57 The All Layers checkbox in the Paint Bucket Options bar.

Shortcuts

You'll be doing a lot of switching between layers, and this can get a bit tedious. Therefore, I'll show you some quick shortcuts. First, you can Command-click (Mac) or Ctrl-click (Windows) anywhere in the image window when using the Move tool to activate the layer directly below your cursor. Then you can find out which layer you're working on by glancing at the Layers palette.

You won't always need the layer below your cursor, so instead of Command-clicking (Mac) or Ctrl-clicking (Windows), try Control-clicking (Mac) or right-clicking (Windows). This will bring up a menu of all the layers that contain pixels directly below your cursor; you just choose the name of the layer you want to work on and Photoshop will switch to that layer.

Remember that you can get to the Move tool temporarily at any time by holding down the Command key (Mac) or Ctrl key (Windows). Therefore, if you hold down Command and Control (Mac) or Ctrl and right-click (Windows) at the same time, no matter what tool you are using, Photoshop will present you with the pop-up menu.

Layer Sets

Have you ever had one of those mega-complicated images with dozens of layers? If so, you are probably familiar with the agony of having to fumble through an endless sea of layers, hoping you won't drown before you find the right one. If this describes you, you'll be ecstatic to know you can group a bunch of layers into a set. A set looks like a folder in the Layers palette. You can view all the layers in the set or just the set name.

To create a set, click the Layer Set icon at the bottom of the Layers palette (it looks like a folder). A folder appears in the list of layers. You can move any number of layers into the set by dragging and dropping them onto the folder icon. The set will have a small arrow just to its left that allows you to collapse the set down to its name or expand the set to show you all the layers it contains

NOTES

You can also create a layer set by linking multiple layers together and then choosing New Set From Linked from the side menu of the Layers palette.

(**Figures 3.58** and **3.59**). This can greatly simplify the Layers palette, making a document of 100-plus layers look as if it's made of only five layers.

Layer sets can also be useful when you want to reorganize the layers in your image. If one of the layers within a set is active, then using the Move tool will affect only that layer (unless it's linked to other layers). If the layer *set* is active, then using the Move tool will move all the layers within that set. You can also move multiple layers up or down in the layers stack by first putting them into a set and then dragging the name of the set up or down in the layers stack.

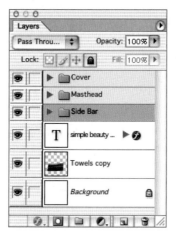

Figure 3.58 Collapsed layer sets.

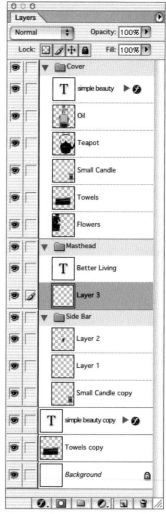

Figure 3.59 Expanded layer sets.

No Thumbnail Mode

If, after organizing your image into layer sets, you still find that the Layers palette is a mess, then you might want to simplify the way Photoshop displays layers. If you choose Palette Options from the side menu of the Layers palette, you'll find the option that allows you to turn off the layer thumbnails. Once you've done that, you should find that the list of layers takes up a lot less space, but you still have the full functionality of all of Photoshop's features (**Figures 3.60** and **3.61**). This also speeds up the screen redraw of the Layers palette.

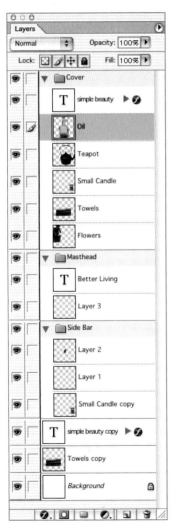

Figure 3.60 The Layers palette using the default thumbnail size.

Figure 3.61 The Layers palette after setting the Thumbnails setting to none.

Figure 3.62 The Layer Properties dialog box.

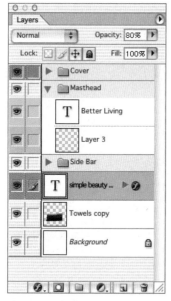

Figure 3.63 Each layer can be color-coded using one of seven colors.

WARNING

Once you've merged two layers, it's awfully hard to get them apart—the only way is to use the History palette. However, even with the History palette, you might lose all the changes you've made since you merged the layers.

Color Coding

If you work within a large group of Photoshop users, it can be useful to assign colors to layers to indicate their current status. Maybe some text needs to be proofed, maybe the client approved a certain part of the image, or perhaps an area needs to be sent off for color-correction. All you have to do is Control-click (Mac) or right-click (Windows) on the name of a layer and choose Layer Properties. That will bring up a dialog box where you can color-code a layer or layer set (**Figures 3.62** and **3.63**).

Merging Layers

When you create a complicated image that contains dozens of layers, your project can start hogging memory, which in turn makes it difficult to manage all the layers. Every time you create a new layer and add something to it, Photoshop gobbles up more memory. Photoshop not only has to think about what's on that layer, it also has to remember what's below the layer (even if that information is completely covered by the information on the layers above).

Whenever possible, I try to simplify my image by merging layers together. This combines the layers into a single layer and thus saves memory (because Photoshop no longer has to remember the parts of those layers that were previously being covered). The side menu on the Layers palette and the Layer menu itself give you several ways to do this:

▶ **Merge Down:** Merges the active layer into the layer directly below it.

▶ **Merge Visible:** Merges all the layers that are currently visible in the main image window.

▶ **Merge Linked:** Merges all the layers that have the link symbol next to them, along with the active layer.

▶ **Flatten Image:** Merges all visible layers into the background, discards hidden layers, and fills empty areas with white.

When I'm creating a complex image, I often end up with a bunch of layers that don't really contribute to the result I was looking for. Maybe they were some experimental layers that I thought I might use later or some extras that I decided made the image look too busy. If that's the case, then I usually turn off the eyeball icons for each of those layers and then choose Photoshop 7.0's new Delete Hidden Layers command from the side menu of the Layers palette. Or, if there are a few hidden layers that I want to keep, I can still link all the disposable layers and then use the new Delete Linked command from the same menu.

If you want to know how much extra memory the layers take up as you're modifying your image, choose Document Sizes from the menu to the right of the numbers that appear at the bottom center of your document (**Figure 3.64**). The number on the left should stay relatively constant (unless you scale or crop the image); it indicates how much memory your image would use if all the layers were merged together. The number on the right indicates how much memory the image is using with all the layers included. This number changes as you add and modify your layers. Keep an eye on it so that you can see how memory-intensive the different layers are.

The number on the right might get huge if you're using a lot of layers; however, keep in mind that you'll know exactly how large the image will be when you're all done by glancing at the left number.

Figure 3.64 Memory usage indicator.

> **NOTES**
>
> To maintain your layers when saving a TIFF file in Photoshop 6.0, you'll need to choose Edit > Preferences > Saving Files and turn on the Enable Advanced TIFF Save Options checkbox. With that active, when you click OK in the Save dialog box, you'll be presented with the same options available in Photoshop 7.0's TIFF Options dialog box.

Done Playing Around?

You've spent hours toiling away on your image, and now you're ready to save your file so it can go on to its next stop (which might be a printing company or one of your clients, or perhaps it's going to be posted to the Web). Then again, maybe it's not going anywhere—you just want to rest your eyes, take a break, and work on it later. Wherever the image ends up, you need to make sure to save it in a format you can work with in Photoshop (complete with layers, paths, channels, and so on). Then you can save it in another format that's appropriate for its destination.

NOTES

The settings used to save GIF and JPEG files are covered in Chapter 19, "Optimization."

It would be wonderful if all software programs could work with the same format, but alas, they can't. Therefore, it's worth your while to get familiar with the various file formats available in Photoshop.

Saving Layered Files

If you're not too familiar with file formats, you might wonder why there are so many options in the Save dialog box. It's like anything else with Photoshop—you just have to think about the end use. If you're going to use the file in Photoshop and keep the layers, you'll want to save it in the Photoshop file format (also known as PSD). Photoshop, TIFF, and PDF are the only formats that recognize layers.

I mainly use the Photoshop format, since Photoshop 5.5 cannot extract the layers from a TIFF or PDF file. Unfortunately, most other programs cannot open files saved in the Photoshop file format, so it's a good habit to save the original image in Photoshop's native PSD format and then make a copy of the image without layers and save it in another format—JPEG or TIFF, for example.

Most formats other than Photoshop's native PSD format and the TIFF format (EPS, JPEG, and so on) can't handle multiple layers, so you'll have to merge all the layers into the background of your image. You can do this quickly by choosing Flatten Image from the side menu of the Layers palette. Flatten Image combines all your layers and any areas that were transparent are filled with white. The transparent areas are filled in because the other file formats don't know what to do with them. I usually save two versions of my files—one in the Photoshop file format (so I can get back to the layers) and one in TIFF or EPS format (to use in my page-layout program) or GIF or JPEG format (for the Web).

Closing Thoughts

Layers play such a huge role in Photoshop that to deny yourself any crucial information about them is asking for trouble. With every new release, Adobe likes to pack more and more functions into the Layers palette. So as time goes on, understanding them will become even more crucial. This is definitely a chapter you should feel comfortable with before you move on to the more advanced areas of Photoshop.

Ben's Techno-babble Decoder Ring

Lock Transparency: A function in Photoshop that "freezes" the transparency of a layer. While Lock Transparency is in effect, you cannot increase or decrease how transparent an area will appear.

Opacity: The Opacity setting determines how opaque (the opposite of transparent) the information on a layer will appear. An Opacity setting of 100% will not allow you to see the underlying image. A setting below 100% will allow the underlying image to partially show through the current layer.

Keyboard Shortcuts

FUNCTION	MACINTOSH	WINDOWS
Show/Hide Layers Palette	F7	F7
New Layer	Shift-Command-N	Shift-Ctrl-N
New Layer Via Copy	Command-J	Ctrl-J
New Layer Via Cut	Shift-Command-J	Shift-Ctrl-J
Toggle Lock Transparency	/	/
Make Top Layer Active	Shift-Option-]	Shift-Alt-]
Make Next Layer Active	Option-]	Alt-]
Make Previous Layer Active	Option-[	Alt-[
Make Bottom Layer Active	Shift-Option-[	Shift-Alt-[
Move Layer Up	Option-Command-]	Alt-Ctrl-]
Move Layer Down	Option-Command-[	Alt-Ctrl-[
Merge Down	Command-E	Ctrl-E
Merge Visible	Shift-Command-E	Shift-Ctrl-E

Courtesy of Gordon Studer, www.gordonstuder.com

Courtesy of Gordon Studer, www.gordonstuder.com

PART II

Production Essentials

Courtesy of Nick Koudis, www.koudis.com

4

Resolution Solutions

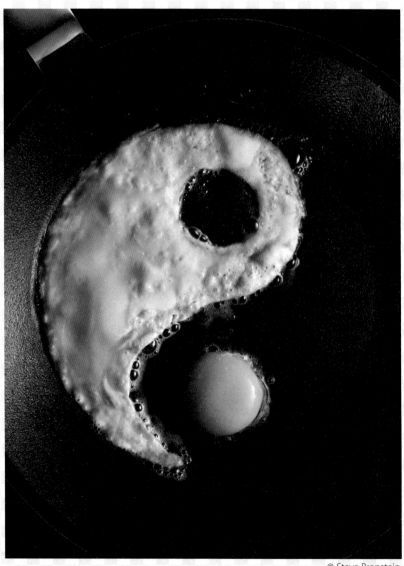

© Steve Bronstein

NEW IN 7

The concepts behind resolution have not changed in Photoshop 7.0, but resolution is such a critical issue that I've decided to completely rewrite this chapter in an attempt to make it easier for you to understand.

The difference between failure and success is doing a thing nearly right and doing it exactly right.

—Edward C. Simmons

Resolution Solutions

Resolution is one of those concepts that have a huge impact on the quality of your images, yet most people don't understand it. Part of the reason is that the term *resolution* can relate to so many things (printers, scanners, digital cameras, images, and more) and with each device it might mean something slightly different. To add to the confusion there are numerous terms used to describe the resolution for each of the different devices (ppi, dpi, lpi, megapixels, etc.). But it's by no means beyond the grasp of someone who is committed enough to read through this chapter a few times. The rewards are smaller file sizes, higher-quality images, and significantly less frustration. Let's start off with the general concept of resolution.

Understanding Pixel Size

NOTES

Notice that I said "every photograph," not every image. There are some features in Photoshop that are not made out of pixels. Those include paths, shape layers, and type layers. They print out with crisp edges regardless of the resolution setting of the document.

Every photograph you ever see in Photoshop is made out of a grid of different-colored squares that are known as pixels. So, imagine that you printed a photograph and then zoomed in on it with a microscope. Once you start to see the individual pixels, you can start to think about how large they are. If you slid a ruler under that microscope, you could measure the size of an individual pixel (**Figure 4.1**). Resolution is simply a measurement of how large a pixel is when it's printed. Maybe you end up with pixels that are 0.0769 inches in size. The only problem is that that's not a very friendly number, because most people don't like dealing with decimals. So, instead, why don't we look at more than one pixel and simply measure how many of them fit in 1 inch? In that case we'd end up with 13 pixels per inch, or ppi (**Figure 4.2**). The smaller the pixels are, the more of them you can fit into an inch, so higher ppi settings mean smaller pixels (**Figure 4.3**). *Resolution* simply means how large a pixel is when you print it, and it's usually measured in pixels per inch.

Figure 4.1 This pixel measures 0.0769 inches.

Figure 4.2 Here, 13 pixels fit in 1 inch.

Figure 4.3 From left to right: 30 ppi, 100 ppi, 200 ppi.

Let's see how that applies to an image. Imagine you have an image that's 4 by 6 inches and you wanted to fit 300 pixels in each inch. With that information and a little simple math, you can figure out the total number of pixels there would be in the width and height of the image. If you add up how many inches you have and multiply that by 300, then you could say you have 1,200 by 1,800 at 300 ppi (**Figure 4.4**). With that information, you could also go the other direction and figure out how many inches wide and tall the image is. Just take the width in pixels and divide it by how many pixels you'll be printing in each inch (1,200/300 = 4). So 1, 200 by 1,800 at 300 ppi is also 4 by 6 inches at 300 ppi. Either way, you would be describing the same image. That's exactly what Photoshop does when you choose Image > Image Size (**Figure 4.5**). At the top of the dialog box, Photoshop shows you the total number of pixels you have in the width and height of your image. At the bottom, it shows you how large those pixels will be when you go to print your image. That's usually the same number you typed into your scanner when you scanned the image, or, if you created the image from scratch, Photoshop would have asked you for the resolution setting you wanted to use. For Photoshop to figure out the width in inches, all it does is take the total width in pixels and divide that by how many pixels you'll be printing in each inch.

Figure 4.4 Adding up the pixel count. (original image © 2002 Stockbyte, www.stockbyte.com)

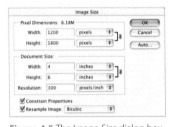

Figure 4.5 The Image Size dialog box.

Printing

Now let's see how resolution applies to printing. You can use many kinds of printers … an inkjet, a dye sub, a laser printer, or a commercial printing press. The problem is

Figure 4.6 Dye-sub output.

Figure 4.7 Inkjet output.

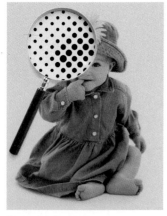

Figure 4.8 Laser printer output.

that most of those printing devices can't reproduce exactly what you see on your screen. Instead, the device simulates what you see onscreen using four solid colors. Look at **Figures 4.6, 4.7,** and **4.8**. The first one shows how a dye-sub printer would reproduce an image, the second how an inkjet printer would, and the third how a laser printer or printing press would output the same image. When you compare them, you'll notice that the dye sub gives the most detail and the laser printer gives the least. Wouldn't it make sense that you will need more info in your scan if it is going to be printed on a dye-sub printer instead of a laser printer or inkjet? Let's look at the different types of printers we can choose from and see how each one reproduces an image differently and why the image needs to have a different resolution.

Resolution and Line Art

When you have a pure black and pure white image, that's known as *line art*. With that type of image, you'll end up needing to use a special setting that you wouldn't normally use for photographic images. With any type of printer, find out the resolution of the printer and type the exact same number into your scanner when you scan it. For instance, my laser printer is 600 dpi, so when I scan a line art image for this printer, I use a scanning resolution of 600. That way the pixels that make up the image will be the same size as the dots that the printer will use to print it. If you're not sure what the resolution of your printer is, then look in the manual for the printer or look in an ad or catalog that features that model and it will usually be listed.

Resolution and Grayscale or Color Images

Inkjet

Let's see how an inkjet printer would simulate shades of gray (**Figure 4.9**). Inkjets use fixed-size dots and just pack them closer and closer together to create darker shades of gray. As long as those dots are so small that your eyes can't focus on them, your eye can't tell the difference between those solid black dots and the original photograph. When you print a full-color photograph, it's just a bit different.

The ink cartridge in your inkjet printer has four colors of ink (some have two shades of cyan and two of magenta, for a total of six). That means that it has to reproduce your color images using only solid cyan, magenta, yellow, and black dots. Just look at **Figure 4.10** and you'll see what I mean. It's the same concept as creating shades of gray, only that it's doing it with four colors of ink instead of just one.

Figure 4.9 Inkjets use tiny dots to simulate shades of gray.

Figure 4.10 Color images are made from four solid inks. (original image © 2002 PhotoSpin, www.photospin.com)

Here's how to find out the optimal image resolution for an inkjet printer: First, find out the resolution of your printer. Next, divide that number by 3 to calculate the resolution at which you should scan your images. You're welcome to use lower settings if you'd like a smaller file size, but I wouldn't go any higher than that. I own an Epson inkjet that has a resolution of 720 dpi. When I scan images, I divide 720 by 3 and end up with a suggested scanning resolution of 240. Some of the newer inkjet printers have resolutions as high as 2,880 dpi, but that doesn't mean that I use 960 ppi when I scan an image (2,880/3 = 960). The printer might be capable of delivering that much detail, but my eyes just aren't good enough to tell the difference between that and a lower-resolution image. In that case, I'd think of 960 as the absolute highest setting to use and I'd experiment with lower settings until I figured out how much quality I really need.

Laser Printer/Printing Press

A laser printer uses a different method than an inkjet printer to simulate shades of gray. Most laser printers are not attempting to deliver the photorealistic quality you can achieve on an inkjet printer. That's mainly because they use opaque toner instead of transparent ink. Since that's the case, they are more a device that would be used as the starting point for an image that will eventually be reproduced on a printing press. If you ever look really close at a grayscale photo in a newspaper, you might notice that it's made out of tiny black circles on a grid

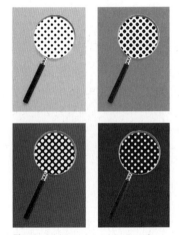

Figure 4.11 Simulating shades of gray using a halftone.

Figure 4.12 Five circles fit in an inch.

(**Figure 4.11**). That's known as a *halftone* and it's used because commercial printing presses that are used to print newspapers, brochures, and magazines can't reproduce those incredibly tiny dots that result in near photographic quality. When you print an image on a laser printer, there's a setting involved that determines how large those circles are. If we were to hold a ruler up to the image and count how many circles fit in an inch (in this case, they are on a grid that's rotated to 45 degrees), you might end up with five (**Figure 4.12**). So, you'd think that would be called 5 circles per inch, right? But it's not. That's because we don't always use a grid of circles. Printers can also use squares, diamonds, ovals, and other shapes (**Figure 4.13**). So we simply call this setting *lines per inch,* or *lpi,* really meaning how many lines (of whatever shape is being used) will fit in 1 inch. Once they get small enough that your eye can't focus on them anymore, then you get to the point when your eye can't tell the difference between those little black circles and a real grayscale photograph (**Figure 4.14**).

With a color image, the same thing happens. The only difference is that we use four colors of ink—cyan, magenta, yellow, and black (**Figure 4.15**). When the moment arrives that you finally click on the Print button (using Adobe Photoshop, Adobe InDesign, QuarkXPress, etc.), the program you're printing from needs a very important piece of information about how you want the printed version of your image to look: lines per inch (lpi). If you don't provide it, the program will use its own default setting, and that could be disastrous.

Figure 4.13 Different printers can output different shapes on a grid.

Figure 4.15 Full-color photo created from four solid colors of ink. (original image © 2002 PhotoSpin, www.photospin.com)

Figure 4.14 Dots small enough that your eye can't focus on them.

So what does all this have to do with resolution? To find out, let's look at the most common lpi settings used for different printing processes. Keep in mind that the cruder the printing process (such as a high-speed newspaper press printing on cheap paper), the harder it is to reproduce tiny dots, and the more precise the process (such as a slow-speed, sheet-fed printing press with high quality paper), the better it can reproduce those tiny dots. So it's the printing *process* (newspaper versus magazine, etc.) you'll be using that usually dictates which setting is necessary, rather than the printer *type* (laser, thermal wax, etc.). **Figure 4.16** shows the most common settings used. It also doesn't matter what the resolution of your printer is. When you go to the Page Setup dialog box, you'll find this setting called lines per inch. Here's how it relates to resolution.

FIGURE 4.16 Common LPI Settings

LPI	GENERAL USE
85	Newspaper advertisements
100	Newspaper editorial section
133	Magazines and brochures
150	High-end magazines and high-quality brochures
175	Annual reports and high-end brochures
53	300-dpi laser printers
106	600-dpi laser printers
212	1,200-dpi laser printers

To determine the best resolution for your image, multiply the desired lpi setting by 1.5 if you want to see a lot of detail, or multiply it by 2 if you would rather have the image look smoother. For example, a portrait used in a newspaper ad would be something that should look smooth; otherwise, you'll exaggerate the detail in the face, which usually makes people look older. Since newspapers usually use an lpi setting of 85 and I want things to look smooth, I'll multiply 85 by 2 and end up with 170, which is the resolution setting I should use when scanning the image. If I use anything higher than that, I'll end up with more information (detail) than I need, which might cause me to do a bunch of retouching on screen (unnecessary because my printer simply isn't capable of reproducing that much detail). If I use a setting lower than that, the pixels might end up being so large that you can see them (giving you the jaggy look).

There is one special instance when you'll want to use higher settings than what I've mentioned here. That would be when your image contains high-contrast lines. Examples would be guitar strings or a sailboat mast. If you're ever going to notice jaggies, it will be in these high-contrast lines. So, to ensure that the pixels are small enough, you'll want to bump up the resolution setting to at least 2.5 times the lpi setting that will be used to print the image (**Figures 4.17** and **4.18**).

You can use Photoshop's Image Size dialog box as a quick resolution calculator. With any image open, choose Image > Image Size and click on the Auto button. When you do, Photoshop will prompt you for the lpi setting that will be used when printing. Use the Good setting if you'd like to multiply the lpi by 1.5 to get crisp detail, or use the Best setting to multiply it by 2 and get a smooth result. The answer to the calculation will appear as the resolution setting once you click OK.

Dye Sub

Instead of using solid cyan, magenta, and yellow dots (like an inkjet or laser printer), dye-sub printers can really print shades of gray and shades of color without using solid dots. For this type of printer, you need to find out how small the pixels are that your printer is capable of printing. That's known as the resolution of your printer. Let's say you have a 300-dpi printer. If that's the case, then you want the resolution of your image to be the same as the resolution of your printer. That will make it so the pixels in your image will be exactly the same size as the dots your printer uses to print them out with. That way you will get the highest quality. You are welcome to use a lower setting than that, but if you do, you'll be sacrificing quality for the convenience of a smaller file size.

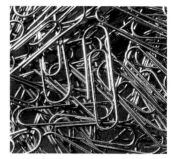

Figure 4.17 Scanned at standard resolution. (© 2002 Stockbyte, www.stockbyte.com)

Figure 4.18 Scanned at optimal resolution for high-contrast lines.

35mm Slides

Slides are similar to multimedia in that the resolution setting attached to the image is ignored. That's because you're always printing to the same-size end result and it will just scale your info up or down to fit that size. Like a dye-sub printer, slides can truly reproduce shades of gray and color instead of using only four solid colors. In this case, we need the pixels in our image to be the same size as the ones that will be used to output the image. If you ask someone who owns a slide recorder, they might tell you they have a 2K or 4K slide recorder. That's just like people saying they have a 300-dpi or 600-dpi laser printer. It's just that slide recorders are measured in K instead of dpi. K stands for 1,024. That means a 2K slide recorder can reproduce 2,048 pixels in the width of the slide (2 x 1,024 = 2,048) and a 4K recorder can handle 4,096 pixels (4 x 1,024 = 4,096). To find the proper scanning resolution, you need to figure out how many pixels your slide recorder can reproduce and then divide that by how wide your original image is in inches. So, if I have a 6-inch-wide original and I'll be printing it to a 4K slide recorder, then I'd want to divide 4,096 by 6 and I'd end up with a scanning resolution of 683. That's the exact setting needed to end up with the right amount of information for that kind of slide recorder—that is, if you want to get the absolute highest quality. You're welcome to use lower settings, but if you do, you simply won't be getting as much quality as what that slide recorder is capable of.

Multimedia/Internet

Let's talk about how your Web browser thinks about your images. It ignores the resolution setting. To show you what I mean, open Photoshop and choose Image > Image Size. Notice that the top describes how many pixels your image is made from and the bottom shows you how large the image will be when printed (**Figure 4.19**). But, if we switch to ImageReady, which is designed for Web graphics, you will notice that it takes a different approach. Since Web

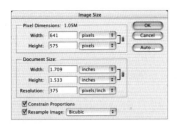

Figure 4.19 The Image Size dialog box.

browsers ignore the resolution setting, ImageReady does-n't even list a resolution setting when you create a new document (**Figure 4.20**) or choose Image Size (**Figure 4.21**). Remember that a number called pixels per inch usually determines how large the pixels will be when they are printed. That's also why you'll never find the width or height of your image measured in inches in ImageReady. It has no idea how large the pixels are on your screen, so it has no idea how much space your image will take up on your screen. When Photoshop is only thinking about onscreen use, it ignores the ppi setting of the image. That's because Photoshop can't control how large the pixels are that make up your screen. Instead, you are in control of it. You can change it by adjusting your operating system's settings. Choose Apple Menu > System Preferences and then click on the Displays icon (in Mac OS X), or Apple Menu > Control Panels > Monitors (in Mac OS 9), or choose Start > Settings > Control Panel, then double-click Display and click on Settings (Windows). That's where you can determine how much information can fit on your screen. (Remember, you might be able to change this setting on your screen, but you won't be able to change it for all the people who will be visiting your Web site. They will choose their settings, and you can't do anything about it.)

The more information you display, the smaller the pixels become. For example, let's say we used a setting of 1,024 by 768. That means that we'll have 1,024 pixels in the width of the screen and 768 in the height. Which means we'd need an image that's exactly 1,024 by 768 pixels to fill that screen. Let's figure out how we'd end up with that. Let's say the physical original that I'm going to put on my scanner is 6 inches wide. Really what we're trying to figure out is how many pixels the scanner should capture in each inch of the original to end up with 1,024 pixels total. It's just simple math. Take the number of pixels we need to end up with and divide that by how many inches wide the original is. In this case 1,024/6 = 171. So that's what I'd need to type into my scanner to end up with exactly 1,024 pixels total.

Figure 4.20 ImageReady's New Document dialog box.

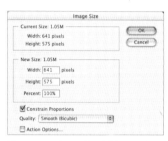

Figure 4.21 ImageReady's Image Size dialog box.

But what if you don't want to fill your entire screen? Instead, maybe you want the image to be about the same size as the original you put on your scanner. When that's the case, just use a generic setting of 85. There really isn't any ideal setting; this is just the average pixel size for most people's screens. Two numbers you'll hear quite often are 72 and 96. That's because the original Macintosh had a built-in screen that displayed exactly 72 pixels per inch. But once Apple stopped making them with a built-in screen, that was no longer true. On other monitors, the "generic" setting has always been 96 ppi. My preference is simply an average of those two: 85 ppi should give you something close to actual size onscreen.

To complicate matters, when you first open an image in Photoshop, it's not trying to show you how large the image will appear when printed or viewed in a Web browser; instead, it's just zooming out until you can see the entire image. To see exactly how large your image will look in a Web browser, you'll want to view it at 100% scale. To view it at 100% magnification, double-click on the Zoom tool, or choose View > Actual Pixels. If you find that that's too large, here's a simple technique I use for resizing things for the Web: Start by viewing it at 100%, then choose Window > Show Navigator. Move the slider at the bottom of the palette to scale the image. If it can't make things small enough, use the large and small mountain icons to go even further. Once you've got it at the size you need, note the percentage that appears in the lower left of the Navigator palette. That indicates exactly how much you need to scale your image to get it to appear that size in a Web browser. Now, to actually scale the image, choose Image > Image Size, turn on the Resample Image checkbox, then change the Inches pop-up menu to Percent and enter the number you saw in the Navigator palette (**Figure 4.22**). When you click OK, you'll notice that the image gets much smaller. To see how large it will appear in a Web browser, double-click on the Zoom tool and you should end up with exactly what you were looking for.

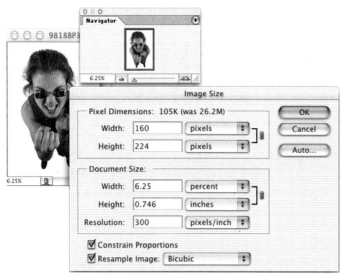

Figure 4.22 Entering the percentage from the Navigator palette. (original image © 2002 Stockbyte, www.stockbyte.com)

Digital Cameras

The resolution of a digital camera is not measured in pixels per inch; instead, it's measured in megapixels. A megapixel is simply 1 million pixels. To find out how many megapixels you need to create a particular image size, try the following: Choose File > New, set the resolution to what's needed for your type of output, and then set the width and height to what you desire. Once you've done that, click on the resolution field and then change the width and height pop-up menus to Pixels. Then multiply the width by the height to find out the total number of pixels you need. Finally, divide the result by 1,000,000 and you'll find out how many megapixels you need to end up with an image of that size. So, if you want to print 8-by-10-inch prints at 300 ppi, then Photoshop would let you know that you need 2,400 by 3,000 pixels. Multiplying 2,400 by 3,000 lets you know that you need 7,200,000 pixels total, which is 7.2 megapixels. Now, when you're out shopping for a digital camera, you know exactly what type of camera you need.

When you open an image from a digital camera, you'll find that the resolution is almost always set to 72 ppi. That's because the camera doesn't know how large you want to print your pixels, so it just plops in the default setting. I'll show you how I deal with that type of image once we get a chance to talk about something that's known as resampling.

Resolution and File Size

Let's see how the resolution setting you scan with affects your file sizes. Let's say you have a 1-by-1-inch original. If you scan it at 200 ppi, the file size will be 117 Kbytes (uncompressed). At 100 ppi, it would be 29 Kbytes, and at 50 ppi, it would be only 7 Kbytes (**Figure 4.23**). In general, it's best to go with the lowest setting that will give you a good result. The settings mentioned earlier in this chapter are the optimal settings, which in general will be the settings that give you the absolute highest-quality result. If you decide to use anything lower than what I mentioned earlier, be sure to do a test to ensure that your image doesn't become pixilated when it's printed.

If you're not sure how the image will be reproduced, then scan for the most demanding type of output you think you'd ever use, because you can always change things later. Let's take a look at what your options are for post-scan resolution changes.

Resampling

If you'd like to change how large the pixels are that make up your image (the ppi setting), just choose Image > Image Size and turn on the Resample Image checkbox. Any changes you make to the resolution setting will make the pixels larger or smaller, but the image will stay the same overall size. See **Figure 4.24** for an example. This is useful when you get an image that was scanned for a high-end purpose (such as a brochure) and you want to, for example, reuse it in a newspaper. So, it might start with a resolution of 300 ppi, but you need it to be only 170 ppi. By making that change, the file size would become less than half of what it was at the higher resolution.

When Resample Image is turned on, it's kind of like printing your image and then placing it on a scanner and scanning it. That would be fine as long as you're not asking to get more info out of it, because there simply isn't any more in the image. It doesn't harm an image to reduce its resolution using resampling because you are asking for less information than what's in the original, but there is no advantage to increasing the resolution. So, when using resampling, you're fine as long as the file size is going down because you're starting with more than what you needed. But if it's going up, then that means that Photoshop doesn't really have enough info to do what you're asking for, which won't improve the quality of your image.

NOTES

You can also choose Help > Resize Image to calculate the proper scale and resolution settings.

Figure 4.23 Top to bottom: 200 ppi, 100 ppi, 50 ppi. (original image © 2002 Stockbyte, www.stockbyte.com)

Figure 4.24 Top to bottom: 50 ppi, 100 ppi, 200 ppi. (original image © 2002 Stockbyte, www.stockbyte.com)

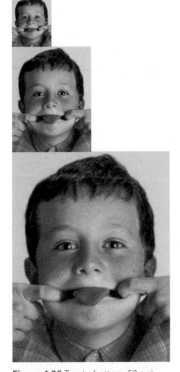

Figure 4.25 Top to bottom: 50 ppi, 100 ppi, 200 ppi. (original image © 2002 Stockbyte, www.stockbyte.com)

If you turn Resample Image off, then you're going to keep the same amount of information and just change the size the pixels will be when they are printed. The entire image will shrink, but you don't lose any information; you just make the pixels smaller (**Figure 4.25**). This is what you need to do to images that come from a digital camera, since it doesn't degrade the image in any way. The resolution is almost always set at 72, but the overall width and height are quite large. For instance, on my digital camera, I get images that are 35 by 26 inches at 72 ppi. With a resolution setting that low, the images always print out jaggy. But, if I go to the Image Size dialog box, turn Resample Image off, and change the resolution to 300, I end up with an 8.5-by-6.5-inch image and it doesn't look jaggy when it's printed.

Another approach is to ignore the resolution setting when scanning and instead shoot for the correct file size. Let's see how that would work. You'd start off by using Photoshop's New dialog box as a file-size calculator. Simply enter the width and height you'd like to print your image at (let's say 12 by 14 inches) and enter the resolution setting required for the type of printing you'll be using (let's say 300 ppi). With that information entered, set the Mode pop-up menu to RGB and then note the file size listed at the top of the New dialog box (**Figure 4.26**). In my example, Photoshop indicated that I'd need a 43.3-Mbyte file. Now let's say we're scanning a 35mm slide, which is a little less than 3 inches in size. Using the file-size trick, I don't have to figure out the proper resolution and scaling settings; instead, I'd just experiment with those settings until my scanner indicates that I'd end up with a 43.3-Mbyte file. Then, once I'm done scanning the image, I'd have to choose Image > Image Size, turn off the Resample Image checkbox, and enter the width I was looking for (12 inches, in my case). That will keep the same amount of information in the file but will make sure that the pixels are set to the proper size to get what I was looking for. I'd end up with a 12-by-14-inch image with a resolution of 300 ppi. Try it out; it sounds much more complicated than it really is.

Figure 4.26 The New dialog box.

If you send out for a high-end scan, the company that scans your image might not care what resolution you are looking for. They often only care about the file size. If that's the case, then use the New dialog box to calculate the file size that is needed for the output you desire, just as we did above.

Other Resolution Tricks

There are a lot of little tricks that I use when working with resolution. In this section I'll share the ones I use the most.

Scan with Maximum Resolution

I often don't know how my images will be printed and am not sure what size I'll need at the time they are scanned. In that case, I look at the most demanding type of printing that I might use (the highest resolution I'd need) and also think of the largest size I'd ever need the image to be and I'll scan for that. That way I'll have enough info no matter how I end up using the image. Once I know the final size and output type, then I'll simply choose Image > Image Size and enter the proper settings, which will cause Photoshop to reduce the file size so the image is optimized for that type of output.

Sharpening

When you sharpen an image, Photoshop will add tiny halos around the edges of objects. This makes it easier to see the detail that was already present in your image. I sharpen images only when they have been scaled to their final size and their resolution has been set to what's proper for the type of output that will be used. If you sharpen an image before scaling or resampling it, then the halos that make the detail easier to see will often get averaged into the rest of the image, resulting in a rather soft-looking image.

Res vs. PPI

If you use a use high-end scanner you may not be able to find a setting called ppi in the scanner software. Instead you'll be able to specify the resolution in small numbers

NOTES

If you plan to scan in 16-bit mode, you'll need to create the document I mentioned above and choose Image > Mode > 16 Bits/Channel. Then to find the file size you need to shoot for, choose Image > Image Size and look at what's listed at the top of the dialog box.

such as res 4 or res 8. All that means is that the particular scanner is using the metric system. Here's how to quickly convert between pixels per inch and resolution. Choose Image > New and enter the Resolution setting you desire. Now, click on the Width field so Photoshop knows you're done entering the resolution, and then change the pop-up menu next to the Resolution setting to pixels/cm. Finally, move the decimal one place to the left and you'll know the res equivalent of the ppi setting you were looking for.

Print Size

The View > Print Size command is supposed to show you how large your image will be when it's printed. But it's not usually accurate because it assumes that 72 pixels fit on each inch of your screen. You can find out if that's true on your screen by creating a document that is exactly 72 pixels wide (the resolution, mode and height don't matter), then double-clicking on the Eyedropper tool to view the image at 100% magnification. Once you've done that, just hold a real physical ruler up to your screen and measure how wide that document is. If it's not exactly an inch wide, then your screen does not display 72 pixels per inch and therefore the Print Size command will not be accurate.

Here's how to get an accurate print preview: Open your image, choose View > Show Guides, then choose Window > Show Navigator. Now hold a real ruler up to your screen and move the slider in the Navigator palette until the onscreen ruler matches the one you are holding in your hand. If the slider can't make things small enough, then experiment with the percentage setting that appears in the lower left of the Navigator palette. Once both rulers match, you're getting an accurate preview of how large your image will be when it's printed (**Figure 4.27**).

Figure 4.27 Matching onscreen with a physical ruler. (original image © 2002 Stockbyte, www.stockbyte.com)

Closing Thoughts

With some practice and a bit of patience you should be able to figure out the proper resolution for any job. The majority of people using Photoshop aren't comfortable with the concept of resolution, so don't feel bad if it takes a while before you feel like you know what you're doing.

Ben's Techno-babble Decoder Ring

Dots per inch (dpi): Determines the size of the dots an output device will use when printing an image. A 300-dpi laser printer uses black dots that are $\frac{1}{300}$ of an inch. This term is often used incorrectly to describe the resolution of an image (which should be measured in pixels per inch).

Dye sub: Short for dye sublimation. A type of output device that produces a continuous-tone result by heating CMY dyes until they turn into a gas (without first becoming a liquid). The output of a dye-sub printer has a continuous-tone glossy look that resembles a photographic print.

Imagesetter: A type of high-end output device that is used to output images onto photographic paper or film. Imagesetters are capable of outputting only pure black and pure white dots. The minimum resolution of an imagesetter is 2,540 dpi.

Inkjet: A type of output device that sprays CMYK inks onto special paper. Upon close inspection, the output of an inkjet printer typically appears "noisy" because the printer uses a dither pattern to simulate shades of gray.

Lines per inch (lpi): Determines the spacing of halftone dots and therefore their maximum size. The higher the lines-per-inch setting, the more apparent detail you can reproduce.

Pixels per inch (ppi): Determines how small the pixels in an image will be when printed. A setting of 150 ppi means that pixels will be $\frac{1}{150}$ of an inch when printed. The higher the setting, the smaller the pixels.

Samples per inch (spi): Determines the area a scanner will measure to determine the color of a single pixel. You can figure out the samples-per -inch setting that you need by multiplying the desired image resolution (ppi) by the amount the image will be scaled. Example: If the desired resolution is 300 ppi and the image will be scaled 200%: 300 x 200% = 600 spi.

Thermal wax: A type of CMYK output device that bonds a waxy substance to a special type of paper. If you scratch the output of a thermal-wax printer with your fingernail, you will usually be able to scratch off some of the waxy substance.

5

Line Art Scanning

Courtesy of Regina Cleveland

NEW IN 7

The tools used for line art scanning haven't changed in 7.0. In this version of the book, you'll find more detail on sharpening and you'll learn to remove the paper texture from a scanned image.

NOTES

Not all scanners use the same names for their scanning modes: line art mode might be parading around under a different name, such as *text* mode.

Only those who have the patience to do simple things perfectly will acquire the skill to do difficult things easily.

—Johann Schiller, German poet and playwright

Line Art Scanning

Scanning line art is a wonderful opportunity to learn how to do a relatively simple thing perfectly. Line art images consist of black lines on a white background. You see examples of line art every day in the text, logos, and signatures that are all around us. You'd think that scanning this type of image would be simple; after all, it's only pure black and white, right? Well, in order to really get control over your line art images, you'll need to go through a few hoops in Photoshop, but with a little effort, you can achieve stunning results.

Almost all scanners have a line art mode that gives you a pure black and pure white end result. However, don't be fooled by your scanner. Scanning in line art mode produces an image that doesn't contain anywhere near the amount of detail found in the original (**Figures 5.1** and **5.2**).

If you scan an image in line art mode, it will open in Photoshop in bitmap mode, which is Photoshop's mode for dealing with pure black/white images. That's practically useless, because Photoshop is not able to enhance images that are in bitmap mode. (For example, you can't use most of the editing tools, rotate the image in precise increments, or apply filters.) This is why so many people end up with line art reproductions that have jagged edges, broken lines, and dense areas that are all clogged up.

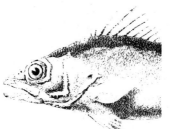

Figure 5.1 A "raw" line art scan.

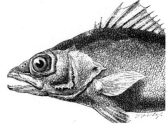

Figure 5.2 Line art scanned using the techniques in this chapter.

But that's not going to happen to *you*. You're going to ignore your scanner's advice and scan in grayscale mode instead of line art mode. After the image is scanned in grayscale mode, you can take full advantage of Photoshop's enhancement controls. With very little practice and a handful of tricks that you'll learn in this chapter, you'll be able to create beautiful line art reproductions as they were intended to be—with crisp edges and sharp detail.

When you're all done producing your line art and are pleased with the result, you should convert your image into bitmap mode. This will keep your file size small and prevent you from accidentally adding shades of gray to the image. After all, true line art contains only pure black and pure white, and no shades of gray. By converting your image to bitmap mode in the end, you'll guarantee that it won't be contaminated with grays. Shades of gray are reproduced using a pattern of black circles, known as a halftone, which makes the lines of your image appear fuzzy (**Figures 5.3** and **5.4**).

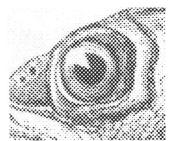

Figure 5.4 Magnified version of grayscale line art as reproduced on a laser printer.

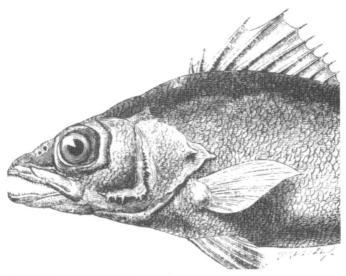

Figure 5.3 A grayscale mode image of line art.

Figure 5.5 Jaggy line art.

NOTES

When scanning a line art image for onscreen display (for multimedia, the Web, and so on), it will usually look better if you leave it in grayscale mode. I know, I know, that really isn't true line art, but it will look better onscreen. Why? Because the pixels that make up your screen are quite large (between 72 and 96 ppi), so it's easy to see the jagged edges of the pixels that make up your image. By including shades of gray, the edges of the image will fade out and have a smoother look. When scanning for onscreen use, use a resolution setting of 85.

Avoiding the Jaggies

The most common complaint I hear about line art is that it has jagged edges (**Figure 5.5**). This happens when the pixels in the image are so large that you can easily see them when the image is printed. Thankfully, avoiding the "jaggies" is the easiest part of dealing with line art.

Resolution Is the Key

Photoshop gives users the ability to try a lot of wild things with images. But the one thing all users have in common is the desire to get the highest quality possible. And when you're working with pure black-and-white line art, that means you'll want each pixel in your image to be the exact same size as the smallest dot your printer can reproduce.

The size of the pixels in your document is determined by the resolution setting of your file. This is measured in pixels per inch, or ppi. The resolution of your printer dictates the smallest dot it can reproduce. This is measured in dots per inch, or dpi. You'll want to find out the resolution of your printer and use that setting when scanning your image. This makes your pixels the same size as the smallest dot your printer can reproduce, thus giving you the best possible results.

Most people think higher settings produce better results, but that's not necessarily the case. If your end result is a restaurant receipt printer, and you feed it an image with 300 pixels per inch, there's no way it can print dots that small. So it must distill the image and discard the extra information—and that's when your image will suffer. You're much better off using the correct resolution setting in the first place.

Printing companies and service bureaus have expensive output devices that offer resolutions of at least 2,540 dots per inch. I've found that files with resolutions above 1,200 ppi don't seem to produce better detail; they just give you huge file sizes and therefore slow down your computer. **Figures 5.6** to **5.11** show the effect of resolution on file size and quality.

Figure 5.6 Resolution: 72 ppi. File size: 28 Kbytes.

Figure 5.7 Resolution: 150 ppi. File size: 28 Kbytes.

Figure 5.8 Resolution: 300 ppi. File size: 36 Kbytes.

Figure 5.9 Resolution: 600 ppi. File size: 53 Kbytes.

Figure 5.10 Resolution: 800 ppi. File size: 68 Kbytes.

Figure 5.11 Resolution: 1,200 ppi. File size: 100 Kbytes.

Photoshop Can Fake It

If your scanner is not capable of using a resolution setting as high as you need, you can have Photoshop increase the resolution of the image and add the extra information your scanner couldn't deliver. To do this, scan with the highest resolution setting available, and then choose Image > Image Size. Select the Resample Image checkbox, set the pop-up menu to Bicubic (that's the kind of math Photoshop will use to add information to your image), type in the resolution of your printer in the Resolution field, and then click OK. Remember, your image must be in grayscale mode; otherwise, this step will not improve image quality. This step is unique to line art images; if you were to increase the resolution of a photographic-quality image, the result would appear blurry. In the case of line art, the extra information will not harm the image, because we're going to convert it to a pure black-and-white bitmap, which is incapable of appearing blurry.

NOTES

Line art file sizes will vary depending on which file format is used. The images above were saved as TIFF files with LZW compression turned on. LZW compression is ideal for images that contain large areas of solid color. The 1,200-ppi image would have been 410 Kbytes if LZW compression had not been used.

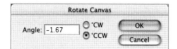

Figure 5.12 Photoshop automatically calculates the rotation amount needed and puts it in the dialog box.

Straighten a scan while it's still in grayscale mode. If your image is in bitmap mode, it can be rotated only in 90-degree increments.

Whenever possible, avoid straightening scans in other software programs, such as your page-layout program. If scans are straightened in other programs, the screen redraw will take longer and printing time will increase. Also, the quality of the art will suffer, and you'll not have a true image preview.

When you scan grayscale images that have already been printed using a halftone screen, you'll often get an unwanted repetitive pattern. You might get a better result by scanning the preprinted image as line art (even though it's a grayscale photo). This method will try to capture the halftone look instead of converting the image into a grayscale file. Using the line art technique described in this chapter, you can scan grayscale images that were printed with a halftone screen of 85 lines per inch or below. If an image was printed with a halftone screen above 85 lines per inch, the image should be scanned as a normal grayscale image instead of using the line art technique.

Straightening the Image

If the image you've scanned needs to be straightened, you can use the Measure tool (it looks like a ruler and is grouped with the Eyedropper tool). Draw a line across an area that should be perfectly vertical or horizontal. If there's more than one area of the image that should be straightened, you can click the middle of the measurement line and drag it around your screen to make sure it matches all the affected areas. If you need to adjust the angle of the measurement line, just drag one of its ends.

When you're certain the line is at the proper angle, check to make sure the background color is set to white and then choose Image > Rotate Canvas > Arbitrary. Photoshop has a great feature that automatically calculates how much the image needs to be rotated, so all you have to do is click OK (**Figure 5.12**). Once you're done, you can get rid of the measurement line by clicking the Clear button in the Options bar at the top of your screen.

Improving Definition

When you convert an image to bitmap mode (which we'll do at the end of this chapter), any areas that are darker than 50 percent gray will become pure black. This usually causes detail in the darkest, most densely packed areas to clog up and become a black blob. You can prevent this from happening by sharpening the image. Sharpening will add more contrast to those densely packed areas and produce better detail. However, before you sharpen an image, you'll want to take a snapshot of the unsharpened image so you can use it later to enhance the result.

Taking a Snapshot

Choose New Snapshot from the side menu of the History palette to record what the image looks like before you sharpen it. Name the snapshot something like "Before

Sharpening" so you can remember what it contains. The snapshot you create will appear near the top of the History palette (**Figure 5.13**). Click the column just to the left of the snapshot thumbnail icon to tell Photoshop to use this version of the image when using the History brush.

Sharpening the Image

Now that you've created a snapshot version of the image, it's safe to proceed with the sharpening process. Double-click the Zoom tool in the Tools palette to view the image at 100 percent magnification; otherwise, the onscreen preview of the sharpening filter will not be accurate. Choose Filter > Sharpen > Unsharp Mask, and set the amount to 500, the radius to 1.2, and the threshold to 2. This is usually a good starting point because it will make the detail in the dark areas more defined.

Now adjust the Radius setting until any tiny elements (which usually come in as light shades of gray) turn dark. You're really looking for a balance between good shadow detail and dark tiny elements. Radius settings between .5 and 5 usually produce the best results (**Figure 5.14**).

A Threshold setting of 0 will sharpen all shades in the image, including the lightest grays. High threshold settings will sharpen only the darker thick lines in the image. I usually keep the Threshold setting at 2, unless any paper texture starts to show up. If you notice that the paper texture is being exaggerated, then increase the Threshold setting until the paper smoothes out again, and then readjust the Radius setting to maintain that shadow/tiny-detail balance I mentioned earlier.

Converting to Line Art

When you print an image that contains shades of gray, your printer uses a halftone screen, which prevents your grayscale image from having crisp edges. In order for you to get nice, crisp edges, the image must contain only pure black and pure white—that's true line art. So, how do you get there?

Figure 5.13 After creating a new snapshot, click to the left of the snapshot thumbnail image to set the History brush to that snapshot.

NOTES

The Unsharp Mask filter is used here because it's the only sharpening filter that gives you enough control over the end result. The other filters deliver a more generic result because there are no user-defined settings involved.

There is no need to apply a Threshold layer if your end result will be used onscreen for the Internet or multimedia. But you might need to enhance the contrast of the image by choosing Image > Adjustments > Levels. Move the upper-left slider until the lines in your image become completely black, and then move the upper-left slider until the background is completely white. If you've done that, then you can stop right here and save your image in the GIF file format.

If you need to have a transparent background for the Web, press Option-Command-~ (Mac) or Alt-Ctrl-~ (Windows) to select the background of the image. Next, choose Select > Inverse to get the line art selected. Then create a new layer, choose Edit > Fill and fill the layer with black, and finally drag the original layer to the trash at the bottom of the Layers palette.

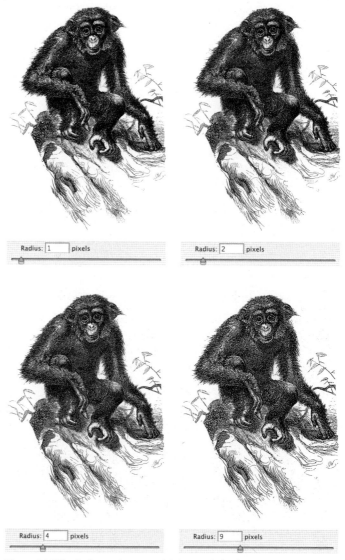

Figure 5.14 The Radius setting controls how much shadow detail will appear.

NOTES

To create a Threshold adjustment layer in earlier versions of Photoshop, choose Layer > New > Adjustment Layer and then choose Threshold from the pop-up menu that appears.

Adding a Threshold Adjustment Layer

You can use the Threshold command to rid the image of all shades of gray, leaving only pure black and pure white. By applying Threshold on an adjustment layer instead of directly to the image, you'll be able to easily make changes after the image is black and white. To achieve an accurate preview, you must view the image at 100 percent magnification. Double-click the Zoom tool in the Tools palette to quickly zoom to 100 percent. Create a new Threshold adjustment layer by choosing Layer > New Adjustment Layer > Threshold. Adjust the slider until the lines in the image have the desired thickness and detail. You can compare the black-and-white result to the grayscale version of the image by turning the Preview option off and on.

The Threshold level forces anything darker than the threshold number to black and anything lighter to white (**Figures 5.15** to **5.20**). Refer to the table in Chapter 6, "Optimizing Grayscale Images," to see what the threshold numbers mean.

Figures 5.21 to **5.23** show the quality improvement that is possible by scanning in grayscale instead of line art mode. Even more detail could be brought out of **Figure 5.23** by using the enhancement techniques that were applied to **Figure 5.24** (page 160).

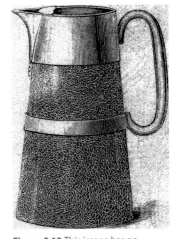

Figure 5.15 The lines appear to be breaking up.

Figure 5.17 This image shows good highlight detail without plugging up the shadow detail.

Figure 5.19 This image has no shadow detail and the lines are too thick.

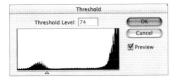

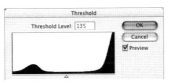

Figure 5.16 The Threshold setting is too low.

Figure 5.18 Proper Threshold setting.

Figure 5.20 The Threshold setting is too high.

Figure 5.21 Raw line art scan (same as scanning in grayscale and using the default Threshold setting). File size: 448 Kbytes.

Figure 5.22 Raw grayscale scan (lines are not crisp, and the file size is very large). File size: 7.9 Mbytes.

Figure 5.23 Grayscale scan with sharpening and a proper Threshold setting (shows good shadow detail). File size: 584 Kbytes.

Refining Areas

To retain additional detail, you must enhance the grayscale image that's below the adjustment layer. To do so, click the name of the layer that contains the original image. There are many ways to enhance the image, including the following. (**Figure 5.24** shows examples of these settings.)

You can change the current brush size at any time by pressing [or] (square brackets).

▶ **Increase shadow detail.** Brush across the image with the Sharpen tool to bring out detail in shadow areas.

▶ **Fix broken lines.** Brush across the image with the Burn tool (with the Range option set to Shadows) to clean up broken lines or to make lines thicker. If the Burn tool doesn't change the image enough, use the History brush with the Mode option set to Multiply or Darken to increase the line thickness. Lower the Opacity setting if the changes are too extreme.

▶ **Reduce line thickness.** Brush across the image with the Dodge tool (with the Range option set to Highlights or Midtones) to reduce the thickness of lines. If the Dodge tool doesn't change the image enough, use the History brush with the Mode option set to Screen or Lighten to make the lines thinner. Lower the Opacity setting if the changes are too extreme.

▶ If the Dodge and Burn tools don't change the image enough, use the History brush with the Mode option set to Hard Light to make lines thinner. Lower the Opacity setting if the changes are too extreme.

▶ **Remove paper texture.** Choose either Despeckle or Median from the Filter > Noise menu (**Figures 5.25** to **5.27**).

▶ **Control text thickness.** If you're scanning text at large point sizes, you can make the text thicker by choosing Filter > Other > Minimum or thinner by choosing Filter > Other > Maximum. If the adjectives used in these menu options seem contrary to common sense, well, they are. Just remember to apply reverse logic when dealing with text thickness (**Figure 5.28**).

Figure 5.28 This image is split into thirds vertically. The middle is the original, the top is after applying Minimum, and the bottom is after applying Maximum.

The Dodge tool with 100% exposure setting.

The History brush using Multiply blending mode.

The History brush using Screen blending mode at 45% opacity.

The History brush using Lighten blending mode.

Figure 5.24 Refining the image.

Figure 5.25 Unrefined image.

Figure 5.26 Result of applying the Despeckle filter.

Figure 5.27 Result of applying the Median filter.

Minimizing File Size

Nobody likes dealing with big, bloated files. They're greedy resource hogs that slow down your system and wreak havoc on your ability to work quickly and efficiently. Any extra white space around the image is a file-fattening waste because it's not necessary for printing the image. One way to simplify the image is to choose Flatten Image from the side menu of the Layers palette and then use the Eraser tool to clean up any stray pixels in the white area surrounding the image. Finally, to discard any extra space, choose Image > Trim, turn on all the checkboxes at the bottom, and then choose whichever top choice would make Photoshop find a white pixel (**Figure 5.29**).

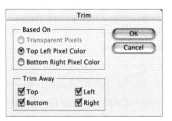

Figure 5.29 The Trim command will discard any extra space in your image.

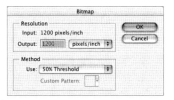

Figure 5.30 The Bitmap dialog box.

Converting to Bitmap

Your image is now pure black and white, but the file itself is still in grayscale mode. You can click the eyeball icon next to the adjustment layer to toggle it off and on and see that it's being applied to a grayscale image. The image must be converted to bitmap mode to save disk space and to make sure that any final editing doesn't produce unwanted shades of gray. Convert the image from grayscale to bitmap by choosing Image > Mode > Bitmap. This brings up the Bitmap dialog box (**Figure 5.30**), which is where you can change the resolution of your image. If you followed the steps mentioned in the Avoiding the Jaggies section at the beginning of this chapter, then the resolution of your image should be just right. If that's the case, then make sure the input and output resolution numbers match, so Photoshop doesn't mess with the Resolution setting, and then click OK.

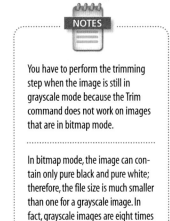

NOTES

You have to perform the trimming step when the image is still in grayscale mode because the Trim command does not work on images that are in bitmap mode.

In bitmap mode, the image can contain only pure black and pure white; therefore, the file size is much smaller than one for a grayscale image. In fact, grayscale images are eight times as large as bitmap images.

NOTES

If you resize an image that's already in bitmap mode, the individual pixels in the image become large black squares. To maintain good quality, convert the image to grayscale mode and then use the Gaussian Blur filter with a setting just high enough to introduce shades of gray (**Figure 5.31**). Now you can use the techniques listed in this chapter to enhance the image and convert it back to bitmap mode.

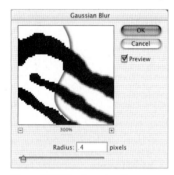

Figure 5.31 The Gaussian Blur dialog box.

Figure 5.32 The EPS Options dialog box.

Choosing a File Format

If your image is destined to be printed, then you'll want to use the EPS or TIFF file formats. The EPS file format allows you to specify whether the white areas should be solid or transparent (**Figure 5.32**).

Line art images that are destined for the Web should be saved in the GIF file format.

Closing Thoughts

Lately I've been noticing that a lot of the line art out there is inferior to what I used to see only a few years ago. Check it out for yourself! Pick up any magazine (even the high-end ones sometimes have this problem) and look through it for line art images. If your experience is anything like mine, you'll probably see some really mediocre stuff—edges are jagged, lines are broken up, and patterns look clogged. My theory is that people stopped sending out for line art scans and started performing them in-house.

That's fine, but only if you're not sacrificing quality for convenience. After reading this chapter, I hope you'll agree with me that you can have both. As long as you know how to get a good scan that captures the right amount of detail, and then know how to enhance the scanned image in Photoshop, there's no reason why you can't end up with exquisite line art.

And as a side note, I want you to know that just because you can achieve high-quality results using these techniques doesn't mean you will want to use them for every line art scan. I occasionally have to scan dozens of images for a single project. In that case, I might decide that speed is more important than quality and just scan in line art mode to begin with. But if I'm scanning my own signature, a high-quality etching, or a logo I'll be using over and over again, then I will definitely spend the extra time to get a high-quality result.

Ben's Techno-babble Decoder Ring

Bitmap. A confusing term, because Photoshop uses it in an unusual way. Technically "bitmap" means a grid of pixels. That means that any image you ever see in Photoshop that contains pixels is technically a bitmap image. That's why the native format for transporting pixel-based images on the Windows platform is called a BMP file. That stands for Windows Bitmap. Adobe has decided to reserve the term to describe images that contain only pure black and pure white (no grays or color). The reason can be attributed to Apple. The Macintosh was one of the first personal computers that were designed to deal with pixel-based images, and in its first incarnation it contained a black-and-white screen (no grays). "Bitmap" got associated with any pixel-based image on that first Mac model, and that's how the dual meaning came about.

Line art: Any artwork that consists of pure black lines on a pure white background. Line art images always contain extremely crisp edges and no shades of gray or color.

Resample: The process of changing the total number of pixels in an image without cropping or adding empty space.

Threshold: An adjustment that converts all shades of gray to pure black or pure white. Any shades of gray brighter than the threshold value will become white, and any shades darker than the threshold value will become black.

Courtesy of Diane Fenster, www.dianefenster.com

6

Optimizing Grayscale Images

Courtesy of Andy Katz

NEW IN 7

The features used to adjust gray-scale images have not changed in Photoshop 7.0. In this chapter you'll find expanded coverage of histograms and sharpening that was not in previous editions of this book.

If you go through life convinced that your way is always best, all the new ideas in the world will pass you by.

—Akio Morita, founder of Sony

Optimizing Grayscale Images

When inexperienced users first try to adjust a grayscale image, they usually look for something familiar and easy, and the Brightness/Contrast dialog box is frequently where they end up (**Figure 6.1**). With a mere flick of the mouse, they can dramatically change their image. Big results, little effort. At first glance, the Brightness/Contrast dialog box seems to hold great promise. But does it *really* do the job?

If you were to compare images adjusted with Brightness/Contrast with the images you see in high-end magazines and brochures, you'd notice that the quality of the Brightness/Contrast images is inferior (**Figures 6.2** and **6.3**). Why? Because the Brightness/Contrast dialog box adjusts the entire image an equal amount. So, if you decide to increase the overall brightness of an image until an area that was 10 percent gray becomes white, then areas that are black will also be changed the same amount and become 90 percent gray. Using controls like these, it is extremely hard to achieve professional quality. When you correct one problem, you usually introduce another.

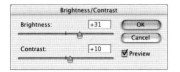

Figure 6.1 The Brightness/Contrast dialog box.

Figure 6.2 Image optimized using Brightness/Contrast. (© 2002 Andy Katz)

Figure 6.3 Image professionally optimized.

Common adjustment complaints include:

▶ Images appearing flat (lacking contrast)

▶ Images printing overly dark

▶ Blown-out detail in the highlights (bright white areas in the middle of people's foreheads)

▶ Lack of detail in the shadows

All of these problems—and others—can be solved in one dialog box.

Levels Is the Solution

The Levels dialog box (choose Image > Adjust > Levels) is the cure for most common complaints about grayscale image quality (**Figure 6.4**). It offers you far more control and feedback than Brightness/Contrast. Instead of having only two sliders to adjust, Levels offers you five, as well as a bar chart that indicates exactly what is happening to the image. And unlike the sliders in Brightness/Contrast, the Levels sliders don't change the entire image in equal amounts.

NOTES

To reset sliders to their default positions, hold down Option (Mac) or Alt (Windows) and click on the Cancel button, which has temporarily become the Reset button. Or, you can type Option-Command-. (that's a period) on the Mac.

If you have a color original that will be reproduced as a grayscale image, be sure to scan the original as color and then convert it to grayscale in Photoshop. Also, be sure to check out the chapters on Enhancement and Channels, where you'll learn how to produce a higher-quality grayscale conversion.

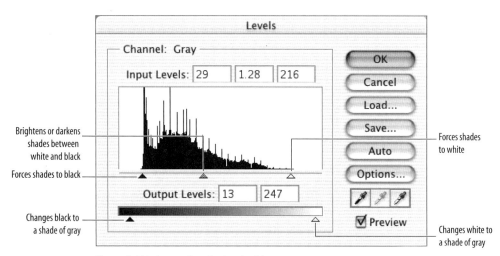

Figure 6.4 Understanding the Levels sliders.

NOTES

The height of the bars in a histogram suggest, visually, how much space the shades take up in an image. The height doesn't indicate an exact number of pixels; instead, it measures how much space the shade takes up—how much it's used compared with the other shades in the image. It's as if everyone in a room stood up and you compared how tall each person was without using a ruler. You wouldn't know exactly how tall anyone was, but you'd have an idea of how tall each person was compared with the others (**Figure 6.5**).

It might take several pages to describe all the controls in the Levels dialog box, but once you know how to use them, it will take you less than a minute to optimize an image. Just remember to apply all of the controls in Levels, because each builds on the last. You can liken the steps in Levels to the ingredients in crème brûlée—leave one out and you might end up with pudding instead of perfection.

The Histogram Is Your Guide

You can use the bar chart (also known as a histogram) at the top of the Levels dialog box to determine if the adjustments you're making are going to harm the image or improve it. The histogram indicates which shades of gray your image uses and how much space those shades take up—that is, how much they are used in the image. If you find a gap in the histogram, you can look at the gradient directly below it to see which shade of gray is missing from your image.

By looking directly below the first bar that appears on the left end of the histogram, you can determine the darkest shade of gray in the image. If there were anything darker than that, then there would have to be some bars above those shades in the histogram. By looking directly below the last bar that appears on the right end of the histogram, you can determine the brightest shade of gray in the image. So if you look at **Figure 6.6,** you might notice the image contains no pure blacks or pure whites. The darkest shade of gray is about 95 percent, and the brightest shade is about 6 percent.

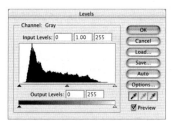

Figure 6.5 This histogram indicates that the shades between around 90% and 75% take up a lot of space (tall bars) and the shades between around 5% and 15% take up little space (short bars).

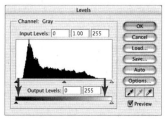

Figure 6.6 Look at the gradient bar directly below the ends of the histogram to determine the brightest and darkest shades present in the image.

There is no ideal when it comes to a histogram; it's simply a reflection of which shades of gray are most prevalent in your image (**Figure 6.7**). Tall bars indicate a shade of gray that takes up a lot of space in the image, and short bars indicate a shade that isn't very prevalent in the image. A histogram that extends all the way across the space available indicates an image that has the full range of shades available and is usually a sign of a good scan or a well-adjusted image.

Figure 6.7 Each image will have its own unique histogram.

© 2002 Andy Katz

© 2002 Andy Katz

© 2002 Andy Katz

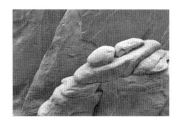

© 2002 Andy Katz

© 2002 Andy Katz

© 2002 Andy Katz

The middle slider will move when you adjust the upper-right or upper-left slider. This happens because Photoshop is attempting to keep the middle slider in the same position relative to the other two sliders. So if the middle slider is centered between the other two, it will remain centered when you move one of the outer sliders.

Evaluate and Adjust Contrast

The brightest and darkest areas of your computer monitor are nowhere near as bright or dark as the objects you'll find in the real world. The difference is even more extreme when you look at the brightest and darkest areas of a printed brochure—the paper is actually pretty dull and the ink isn't all that dark. Because of this, you'll need to use the full range of shades from black to white in order to make your photos look as close to reality as possible.

By adjusting the upper-right and upper-left sliders in the Levels dialog box, you can dramatically improve the contrast of an image and make it appear more lifelike. When you move the upper-left slider in the Levels dialog box, you force the shade of gray directly below it and any shade darker than it (see the gradient) to black. So moving that slider until it touches the first bar on the histogram forces the darkest shade of gray in the image to black, which should give you nice dark shadows.

When you move the upper-right slider, you will force the shade that appears directly below the slider and any shade brighter than it to white. So, as above (for dark colors), moving the right slider until it touches the last bar on the histogram forces the brightest shade of gray to white, which should give you nice white highlights.

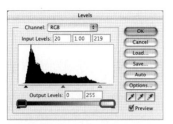

Figure 6.8 The shades that are beyond the upper-right and upper-left triangles will become pure black and pure white.

By adjusting both sliders, your image will be using the full range of shades available to a grayscale image (**Figure 6.8**). If you move the sliders past the beginning and end of the histogram, you will get even more contrast, but you risk losing important detail in the process.

Hidden Features to the Rescue

To achieve maximum contrast without sacrificing detail, Adobe created a hidden feature in the Levels dialog box. It's known as Threshold mode because it acts like the Threshold dialog box that we used in the previous chapter. This feature allows you to see exactly which areas are becoming black or white, and it's the key to ensuring that you don't sacrifice detail. To get to the hidden feature, hold down the Option key (Mac) or Alt key (Windows) when you move the upper-right or upper-left sliders in the Levels dialog box.

When you move the upper-left slider with Threshold mode turned on, your image should turn white until the slider touches the first bar on the histogram; then small black areas should start to appear. These are the areas that will become pure black. With most images, you'll want to make sure you don't force a large concentrated area to black, so move the slider until only small areas appear. You also want to make sure the areas that are becoming black still contain detail. Detail will show up looking like noise (not the kind you hear—the kind you see on television when you don't have an antenna hooked up), so make sure those small areas also look noisy. You'll need to repeat this process with the upper-right slider to make sure you get optimal contrast (**Figures 6.9** to **6.18**).

There are three things that might cause an image to have large areas of black or white from the start:

1. Your scanner isn't capable of capturing good shadow detail.

2. The image simply didn't have any detail in the shadows to begin with.

3. The image has been adjusted without Photoshop's Threshold mode.

NOTES

If you're in the market for a new scanner, be sure to compare the D-max specifications for each scanner you are considering. Higher D-max specs indicate a scanner that is capable of capturing more shadow detail than a scanner with a lower D-max spec. It's often worth the extra money to get a scanner that can deliver good shadow detail.

Figure 6.9 Original. (© 2002 Andy Katz)

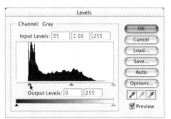

Figure 6.10 Upper left slide adjusted way too far.

Figure 6.11 Large areas of the image are losing detail and becoming pure black.

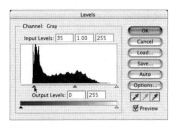

Figure 6.12 Upper left slider adjusted correctly.

Figure 6.13 Small areas become black but still contain detail (noise).

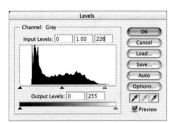

Figure 6.14 Upper left slider adjusted too far.

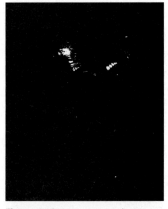

Figure 6.15 Large areas are losing detail and become pure white.

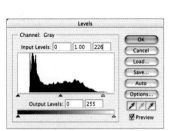

Figure 6.16 Upper right slider adjusted correctly.

Figure 6.17 Small areas become white but still contain detail (noise).

Figure 6.18 Final result.

The Histogram Gives You Feedback

Once you have applied an adjustment to your image, you can see an updated histogram by choosing Image > Adjust > Levels again. You should notice that after adjusting the upper-right and upper-left sliders, the histogram will stretch all the way across the area available. It's just like stretching out a Slinky … you remember, "it walks down stairs alone or in pairs" (**Figure 6.19**). As you pull on the ends of the Slinky, the loops stretch out and start to create gaps. The same thing happens to a histogram—because Photoshop can't add more bars to the histogram, it can only spread out the ones that were already there. And remember, gaps in the histogram mean that certain shades of gray are missing from the image. So the more you adjust an image using Levels, the more you increase the possibility that you'll lose some of the smooth transitions between bright and dark areas (**Figure 6.20**).

If you see large spikes on either end of the histogram, as shown in **Figure 6.21**, it's an indication that you've lost detail. That's because you forced quite a bit of space to white or black using Levels. But you'd know you did that, because you were using the hidden feature, right? Or maybe you couldn't control yourself and were using that Brightness/Contrast dialog box, where you can't tell if you damage the image! You might also get spikes on the ends of the histogram if you scan an image with a brightness setting that is way too high or low, or if your scanner wasn't capable of capturing enough shadow detail (see information about D-max above).

Figure 6.19 A Slinky.

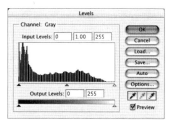

Figure 6.20 After adjusting the top two sliders, your image should use the full range of shades available.

NOTES

If you find evenly spaced spikes in the histogram of an unadjusted image, it usually indicates a noisy scan (**Figure 6.22**).

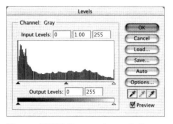

Figure 6.21 Spikes on the end of a histogram usually indicate lost detail.

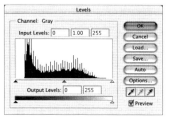

Figure 6.22 Noise.

NOTES

Spikes that show up after an image has been adjusted with Levels do not indicate noise. It's as if you took your trusty Slinky and tried to squish it down to a centimeter wide. Something would have to budge. The only way I can do it is to bend the Slinky into a V shape where the loops start piling up, one on top of the other. Otherwise, the loops just line up in a nice row and limit how much I can compress the Slinky. Well, the same thing happens with the histogram. Let's say you try to squish 20 bars into a space that is only 15 pixels wide on the histogram. Five of the bars have to disappear. They are going to just pile on top of the bars next to them and make those bars about twice as tall. When this happens, you get evenly spaced spikes across part of the histogram.

Improve Brightness

After you have achieved good contrast, your image might look too dark. The middle slider in the Levels dialog box can fix that. (Techies love to call this slider the Gamma setting, but we plain folks call it the midpoint.) If you move the middle slider to the left, the image will become brighter without messing up the dark areas of your image. Black areas will stay nice and black. Or you can move the middle slider to the right to darken the image without messing up the bright areas of the image. White areas will stay bright white.

If you want to know what this adjustment is doing, just look directly below the middle slider; the shade of gray there will become 50 percent gray. If you look at an updated histogram of the image, it will look like you stretched out a Slinky, then grabbed one side and pulled it to the middle (**Figure 6.24**). Some bars will get scrunched (is that a technical term?) together, while others get spread apart.

Setting Up Your Images for Final Output

If your images are going to be printed, especially with ink on paper, chances are that they will end up looking a lot darker than they did when you viewed them onscreen. This is known as dot gain. Fortunately, Photoshop allows you to compensate for it. You can tell Photoshop ahead of time how you intend to output your images, and it will adjust the onscreen appearance of your image to look as dark as it should be after it's printed.

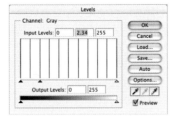

Figure 6.23 Effects of the middle slider.

Figure 6.24 The adjustment shown at the top results in the histogram shown at the bottom.

To select or enter dot-gain settings, choose Edit > Color Settings (Photoshop > Color Settings in OS X). In the Working Spaces area, you'll use the Gray pop-up menu, as shown in **Figure 6.25**. You'll definitely want to ask your printing company about what settings to use; otherwise, you'll just be guessing and you might not like your end result. But just in case you're working at midnight or don't have time to ask your printing company, then use the settings that appear in the table on this page (see table 6.1).

TABLE 6.1 Dot-Gain Settings

Newspapers	34%
Magazines and brochures	24%
High-end brochures	22%

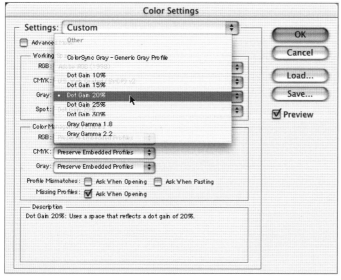

Figure 6.25 The Color Settings dialog box.

Prepare for a Printing Press

Take a close look at the black-and-white image in **Figure 4.14**, and imagine that you took that image to Kinko's and made a copy of it. Then you took the copy and copied it again at your local library. Then you took the library copy and ran it through the copy machine in your office. Then you held the version that had been copied three times next to the original. Would you expect them to look the same? Of course not. In fact, the tiny dots that are in the brightest part of the image would have begun to disappear and become pure white, because every time you make a copy, you lose some quality. Well, the same thing happens when you hand over your

NOTES

Printing a grayscale image on a color inkjet printer will usually produce an image that has a color cast. To avoid that problem, be sure to print grayscale images using only black ink. This can usually be accomplished in the print settings for your inkjet printer.

If the dot-gain setting you need isn't listed in the Working Spaces area, you'll need a custom setting. Turn on the Advanced Mode checkbox at the top of the dialog box, and then choose Custom Dot Gain from the Gray pop-up menu. To get a traditional dot-gain measurement (in which you measure only 50 percent gray), just add 50 to the dot gain setting you need, and enter the result in the 50% field.

If your image will be displayed only onscreen (and not printed), then change the Gray pop-up menu to Gray Gamma 1.8 (for Mac) or Gray Gamma 2.2 (for Windows).

If your images are destined for multimedia output (Web, video, animation, etc.), then you can skip over the next few steps and go directly to the "Sharpening" section later in this chapter.

image to a printing company. When you give your printing company your original output, they will have to make three copies of it before it makes it to the end of the printing process. They start by converting the original into a piece of metal called a printing plate, to make the first copy. Then they put the plate on a big, round roller on the printing press and flood it with water and ink. The oily ink will stick to the plate only where your images and text should be; the water will make sure it doesn't stick to the other areas (using the idea that oil and water don't mix). Next to that roller is another one known as a blanket; it's just covered with rubber. The plate will come into contact with the blanket so the ink on the plate will transfer over to the blanket—that's your second copy. Finally, the blanket will transfer the ink onto a sheet of paper to create the last copy (**Figure 6.26**). Each time a copy is made, you lose some of the smallest dots in the image. Until you know how to compensate for this, you're likely to end up with pictures of people with big white spots in the middle of their foreheads.

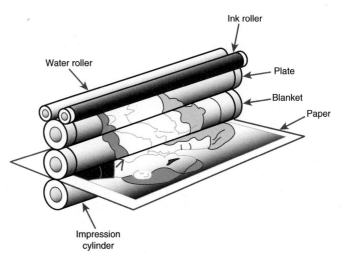

Figure 6.26 Three copies are made before your image turns into a printed page.

Before I show you how to compensate for the loss of detail in the bright areas of your image, let's look at what happens to the darkest areas, since we'll have to deal with them as well. When you print with ink on paper, the ink always gets absorbed into the paper and spreads out—just like when you spill coffee on your morning newspaper. This will cause the darkest areas of an image (97 percent, 98 percent, 99 percent) to become pure black. If you don't adjust for this, you will lose detail in the shadows of your image.

Most printing companies create a simple test strip that they print on the edge of your job, in the area that will be cropped after it's printed. This test strip contains shades of gray from 1 percent to about 5 percent to determine the lightest shade of gray that doesn't disappear on press and become pure white. Of course, the folks in the printing industry don't just use plain English to describe it; instead, they invented the term "minimum highlight dot reproducible on press." The test strip area also contains shades of gray from 99 percent to about 75 percent so they can see the darkest shade of gray that doesn't become pure black. For that one, they came up with the term "maximum shadow dot reproducible on press." If you ask your printing company, they can usually tell you exactly which settings to use. I know you don't always know who will print your images or don't have the time to ask, so I'll give you some generic numbers to use (**Tables 6.2 and 6.3**). But first, let's find out how we adjust for minimum highlight and maximum shadow dots.

Here's where you come in, and also where we get back to Levels. By moving the lower-right slider in the Levels dialog box, you will change white to the shade of gray the slider is pointing to. You want to move this slider until it points to the minimum highlight dot—that is, the lightest shade of gray that will not disappear and become white on press.

You don't want to just eyeball this setting, so instead of just looking at the shades of gray, we'll use the Output Level numbers in the Levels dialog box. There is one problem with these numbers: they range from 0 to 255 instead of 0 to 100 percent! This is because you can have up to 256 shades of gray in a grayscale image and Photoshop wants you to be able to control them all. When you're using this numbering system, think about light instead of ink. If you have no light (0), then it would be pitch black; if you have as much light as possible (255), you could call that white. So that you won't need a calculator, I'll give you a conversion table (**Table 6.4**).

TABLE 6.2 Common Minimum Highlight Settings

Newspapers	5%
Magazines and brochures	3%
High-end brochures	3%

TABLE 6.3 Common Maximum Shadow Settings

Newspapers	75%
Magazines and brochures	90%
High-end brochures	95%

NOTES

If you'd like to measure the minimum highlight and maximum shadow settings for an output device that you own, be sure to try the highlight/shadow test that's available on the companion website at www.digital-mastery.com/companionsite.

TABLE 6.4

PERCENTAGE CONVERSION TABLE

%	Value	%	Value	%	Value
100%	0	66%	87	32%	173
99%	3	65%	89	31%	176
98%	5	64%	92	30%	179
97%	8	63%	94	29%	181
96%	10	62%	97	28%	184
95%	13	61%	100	27%	186
94%	15	60%	102	26%	189
93%	18	59%	105	25%	191
92%	20	58%	107	24%	194
91%	23	57%	110	23%	196
90%	26	56%	112	22%	199
89%	28	55%	115	21%	202
88%	31	54%	117	20%	204
87%	33	53%	120	19%	207
86%	36	52%	122	18%	209
85%	38	51%	125	17%	211
84%	41	50%	128	16%	214
83%	44	49%	130	15%	217
82%	46	48%	133	14%	219
81%	49	47%	135	13%	222
80%	51	46%	138	12%	224
79%	54	45%	140	11%	227
78%	56	44%	143	10%	229
77%	59	43%	145	9%	232
76%	61	42%	148	8%	235
75%	64	41%	150	7%	237
74%	66	40%	153	6%	240
73%	69	39%	156	5%	242
72%	71	38%	158	4%	245
71%	74	37%	161	3%	247
70%	77	36%	163	2%	250
69%	79	35%	166	1%	252
68%	82	34%	168	0%	255
67%	84	33%	171		

By moving the lower-left slider in the Levels dialog box, you will change black to the shade of gray the slider is pointing to (**Figure 6.27**). You want to move this slider until it points to the darkest shade of gray that will not plug up and become black (known as the maximum shadow dot).

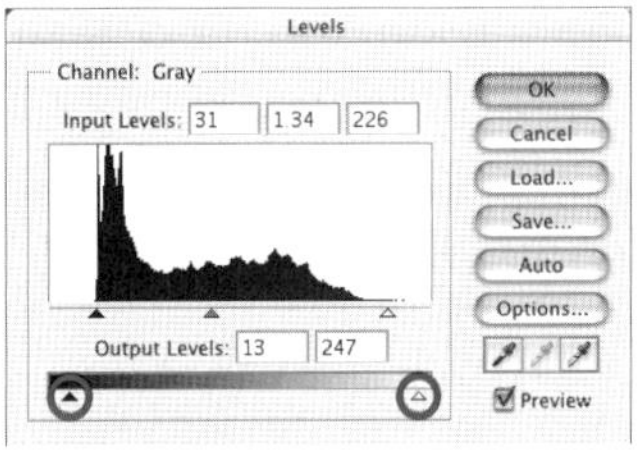

At first glance this stuff might seem complicated, but it is really quite simple. All you do is use the numbers from the tables or ask your printing company for settings. If you always print on the same kind of paper, you'll always use the same numbers.

Figure 6.27 The bottom sliders reduce image contrast to compensate for the limitations of the printing press.

A Quick Levels Recap

There are several steps to using Levels to adjust grayscale images, but as I've said, they're all quick and easy once you get used to them. Here's a brief recap of the role of each of the sliders in the Levels dialog box:

1. Move the upper-left slider until it touches the first bar on the histogram to force the darkest area of the image to black. Use the hidden Threshold feature—hold Option (Mac) or Alt (Windows)— to go as far as possible without damaging the image (**Figure 6.28**).

2. Move the upper-right slider until it touches the last bar on the histogram to force the brightest area of the image to white. Again, use the hidden feature to go as far as possible without damaging the image (**Figure 6.29**).

3. Move the middle slider to the left until the image looks nice and bright (**Figure 6.30**).

4. Move the lower-left slider to make sure the shadows won't plug up and become pure black on the printing press. Use the tables I've provided for settings, or ask your printer for more precise ones (**Figure 6.31**).

5. Move the lower-right slider to make sure you don't lose detail in the highlights when the smallest dots in your image disappear on the printing press. Use the tables for settings, or ask your printer for more precise ones (**Figure 6.32**). I usually adjust all five sliders before clicking OK to apply them.

Figure 6.28 Result of adjusting upper-left slider.

Figure 6.29 Result of adjusting upper-right slider.

Figure 6.30 Result of adjusting middle slider.

NOTES

If you own a 30-bit or higher scanner and your scanning software contains a histogram and has the same adjustment controls available, you can make adjustments within your scanning software. Most scanners can deliver a histogram without gaps because they can look back to the image and pick up extra shades of gray that would fill the gaps. These days, almost all scanners are 30-bit or higher. If your scanner is more than seven years old, there is a chance you might own a 24-bit model. If you are using one of those 24-bit scanners, there is no advantage to making the adjustments within your scanning software.

Figure 6.31 Result of adjusting lower-left slider.

Figure 6.32 Result of adjusting lower-right slider.

Postadjustment Analysis

Anytime you adjust an image, you run the risk of introducing some artifacts that might not be all that pleasant. So let's take a look at what can happen to your image after applying Levels. But don't worry—remember, in Photoshop there is usually at least one "fix" for every artifact.

Recognizing Posterization

When you look at an updated histogram, you might see wide gaps in the histogram—this indicates *posterization* (**Figure 6.33**). Posterization is when you should have a smooth transition between areas and instead you see a drastic jump between a bright and dark area. Some call this banding or stair-stepping. As long as the gaps in the histogram are smaller than three pixels wide, you probably won't notice it at all in the image.

Adjusting the image usually causes these gaps. As you adjust the image, the bars on the histogram spread out and gaps start to appear (remember that Slinky). The more extreme the adjustment you make, the wider the gaps. And if you see those huge gaps in the histogram, it'll probably mean that the posterization is noticeable enough that you'll want to fix it (it usually shows up in the dark areas of the image).

Eliminating Posterization

Here's a trick that can minimize the posterization. I should warn you that you have to apply this technique manually to each area that is posterized. Although it might take you a little bit of time, the results will be worth it.

To begin, select the Magic Wand tool, set the Tolerance to zero, and click on an area that looks posterized. Next, choose Select > Modify > Border, and use a setting of 2 for slight posterization or 4 for a moderate amount of posterization. Now apply Filter > Blur > Gaussian Blur until the area looks smooth (**Figures 6.34** and **6.35**). Repeat this process on all of the posterized areas until you're satisfied with the results. If you find that a large number of your images end up with post-scan posterization, then you might want to look into getting a scanner that's capable of delivering 16-bit images to Photoshop. A typical grayscale image will contain no more than 256 shades of gray, which is technically known as an 8-bit image. That's sufficient for most images, but extreme adjustments will cause posterization. One way to avoid posterization is to use a scanner that can produce images that contain thousands of shades of gray,

To see an updated histogram after adjusting the image, you must first apply the adjustment and then reopen the Levels dialog box.

I don't use this technique on every image, just on those that have extremely noticeable posterization.

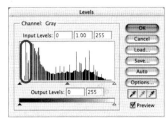

Figure 6.33 Gaps in a histogram indicate posterization.

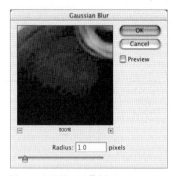

Figure 6.34 Turn off the Preview checkbox to see the edges of the posterized area.

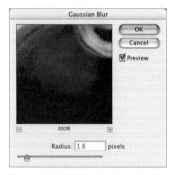

Figure 6.35 With the Preview checkbox turned on, increase the Radius setting until the posterized area appears smooth.

NOTES

To see the effects accurately when you're applying Unsharp Mask, you must view your image at 100 percent magnification. A quick way to view an image at 100 percent is to double-click the Zoom tool.

which is technically known as a 16-bit image. Most scanners are capable of capturing more than 256 shades of gray from a photograph, but few are capable of actually delivering all those shades to Photoshop. So, the next time you shop for a scanner, be sure to ask if it is capable of delivering 16-bit images to Photoshop. The only problem with 16-bit images is that only a fraction of Photoshop's features are available when working in that mode (no layer support for one). But you can easily adjust your image in 16-bit mode, then choose Image > Mode > 8 Bits/Channel to convert it to 8-bit and then all of Photoshop's features should be available.

Sharpening

By now your image should have great contrast, and it should reproduce nicely on a printing press. But I gotta tell you: Almost all images that are scanned need to be artificially sharpened. First I'll show you the controls available when sharpening; then I'll show you exactly how I go about sharpening an image.

To sharpen an image, choose Filter > Sharpen. Photoshop will present you with a submenu of choices. The top three might sound friendly (Sharpen, Sharpen More, Sharpen Edges), but you need to use the bottom one (Unsharp Mask). It's the only choice that allows you to control exactly how much the image will be sharpened. You can think of the other choices as being simple presets that just enter different numbers into the Unsharp Mask filter.

The reason it has the scary name is because way back before people used desktop computers, they sharpened images in a photographic darkroom. They would have to go through a process that involved a blurry (unsharp) version of the image. This would take well over an hour (don't worry, in Photoshop it takes only seconds) and would not be much fun. The process they'd go through in the darkroom was known as making an Unsharp Mask, so Adobe just borrowed that term.

The Unsharp Mask filter increases the contrast where two shades of gray touch in the image, making their edges more prominent and therefore easier to see. To easily view the effect of the Unsharp Mask filter (**Figure 6.36**), I'll demonstrate with a document that contains only three shades of gray (20 percent, 30 percent, and 50 percent), as shown in **Figures 6.37** to **6.40**. When you choose Unsharp Mask, you'll be presented with three sliders: Amount, Radius, and Threshold.

Figure 6.36 The Unsharp Mask.

▶ **Amount:** How much the contrast will be increased and, therefore, how obvious the sharpening will be.

▶ **Radius:** How wide a halo will be used. If you use too much, it will be obvious.

▶ **Threshold:** How different two touching shades have to be for sharpening to kick in. With Threshold set at 0, everything will get sharpened. As you increase this setting, only the areas that are drastically different will be sharpened.

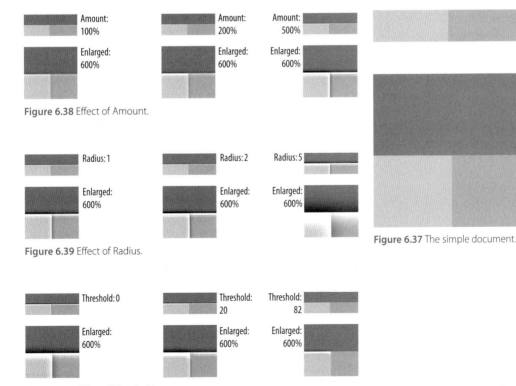

Figure 6.38 Effect of Amount.

Figure 6.39 Effect of Radius.

Figure 6.37 The simple document.

Figure 6.40 Effect of Threshold.

Figure 6.41 Amount 150, Radius 1, Threshold 0.

Figure 6.42 Amount 20, Radius 20, Threshold 0.

Now that we've explored all the options that are available with the Unsharp Mask filter, let's get down to business and find out how to apply them to an image.

Each time you apply the Unsharp Mask filter, it will remember the last settings you used. Because this filter is used on a wide variety of images (remember, we used it for line art scanning), the first thing we'll need to do is make sure it isn't using an extreme setting. So choose Filter > Sharpen > Unsharp Mask and type in the generic numbers of Amount=100, Radius=1, Threshold=0, just to make sure you're in the normal range.

Next, start to experiment with the Amount setting. I usually end up with a setting between 15 and 200. Grainy images usually require a low setting, while others can handle a much higher setting. Let your eyes be your guide. If things start to look overly grainy, then back off on the setting; otherwise, just keep raising it until things look nice and sharp without appearing artificial. There are two common indicators that you've gone too far:

▶ Obvious bright halos start to appear around the edge of objects (there will always be halos; you just want to make sure they aren't very noticeable).

▶ Very fine detail (like hair, or texture in bricks) will become overly contrasty; where it's almost pure black and pure white.

The Radius setting can have a radical effect on sharpening. You'll need to achieve a balance between Amount and Radius. High Amount settings (90–250ish) will require low Radius settings (.5 to 1.5), and low Amount settings (10–30) will require higher Radius settings (5–20). For instance, a grainy image will start to look unusual when you get an Amount setting anywhere near 100; you might even need to bring the Amount setting down to near 20 before the grain stops being exaggerated too much. At that point, you'll barely be able to tell that the image has been sharpened, so to compensate for that, you'll need to get the Radius setting up until the image starts to look sharp (maybe up to 15 or so) (**Figures 6.41** and **6.42**). But on most images, you'll find that you'll be able to get away with much higher Amount settings without causing grain problems. In that case, you might end up with an Amount setting around 120, and then you'll need to experiment with the Radius setting to see what looks best (probably between .5 and 1.5).

If you find that you ended up with a high Amount setting, then you might need to experiment with the Threshold setting (**Figures 6.43** to **6.45**). With it set to 0, everything in the image will be sharpened. That can cause areas that used to have fine detail (like a brick wall) or areas that used to look relatively smooth (like a skin tone) to suddenly have overly exaggerated detail. That will make those bricks look noisy and will add years to anyone's face because you've exaggerated every imperfection in their face. To avoid that, slowly increase the Threshold setting until those areas smooth out. You'll usually end up using settings in the single digits. You'll find that the higher you get the Threshold setting, the less effect the sharpening will have. That means that you'll most likely need to readjust the Amount setting to compensate.

Now, I know you're not going to want to hear this, but I'll mention it anyway. If you are going to print this image, you should sharpen it until it looks just a little bit over-sharp because the printing process isn't capable of delivering as much detail as you see onscreen.

Closing Thoughts

We've covered two main dialog boxes, Levels and Unsharp Mask. Remember, after you've practiced a few times, the whole process takes about a minute. When you feel that you have mastered Levels, you will be ready to take on the ultimate adjustment tool—Curves. Curves is equipped to do the same basic corrections as Levels, but can also do much, much more. In general, with grayscale images I always start out using Levels, and then move on to Curves to fix any problems that Levels can't handle; I also use Curves to work with color. It's like graduating from a Chevette to a Ferrari. The Ferrari takes more skill and coordination to master, but you get one hell of a ride. But that's another chapter.

Figure 6.43   A = 100, R = 1, T = 0   A = 150, R = 1, T = 0   A = 200, R = 1, T = 0

Adjust the Amount setting until the image looks nice and sharp. You'll know this setting is too high when the white halos become overly dominant or when the fine detail starts to break apart into pure black and pure white.

Figure 6.44   A = 150, R = 1.2, T = 0   A = 150, R = 2, T = 0   A = 150, R = 5, T = 0

If the Amount setting doesn't make the image look sharp enough, adjust Radius a small amount (1.1, 1.2, 1.3). I usually end up using really low settings unless I'm sharpening an image that has a lot of grain.

Figure 6.45   A = 150, R = 1.1, T = 3   A= 150, R = 1.1, T = 7   A = 150, R = 1.1, T = 15

If your image contains skin tones or other areas that should look very smooth, increase the Threshold slider until those areas do look smooth. I usually use Threshold settings between 0 and 9.

Ben's Techno-babble Decoder Ring

30-bit: Designates how many colors a scanner can capture (10 bits of red + 10 bits of green + 10 bits of blue = 30 bits total). So 10 bits per channel (RGB) is the same as 30 bits total. 10 bits = 2 to the tenth power, which equals 1,024. So a 30-bit scanner can capture 1.1 billion colors (1,024 x 1,024 x 1,024 = 1.1 billion), whereas a 24-bit scanner can capture only 16.7 million colors. When scanning in grayscale, a 24-bit scanner captures 256 grays and a 30-bit scanner captures 1,024 grays.

Maximum shadow dot: The largest halftone dot that will not combine with the surrounding halftone dots to become pure black. This is usually measured as a percentage and reflects the highest percentage of ink that could be used without losing detail when printed. The type of paper usually determines what the Maximum Shadow Dot setting will be.

Minimum highlight dot: The smallest halftone dot that is reproducible using a particular printing process. This is usually measured as a percentage and reflects the lowest percentage of ink that will not lose detail when printed.

Unsharp Mask: A term used to describe the traditional process of sharpening an image by combining a blurry (unsharp) version of the image with a normal version. The idea behind Unsharp Mask is to increase contrast and therefore detail.

Keyboard Shortcuts

Function	Macintosh	Windows
Levels	Command-L	Ctrl-L
Auto Levels	Shift-Command-L	Shift-Ctrl-L
Reapply Previous Setting	Option-Command-L	Alt-Ctrl-L

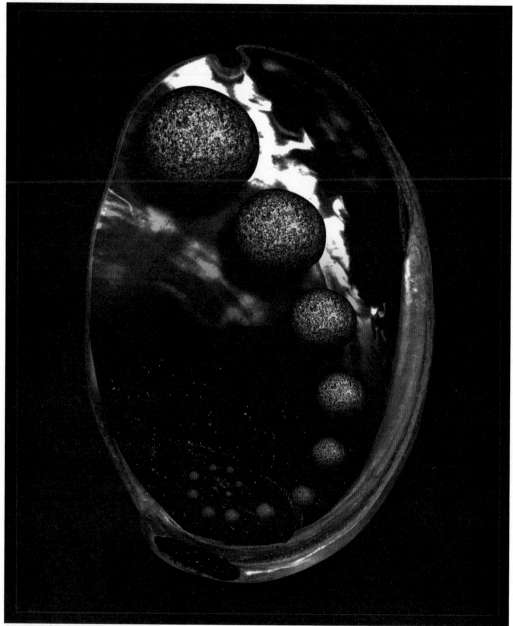

Courtesy of Gregg Lauer, www.gregglauer.com

Understanding Curves

Courtesy of Michael Slack, www.slackart.com

NEW IN 7

The only change to Curves in 7.0 is the addition of the Auto Color settings. But instead of covering that feature here, it's actually more useful to review it in the chapter on color correction. In this chapter, you'll find new information about working in Lab mode and using a histogram to help determine which areas of an image can be safely adjusted.

Have patience. All things are difficult before they become easy.

—Saadi

Understanding Curves

If I were going to be dropped on a deserted island and could bring only one thing with me, I might choose a Swiss Army knife. With that knife, I could cut firewood, spear fish, and clean my teeth (remember the toothpick?). Much like a Swiss Army knife, Image > Adjust > Curves can be used for just about anything. In fact, if I had to pick one adjustment tool to use all the time, it would definitely be Curves. By mastering the Curves dialog box, you have so much control over your images that you might wonder why you would ever need to use the Levels or Brightness/Contrast dialog box. Let's take a look at some of the things you can do with the Curves dialog box. You can

▶ Pull out far more detail than it's possible to see with the Sharpening filters (**Figures 7.1** to **7.3**).

▶ Lighten or darken areas without making selections (**Figures 7.4** and **7.5**).

▶ Turn ordinary text into extraordinary text (**Figures 7.6** and **7.7**).

▶ Color-correct your images without guesswork (**Figures 7.8** and **7.9**).

Figure 7.1 The original image. (© 2002 Stockbyte, www.stockbyte.com)

Figure 7.2 After applying the Unsharp Mask filter.

Figure 7.3 After a simple Curves adjustment.

Figure 7.4 The original image. (©2002 PhotoSpin, www.photospin.com)

Figure 7.5 After a simple Curves adjustment.

Figure 7.6 The original text effect.

Magical

Figure 7.7 After a simple Curves adjustment.

Figure 7.8 The original image. (© 2002 Stockbyte, www.stockbyte.com)

Figure 7.9 After a simple Curves adjustment.

None of these changes could be made by using Levels or Brightness/Contrast (that is, not without making complicated selections or losing control over the result). Now you can see why you'll want to master Curves!

Using Curves, you can perform all the adjustments available in the Levels, Brightness/Contrast, and Threshold dialog boxes, and much, much more. In fact, you can adjust each of the 256 shades of gray in your image (**Figure 7.10**).

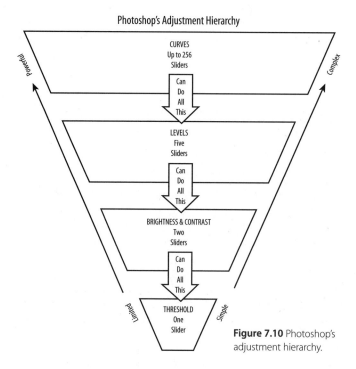

Figure 7.10 Photoshop's adjustment hierarchy.

With Power Comes Complexity

I find that the majority of Photoshop users never truly master (or even become comfortable with) Curves, just as some people never drive cars with manual transmissions. Perhaps the first time they tried to drive with a clutch, they drove up a really steep hill and encountered a stop sign at the top. Then, maybe a big garbage truck pulled up behind them within what seemed like an inch of their bumper.

If you've ever driven a car with a clutch, you know what I'm getting at. When you're not comfortable with some-thing and are forced to use it in a challenging situation, the tendency is to give up. However, if you've spent enough time getting comfortable with a manual transmission, you don't even think about it when you're driving. Curves works the same way. If you just play around with it, you might get scared off, but if you hang in there, it becomes easier to use, and you'll find yourself doing some amazing things to your images. This chapter might seem long-winded, but the truth is that until you truly "get" Curves, you will be a prisoner of Photoshop's less powerful tools. So, fasten your seatbelt, adjust your rearview mirror, and settle in for the ride.

NOTES

All the techniques mentioned in this chapter apply equally to images prepared for Web pages and those prepared for print. You might notice that I concentrate on ink settings throughout this chapter. I find that most users are more comfortable thinking about how ink would affect their image instead of light. Ink is the exact opposite of light, so Photo-shop can easily translate what you're attempting to do, even if your image will be displayed using light.

But First, a Test!

Before we delve into Curves, I want to test your present knowledge of the Curves dialog box. Don't worry, though, because the lower your score, the more you should enjoy this chapter.

Look at the curve shown in **Figure 7.11** and see if you can answer the following questions:

▸ Which areas of the image will lose detail from this adjustment?

▸ Which areas of the image will become brighter?

▸ What happened to 62% gray?

▸ What happened to the image's contrast?

If you truly understand the Curves dialog box, then you found these questions extremely easy to answer. However, if you hesitated before answering any of them or couldn't answer them at all, then this chapter was designed for you.

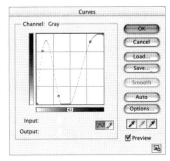

Figure 7.11 Can you figure out exactly what this curve will do to an image?

The Idea Behind Curves

Because the Curves dialog box allows you to adjust every shade of gray in an image (256 in all), it works quite a bit differently from the other adjustment tools. To get a clearer picture of what Curves does, let's construct our own Curves dialog box from scratch, using something you're already familiar with: the plain old vanilla bar chart. You know what I'm talking about—those wretched bar charts that can't be avoided in magazines, brochures, television, and pretty much everywhere you look. Now we can finally put one to good use by using it to help us understand Curves.

What if you create a bar chart that indicates how much light your monitor uses to display each color in an image? This bar chart would be just like any other that you've seen, where taller bars mean more light and shorter bars mean less. You could show the shade of gray you are using below each bar, and then draw a line from the top of each bar over to the left so you could label how much light is being used for each shade. I think you'd end up with something that looks like **Figure 7.12.** Or you could just as easily change the chart to indicate how much ink your printer would use to reproduce the image. Now that we're talking about ink, short bars would mean less ink, which would produce a light shade of gray, and tall bars would mean a lot of ink and would produce a dark shade of gray. To make the change, all we'd have to do is flip all the shades at the bottom of the graph so the dark ones are below the tall bars and the bright ones are below the short bars. The result would look like **Figure 7.13,** right?

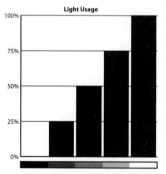

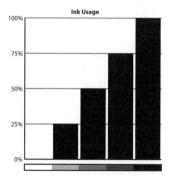

Figure 7.12 This bar chart indicates the amount of light used to display the shades of gray shown at the bottom.

Figure 7.13 Flip the shades at the bottom, and you've got a graph that represents ink usage.

OK, now that you've got the concept, let's expand on that to accommodate the real world. Our basic bar chart might work for a simple logo with just a few shades of gray (one bar representing each shade), but most of your images will contain many more than that. So, we just increase the number of bars (**Figure 7.14**), right? Well, sort of. The fact is, your image can contain up to 256 shades of gray. But if we jam 256 bars (one for each shade) into our chart, then they won't look like bars anymore; they'll just turn into a big mass (**Figure 7.15**). You can't see the individual bars because there isn't any space between them.

All the same, our images contain up to 256 shades of gray, so we really need that many bars in our chart. Now that they're all smashed together, we don't have room to label each bar, so why don't we just overlay a grid (**Figure 7.16**) and label that instead? If that grid isn't detailed enough for you, we could add a more detailed grid, such as the one shown in **Figure 7.17.**

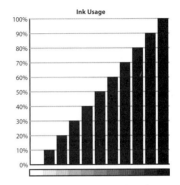

Figure 7.14 Add more bars for additional accuracy.

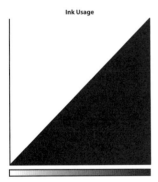

Figure 7.15 The 256 bars take up so much space that the chart no longer looks like a bar chart.

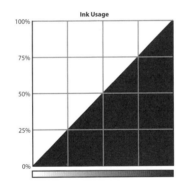

Figure 7.16 A grid can help you figure out how much ink is used.

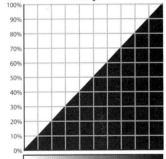

Figure 7.17 The more detailed grid allows you to be even more accurate.

If you've followed along and this makes sense to you, then you have grasped the principle behind Curves. We have just a bit more to go. Stick with me, and trust me—all these details are well worth slogging through because they'll help you get a much deeper understanding of Curves.

The sample chart we've created isn't really all that useful…yet. It's not telling you anything you can't find in the

Info or Color palettes. For example, if you really want to know how much ink (or light) you'd use to reproduce a shade of gray, you could just open the Info palette by choosing Window > Show Info (**Figure 7.18**), and then move your pointer over the image; the Info palette would indicate how much ink would be used in that area. The Color palette (Window > Show Color) is set up similarly and will tell you how much ink or light makes up a shade of gray (**Figure 7.19**). The main difference between the two methods is that the Info palette gives you information about your image—specifically, what's under the pointer. The Color palette isn't image-specific but gives you generic information about how much ink or light makes up a shade of gray.

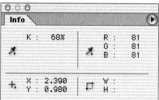

Figure 7.18 The Info palette indicates how much ink would be used to reproduce the color that is under the pointer.

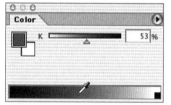

Figure 7.19 The Color palette indicates how much ink would be used to reproduce your current foreground color.

The Curves dialog box, meanwhile, is really just a simple bar chart—with a lot of bars that are very close together—that shows how much ink or light will be used in your image. The gradient at the bottom shows all the shades of gray you could possibly have, and the chart above shows how much ink or light will be used to create each shade. But the wonderful thing about the Curves dialog box is that it doesn't just sit there like a static bar chart that only gives you information. It's interactive—you can use it to change the amount of ink (or light) used to reproduce your image (**Figure 7.20**).

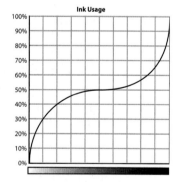

Figure 7.20 Changing the shape of the line in the Curves graph changes how much ink is used throughout the image.

Think of our Ink Usage bar graph: As the shades of gray get steadily darker, each shade uses slightly more ink, resulting in a straight diagonal line. But in the Curves graph, you can move points on the line. For example, you can flatten the line so that in your modified image, many shades of gray are represented by a single shade. Or you can make a dramatic change to the line, dragging a point up or down so that a shade changes to become much darker or lighter.

The Gradients Are Your Guide

Go ahead and pick any shade of gray from the gradient, and then look above it to figure out how much ink would be used to create it (**Figure 7.21**). You can use the grid to help you calculate the exact amount of ink used (about 23% in this case). But wouldn't you rather see what 23% looks like? Suppose we replace those percentage numbers with another gradient that shows how bright each area would be (**Figure 7.22**). Just to make sure you don't get the two gradients confused, read the next two sentences twice: The bottom gradient represents the shades of gray you are changing. The side gradient indicates how bright or dark a shade will be if you move the line to a certain height (**Figure 7.23**).

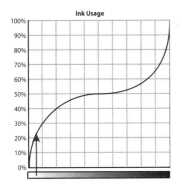

Figure 7.21 Use the grid to help determine how much ink is used in an area.

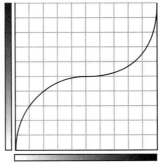

Figure 7.22 The gradient on the left indicates how dark an area will become if the curve is moved to a certain height.

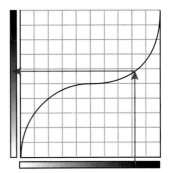

Figure 7.23 The bottom gradient scale is what you're changing. The left gradient scale is what you changed it to.

Congratulations. You've survived Ben's Bar Charts 101. Now you're ready to graduate from charts and take flight with the full-fledged Curves dialog box (**Figure 7.24**). Does it look familiar? It should. You might notice that the Curves dialog box is a bit smaller than the bar chart we were using.

To get a larger grid, click the zoom icon in the lower right of the Curves dialog box. Each time you click this symbol, it toggles between a grid that's 171 pixels wide and one that's 256 pixels wide (**Figure 7.25**). I generally use the large grid because it shows all the grays you can have in your image, which makes it easier to be precise. In fact, if you use the small version, you can't control every shade of gray (your image contains 256 shades of gray, and the smaller grid is only 171 pixels wide). I use the 171-pixel version only when working on a small screen, because then the large version covers up too much of the image.

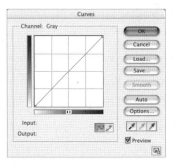 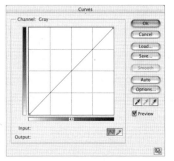

Figure 7.24 The grid in the small version of the Curves dialog box is only 171 pixels wide.

Figure 7.25 The grid in the large version of the Curves dialog box is 256 pixels wide.

Ben, Are We There Yet?

I know what you're thinking. "I wanna play with Curves, now!" Be calm, you're *almost* ready. There are just a couple of thoughts I need to plant in your brain first.

If you go back to when we first started to create the bar chart, you'll remember that we started measuring how much light our monitor was using to display things. Then we flip-flopped and measured how much ink we'd use for printing. The same thinking applies to the Curves dialog box. Remember how we accomplished that switch earlier in the chapter—didn't we just reverse the shades of gray at the bottom of the chart? Hold that thought, and look at the middle of the gradient at the bottom of the Curves dialog box. Clicking those arrows reverses the gradient, which toggles the chart's context between light and ink (**Figures 7.26** and **7.27**).

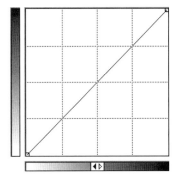 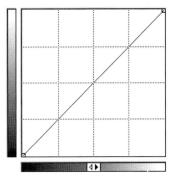

Figure 7.26 When black is at the top, you are using ink (remember, up means more).

Figure 7.27 When white is at the top, you are using light (again, up means more).

The *mode* of your image determines what you'll start with. Photoshop assumes that images that are in grayscale, CMYK, or Lab mode will be printed, and therefore it defaults to using the gradient that represents ink. Since your monitor displays everything using red, green, and blue light, images in RGB mode will cause Photoshop to use the gradient that represents light.

Photoshop doesn't care which system you use. It can easily translate between the two, because light is the exact opposite of ink. When you switch from one scale to the other, not only do the light and dark ends of the gradients get swapped, but the curve flips upside down. Be sure to look out for which mode I use throughout the examples in this chapter; otherwise, you might end up getting the exact opposite result of what you see in this book! I'll stick to the default settings unless there's a good reason to change them, and when I do, I'll clue you in.

Remember, the side gradient indicates what you'll end up with if you move a point on the curve to a certain height. You can always glance at the side to find out how much light or ink you're using. Just remember that up means more of something and that you can use either light or ink.

NOTES

You can press the Option (Mac) or Alt (Windows) key when choosing Image > Adjust > Curves to apply the last settings used on an image.

Next comes the grid. Remember how we ended up with one that is more detailed than the one we started with? Well, you can toggle between those two grids by Option-clicking (Mac) or Alt-clicking (Windows) anywhere within the grid area. It's up to you which grid you use. It doesn't affect the result you'll get in Curves; it's just a personal preference (**Figure 7.28**).

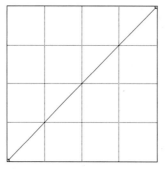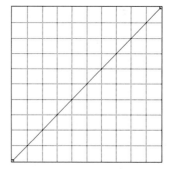

Figure 7.28 Option-click (Mac) or Alt-click (Windows) anywhere on the grid to toggle between a 25% increment grid (left) and a 10% increment grid (right).

Take Curves for a Test Drive

OK, start your engines. We're going to stop babbling and start driving! Go ahead, open an image, choose Image > Adjust > Curves, and start messing with the curve. Just click anywhere on the curve to add a point, and then drag it around to change the shape of the curve. If you want to get rid of a point, drag it off the edge of the grid. You can also click a point and then use the arrow keys on your keyboard to nudge it around the grid. You can even add the Shift key to the arrow keys to nudge it in larger increments.

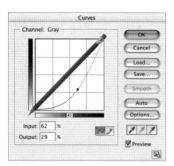

Figure 7.29 Use a pencil to represent the original line.

You should quickly find that it's pretty easy to screw up your image! That's because we haven't talked about specific types of adjustments yet. So, let's explore the final piece of the Curves puzzle. To understand what you're doing, you must compare the curve you're making to the original line. After all, how can you know how much of a change you've made unless you know where you started? I usually just grab a pencil and hold it up to the screen to represent the original line (**Figure 7.29**). Now let's see what we can do with all this.

Improving Dark Images

Try this: Open any grayscale image you think is too dark (I'll show you how to work with color in a minute), as shown in **Figure 7.30**. Next, choose Image > Adjust > Curves, and add a point by clicking the middle of the line. Pull the line straight down, and see what happens to your image. Compare the curve with the gradient at the left of the Curves dialog box (**Figures 7.31** and **7.32**). The farther you move the curve down, the less ink you use and therefore the brighter the image becomes. If part of the curve bottoms out, the shade represented by that area becomes pure white because there will be no ink used when the image is printed.

Figure 7.30 Start with a dark grayscale image. (© 2002 Stockbyte, www.stockbyte.com)

Figure 7.31 Move the curve down to reduce how much ink is used.

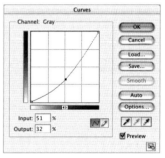

Figure 7.32 Comparing the curve with the gradients.

Any part of a curve that's below the original line indicates an area that is using less ink, which means that it has been brightened. Look at the gradient directly below those areas to determine which shades of the image were brightened (**Figure 7.32**). The farther the line is moved down from its original position, the brighter the image will become (**Figure 7.33**).

Previewing the Changes

You can compare the original and changed versions of the image by checking and unchecking the Preview checkbox. As long as the checkbox is unchecked, you'll see what the image looked like before the adjustment. When you click to check it, you'll see the changes you just made.

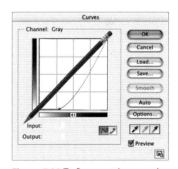

Figure 7.33 To figure out how much ink you've removed, look below where the line used to be.

Color Is Different

The concepts and adjustments we talk about with Curves apply equally to grayscale and color images. But when you

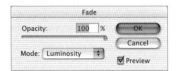

Figure 7.34 Choose Edit > Fade Curves to limit your changes to the brightness of your image.

Figure 7.35 When creating an adjustment layer, change the Mode menu selection to Luminosity.

work on a color image, you have to be more careful; otherwise, you might end up shifting the colors, rather than just the brightness, of your image. There are two ways to apply Curves to your image and therefore two methods for limiting its effect on the brightness of a color image. First, you can apply Curves to the currently active layer by choosing Image > Adjust > Curves. Immediately after applying Curves, you can choose Edit > Fade and set the Mode pop-up menu to Luminosity (**Figure 7.34**). The Fade command will limit the last change you made (Curves, in our case) to changing only the brightness (*luminosity* is just another word for brightness) of the image—it will not be able to shift the colors or change how saturated they are.

Your other choice would be to apply Curves to more than one layer by choosing Layer > New Adjustment Layer > Curves. Then, when prompted (**Figure 7.35**), you would set the Mode pop-up menu to Luminosity. An adjustment layer will affect all the layers below it but none of the layers above it. It's also a nonpermanent change, because you can click twice on the adjustment-layer thumbnail in that layer to reopen the Curves dialog box and make changes. That means that any Curves techniques you use for adjusting grayscale images will work on color images if you use the Luminosity blending mode (**Figures 7.36** to **7.38**).

Figure 7.36 Original image. (© 2002 Stockbyte, www.stockbyte.com)

Figure 7.37 After brightening the image with Curves, the color and saturation change.

Figure 7.38 Using the Luminosity blending mode prevents adjustments from shifting the colors in the image.

Color shifts aren't the only problems you'll encounter when adjusting color images with Curves. The *mode* your image is in might be having an adverse effect on the adjustment. RGB color images are made from three components (red, green, and blue). A bright green color might be made out of 0 red, 255 green, and 128 blue. When you first open the Curves dialog box, the pop-up menu at the top of the dialog box will be set to RGB, which will cause any points to affect the exact same R, G, and B value. Clicking on that green color in your image will display a circle at 165 on the curve, which will affect all the areas that contain 165 red, 165 blue, and 165 green. Equal amounts of R, G, and B create gray. So, simply clicking on the curve of a color image will usually cause the colors to shift in an unsatisfactory way, because the circle that appears when clicking on your image will not accurately target the area you clicked on. While working in RGB mode, all color areas will shift because their RGB mix will change as the Curves dialog box shifts the RGB values in equal amounts. Ideally it would affect only the exact mix of RGB that the color is made from, but it doesn't work that way in RGB mode. The solution to this problem is to convert your image to Lab mode by choosing Image > Mode > Lab Color. In Lab mode, your image is made from three components: Lightness, A, and B. When you adjust your image, the Curves dialog box will automatically set itself to work on the Lightness information, which will prevent your adjustment from shifting the color of your image and will also make it so that the circle will show up in the correct position to make accurate adjustments. Once you're done with your adjustment, I'd suggest that you convert the image back to RGB mode because many of Photoshop's features are not available in Lab mode. I don't use Lab mode for every color image; I reserve it for those images that are troublesome in RGB mode.

Ghosting an Image

Curves can also be helpful when you plan to add text to a photograph. When you place text on top of a photo, it's often difficult to read because there isn't much contrast

NOTES

You can hold down Option (Mac) or Alt (Windows) to set options such as the Blending mode when you are creating an adjustment layer.

between the text and the image. However, if you lighten the photo, the text will be easier to read (**Figure 7.39**). This is known as *ghosting,* or *screening back,* an image.

Figure 7.39 Ghosted image. (© 2002 Stockbyte, www.stockbyte.com)

Try this: Open any color photo (make sure it's in RGB mode), and then use the Marquee tool to select about half the image. Choose Image > Adjust > Curves, and click the control point in the lower-left corner of the grid area to select it (use the upper-right point for CMYK images). Now move that point up (down, in CMYK mode) using the up arrow on your keyboard. You have just lightened (or *ghosted)* the dark part of the image. This technique is often used to lighten a photo so that any text placed on top of it is easier to read.

Compare the line you just made with the original (remember to use your pencil). See how the dark areas of the image have changed a large amount, and the bright areas have not changed as drastically (**Figure 7.40**).

Using Curves to screen back an area of an image provides professional-looking results. Resist the temptation to resort to this commonly used quick-and-dirty method: Create a new layer above the image, make a rectangular selection on the new layer, and fill it with white; then reduce the

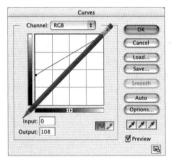

Figure 7.40 This curve brightens the dark areas of the image more than the bright areas.

opacity of the new layer until it forms a ghostly box. Cheating like this tends to change all the shades in the image an equal amount and could easily blow out the detail in the highlights of the image.

Increasing Contrast and Detail

So far, we've learned that moving the curve up or down will increase or decrease the amount of ink used to make the image. Now let's look at how changing the angle of the curve can help us. What if you had an image where the brightest area was white and the darkest area was only 25% gray? Would it be easy to see the detail in the image? I don't think so (**Figure 7.41**).

Now think about how that image would change if we applied the curve shown in **Figure 7.42.** If you look closely at this curve, you'll notice that areas that are white in the original image wouldn't change at all and areas that used to be 25% gray would end up being around 75% gray. Wouldn't that make it much easier to see the detail in whole image? In an overexposed image like this one, you have to make the curve steeper in the lighter part of the curve. (We already learned that in an underexposed image, like the one in **Figure 7.30,** you have to make the dark part of the curve steeper to bring out the detail.) You always have to compare the curve with the original line to determine how much of a change you've made. If you make the curve just a little steeper than the original, then you'll add just a little contrast to that area. Anytime you add contrast, it becomes easier to see the detail in that area because the difference between the bright and dark parts becomes more pronounced. Remember to look at the gradient below to figure out which shades of gray you are changing.

Open any grayscale image, and choose Image > Adjust > Curves. Move your pointer over the image, and then click and drag across the area where you want to exaggerate the detail. You'll notice that a circle appears in the Curves dialog box. Photoshop is simply looking at the bottom gradient to find the shade of gray under your pointer; it then puts a circle on the curve directly above that shade. This

Figure 7.41 You can't see much detail in this image because the brightness is limited to 0%–25%. (© 2002 Stockbyte, www.stockbyte.com)

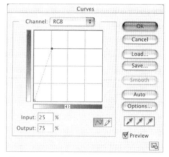

Figure 7.42 This curve adds more contrast, making it easier to see the detail in the whole image.

Figure 7.43 After making the curve steeper, it's easier to see the detail.

circle indicates the area of the curve that needs to be changed to affect the area you're dragging across. Add control points on either side of this area of the curve. Next, move the top point you just added up toward the top of the chart, and move the bottom point down toward the bottom of the chart. The area you dragged across should appear to have more detail (**Figures 7.44** to **7.46**).

Figure 7.44 Original image. (© 2002 Stockbyte, www.stockbyte.com)

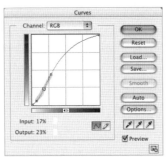

Figure 7.45 Find the range you'd like to change, and then make the curve steeper in that area.

Figure 7.46 After making the curve steeper.

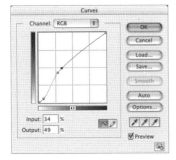

Figure 7.47 Fix the rest of the curve so you don't exaggerate the contrast in other areas.

You might also need to fix the rest of the curve to make sure that the contrast in those areas doesn't change radically. You can do this by adding another point and moving it so that the majority of the curve looks normal—that is, diagonal (**Figure 7.47**).

Decreasing Contrast and Detail

Any part of the curve that's flatter (more horizontal) than the original line indicates an area where the contrast has been reduced (shades of gray become more similar). Look at the gradient directly below these areas to determine which shades of the image were changed. The flatter the line becomes, the less contrast you'll see in that area of the image. When you lower the amount of contrast in an image, it becomes harder to see detail. This can be useful if you *want* detail to be less visible. If the curve becomes completely horizontal in an area, you've lost all detail there (**Figures 7.48** to **7.50**). Remember, it's a bar chart— the same height means the same brightness.

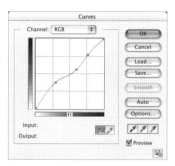

Figure 7.48 Original image. (© 2002 Stockbyte, www.stockbyte.com)

Figure 7.49 Curve used to reduce apparent detail in stonework.

Figure 7.50 Result of applying Curves to reduce apparent detail.

Using a Histogram with Curves

Flattening a curve is usually harmful to an image because the detail in the area you are adjusting will be very difficult to see. You can often analyze the histogram that is found in the Levels dialog box (see Chapter 6, "Optimizing Grayscale Images") to determine which areas of the image won't be harmed by flattening the curve. Since short lines in a histogram indicate shades that are not very prevalent in the image, those areas can often be flattened in a curve without noticeable degradation to the image. Flattening one part of the curve will allow you to make the rest of the curve steeper, which will increase the contrast of those areas and make the area appear to have more detail.

Here's how it works: Before adjusting an image, choose Image > Adjust > Levels and look for flat areas in the histogram. When you find a flat area (not all images will have them), move the upper-left slider over until it points to the beginning of the flat area and not the 0–255 number that appears in the upper left of the dialog box (**Figure 7.51**). Now move the slider to the end of the flat area and make a note of the 0–255 number again. Next, click Cancel in Levels and choose Image > Adjust > Curves. Move your cursor around the dialog box to see if the numbers at the bottom of the Curves dialog box are 0–100% or 0–255 numbers. If they are ranging from 0–100%, then click the arrows that appear in the center of the bottom gradient in the Curves dialog box to switch to the 0–255 numbering system. Now

NOTES

You can reset the Curves dialog box back to the default line by pressing and holding Option (Mac) or Alt (Windows) and then clicking the Reset button.

If you're trying to exaggerate the detail in the darkest areas of an image, you'll have to be very careful not to force areas to pure black (if an area becomes pure black, it will contain absolutely no detail). You can do this by making sure no part of the curve bottoms out. The same problem will happen if the curve flattens out on the other end, which forces areas to pure white.

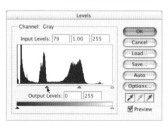

Figure 7.51 Move the upper-left slider to the beginning of the flat area.

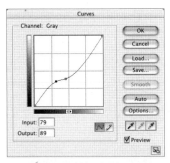

Figure 7.52 Use the number you saw in Levels as the Input number in curves.

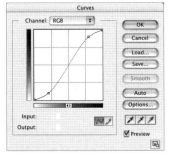

Figure 7.53 A classic S curve.

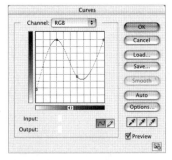

Figure 7.54 After this adjustment, the image won't contain any areas darker than 90% or brighter than 18%.

click in the middle of the curve and then enter the first number you wrote down from the Levels dialog box for the Input and Output settings. Add a second point and do the same for the second number you saw in the Levels dialog box. Now, move the upper dot straight down and the lower dot straight up until the area between the two becomes flat. That should increase the contrast across most of the image, while reducing contrast in those pixels that are not very prevalent in the image (**Figure 7.52**).

Let's Analyze a Classic Tip

Have you ever heard the tip "make an S curve"? Well, let's explore exactly what an S curve does (**Figure 7.53**).

Remember, to find out what a curve is doing to your image, you should compare the curve with the original line. Look at the areas of the curve that are steeper than the original line—namely, the middle of the curve. The shades represented by these steeper areas appear to have more detail. Whenever you pull detail out of one part of an image, you'll also lose detail in another part. Therefore, look at either end of the curve, at the areas of the curve that are flatter than the original line (more horizontal). These areas appear to have less detail. Thus, an S curve attempts to exaggerate detail in the middle grays of the image. However, it also gives you less detail in the highlights and shadows.

Checking Ink Ranges

Look at **Figure 7.54** and concentrate on the gradient at the left side of the Curves dialog box. This gradient indicates how dark an area will become if you move the curve to a particular height. Pick a shade of gray from that gradient (such as 90%); then look directly to the right of it to determine if you'll have any areas that shade of gray. Pick another shade and do the same thing. If the curve starts in the lower-left corner and ends in the upper-right corner, each one of the shades should be used somewhere in the image. However, there might be a few shades that are used in more than one area of the curve.

Inverting Your Image

Think of a stock-market chart that indicates what's happening to the market over a month's time. If you're like most investors, whenever the market's going up, you're happy. However, you're always carefully watching that chart to see if the market starts to dip. If it does, that's when you start to panic. You can think of curves in the same way. As long as the curve is rising, you're fine; however, if the curve starts to fall, you should expect unusual results. Look at **Figure 7.57**, and try to figure out what's happening in the area that's going downhill. The dark areas of the image (around 75%) became bright, and the bright areas (around 25%) became dark. That means you've inverted that part of the image. You'll usually want to minimize or avoid this situation unless you're going for a special effect (**Figures 7.55** and **7.56**).

Figure 7.55 Original image. (© 2002 Stockbyte, www.stockbyte.com)

Figure 7.56 Result of applying the curve shown in Figure 7.57 and fading it using Luminosity mode.

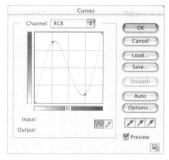

Figure 7.57 Areas between 25% and 75% have been inverted.

Freeform Curves

To change the curve, you're not limited to adding and moving points. Another way to define a curve is to click the pencil icon at the bottom of the Curves dialog box and draw a freeform shape (**Figure 7.58**). However, the shape you draw has to resemble a line moving from left to right. Go ahead, just try to draw a circle. You can't do it. That's because the Curves dialog box is just like a bar chart, and you can't have two bars for a single shade. Just for giggles, draw a really wild-looking line across the grid area, and then look at your image. Drawing your own line

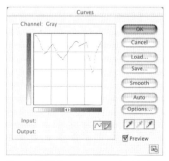

Figure 7.58 A curve created with the Pencil tool.

with the Pencil tool is usually better for special effects than for simple image adjustments.

Let's take a quick look at some of the things you can do when working with a freeform curve:

▶ **Smoothing.** After creating a curve with the Pencil tool, you can click the Smooth button to smooth out the shape you drew (**Figure 7.59**). Go ahead and click it multiple times to keep smoothing the curve.

▶ **Converting to points.** To convert any line drawn with the Pencil tool into a normal curve, click the curve icon (**Figure 7.60**).

▶ **Drawing straight lines.** You can also draw straight lines with the Pencil tool (**Figure 7.61**). Just Shift-click across the graph area, and Photoshop will connect the dots to create a straight line.

▶ **Posterizing.** By drawing a stair-step shape with the Pencil tool, you can accomplish the same effect as if you had used the Posterize command (**Figure 7.62**).

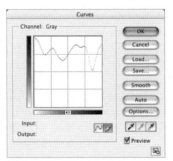

Figure 7.59 A freeform curve after Smooth is applied.

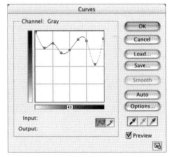

Figure 7.60 The result of converting a freeform curve into a normal curve.

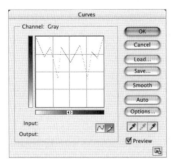

Figure 7.61 Straight lines drawn by Shift-clicking with the Pencil tool.

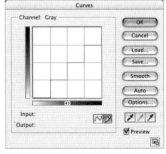

Figure 7.62 Drawing stair-steps is the same as choosing Image > Adjust > Posterize.

To try this out, open the image called "chrome.jpg" from the CD, and then play around with the Pencil tool in the Curves dialog box. Try making a huge M or W, and experiment with different shapes. You should be able to transform the 3D type into some cool-looking chrome text if you experiment long enough (**Figures 7.63** to **7.65**).

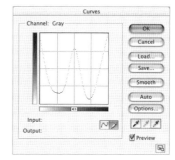

Figure 7.65 Freeform curve used to create chrome effect.

Chrome Chrome

Figure 7.63 Image from the CD.

Figure 7.64 Result of applying the curve in Figure 7.65.

Input and Output Numbers

The Input and Output numbers at the bottom of the Curves dialog box allow you to be very precise when adjusting an image. Input is the shade of gray being changed; Output is what it will become. When the points on the curve appear as hollow squares, the Input and Output numbers relate to your pointer. The Input number tells you which shade of gray is directly below your pointer. The Output number will tell you what the shade of gray (height of the bar chart) would be if you moved the curve to the height of your pointer.

Try it. First, click the curve icon (not the pencil), and then make sure that none of the points on the curve are solid. Do this by moving your pointer around until it looks like a white arrow, and then click the mouse. Now move your pointer around the grid area. You'll notice the Input and Output numbers changing. All they're doing is telling you which shades of gray are directly below and to the left of your pointer (**Figure 7.66**). If you trace over the shape of a curve, the Input and Output numbers will show you exactly what the curve is doing to all the shades of gray in your image.

Two Numbering Systems

Two different numbering systems can be used in the Curves dialog box. You can switch between the 0–100% system and the 0–255 numbering system (which we used in Levels) by switching between light and ink (remember

NOTES

Clicking the Save button brings up a standard Save dialog box, which allows you to save the current settings for future use. The file that's created contains the Input and Output settings for each of the points used on the current curve. To reuse a saved setting, click the Load button.

When you're changing the Input and Output numbers, press the up or down arrow key to change a number by 1, or press Shift–up arrow or Shift–down arrow to change a number by 10.

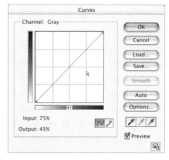

Figure 7.66 Input and Output numbers indicate the location of your pointer relative to the two gradients in the Curves dialog box.

the little arrows that appear in the middle of the bottom gradient). Go ahead and give it a try (**Figure 7.67**).

If you're working on an image that's in RGB mode, Photoshop assumes you're going to use the image onscreen instead of printing it. Therefore, when you open Curves, it uses Input and Output numbers ranging from 0 to 255. These numbers represent the amount of light your monitor will use to display the image onscreen (0 = no light, or black; 255 = maximum light, or white). Using this numbering system allows you to have control over each shade.

Figure 7.67 Click the arrow symbol to switch numbering systems.

If you're working on an image that's in grayscale or CMYK mode, Photoshop assumes you'll be printing the image. Therefore, when you open Curves, it uses numbers ranging from 0% to 100%. These numbers represent the amount of ink used to reproduce each level of gray in the image (0% = no ink; 100% = solid ink).

When you click the arrows that switch between the two numbering systems, Photoshop also reverses the gradients at the bottom and left of the graph. It does this to keep the zero point of each numbering system in the lower-left corner of the graph, which effectively changes between light and ink. You don't have to remember or understand why this happens—it's just nice to know there's a reason behind it.

When you switch the numbering system, this also changes the gradient on the left side of the Curves dialog box. Therefore, if you're using the 0–255 numbering system, you have to move a curve up to brighten the image and down to darken it (the exact opposite of what you do in the 0–100% numbering system). I always look at the gradient on the left to remind me; if black is at the top (the 0–100% system), you're using ink, and moving a curve up will darken the image. If white is at the top of the gradient (the 0–255 system), you're using light, and moving a curve up will brighten the image.

Entering Numbers

After you've created a point, it will appear as a solid square. This represents the point that's currently being edited. The Input and Output numbers at the bottom of the dialog box indicate the change this point will make to an image. The Input number represents the shade of gray that's being changed. The Output number indicates what's happening to the shade of gray—the value that you're changing it to. As long as the point appears as a solid square, you can type numbers into the Input and Output fields to change the location of the point (**Figure 7.68**).

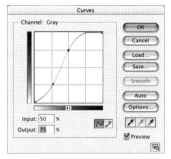

Figure 7.68 To alter the position of a point on the curve, just change one of the numbers.

Those numbers can be very useful. We'll end up depending on them once we get into the chapter on color correction. But for now, let's see how they can be useful when attempting to change the brightness of an image. Remember that you can click on your image and a circle will appear in the Curves dialog box that indicates what part of the curve would affect the shade in that area? Well, you can also Command–click (Mac) or Ctrl–click (Windows) on your image and Photoshop will add a point where that circle would show up. So, what if you'd like two areas of your image to have the same brightness level? Command–click or Ctrl–click one of them to lock in its brightness level. Then, before you release the mouse button, glance at the numbers at the bottom of the Curves dialog box to see exactly how bright that area is. Command–click or Ctrl–click the second area, and change the Output number to match that of the first object (**Figure 7.69**). The bar chart will be the same height in both areas, which means that both areas will end up with the same brightness. But you have to be careful when doing this, because the bar chart will flatten out between those two points. When that happens, there won't be any detail in those shades, so other parts of your image might seem to disappear (**Figures 7.70** and **7.71**).

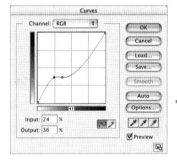

Figure 7.69 When two points are at the same height, those two areas will have the same brightness level.

Figure 7.70 Original image. (© 2002 PhotoSpin, www.photospin.com)

Figure 7.71 Result of making the far and close buildings the same brightness levels.

The Info Palette

The Info palette can also show you how Curves affects your image (**Figure 7.72**). When you move your pointer over the image, the Info palette indicates what's happening to that area of the image. (If you want a more precise cursor, press the Caps Lock key to change your cursor from the default eyedropper to the crosshairs.) The first number in the Info palette tells you how dark the area is before using Curves. The second number tells you how dark it will be after Curves is applied.

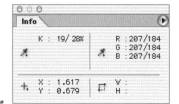

Figure 7.72 The first number is what you have before using Curves; the second is what you get after using Curves.

A Quick Recap

Now, to verify that you're ready to move on, you should make sure you understand the general concepts. Take a look at the curve in **Figure 7.73** and see if you can answer the following questions:

▶ Which areas of the image will lose detail with this adjustment?

▶ Which areas of the image will become brighter?

▶ What happened to 62% gray?

▶ What happened to the image's contrast?

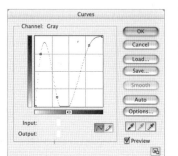

Figure 7.73 Can you figure out what this curve will do to an image?

Just in case you couldn't answer all these questions, let's recap what we've covered:

▶ Flattening a curve will reduce contrast and make it more difficult to see detail.

▶ Making a curve steeper will increase contrast and make it easier to see detail.

▶ Up means darken in the 0–100% system.

▶ Down means darken in the 0–255 system.

▶ Up means brighten in the 0–255 system.

▶ Down means brighten in the 0–100% system.

Closing Thoughts

My hope is that after you've read this chapter you'll have come to the conclusion that the Curves feature really isn't such a brain twister. And if you come out of it thinking of ways you might use Curves in the future, even better. The Curves dialog box is one of a handful of Photoshop features that separate the experts from everyone else. But there's no reason why you can't propel yourself into the expert category. Once you get comfortable with Curves (OK, it might take a while), you'll be able to do so much more than you can do with any other dialog box. So hang in there and stick with it. The initial learning curve might be somewhat daunting, but the fringe benefits are dynamite.

Ben's Techno-babble Decoder Ring

Contrast: The range between the brightest and darkest areas of an image (or a portion of the image).

S curve: A generic curve used to exaggerate the detail in the midtones of an image by suppressing the detail in the highlights and the shadows.

Keyboard Shortcuts

FUNCTION	MACINTOSH	WINDOWS
Curves	Command-M	Ctrl-M
Move point up 1	Up arrow	Up arrow
Move point down 1	Down arrow	Down arrow
Move point left 1	Left arrow	Left arrow
Move point right 1	Right arrow	Right arrow
Move point up 10	Shift–Up arrow	Shift–Up arrow
Move point down 10	Shift–Down arrow	Shift–Down arrow
Move point left 10	Shift–Left arrow	Shift–Left arrow
Move point right 10	Shift–Right arrow	Shift–Right arrow
Select next point	Command–Control–Tab	Ctrl–Tab
Select previous point	Shift–Command–Control–Tab	Shift–Ctrl–Tab
Deselect all points	Command–D	Ctrl–D

Color Management

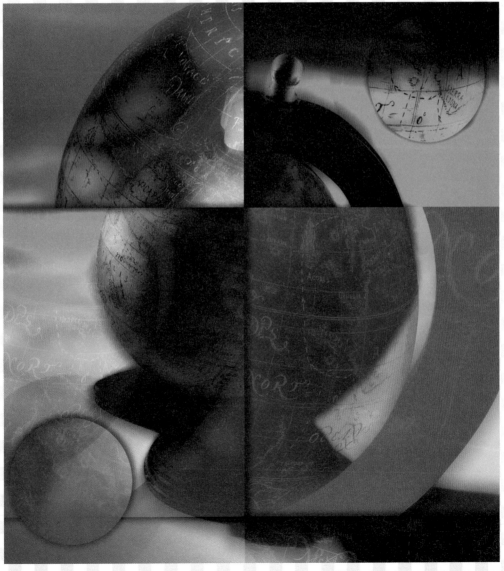

© 2002 Jim DiVitale, www.divitalphoto.com

NEW IN 7

The color mangement settings are not new to Photoshop 7.0. This chapter is brand new to this version of this book, so I'm sure you'll want to read it even if you've read a previous edition of this book.

This would be so much easier if I weren't color-blind.
—Donkey from the movie "Shrek"

Color Management

This chapter should probably be named "Confessions of a Photoshop Expert," and it's the chapter that I wish I could have read myself a few years ago. My embarrassing secret? Until recently I've found color management to be so painstakingly cumbersome and time consuming that I found every reason to avoid it. That all changed with the introduction of Photoshop 6, and I'm now pleased to be able to help you successfully negotiate the rat maze of issues that are involved in getting your colors to behave themselves.

For years, I was frustrated because I'd scan an image and adjust it so it looked great onscreen, then I'd print it on my desktop color printer and it just never looked right. The colors were oversaturated, or the whole thing looked bluish. Then I'd work with it more until it was "acceptable" on both my screen and desktop printer, but when I sent it out to be printed in a brochure, it would look quite different. I just couldn't fathom why the colors were never consistent. That was back in prehistoric times when I was using Photoshop 3. Later, when Photoshop 5 was released, there was a great deal of hype about its wonderful "new and improved" color-management features. It was supposed to make everything perfect. Your screen would match your desktop printer and you could have either one of them simulate a printing press. But when I tried to learn what was necessary to get everything set up, the experts just seemed to talk in a foreign language that I simply didn't understand. They loved to talk about gamut, profiles, delta E, colorimeters…and the terms just kept coming. They just didn't speak my language, and when I tried to implement everything they were telling me about, I got so frustrated that I just ended up turning off all those fancy features. I mean, I'm supposed to be a Photoshop expert and here I was turning off the one feature was supposed to help me the most. I was even on a first-name basis with the people who write Photoshop and with many

Figure 8.1 The color wheel.

color-management "experts" around the country, and I couldn't get my head around it.

Every time Adobe released a new version of Photoshop, I'd throw myself back into the color-management labyrinth, driving my "expert" friends crazy as I tried to distill all the terms, technology, and techniques into something workable. But it was still too complicated for me to get it to really work comfortably in my situation. Along came Photoshop 5 and I went at it again. But, still, there were just too many details and far too many settings. I'd have to have a color-management expert on staff just to keep things running correctly. At last, Photoshop 6 came along, and that's when I felt things had matured to the point that I could get some traction with all this wizardry. I finally realized that all those highfalutin terms were just the technical people strutting their stuff. It's not rocket science we're talking about, after all. The truth is that all this stuff can really work if you can just get over a bunch of terms and figure out how to deal with a few simple settings. And once it's all set up, you don't have to do that much to maintain everything. Not only that, but with things working properly, you can do some amazing things. You can get your screen to match your printer, get your desktop printer to simulate a printing press, and much more. So, now that I've bared my soul, let's jump in and see what all the fuss is about.

For me to truly understand anything in Photoshop, I usually have to simplify it to such an extent that it becomes almost obvious. So, let's start out from the beginning and slowly work our way into the more technical bits. I promise this will all make sense and will be easy for you to set up things for your situation. Stick with me, because once you've gotten this nailed, your Photoshop life will be infinitely easier. Here goes:

In figuring out color management, I read all about how our eyes work and that's when I learned that we could see only three colors of light—red, green, and blue. Everything we see is a combination of those colors. That's right, when you look at a rainbow, all your eyes see are red, green, and blue (**Figures 8.1** and **8.2**). When we see all three of those

Figure 8.2 The RGB components of the color wheel.

colors in a balanced amount (equal amounts of red, green, and blue), we see white light. The more light there is, the brighter it is; the less light there is, the darker it is. We often call dark white *gray*, so that's what I'll call a balanced amount of red, green, and blue. When they aren't balanced, we see color. Photoshop works the same way. Go ahead and launch Photoshop, click on your foreground color, and pick any color you'd like. Now glance over at the RGB numbers that appear in the right side of that dialog box—they show you how that foreground color can be made out of a combination of red, green, and blue (**Figure 8.3**). That's also how your computer screen works (**Figure 8.4**). Each pixel that makes up your screen is really just three bars of color right next to each other— again RGB. A digital camera works on the same principle; it just measures how much RGB light travels through the lens. So, it really is an RGB world out there. But things change just a tiny bit when you print things.

Figure 8.4 A magnified view of your screen.

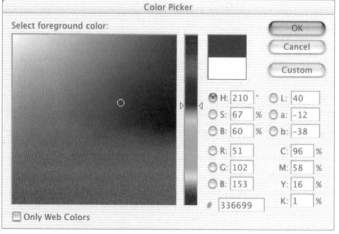

Figure 8.3 Photoshop's Color Picker.

Remember that white light is made from a balanced amount of red, green, and blue light. So, for red ink to look red when you shine white light at a sheet of paper, it has to let only red light reflect off it and into your eyes;

otherwise, it wouldn't look red (**Figure 8.5**). That means that red ink absorbs green and blue in order to just let the red light bounce off the sheet of paper. So if that's the case, then blue light must absorb everything but blue, and green light must absorb everything but green. So, when you combine any two of those inks (let's say red ink printed on top of green ink), all you'd get is black because the inks end up absorbing all three colors of light (**Figure 8.6**). That presents a problem that is easily solved. When we print, we don't need red, green, and blue inks; instead, we need three inks that control how much RGB bounces off a sheet of paper. We need one ink that controls how much red light enters our eye, another to control green light, and a third to control blue.

So, let's figure out what we need. Take a look at **Figure 8.7**. It represents three flashlights, one with a red filter, one with green, and one with blue. Now, check out the area where the blue and green flashlights overlap, but the red one does not; you should see cyan. That means that cyan ink simply absorbs red light, while allowing the other two colors of light to bounce off the sheet of paper. If you analyze Figure 8.7 further, you might be able to figure out that magenta ink absorbs green light and yellow ink absorbs blue light. That's why the Info palette is arranged the way it is (**Figure 8.8**). One side looks at light and the other looks at ink. If you're wondering about the *K* in CMYK, it stands for *key*, which is really just a term used for black ink. It's used because a lot of people in the printing industry call cyan *blue* and they didn't want to confuse anyone by calling black *B*, so they came up with *K* instead to confuse the rest of us. Since black ink can't shift the color of anything, we'll talk about it later in this chapter. I know we haven't really gotten into color management yet, but this information is completely relevant to what we need to accomplish in this chapter. Now that we've got a basic idea of how color is reproduced, let's take a look at why your screen doesn't match your desktop printer and why your printer delivers a different result than your next-door neighbor's—in essence, why we need to bother with color management.

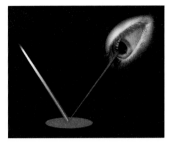

Figure 8.5 Red ink absorbs green and blue light.

Figure 8.6 Red and green ink create black.

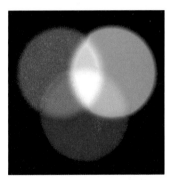

Figure 8.7 Three overlapping flashlight beams.

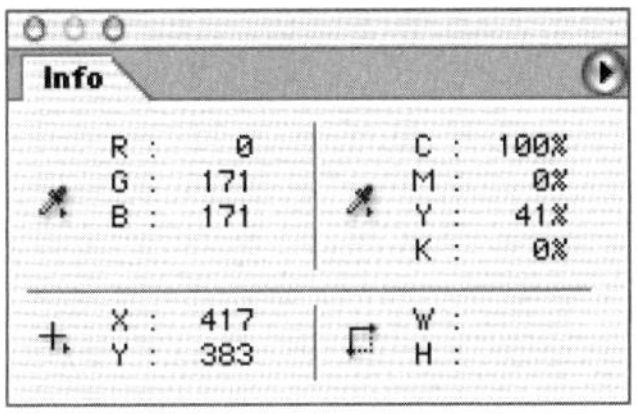

Figure 8.8 The Info palette.

NOTES

Some inkjet printers use two shades of cyan ink and two of magenta, but the general principles still apply.

Here are the problems we need to overcome: If you were to purchase a red felt-tip marker from three different manufacturers (maybe Crayola, Sharpie, and a generic brand), would you expect them to produce identical results? It's true that they are all red, but each one would, in fact, be a different shade of red. Maybe a Sharpie marker would produce a darker red and a Crayola a more vivid red. Not only that, but buying two red markers from the same company doesn't even guarantee consistent results; after all, they could be from different batches or one could be older than the other. Well, the same thing goes for printing. Each printer will deliver a slightly different result when printing the same image because the inks are slightly different, so don't expect to send the same info to an Epson and a Canon printer and get the same results. The problems don't stop there. Would you expect a Sony television set to look the same as a Panasonic? Just take a stroll through your local electronics superstore and look at all the TVs that are tuned to the same station. Even though they are being sent the exact same signal, they all look different. That's because they all use different shades of red, green, and blue. So why would you expect two different brands of monitors to look the same? They also use different shades of RGB. This is why color management is needed. It's designed to deal with all these variations among devices (monitors, scanners, printers, cameras, etc.). All we have to do is measure the exact color of red, green, and blue that your scanner and monitor use and also measure which shades of CMY that your printer uses (I'm ignoring the K in CMYK because black ink won't shift the color of things). Then Photoshop can use its wizardry to send different information to each device in an attempt to get consistent results on all those devices.

There is one more issue to deal with before we figure out how to get all this stuff to work in our favor. Remember when I said that your eyes see white light when a balanced amount of red, green, and blue light enters your eye? Well, you don't end up with white when you use a balanced amount of RGB or CMY on your monitor, printer, or scanner. Remember that all your equipment uses slightly different shades of RGB or CMY (just like those felt-tip pens), which means that equal amounts of red, green, and blue would produce different results on each device. So balanced RGB on one device might look a little greenish or bluish instead of looking gray. That can cause a lot of problems because many of Photoshop's features (such as color correction) make the assumption that equal amounts of R, G, and B produce no color at all. The solution to that problem is to make your images out of idealized shades of red, green, and blue that have nothing to do with your monitor, scanner, or printer. This special set of RGB colors is what all our images will be made from; then Photoshop will go to work to make sure it can print and display things correctly using the less-than-ideal colors of RGB or CMY used by our monitor and printers (**Figure 8.9**).

Figure 8.9 The overall concept of different RGBs being used.

Implementing Color Management

This is where things will become a little technical, but don't worry, I'll be here as your plain-English translator. First, let's see how all this relates to Photoshop's color-management features. When we measure the exact shade of RGB or CMY that a device uses, the end result will be an *ICC profile*. An ICC profile is just a small file that describes how something reproduces color. It's in a format that is approved by the

International Color Consortium (ICC). That's the file you feed Photoshop so it can do the magic necessary to produce consistent color on each device. You'll end up with a profile for your monitor, your desktop printer, your scanner, and even your digital camera, with each profile telling Photoshop which shades of RGB or CMY it uses to make color.

If you compare two printers and one has a more vivid set of CMY inks loaded, then that printer will be capable of reproducing a more vivid range of colors than the other one (just like different brands of markers). Each set of RGB colors (or CMY, for that matter) will display color in a unique way. The range of colors you can reproduce on any given device is known as its *gamut.* Let's say that you can reproduce a nice deep blue on your inkjet, but you can't on your friend's inkjet (maybe it comes out as a more muted blue). That just means the particular color was *in gamut* on your printer but was *out of gamut* on your friend's printer. And, as you might already know, more exotic colors like fluorescent orange are out of gamut on just about any desktop printer.

There's just one more term with which I want you to get familiar. Remember that idealized version of RGB out of which we're going to create our images? The one where a balanced amount of RGB makes gray? Well, that's known as our *RGB working space.* A working space indicates what you'll make your images out of when you create a new document instead of opening an existing one.

So, now that we know some of the terms Photoshop will be throwing at us, we can get to the business of getting all this stuff set up properly. We'll figure out the details of picking that idealized version of RGB, measuring the shades of RGB and CMY that our devices use, and learn how to tell Photoshop how to deal with all that information.

The first order of business is to pick that idealized version of RGB (known as your RGB working space) out of which we'll make our images. Picking a working space is just like picking which brand and type of film to use for a 35mm camera. If there was one best choice in that area, then that would be all that's available. A lot of people just grab Kodak

400-speed film, but there are legions of photographers who will happily debate the merits of each film type. It's the same with RGB working spaces. One might be better for your specific situation than another, but they will all work. Let's see what's available: To see your choices, choose File > Color Settings and click on the RGB pop-up menu (**Figure 8.10**). Here's my general take on this menu: With most of the choices, equal amounts of R, G, and B make gray. The main difference is in the *range* of colors that you can create (also known as gamut). Don't stress about it. It's just like film for a camera—they all take OK photos, but there might be one that's better for your specific needs.

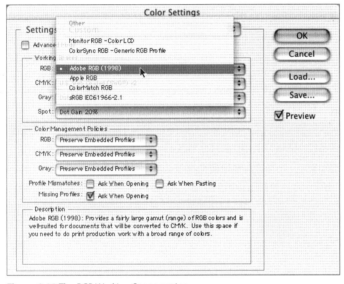

Figure 8.10 The RGB Working Space setting.

RGB Working Spaces

▶ **Adobe RGB:** The best general choice for people who end up printing their images on desktop inkjet printers or send them to commercial printing presses.

▶ **Apple RGB:** A less-than-ideal choice because adjustments won't affect the image evenly from light to dark. Useful if you have old untagged images, which will be talked about below.

NOTES

Make sure the Color Management Policies pop-up menus are all set to Preserve Embedded Profiles, otherwise you just might want Photoshop to warn you when opening an image or when pasting.

▶ **ColorMatch RGB:** Not a bad choice for images that will end up on a commercial printing press, but not quite as ideal as Adobe RGB for that purpose.

▶ **ProPhotoRGB:** Ideal for photographs that are scanned in 16-bit mode from color transparencies, because it offers a very wide gamut. Can cause posterization in 8-bit images.

▶ **Monitor RGB:** Use when you'd like your images to look identical in both Photoshop and your Web browser. An alternative to sRGB, but it does not take into consideration what other people will see when viewing your Web site.

▶ **sRGB:** Good for people who create Web graphics and would like to limit the colors used in their images to those that can be seen on an average user's screen. Less than ideal for anyone who will end up printing on a commercial printing press or photographic process because it has such a limited range of colors available.

While we're at it, let's make sure that Photoshop will interrupt our work only when it really has to; otherwise, it will constantly remind us whenever we open an image that happens to be created with a different RGB working space than what we currently have set up. I suggest that you turn off the Ask When Opening and Ask When Pasting checkboxes at the bottom of the Color Settings dialog box.

Now that we've gotten our RGB working space out of the way, let's make sure that our images will be friendly to others. We'll do that by including a profile of our working space with each image. That way when someone else opens it, their copy of Photoshop will know what colors of RGB the image was made from, so it can display it properly. When you save an image, make sure the Embed Color Profile checkbox is turned on (**Figure 8.11**). That will "tag" the image with an ICC profile.

Figure 8.11 Turn on the Embed Color Profile checkbox to "tag" an image.

Figure 8.12 The Missing Profile dialog box.

If you don't tag your images, Photoshop will ask you to guess which colors of RGB the image was made from (**Figure 8.12**). If you guess wrong, the image won't look right. I get a lot of untagged images, but I really don't like the way Photoshop makes you blindly choose a profile without seeing the consequences. If you get an untagged image, here's what I suggest you do: Just choose the "Leave as is" option and then click OK. Then, immediately after opening it, choose Image > Mode > Assign Profile. Then try all of the profiles (just make sure the Preview checkbox is on). Each time you change that setting, you should see your image change. Keep cycling through until you find one that makes your image look good. The person who sent you the image didn't include enough info for Photoshop to know what the colors should look like, so you're just guessing. And, no, it's not worth calling the person who sent it to you because they obviously don't know enough about color management to have it set up correctly, so you'll just end up confusing them by asking which setting to use.

Device Profiles

Now that you have Photoshop set up for creating new images and opening pre-existing ones, let's get all your devices set up. Remember, a profile tells Photoshop what color of RGB or CMY your device uses. This is also where you're going to need to start thinking about how accurate you need things to be and therefore how much money you are willing to spend.

The more precise the profile, the more accurate your color will be. There are three ways to get a profile and they each come with their own level of cost and quality:

▶ **Canned profiles:** Just like canned spinach, it's nothing like the real thing. These profiles are usually free and are usually created at the factory and do not take into account the variations among products and the specifics of your situation (paper lot and ink batch for printer, etc.). They can often be found on the CD that came with the device or on the manufacturer's Web site.

▶ **Visual adjustment:** Like 14-day-old carrots—better than frozen, but not by much. These profiles are created using low-cost or free software that depend on your eyes to be the measurement devices to create a profile. This method is mainly used for computer displays and usually involves much guesswork.

▶ **Custom profiles:** Like fresh-picked garden vegetables, nothing compares to it. These profiles are the most accurate and are completely customized to your specific situation. They are created using sophisticated measurement devices and will deliver the most accurate color matching between devices.

If you're on a budget, then you'll be working with one of the first two choices. But if you're really serious about color, then you'll want to look into the last option.

Let's start by making sure Photoshop knows how to display images correctly on your screen. We'll do that by measuring the exact colors of RGB that your monitor uses and also measuring how bright your monitor is. I wouldn't even think about using a canned profile for a monitor unless it's an LCD screen. Unlike standard CRT monitors, LCDs are much more consistent among batches and over time. The method for creating visually measured profiles varies depending on which operating system you use. In Mac OS 9, choose Apple Menu > Control Panels > Monitors, click on the color icon, and then click the Calibrate button. In Mac OS X, choose System Preferences from the Apple Menu, click the displays icon, then click the Color tab, and finally click the Calibrate button. In Windows, choose Start > Settings > Control Panel and then double-click on the Adobe Gamma icon. No matter which operating system you are using, the setting will be very similar to what you see below. You'll get different choices depending on what type of monitor you have (LCDs have fewer settings). Let's take a look at what you might expect when creating a profile in Mac OS X. Not every option that you see here will be available when you try it—it depends on the type of monitor you own and how much information your monitor can share with the calibration software. Since you'll find similar settings in Adobe Gamma on Windows, this information should apply to everyone, regardless of what type of computer you have.

Using Apple's Calibration Utility

When the calibration utility starts up, you'll be presented with an Introduction screen. Checking the Expert Mode checkbox requires you to make more adjustments than the standard mode, so I suggest you turn it on because you'll end up with a more accurate profile (**Figure 8.13**).

NOTES

It's most ideal to perform this calibration while you are working under the same lighting conditions that you'll use throughout the day. So, make sure you don't have radically different lighting conditions between the time you calibrate and the time you want to use your monitor for critical color judgments.

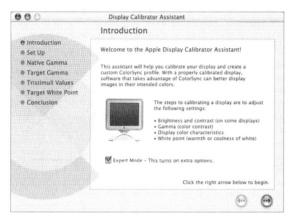

Figure 8.13 The Introduction screen.

The second screen (**Figure 8.14**) will ask you to adjust the brightness and contrast of your display so that it can use the full range of your monitor's capabilities. There's not much to say here, so let's continue to the next step. The third screen will ask you to adjust the gamma of your monitor. It's really just trying to figure out what it takes to get all three colors (red, green, and blue) at the same brightness level, which will make it possible to display a true gray when it's requested. The outside of the three squares are created from alternating stripes of solid black and whichever color you are adjusting. The general idea is to squint your eyes so those strips blur into a single tone and then move the slider until the middle portion of the square matches the edges in brightness. After you've done that, it will ask you what gamma setting you'd like to use (**Figure 8.15**). *Gamma* is a technical term that describes how bright your monitor will be. The standard setting for a Mac is 1.8, so go ahead and choose that. The next screen is the challenging one (**Figure 8.16**). That's where you're supposed to indicate which shades of red, green, and blue are used by your specific display (known as phosphor colors). For most people, this will be a total guessing game because their specific brand of monitor is not likely to be listed. Trinitron displays are rather popular and you can find out if you have one by looking very closely at your screen. See if you can find two very thin dark lines running horizontally across your screen. They will be about ⅓ and ⅔ of the way down your screen. If you can see them, then you have a Trinitron; if you don't, then it's anyone's guess which choice to use (although you might be able to find your phosphor colors listed in the specifications page of your monitor's manual). If your brand of display isn't listed and you don't find those two thin lines on your screen, then you're going to completely end up guessing—that's why I really would prefer to use a different method to create a profile. After you're done fumbling around trying to find the name of your monitor from that list, you'll be asked to select a white point (**Figure 8.17**). That will determine what color you get when your screen is displaying the brightest white of which it is capable. I find that most of these settings darken of your screen too much, so I'd use the "No white point correction" setting. The last step is to give your newly created profile a name (**Figure 8.18**). I usually call it something like "Ben's display 6/17/2002" so I can remember how long it's been since I created it.

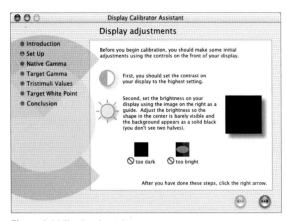

Figure 8.14 The Display Adjustments screen.

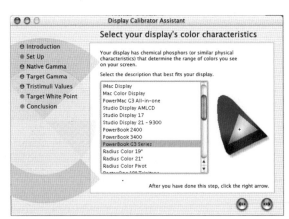

Figure 8.15 Current Gamma setting.

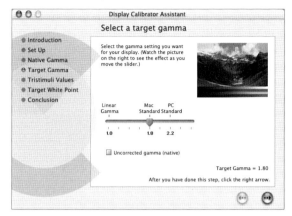

Figure 8.16 Target Gamma setting.

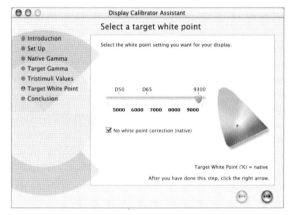

Figure 8.17 White Point setting.

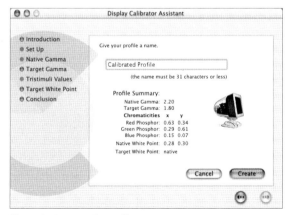

Figure 8.18 Saving the profile.

Once you've saved your profile, the Calibration utility will automatically save it in the proper location so that Photoshop uses the proper information. You can always check which profile is being used by clicking the Device Profiles tab in the ColorSync control panel (**Figure 8.19**). (Photoshop only uses the Display Profile setting and ignores the rest). The color and brightness of your screen changes over time, so you should create a new profile at least every three months. Now, I don't know about you, but I didn't feel overly confident when I was creating that profile. After all, I had to guess at what colors of RGB my display uses, and it seemed to be overly easy to screw things up (such as choosing an unusual white-point setting). Because of that, I don't suggest you rely on a visually measured profile if you do any serious color work in Photoshop. Instead, I'd invest in a color-measurement device that will do all the work for you and will deliver a much more accurate profile.

Creating a Custom Profile

This is where you'll have to start shelling out some bucks if you want accurate color. I think it's well worth the money for anyone who is a true Photoshop professional. After all, you can easily end up paying just as much to fix a mistake

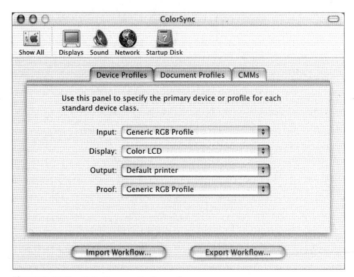

Figure 8.19 The ColorSync control panel.

that was made because of inaccurate color (such as reprinting a brochure). You'll need to purchase a colorimeter (**Figure 8.20**), which start at about $200, to get an accurate profile. You can purchase one from computer catalogs or Web sites such as www.rodsandcones.com or www.profilecity.com. When you open the box, you'll find three things: the colorimeter, a manual, and a CD. So, plug the thing in (it usually connects via a USB port), pop the CD into your computer, and install the software. Then, when you run the software, it will ask you to put the colorimeter on the middle of your screen. Then it will flash a bunch of colors in front of it, and before you know it, you'll have a custom profile. In general, this hardware/software combo ends up measuring the exact shades of RGB that your specific display uses and it measures how consistent it is across the range from bright to dark.

Figure 8.20 A colorimeter.

If you're going to drop the cash needed to purchase a colorimeter, then you might as well profile your display once a week. After all, it takes only a few minutes, and you never know how much your display has changed over time.

Creating a Printer Profile

The next step is to create a printer profile so that we can get the printer to accurately simulate what you see on that newly profiled display of yours. When profiling a printer, you have three choices: a canned profile, a scanner-based profile, and a custom profile. Let's see what's needed to get those set up.

Most desktop color printers come with an ICC profile right on the CD that shipped with the unit. If you don't find it there, try visiting the manufacturer's Web site. It will often be part of the driver software you can download. They don't always mention that it contains a profile on the Web site, though. That's what happened to me with my Epson 2000P inkjet printer. I went to Epson's Web site and didn't find any downloadable item that mentioned a profile, but when I downloaded the drivers for my printer, the profiles just happened to be part of the installation. This is what would be considered a canned profile because it was created using someone else's printer (same model though), using their batch of paper and ink. Canned profiles are usually perfectly acceptable for casual Photoshop users. You just have to be aware that they are specific to the ink and paper set used when the profile was made. That means that the profile might produce unsatisfactory results if you use a brand of paper or ink that is different from what the profile was designed for. Once you download that canned profile, you'll need to put it in a special place on your hard drive so that Photoshop knows where to find it. Here's where they belong:

▶ **Windows 2000:** WinNT/System/Spool/Drivers/Color

▶ **Windows NT:** WinNT/System32/Color

▶ **Windows 98:** Windows/System/Color

▶ **Mac OS 9:** System Folder/ColorSync Profiles

▶ **Mac OS X:** Users/CurrentUser/Library/ColorSync/ Profiles

While you're playing around in that folder, you might as well throw away the profiles that are for devices that you'll never use. That way Photoshop's Profile pop-up menu (we'll talk about that in a little bit) won't be so cluttered with choices.

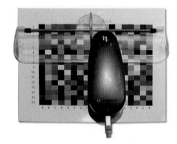

Figure 8.21 A $3,000 device used to create a printer profile.

If you really want the most accurate color reproduction from your desktop color printer, you should think about having a custom profile made. Creating a profile isn't very difficult. All you do is purchase a color-measurement device and install the software. Then you get the reference image that comes with the software and measure the result using the measurement device (**Figure 8.21**). The only problem is that the measurement device can easily set you back $3,000 or more! That's fine if you work for a large company that has dozens of printers or if you are a commercial printing company, but it's out of reach for most other users. But that's OK, because there is a way to get the benefit of a custom profile without parting with the money for that spiffy measurement device. You can visit a Web site such as www.profilecity.com, where they will create one for you. Here's how it works: You pay them just under $100 (don't quote me on that now) and they email you a reference image. Then, you print that image and snail mail it back to them. They use one of those expensive measurement devices to create a profile and then they email it to you. The only problem is that you really should have a profile for each ink and paper combination that you'll end up sending through your printer. That means one for the extra-glossy stuff that almost feels like plastic and works great for photos and another for the slightly shiny version you use for brochures and maybe a third for that dull cheap paper that you have loaded most of the time. As you can guess, the money can add up quite quickly. But that kind of money is pocket change if you work for a commercial printing company and you want to make sure that you can supply your customers with an accurate profile of a particular ink/paper/press combination.

There is one more alternative, and this one will cost about as much as two of those custom profiles. You can purchase a special piece of software (such as Monaco EZcolor 2) that will allow you to use your flatbed scanner as a measurement device to create a printer profile. Let's see how it works: You start by choosing what type of profile you'd like to create (**Figure 8.22**). The software is capable of creating display, printer, and scanner profiles and can use a colorimeter for the display portion if you own one.

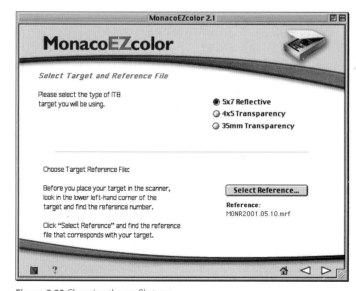

Figure 8.22 Choosing the profile type.

When you indicate that you'd like to create a printer profile, it will walk you through a series of steps that include printing a reference image (**Figure 8.23**). Then, once that print has dried, you grab a special image that was supplied in the box for the product and put both the special image and the image you just printed onto your scanner and scan them. Then you indicate where the edges of the images are (**Figure 8.24**) and the software measures all the colors based on what your scanner captured. The end result is a set of profiles—one for your scanner and one for your printer. That way you can create as many profiles as you'd like and you don't have to pay $100 a pop for each one. The profiles you get are only as good as your scanner, but I've found that these profiles are good enough for most Photoshop users.

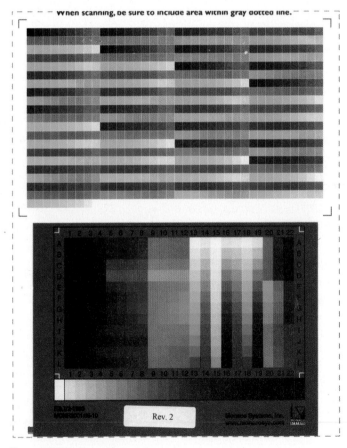

Figure 8.23 Printing a reference image.

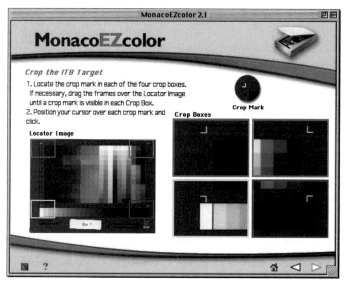

Figure 8.24 Defining the edges of the image.

Profiling a Printing Press

If you ever plan to reproduce your images on a commercial printing press, you'll have to convert your images to CMYK mode before you send them off. For Photoshop to correctly convert your image to CMYK mode, it will need a bunch of information about how the image will be reproduced (supplied by an ICC profile). When I'm creating an image that will be printed at a commercial printer, the first thing I do is call my sales rep and ask if he or she has an ICC profile for the press/paper combination that I'll be using. Most of the time he tells me that he doesn't. I don't blame him because commercial printers deal with hundreds of ink and paper combinations, so it would be very time consuming and expensive to profile each one. But sometimes I get lucky, and if so, I simply plop the profile in the proper folder, choose File > Color Settings, and set the CMYK Working Space pop-up menu to that choice. Most of the time, though, I have to take a different approach.

Adobe was nice enough to include a bunch of profiles that can be used for different printing conditions. They show up in the CMYK Working Space pop-up menu that

I mentioned above. You just have to make sure you have a profile selected that accurately reflects the printing conditions that will be used to reproduce your image before you convert to CMYK mode. I'll attempt to translate their names and then show you how to get better results.

Here's the rundown on choosing a profile for many standard publication types:

▶ Use U.S. Sheetfed Coated for glossy brochures.

▶ Use U.S. Sheetfed Uncoated for dull-finish brochures.

▶ Use U.S. Web Coated (SWOP) for magazines.

▶ Use U.S. Web Uncoated for dull-finish publications.

The profiles that come with Photoshop are making huge assumptions about the paper and inks that you are using. That means it's possible to get a much better result if you happen to have a custom profile created specifically for the paper and press on which you'll be printing. If you find that your printing company doesn't have a custom profile available and you aren't getting acceptable results from the profiles I mentioned above, then you might want to bypass profiles altogether and set up the CMYK conversion the traditional way. You'll find information about that on my website at www.digitalmastery.com/companionsite/book.

Profiling Your Scanner

You don't have too many options when it comes to scanners. There aren't too many manufacturers that provide canned profiles (some high-end ones do), and you can't visually create a profile. But the good news is that you don't have to buy any expensive hardware to get the job done. All you need is a piece of software (such as Monaco EZcolor 2). The software will come with a reference image that's known as an IT8 target (**Figure 8.25**). All you have to do is scan the image and then feed it to the software and out pops an ICC profile for your scanner. You'll want to place it in the same location I mentioned when I was talking about printer profiles.

WARNING

An error was made when the default settings were determined in OS X. So be sure not to use the default CMYK setting. If you'd like to get it back to normal, then choose Custom CMYK from the CMYK pop-up menu and set the Total Ink Limit setting to 300%.

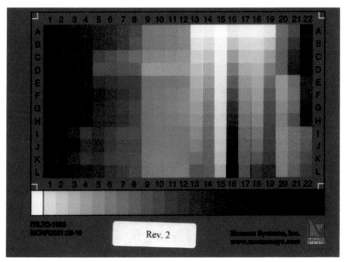

Figure 8.25 An IT8 target.

Color Management in Action

Now that we have everything set up and placed in the proper location, let's see what we can do with all this fancy stuff. Let's say you've used a colorimeter to profile your screen, and you used some software to create scanner and printer profiles (just don't forget to put those profiles in the proper location, as I mentioned above). Now here comes the fun part.

Accurate Scans

From now on, when you scan an image, you won't have to worry about all the color settings that are in your scanner. You just turn all that stuff off and let color management take over. You simply specify the resolution and scaling settings you'd like to use and then press the Scan button. Then, once the image is in Photoshop, choose Image > Mode > Assign Profile (**Figure 8.26**) and choose your scanner profile from the Profile pop-up menu. That's it! The profile supplies the information needed for Photoshop to know how your scanner captures color and therefore should produce an accurate scan (assuming your profile is accurate, that is).

NOTES

Some scanners will automatically assign the proper profile to your images. You can find out if your scanner does this by clicking on the black arrow that appears at the bottom of a Photoshop document and choosing Document Profile. Then scan an image and see if your scanner's profile is listed at the bottom of the document window. If it is, then there is no reason to assign a profile because it already has the correct one assigned.

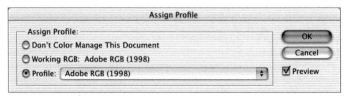

Figure 8.26 The Assign Profile dialog box.

Well, actually that's not quite it, after all. Remember when I talked about equal amounts of red, green, and blue creating gray and that that's not what you get when you use the less-than-ideal shades of RGB that your monitor, printer, and scanner use? Well, if you plan to manipulate your image, you'll most likely want to convert it into that idealized version of RGB that we call our RGB working space. To do that, choose Image > Mode > Convert to Profile (**Figure 8.27**). When that dialog box pops up, you might get a little scared because it's full of overly techie terms, but don't worry about it. At the top it simply lists the profile you assigned after you scanned the image. Next, it asks you for the profile you'd like to convert it to. That's where you want to choose Working RGB, which should be the top choice (the name will also have something like "Adobe RGB" attached to it to remind you of what you chose when you set up that part of Photoshop). Leave the Engine setting at its default. There aren't too many reasons to change that one, and if you knew about the reasons, you'd be writing this book instead of reading

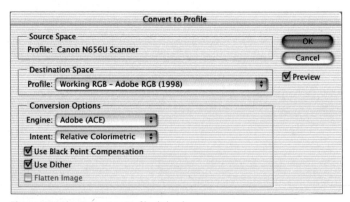

Figure 8.27 The Convert to Profile dialog box.

it—you'd have to be that color savvy. Then experiment with the choices that appear under the Intent pop-up menu. Just look at your image and try the different choices to see which one gives you the best result. I'll talk about what those settings really mean later in this chapter. Now, there is an important difference between assigning a profile and converting to a profile. They might sound similar but so does being pulled over for speeding versus being arrested for speed. With one, you'd just be out a few bucks, while with the other you just might end up in jail! Assigning a profile is informing Photoshop what colors of RGB the image is made out of. That will make the colors shift in your image as Photoshop uses the same amount of red, green and blue, but uses different shades of color (like different brands of markers). Converting to a profile means to simulate the current look of the image (trying not to change the overall look of the image), but to make it out of different shades of RGB than the original. Read over those last three sentences three times to make sure you really understand the difference because it can sound rather subtle, but it's not.

Simulate a Printing Press Onscreen

I often create images that will end up being reproduced on a commercial printing press. Sometimes it's for a brochure and other times it's for a magazine article, but whatever it is for, I want to see what the printed result will look like onscreen in Photoshop. To accomplish that, I usually choose View > Proof Setup > Working CMYK. That should do two things: It will go to the Color Settings dialog box to see what type of printing conditions will be used (we talked about that earlier in this chapter) and it turns on the View > Proof Colors setting. With Proof Colors turned on, Photoshop will attempt to simulate what your image will look like when it's printed on a commercial printing press. I use this setting anytime I'm making an adjustment to the saturation of the image because the range of colors that can be reproduced on a printing press (known as its gamut) is much smaller than what you can see onscreen. Deep blues and vivid colors can shift wildly. That happens because those colors simply can't be reproduced using the CMYK inks that are used in commercial printing. To stop this simulation, turn off the Proof Colors setting from the View menu.

Accurate Prints

Now that you have a profile for your printer ready, Photoshop can give you much more accurate prints, but you'll find have to make sure everything is set up correctly to deliver what you want. Choose File > Print with Preview, turn on the Show More Options checkbox, and choose Color Management from the pop-up menu. Photoshop will now prompt you to make some choices (**Figure 8.28**). Let's take a look at them one by one: First, under the Source Space heading, choose Document if you'd like the printer to simulate what you saw on your screen, or choose Proof Setup if you'd like your desktop printer to simulate what your image will look like when printed on a commercial printing press (or a different device if you have changed the View > Proof Setup settings).

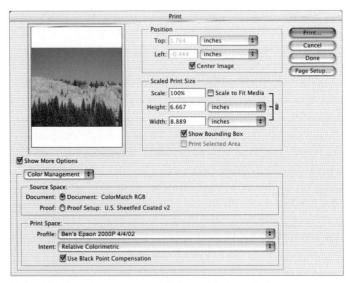

Figure 8.28 The color-management choices used when printing.

Second, for Photoshop to accurately simulate colors on your desktop printer, you have to feed it an ICC profile for that device. Do that by changing the Profile pop-up menu in the Print Space area of the Print with Preview dialog box. And finally, you can choose whether you'd like to simulate the paper color of a printing press. Choose Relative Colorimetric if you don't want to see the paper color or Absolute Colorimetric if you would like to simulate the paper stock (which might be a lot darker than the sheet of paper you have loaded into your desktop printer). I also recommend that you leave the Black Point Compensation checkbox turned on for most images. The only other thing you have to do is turn off any color-adjustment controls that your printer driver offers, since we're letting Photoshop do all the work instead.

Better CMYK Conversions

You'll want to convert your images to CMYK mode if they will be printed on a commercial printing press. The traditional way of doing that is to simply choose Image > Mode > CMYK. That's fine if you're in a hurry, but by doing that you are bypassing a bunch of settings that might make your image look better. Here's your alternative: Choose Image > Mode > Convert to Profile (**Figure 8.29**). It looks complicated, but it's not. The top just tells you the colors of RGB that your image is made from (that's known as your source space). Then, as long as you've set up the CMYK working space to what's right for your printing conditions, all you have to do is choose Working CMYK from the Destination Space pop-up menu. And now all that's left is to play with the Intent pop-up menu and those two checkboxes to see which combination of settings will produce the best result. Earlier, I kind of glossed over what the Intent pop-up menu does, so let's take a look at the choices that are available. Most images will start off with many colors that are just too vivid to be reproduced in CMYK mode (known as colors that are out of gamut for you techie folks). When you convert to CMYK mode, Photoshop has to do something with those colors to get them into the range of what can be reproduced on a printing press. The choices in the Intent pop-up menu determine how Photoshop will deal with those out-of-gamut colors.

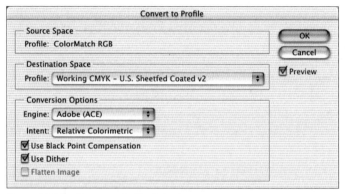

Figure 8.29 The Convert to Profile dialog box.

Perceptual

With this option, Photoshop will alter not only those colors that are not printable, but also the ones that *can* be reproduced just to make sure the relationship between the colors remains consistent. That way you don't have to worry about one overly vivid color becoming the exact same shade of a less vivid color that's right next to it. The only problem with this feature is that it has no idea which colors are actually in your image, so it shifts colors around even if all the colors in your image are within the range of colors that can be reproduced in CMYK mode.

Saturation

This choice will take the most saturated colors in your image and make sure they end up as the most saturated colors that are possible in CMYK mode. That might sound nice, but it doesn't take into account the brightness, color, and saturation differences between colors. That limits its usefulness to solid-colored graphics such as bar charts and business graphics where the relationship between colors isn't important and you just want to maintain vivid colors no matter what.

Relative and Absolute Colorimetric

Both Relative and Absolute Colorimetric shift only those colors that are not reproducible in CMYK, leaving the rest of the colors largely unchanged. The main difference between the two is that Relative Colorimetric makes sure that white in the original image will end up as white in CMYK mode. That's not overly important unless you're using an RGB working space that creates a white that is darker than what you can create in CMYK mode. This feature is mainly used in the Print dialog box when printing an image to a desktop color printer that can reproduce a brighter white than a printing press. In that situation the difference between relative and absolute is the difference between simulating the "whiteness" of the paper that will be used on the printing press (such as newsprint) or not. If your image doesn't contain too many overly vivid colors, you might find that Relative Colorimetric might not be a bad choice.

When I'm converting an image to CMYK, I'm not consciously thinking about what all these choices mean; instead, I'm just trying each one and looking at my image to see which choice produces the most pleasing result. Each choice has both advantages and disadvantages, and the only way to find the best setting is to experiment.

Closing Thoughts

If you worked up a sweat reading this chapter and thought to yourself, "This is truly a cesspool of unending terms and settings, and I'm never going to get through it all," you're not alone. That's what I thought at first. But after going through the motions a few times, and perhaps reading this chapter again, you'll get more comfortable with the concepts here and find some sanity in the chaos. In a perfect world we wouldn't have to deal with all this, but the truth is that, from the viewpoint of your hardware, you're really asking for a gargantuan thing when you want your screen to match your printout. All your devices are different, and Photoshop really needs all this info to manage everything gracefully. But if you spend the time, effort, and money it takes to get everything working properly, you will be generously rewarded with very consistent color across all your devices. And your life will become a lot easier when you can trust your screen and know that your $200 inkjet printer is doing a darn good job of both simulating what you saw onscreen and what will appear on a printing press.

Ben's Techno-babble Decoder Ring

Color management: A system used to achieve consistent color between scanner, monitor and printer.

Gamut: The range of colors that are reproducible on a particular device.

ICC profile: A standard file format used to describe the unique characteristics of a scanner, monitor, or printer.

Color Correction

Courtesy of Andy Katz

NEW IN 7

The color-correction tools have changed with the introduction of Photoshop 7.0's new Auto Color command. If you've read this book before, you'll find that I've greatly simplified the techniques to make them easier for you to understand and apply.

The camera, you know, will never capture you.
Photography, in my experience, has the miraculous
power of transferring wine into water.

—Oscar Wilde in "Lillie"

Color Correction

In the previous chapter, "Color Management," we learned how to get colors to be consistent among our various devices (monitor, scanner, printer, camera, etc.) In this chapter we're dealing with color correction, which is an entirely separate matter. This chapter is all about controlling the colors in your image and getting rid of color-casts that might be having an adverse effect on the final result.

After presenting hundreds of seminars, I've learned that the majority of people perform color correction by picking their favorite adjustment tool (Color Balance, Hue/Saturation, Curves, etc.) and then using a somewhat hit-or-miss technique. They blindly move a few sliders back and forth in the hope that their onscreen image will improve. If that doesn't work, they simply repeat the process with a different adjustment option. Those same people often turn to me asking for "advanced color-correction techniques" because they're frustrated and don't feel like they're really in control of the color in their images. If this describes the way you're adjusting your colors, you'll be pleasantly surprised when you learn about the science of professional color correction, where 95 percent of all guesswork is removed and where you know exactly which tool to use and what settings to use to achieve great color. First, let's look at a general concept that will help us to color-correct an image. Then I'll walk you through the step-by-step technique I use to get good-looking color in Photoshop.

Use Gray to Fix Color?!?

For the time being I want you to wipe out any thoughts of color. And, no, I'm not crazy. This approach really works, so stick with me. Do you remember how to make gray in the idealized RGB mode that we talked about it in the "Color Management" chapter? Equal amounts of red, green, and blue, right? With that in mind, let's open an image and see if we can find an area that should be gray. Then we can look in the Info palette to see if it really *is* gray in Photoshop—all without having to trust your monitor or your eyes! On the CD, open the image that's called "make gray.jpg." The door on the right should be a shade of gray. If the RGB numbers in the Info palette aren't equal—no matter what it looks like on your monitor—it's not gray. If it's not gray, then it must be contaminated with color (**Figure 9.1**). But could that color be contaminating more than the gray area? Most likely. Then why not use the door as an area to measure what's wrong with the entire image so we have the information we need to fix it? Let's give it a try.

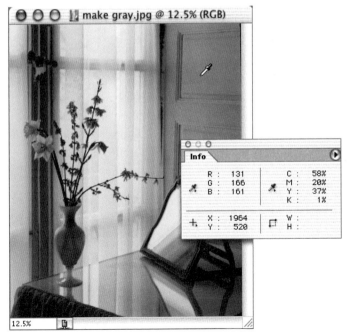

Figure 9.1 If the RGB numbers are not equal, then that area is not gray. (© Andy Katz)

Using the example image, you'll see that the RGB numbers are not equal, telling us that there is indeed color lurking somewhere in that gray. How could those contaminating colors get in there? Here are a few potential culprits: indoor, artificial lighting (you *know* how "off" that can be); temperature of the chemicals used to develop the film being too hot or too cool; inappropriate filters used in a photographic enlarger when your prints are being made; and aging bulbs in a scanner that might shift the colors during the scanning process. We're going to use the Curves dialog box to make our adjustment. But don't worry, you don't have to remember everything from the Curves chapter to do this. For what we're trying to accomplish, here's what you need to know:

▶ Clicking on the curve will add a point.

▶ The Input number indicates what you are changing.

▶ The Output number determines what you'll end up with in the area you are changing.

Put your cursor on the gray door. Now glance over at the Info palette and write down the RGB numbers. To make that door area a *real* gray, we'll need to make those RGB numbers equal. But we don't want to change the *brightness* of the door. To make sure that doesn't happen, let's just average the RGB numbers so we maintain the same amount of light that is currently there, using a balanced amount of red, green, and blue. You can use a calculator to average the numbers. Now that we know what we're starting with (from the Info palette) and what we want to end up with (from the calculator), we can adjust our image.

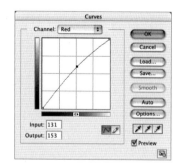

Figure 9.2 The numbers you enter will move the point to the correct position.

If you choose Image > Adjust > Curves and leave the menu at the top set to RGB, you'll end up changing red, green, and blue in equal amounts, which would just change the brightness of the image (which is what we did in the Curves chapter). But for our purposes, start by choosing Red from the pop-up menu at the top of the Curves dialog box. Next, click anywhere on the curve to add a point. Then let's make sure that point is in the right place to make the change we need (**Figure 9.2**). Click on the Input number and type in the red value you wrote down from the Info palette. That should move the point horizontally until it's above the shade we need to change. Your image might look pretty weird now, but pay no attention to that until we're done with everything. Now click on the Output number and enter what you got when you averaged the Info palette numbers. That should move the point up or down until it's at the correct height to make the change we need. Now choose Green from that menu and do the same thing all over again—just add a point and then enter the Info palette number for green (the one you wrote down) for Input and the other number (the averaged one) for Output. Finally, choose Blue from the menu, and repeat the process. It's now safe to peek at your image (**Figure 9.3**). The door should be gray! If it's not, and you're quite sure you followed the steps correctly, your monitor is way out of whack and may need calibration (see the previous chapter on color management for details on how to do that).

NOTES

When performing RGB color correction, make sure that white appears at the top of the gradient that is on the left of the Curves dialog box; otherwise, the numbers will range from 0-100% instead of 0-255. If black appears at the top of that gradient, click on the symbol in the center of the horizontal gradient at the bottom of the Curves dialog box. That will flip the gradients and use the numbering system needed for RGB color correction.

Figure 9.3 When you're done, the area should be gray. The left numbers indicate what was originally in the image; the right numbers indicate the result of our adjustment.

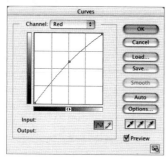

Figure 9.4 The red curve.

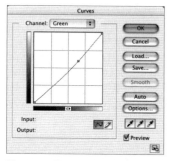

Figure 9.5 The green curve.

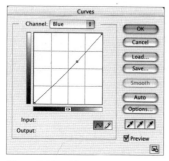

Figure 9.6 The blue curve.

But now, look back at the three curves we applied to this image (**Figures 9.4** to **9.6**). We measured what was wrong with the image in the gray areas, but our adjustment changed the entire image. That's logical enough, because whatever is wrong with the gray areas is also affecting the rest of the image. But when you look at those curves, does it look like we *really* changed the whole image? Almost— but not quite. We didn't change the brightest and darkest areas. So, we really haven't accomplished our color correction, and we won't until we've taken some more steps. But from this exercise, we saw that our concept of measuring and adjusting gray works. Now let's see how we can make this process faster and easier, and then we'll move on to adjusting the brightest and darkest areas.

It might feel quite low tech to be scribbling a bunch of numbers on a sheet of paper and grabbing a calculator when we have a multi-thousand-dollar computer in front of us. The folks at Adobe realized that and gave us a tool that will do 99 percent of the work for us, so let's see what they came up with. Choose File > Revert to get that door and flowers image back to its original state, then choose Image > Adjust > Curves. Click on the middle eyedropper in the lower right of the dialog box, and then move your cursor out onto the image and click on that gray door again. With a single click, it should change to gray. Photoshop is using the same concept we used when we wrote down the RGB numbers and averaged them; it's just doing it in a fraction of a second and there is no paper involved. In fact, those eyedroppers will help us even more if we adjust the full range of shades from the brightest to the darkest. Let's see how it works.

Professional Color Correction

OK, you can start thinking in color again. We will look at the process of professional color correction in four parts: balancing colors, adjusting skin tones, saturation, and sharpening. You don't always have to perform all four parts, but the more you do, the better your result.

Balancing Your Colors

To eliminate any colorcasts that are in your image, you'll need to look for color contamination in the gray areas of your image and then use that information to help correct the whole image. There are three standard areas of your image that will usually contain a shade of gray. The first one is the brightest area of the image, which is known as the *highlight*. The second is the darkest area of the image, which is known as the *shadow*. (On most photos, the highlight and shadow areas shouldn't contain color.) The third area is a gray object in the image.

Now that we know which areas need to be adjusted, let's go ahead and make the actual adjustment. Start by choosing Image > Adjust > Curves. We'll be working with all three eyedroppers that show up in the lower right. One is full of black, the second is full of gray, and the third is full of white. We'll use those to adjust the shadow, gray, and highlight areas, respectively. But we first have to set up things correctly.

Double-click on the rightmost eyedropper to bring up the Color Picker. This eyedropper will be used to adjust the brightest part of the image (the highlight). You don't want the highlight to become pure white because it would look too bright. You want to reserve pure white for those areas that shine light directly into the camera lens (lightbulbs, shiny reflections, etc.). That means you want the highlight to be just a tad bit darker than white. If you remember back to the chapter on grayscale images (Chapter 6), I mentioned that the lightest percentage of ink you can use on a printing press is usually 3 percent (5 percent for some newspapers). That means we don't want to use less than 3% of any ink in the brightest part of our image; otherwise, we might lose critical detail. But we're adjusting our image in RGB mode, and when you do that, you'll be using a numbering system that ranges from 0 to 255, not 0 to 100%. So let's figure out how to create a minimum of 3% ink in RGB mode. After double-clicking the rightmost eyedropper, set the saturation setting (S) to 0 and the brightness setting (B) to 100%, and click on the number

Black ink is usually limited to the darkest areas of the CMYK printing process, so no black will show up when you're looking for 3% ink values.

next to the letter B (brightness). Use the down arrow key to change that setting until the magenta (M) and yellow (Y) readouts indicate at least 3%. Cyan (C) will be higher, but don't worry about that. At this point, the numbers will show you exactly what RGB values are needed to produce that much ink—in my case, 240R 240G 240B (**Figure 9.7**). Once the numbers are at the proper settings, click OK, to save those settings.

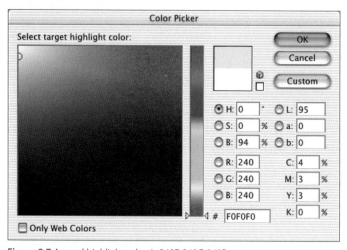

Figure 9.7 A good highlight value is 240R 240G 240B.

Now, on to the dark side. We're going to make the darkest area of your image pure black (0R 0G 0B) in order to use the full range your computer monitor is capable of displaying. Black wouldn't be a good choice if you are really outputting to a printing press (you'd lose a lot of detail), but we'll set it up so that Photoshop will adjust your image automatically if you have to convert to CMYK mode. That way we'll be guaranteed that no detail will be lost no matter what the output. So, double-click on the leftmost eyedropper and make sure it's set to black. You should need to change these settings only once and Photoshop will use them from that time forward.

Now that we have everything set up properly, let's start adjusting images. Open any image that needs to be color-corrected and then choose Layer > New Adjustment

Layer > Curves. Click the black eyedropper and then click on the shadow area. When I mention the shadow, I don't mean a traditional shadow like the kind cast from an object; instead, I'm talking about the darkest area of an image. All images have a shadow area, but it can sometimes be hard to locate because there may be multiple candidates. Once you've done that, then click on the white eyedropper and then click on the brightest part of the image. That is the brightest area that should still contain detail. You'll often find it in a white shirt collar or button, a Styrofoam cup, the whites of someone's eyes, or a sheet of paper. In **Figure 9.8**, the brightest white falls on a fold in the sheer curtain material. Finally, click on the middle eyedropper and then click on any area that should be gray in the final image—not bluish gray or pinkish gray, but pure gray (also known as neutral gray). You might have to really hunt for a gray; it is not always obvious. It could be a sweatshirt, a white shirt, or the edge of a book. On the other hand, you might run across an image that has dozens of gray areas to choose from. In that case, try to pick one that is not overly bright or dark, because we are already adjusting the highlight and shadow of the image. The closer we get to a middle gray, the more effective your adjustment will be. If you have any doubt at all that the area you have chosen should be gray, just experiment by clicking on one area to see what happens, then press Command-Z (Mac) or Ctrl-Z (Windows) to undo the change, and then try another area. Repeat this process until you've found an area that really causes the image to improve, but don't try too hard; not every image contains a true gray. For example, you might not be able to find one in a photograph of a forest. If you can't find one, then (of course) don't adjust it.

Figure 9.8 Finding the highlight of the image.

Using Threshold to Locate Highlight and Shadow

If you hate having to guess at anything, here's how to find the highlight and shadow areas without guessing. Choose Image > Adjust > Threshold and move the slider all the way to the right; then slowly move it toward the middle

(**Figure 9.9**). The brightest area of the image will be the first area that shows up as white (you can use the up and down arrow keys to move the slider). You don't want to find the very brightest speck (that could be a scratch), so be sure to look for a general area at least five or six pixels in size. Once you've found the correct area, you can hold down the Shift key and click on that part of your image to add a color sample to that area (**Figure 9.10**). (You have to hold Shift only if you're still in an adjustment dialog box like Threshold.) A color sampler is simply a visual reminder of where that area is.

Figure 9.10 After using the Color Sampler tool, you should see a crosshair on the image.

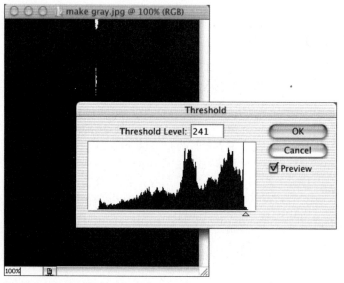

Figure 9.9 Use the Threshold command to find elusive highlights.

Now let's use Threshold to find the darkest area of the image. This time, start with the slider all the way to the left, then slowly move it toward the center. This will show you where the darkest area of the image is hiding. You don't want to find the darkest speck (that could be dust), so be sure to look for a general area at least five or six pixels in size. Once you've located the shadow, Shift-click on that area to place a sample point on top of it, and then click Cancel to get out of the Threshold dialog box. Now you should have two crosshairs on your image, one for the highlight and one for the shadow, as shown in **Figure 9.11.** When you use the eyedroppers in the Curves dialog box, you can press Caps Lock to turn your cursor into a crosshair, which will make it easy to tell when you're lined up with those color samplers. You can get rid of those color samplers by choosing the Color Sampler tool (it's hidden under the Eyedropper tool) and clicking the Clear button in the Options bar.

Now let's explore two alternative methods for adjusting the highlight, shadow, and gray areas of an image.

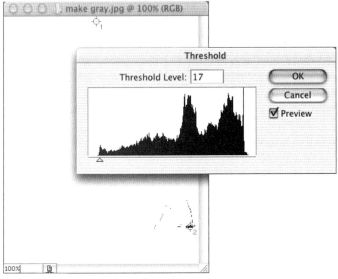

Figure 9.11 After adding a second sample point, you should see two crosshairs on your image.

Using a Gray Wedge to Correct Multiple Images

Here's an interesting trick I like to use when I know I'll be color-correcting a large number of images that will be shot under the same lighting conditions. If you stop by a high-end camera store, you can ask for a gray wedge (**Figure 9.12**). Once you have one, you can place it in the scene where you are about to take a large number of photos (let's say for a yearbook or a product brochure). Now, this is important—before you start shooting your actual scenes, you will want to take a photograph of the wedge under the exact same lighting conditions and exact same film type that you'll be using for the rest of the photos. That way you can use it as a reference that will pick up the color influence of the lighting and film. Once the images are developed, scanned, and loaded into Photoshop, create a new Curves adjustment layer. Click on the white eyedropper and then click on the brightest gray rectangle on the gray wedge. Next, click on the black eyedropper and then click on the darkest rectangle; and finally, click on the middle eyedropper and then click on the middle gray rectangle. That should remove any colorcast that was present in the image.

Figure 9.12 A gray wedge from a high-end camera store.

You can apply that same adjustment to the other images by dragging the Curves adjustment layer from the gray wedge image and dropping it onto another image that was photographed under the same lighting conditions. That way you can perform color correction with no guesswork and quickly apply the same adjustment to a large number of images.

Adjusting the highlight, shadow, and gray areas of an image can dramatically improve the quality of an image. But even with those adjustments, you occasionally need to fine-tune any skin tones that might be in the image.

Auto Color

Photoshop 7.0 includes a great new feature that attempts to automate the process of color correction: Auto Color (**Figure 9.13**). It uses the same general concepts we've been talking about in this chapter, and you'll find that it works well with a large variety of images. You can access Auto Color by creating a new Curves adjustment layer and then clicking on the Options button. The Shadows, Midtones, and Highlights settings use the same setting that we specified when we double-clicked on the eyedroppers in the

Curves dialog box. The only difference is that Photoshop attempts to locate the highlight, shadow, and gray areas automatically. This dialog box is interactive—changes will immediately affect the image. I'd set the Shadows and Highlights Clip values to 0.25% and then experiment with the top settings to see which ones produce the best results. I find that this automated feature works on a surprising number of images. But as with most automated features, you'll find that you have to take over and use the old eye-droppers technique whenever Auto Color fails to deliver a satisfactory result.

Figure 9.13 The Auto Color Correction Options dialog box.

Adjust Skin Tones

You might be thinking that I'm going to give you some kind of magic formula for creating great skin tones (kind of like what I did with grays), but if I give you just one for-mula, then every skin tone in nature's vast diversity would look identical in your images! I'd much rather show you how to get a unique formula for each color of skin you might run across—Asian skin, olive skin, sunburnt skin, fair skin, and all the different shades of black skin. Even better, we can do all that without trusting your monitor at all. (Of course, they will still look good on your screen, but unless you've calibrated your screen using a hardware device, then you shouldn't make critical decisions based on your screen image.)

You know how you can buy stock images from companies such as Stockbyte—there are literally dozens of companies that sell royalty-free stock photography. If you call these companies and ask for a catalog of images, they'll be more than happy to send you a really thick book chock-full of images (it will either be free, or they might charge you for shipping and handling). At the back of that book will be a CD that contains tiny versions of those images, complete with the stock photo company's logo slapped in the mid-dle of it so you'd never use it for a real project. But we don't care about that, because right now we're after some-thing else—most of them contain a veritable treasure trove of flesh that you can transform into your own personal stockpile of skin tones. So, flip through one of those won-derful catalogs, pick the person who has the skin tone that

Figure 9.14 Reference photo from a stock photo catalog. (© 2002 Stockbyte, www.stockbyte.com)

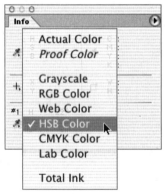

Figure 9.15 Note the brightness of the area you are working on.

best matches your needs, and then open the corresponding image from the CD at the back of the catalog. Next, use the Eyedropper tool and click on an area of the skin that is a medium brightness (**Figure 9.14**). Now click on your foreground color to see the RGB formula needed to create that exact color.

Now let's figure out how to use that information to improve your image that contains skin tones. Open the one you need to correct and use the Color Sampler tool to click on the area that contains the troublesome skin. Be sure to click in an area with medium brightness, similar to the level in the other (stock photo) image. That should give you an extra readout in the Info palette (readout #4 if you still have the three we used earlier in this chapter).

Next, click on the tiny triangle that shows up next to that new readout in the Info palette (**Figure 9.15**). Choose HSB from the menu, note the brightness (B) setting, and then set that menu back to RGB. Now, click on your foreground color to look at the color from the stock photo again. We want to use that basic color, but we don't want to change the brightness of our image much. To accomplish that, change the brightness (B) setting to what you saw in the photo you are attempting to color-correct and then write down the RGB numbers that show up in the Color Picker (**Figure 9.16**). That tells us how to use the color from the stock photo after changing its brightness to match the image we're going to apply it to.

Now it's time to isolate any skin tones in your image and then make our adjustment. I usually choose Select > Color Range to isolate the skin. If you've never used it before, then be sure to read about it in the "Selection Primer" chapter. Once you have a general selection of the skin (don't worry if it's not perfect), it's time to make the adjustment.

Remember earlier when we used an adjustment layer to change the highlight, shadow, and gray areas? That adjustment layer should still be in the Layers palette. Make sure that layer is active and then choose Layer > New Adjustment Layer > Curves. We'll add one point to each of the red, green, and blue curves. Then type in the number you see in the Info palette (the one on the left) and then type in the number we calculated a few minutes ago for the Output. Repeat the same steps for green and blue, and your skin tone should look much better (**Figure 9.17**).

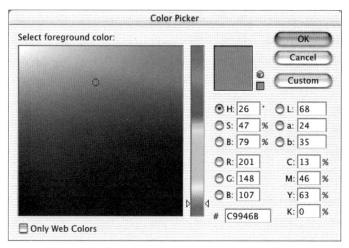

Figure 9.16 Change the brightness (B) setting to find the perfect skin-tone setting.

Figure 9.17 After adjusting for skin tones, the skin should look similar to the stock photo version. (original images © 2002 Stockbyte, www.stockbyte.com)

The more you get used to using this technique, the less you'll have to rely on that catalog. You'll get used to knowing that the more red you pull out of your image, the more tan someone looks, and that the balance between green and blue determines the fairness of someone's skin.

If the skin-tone adjustment was a little too much for you to handle, then just start off by adjusting the highlight, shadow, and gray areas, and come back to this chapter after you've gotten comfortable with those. That might make it a little easier to understand and implement. The general concept is easy (and sneaky), but the execution isn't quite as simple as all that, because we have to make sure we don't mess up our earlier adjustments.

Refine the Result

Now that the colors have been optimized, let's explore some methods for improving the image even more. These steps are optional, but I usually end up performing them on the majority of images that I adjust.

Refinements to Brightness and Contrast Adjustments

The process we've gone through up until now was designed to correct the colors in the image. Now that the colors are better, you can also use all the ideas I showed you in the Curves chapter to further enhance the brightness and contrast of the image. Just be careful not to shift the colors of the image. (You can prevent that by setting the blending mode of all future curves adjustments to Luminosity, as was explained in the chapter on Curves.)

But adjusting color, contrast, and brightness still won't guarantee that your images are as vivid as they could be. Following are two more techniques for making the colors in your images really pop.

Optimize Saturation

Once you've adjusted your colors, you can choose Layer > New Adjustment Layer > Hue/Saturation and increase the Saturation setting. Choose View > Gamut Warning to see how you're doing; if no gray appears over your image, then you can keep increasing the saturation until you start seeing small areas of gray (**Figure 9.18**). You've gone too far if you see large, concentrated gray blobs on your image. After you've adjusted the image, you can get rid of those gray areas by turning off the Gamut Warning.

The Gamut Warning feature is only accurate if you have properly set up Photoshop to convert images to CMYK mode. The settings used when converting to CMYK mode are found by choosing Photoshop > Color Settings (Mac OS X), or Edit > Color Settings (Mac OS and Windows) and clicking on the CMYK pop-up menu.

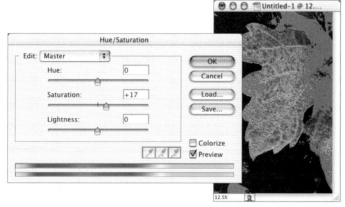

Figure 9.18 Keep increasing the saturation until a lot of gray shows up. (original image © Andy Katz)

Once you've gotten to this point, you should simplify your document before you move on to sharpening the image. You can do that by clicking on the bottom layer (the one that contains your original image) and then clicking on the box that appears on the left side of each of the adjustment layers. Now you can choose Merge Linked from the side menu of the Layers palette to combine those adjustment layers with your image (**Figure 9.19**).

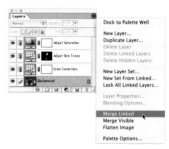

Figure 9.19 Merge the adjustment layers into the main image to simplify the document.

Sharpen the Image

I find that almost every image I work with can be improved by applying the Unsharp Mask filter. We dealt with that filter back in Chapter 6, "Optimizing Grayscale Images," where we learned how to make our grayscale images look good. When it comes to color images, you can use the same concepts we discussed in the grayscale chapter, but you might find that the halos that show up after sharpening an image will be distracting. For instance, you

In versions of Photoshop before 6.0, the Fade command is found on the Filter menu.

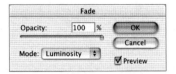

Figure 9.20 Choose Fade from the Mode pop-up menu.

might find that after sharpening the image of a pink dress, bright red halos appear around the edge of the dress.

To prevent off-color halos, you can use a special blending mode in Photoshop: Choose Filter > Sharpen > Unsharp Mask and sharpen the image just as we did with a grayscale image. Once you are done sharpening the image, choose Edit > Fade, and then choose Luminosity from the Mode pop-up menu (**Figure 9.20**). This will make it so that whatever you did last—in this case, sharpening—can change only the brightness of the image, not the colors!

Closing Thoughts

The techniques described in this chapter are the very same ones used by the high-paid color maestros who are responsible for all of those ever-so-perfect glossy magazine ads. It will take you a while to really get the hang of these techniques, but once you do, it should take you less than two minutes to correct most images.

Here's one last bit of advice: Make sure to always correct your images separately before blending them together. That way, you will be able to maintain the color integrity of each component of your big picture.

Ben's Techno-babble Decoder Ring

Gamut: The range of colors that are reproducible on a particular device (monitor, printer, etc.).

Neutral gray: A pure gray that does not have any hint of color.

Specular highlight: An intense reflection that contains little or no detail. You'll find specular highlights in jewelry, metallic objects, and very shiny surfaces.

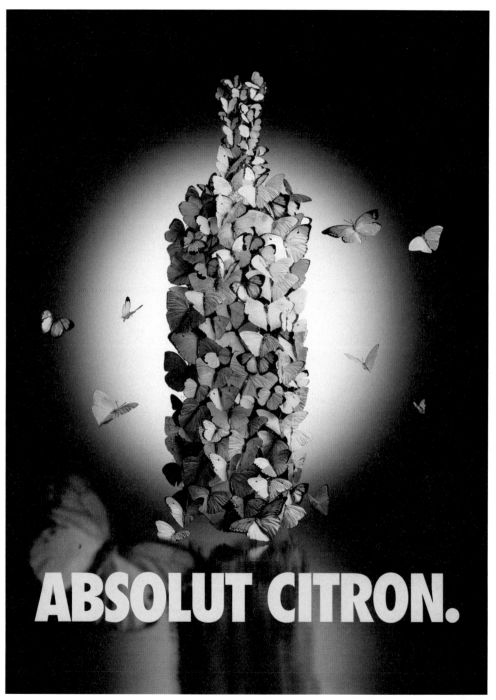

© Steve Bronstein

Courtesy of Andy Katz

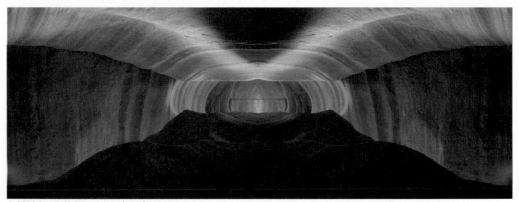

© 2002 Lewis Kemper, www.lewiskemper.com

10

Channels

Courtesy of Michael Slack, www.slackart.com

NEW IN 7

Adobe hasn't added any new features to Channels, but I've added coverage of the Edge Cleanup and Smart Highlighting options in the Extract command.

Why take the escalator when I have a perfectly good canoe right here?

–Austin Powers in the movie
"Austin Powers, International Man of Mystery"

Channels

If you just did a double take on the chapter quote and said, "huh, what?" then you reacted the same way that most people do the first time they hear about channels. To get to the root of all this confusion, you have to go back to when channels were first conceived and given their misbegotten name. The very name "channels" breeds confusion because it doesn't relate to anything in the real world, and so it doesn't mean anything to anybody. As a result, most people just give it a nickname. I've heard them called stencils, masks, friskets, rubyliths, and amberliths, to name a few. I don't know about you, but in the course of normal conversation (as opposed to Photoshop-speak), when I hear someone talk about channels, things like HBO, NBC, and CNN are the first ones that come to mind.

So, taking all of that into consideration, you might wonder what in blazes was Adobe thinking when they came up with that name? I can't answer that. But I can tell you that regardless of the hopeless misnomer, channels are absolutely essential to your work in Photoshop. Once you've mastered them, you will have one of Photoshop's most powerful tools at your beck and call.

Channels Are Worth the Pain!

To be fair, I have to tell you that a lot of people who try channels for the first time throw their hands in the air and give up. They convince themselves that they don't really need channels, and they learn how to patch things up in other ways. But I believe that if they really knew what they were missing, they'd take another crack at it.

Let's say you just met a secretary named Minnie. In her office there are two pieces of equipment: an old IBM Selectric typewriter and the best personal computer that money can buy. Whenever Minnie's boss gives her a memo to type, she immediately loads up the Selectric with a fresh piece of paper and starts rat-tatting away. "Minnie!" you ask, "Why don't you use the computer for that?" Minnie just gives you a dirty look over her bifocals. So you try to reason with her: "But, Minnie, what if you make a mistake or the boss changes his mind? Wouldn't it be easier to have that memo stored in your computer?" Minnie lets out a long impatient sigh (the kind that only mothers can do justice to). Then she gives it to you straight: "Look, smarty-pants, maybe it *would* be easier, maybe it *wouldn't*, but whichever way you look at it, that thing is just too doggoned hard to learn." And with that, she swivels around, hunches over her beloved Selectric and finishes her memo.

Of course, everybody knows that Minnie is crazy as a loon not to use the computer. And anyone who uses a computer knows that, yes, it might have been a little challenging at first, but once you've learned it, how could you possibly live without it? That's exactly how it is with channels! Channels are so completely integrated into Photoshop that there's nothing you can do to your images without affecting the information that's stored in the Channels palette. And if they have that much influence on your images, wouldn't you want to know what they are all about? Of course you would.

Without channels, it would be impossible to save the shape of a selection so that you can get it back later. It would also be impossible to force a shadow to print with only black ink (which makes it look better). And you'd have terrible troubles working with metallic or fluorescent inks without the help of channels. So, let's take a headlong plunge into the not-so-mysterious world of channels. And for the purposes of this chapter, when we talk about them, we're going to be using just two terms: *channels* and *masks*.

Three Varieties of Channels

There are three varieties of channels: color channels, spot channels, and alpha channels (**Figure 10.1**). They all look about the same, but they perform completely different tasks. However, they do have some things in common: They have the same dimensions as the document that contains them; they can contain up to 256 shades of gray; and Photoshop treats them as if they were individual grayscale documents. Let's take a surface look at them; then we'll explore each one in depth.

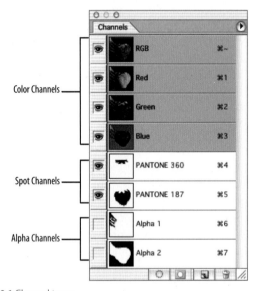

Figure 10.1 Channel types.

Color Channels

The topmost channels in the Channels palette are known as color channels because they keep track of all of the colors that will be printed and displayed. The names of these channels correspond to the mode your image is in (an RGB image will contain Red, Green, and Blue channels; a CMYK image will contain Cyan, Magenta, Yellow, and Black channels). So when you paint, edit, or apply a filter to your image, you're really changing the information in the color channels.

Sample Use: You have an image taken by a digital camera. It's not just any image; it's your Granny blowing out candles on her 90th birthday. You know that pictures from digital cameras are notorious for looking "noisy," but this one takes the cake (so to speak). Your beloved Granny looks like her face is covered with blackheads. If you didn't know better, you'd probably just try to blur the image to get rid of the noise. But you *do* know better, because you've learned that if you did that, you'd end up removing the majority of the detail in the image. So instead, you switch over to color channels and start working on your image "under the hood." In just a few moments you've gotten rid of the noise and sharpened the overall image as well. Granny looks much better.

Spot Channels

Directly below the color channels are the spot channels. This type of channel is used in documents that will be printed using colors other than (or in addition to) cyan, magenta, yellow, and black. The name of a spot channel is usually the name of the ink that will be used (like PANTONE 185 CVC). Only documents that have been specifically set up for spot color work will contain this type of channel.

Sample Use: You're asked to create a "look" that resembles the cover of *Wired* magazine. You thumb through a few copies and notice that they go for the big eye-stopping colors: neon, fluorescent, metallic. You know—disco colors. You go to the standard Color Picker and choose a far-out shade of metallic purple not seen since the days of *Saturday Night Fever*. But you get flagged down by the CMYK Police: "Gamut Warning! Color Cannot Be Reproduced in CMYK, you idiot!" Nooo problem. Like a flash, you switch over to spot channels, where you confidently create your spaced-out color, knowing that you are also creating the necessary information needed by your printer to reproduce it accurately. Groovy.

Alpha Channels

Channels that appear at the bottom of the palette are called alpha channels. This is the real McCoy—the stuff people are usually talking about when they bring up channels, and the stuff they're most scared of. Alpha channels have user-defined names; or, if a name isn't supplied when a channel is created, Photoshop uses a generic name like

"Alpha 1." An alpha channel is a saved *selection*—it's that simple (well, almost that simple).

Sample use: You just spent the good part of an hour making an eye-straining selection of every curl and wisp of hair on a model who's got a mane bigger than Tina Turner's. You're doing this because your client requested a redhead when you only had a blonde, but you're on to this guy and justifiably suspicious that in the end he'll probably want a brunette. So, as usual, you outsmart him and save that selection as an alpha channel, knowing that you will be prepared for anything, even zebra stripes if necessary. (Then you have the option of charging the client for all the time you saved, or not.)

Navigating the Channels Palette

OK, you've been briefly introduced to the channels family. You know their names (color, spot, and alpha); and you know, in the most general sense, what they're intended for. Before we look at them any more closely, let's take a moment to get familiar with their place of residence—the Channels palette.

If you've read the Layer Primer chapter (I hope you did) and now you're sitting there staring at the Channels palette, you'll probably notice that channels look almost identical to layers. Well, Adobe did this for a good reason. They want you to get used to one style of palette. They assumed that if you became comfortable with one kind of palette, you would quickly adapt to other palettes that were similar in design and function. So the Layers, Channels, and Paths palettes look almost identical (**Figures 10.2** to **10.4**). Just a few of the icons at the bottom of each palette are different. And even with these they tried to be consistent. For instance, the icon you use to create a new layer looks the same as the one you use to create a new channel or path.

As with layers, the eyeballs in the Channels palette control what is being displayed within the main image window. Just click in the column that contains the eyeballs to toggle them on or off. The channels that are active for editing are the ones that are highlighted. Click the name of a channel to make it active; to activate more than one channel at a time, Shift-click their names (I wish I could do that with layers). To change the stacking order of the channels, drag the name of a channel up or down within the stack (you can't change the order of the color channels). To create a new empty channel, click on the icon that resembles a piece of paper with a folded corner. To change the name of a channel, double-click its name. Finally, to delete a channel, drag it to the trash can icon (**Figure 10.5**).

OK, that's enough for now. We'll cover the rest of the palette as we go through the different types of channels. So put on your thinking cap and let's get started.

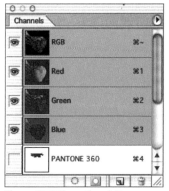

Figure 10.2 Channels palette.

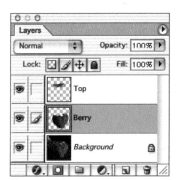

Figure 10.3 Layers palette.

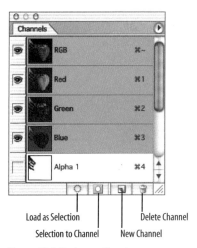

Figure 10.4 Paths palette.

Understanding Color Channels

Using color channels is like peeking behind the scenes and seeing how Photoshop is creating your image. You might think of color channels as the engine in your car: When you push the gas pedal, you are causing a whole chain reaction of events under the hood. In this case, while you are working in layers, the chain reaction is occurring in the color channels. They store up-to-the-minute information about RGB colors (red, green, and blue light), CMYK colors (cyan, magenta, yellow, and black ink), or any other color modes you are using. If you don't tamper with the channels, Photoshop will assume that whatever you're doing, you want it to affect all of the channels at the same time. But if you pop the hood and designate specific channels, you can do some very precise sculpting and manipulations that would be virtually impossible without using color channels.

Load as Selection

Selection to Channel

New Channel

Delete Channel

Figure 10.5 Understanding the Channels palette.

NOTES

Most non-PostScript printers (read: inexpensive printers, like inkjets) must convert CMYK files to RGB before they are sent to the printer driver, which means it's best to print to them from RGB mode. That's right—even though these printers have CMYK inks built in, it's best to print to the files from RGB mode and let the printer driver make the conversion, instead of feeding them CMYK files that the printer will convert twice (once to RGB, then again to CMYK in the printer driver). I know it sounds odd, but that's how it works.

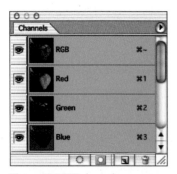

Figure 10.6 RGB channels.

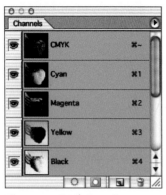

Figure 10.7 CMYK channels.

You'll need to choose a color mode to work in, but before you do, you might want to know a little something about your options.

Choosing a Color Mode

In RGB mode, Photoshop constructs your image out of red, green, and blue light (**Figure 10.6**). This is the mode most images start in, because all scanners and digital cameras use RGB light to capture images, and all computer monitors use RGB light to display images. Some fancy (and very expensive) high-end scanners might deliver a CMYK result, but that conversion occurs in software after the RGB scan. RGB mode is ideal for images that will be displayed using light (including those that will be used onscreen for multimedia or the Internet and those that will be output to video). You'll also want to use RGB mode when outputting images to 35mm slides, because the output device (a film recorder) will use RGB light to expose the photographic film. And since you view all your images on an RGB monitor while you are editing them, RGB turns out to be an excellent "working mode." Once you have finished editing the image, you can convert it to any mode you desire.

CMYK mode creates your image out of cyan, magenta, yellow, and black ink, also known as process colors (**Figure 10.7**). This is the mode that your image should end up in if your final destination is a printing press. When you convert an image to CMYK, Photoshop compensates for many factors (dot gain, total ink limit, etc.) that are specific to the type of paper and press that will be used. I recommend that you perform most editing and adjusting in RGB mode. This will allow you to adjust an image once and use it for multiple types of printing.

Lab mode is a different animal. It separates your image into *lightness*, which means how bright or dark the image is, and two channels called A and B (**Figure 10.8**). The A and B channels are weird because they don't contain just one color. The A channel contains colors that are between green and red, and the B channel contains colors that are between blue and yellow. This makes it the only mode that separates how bright your image is from the color information, and that's what makes it so useful. Lab mode safeguards the brightness of your image so you can adjust the colors without shifting its brightness, whereas with RGB and CMYK mode, if you tried to do the same adjustments, the brightness would probably change. Lab mode is usually a temporary stop on your way to one of the other modes. It's not usually your final destination.

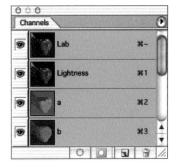

Figure 10.8 Lab channels.

How Channels Relate to Layers

All of the information in the color channels is assembled from the elements in the Layers palette. If you view a single layer, the color channels display just that particular layer's content, as shown in **Figure 10.9**. If you view multiple layers, the color channels show the result of combining those layers, as shown in **Figure 10.10**. Because you can edit only one layer at a time, any changes made using the color channels will affect the currently active layer only.

Because of impurities in the CMYK inks, the CMYK mode cannot reproduce all the colors available in RGB mode. When using the Color Picker to choose a color, a small triangular Warning symbol (known as the gamut warning) will appear next to the color you have chosen if it is one of the colors that are not reproducible in CMYK mode. Clicking on the triangle will give you the closest reproducible color.

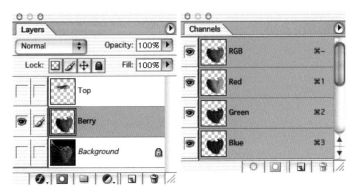

Figure 10.9 When a single layer is visible, the channels indicate what is contained in that layer.

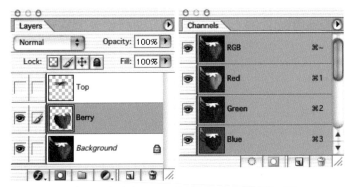

Figure 10.10 When multiple layers are visible, the channels reflect the combination of those layers.

The Composite Color Channel

If the image contains more than one color channel (RGB, CMYK, or Lab), then the topmost channel will be a special one known as the composite channel (**Figure 10.11**). This composite channel doesn't contain any information; it's just a shortcut to make all the color channels visible and active for editing, which is their default state if you haven't been editing the individual channels. So, in effect, this is how you get things back to normal after messing with the individual channels.

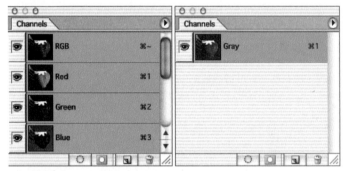

Figure 10.11 When multiple color channels are present, the topmost channel is known as the composite channel.

Viewing Channels in Color

When viewing a single-color channel (by clicking on its name in the Channels palette), it will appear as a grayscale image. This was done on purpose to make it easy for you to see exactly what the channel contains. If you view more than one color channel at a time (by turning on more eyeballs in the palette), the channels will appear in color.

Figure 10.12 The Display & Cursors dialog box.

You can force Photoshop to display individual channels in color (instead of grayscale) by choosing Edit > Preferences > Display & Cursors and turning on the Color Channels in Color check box (**Figure 10.12**). I don't find this all that useful because it becomes much harder to see exactly what is in each channel, especially when viewing the yellow channel of a CMYK image (it's just so light!). Go ahead and try it: Open an image, convert it to CMYK mode, and take a peek at the yellow channel; then turn the preference on and off

(**Figures 10.13** and **10.14**). Then you'll understand why they chose grayscale as the best way to view a channel.

Figure 10.13 Color Channels in Color check box off. (©2002 Stockbyte, www.stockbyte.com)

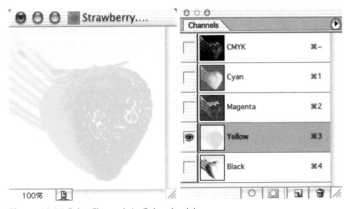

Figure 10.14 Color Channels in Color check box on.

Editing Multiple Channels

When you are adjusting an image using Levels or Curves, you'll notice a pop-up menu at the top of the dialog box, such as the one in **Figure 10.15**. This little menu determines which color channels you are editing (you can either edit a single channel or all of them).

But by using the Channels palette, you can force Levels or Curves (or any control, for that matter) to affect more than one channel at a time (**Figure 10.16**). Just click on the first channel you would like to change, and then Shift-click on

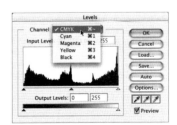

Figure 10.15 When applying Levels, you can adjust either a single color channel or all of them.

another channel. Finally, turn on the eyeball of the composite channel (the topmost one) to make the rest of the color channels visible without making them all active. This can be extremely useful when working on flesh tones, because they are mainly made from magenta and yellow ink.

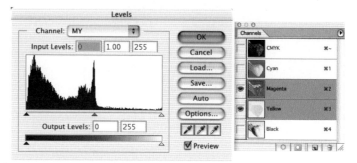

Figure 10.16 By messing with the Channels palette, you can get the Levels dialog box to affect the channels of your choice.

Applying a Filter to a Single Channel

Without using the Channels palette, it's impossible to get a filter to affect only one channel. When you don't use the Channels palette, a filter will always apply to all the color channels that are present in the document.

Images taken from digital cameras often appear noisy. If you blur the entire image to get rid of the noise, it usually looks terrible because you discard most of the important detail. But if you click through the channels, you might notice that the noise is most prominent in one channel (usually blue). By blurring just the blue channel, your image will look better without throwing away too much detail. To blur just the blue channel, click on its name in the Channels palette, and then apply the Blur filter (**Figures 10.17** and **10.18**). You might also try the Despeckle and Median filters. If you would like to see the image in full color, turn on the eyeball on the composite channel before applying the filter.

You can also improve the image by sharpening only those channels that don't contain a large amount of noise (usually the red and green channels), as shown in **Figures 10.19** and **10.20**.

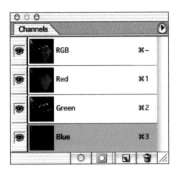

Figure 10.17 Viewing all the channels, but editing the blue channel only.

Figure 10.18 Apply the Gaussian Blur filter to remove noise.

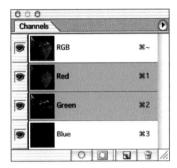

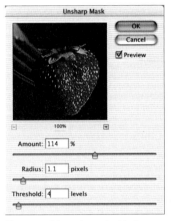

Figure 10.19 Viewing all the channels, but editing the red and green channels only.

Figure 10.20 Applying the Unsharp Mask filter to bring out detail.

Black-only Grayscale Images

Even with color images, there will be times when you want to force a portion of an image to black and white—for example, to make a color image pop all the more in contrast to a drab background. The most common way to force a portion of an image to black and white is to select the area and choose Image > Adjust > Desaturate. On screen, Desaturate will make it appear as if the image will be printed with black ink only. But if you open the Info palette and move your cursor over that now-black-and-white area, you'll notice that the image contains equal amounts of cyan, magenta, and yellow

Figure 10.21 Choosing Image > Adjustments > Desaturate produces a four-color grayscale image, which often appears brownish. (©2002 Stockbyte, www.stockbyte.com)

Figure 10.22 After pasting into the black channel and deleting the remaining information from the other channels, you should have an area that prints with only black ink.

ink (**Figure 10.21**), which will look brown if you remember the basic concepts from the "Color Management" and "Color Correction" chapters.

To get the image to print with only black ink, you'll need to use the Channels palette. To begin, select the area you want to print with black ink, choose Edit > Copy, and then click on the black channel and choose Edit > Paste. That doesn't just paste the black channel information, but instead converts everything you copied to grayscale and then pastes the result into the black channel. But because you chose Copy instead of Cut, there will still be information left in the other channels, so click on each of the color channels (*except* black) and press the Delete (Mac) or Backspace (Windows) key to remove all information from those areas (**Figure 10.22**). Remember, only one layer can be active at a time, so pressing Delete or Backspace will delete the channel information only from the currently active layer.

You can get the same result by choosing Image > Adjust > Channel Mixer and turning on the Monochrome check box. You can even create a Channel Mixer adjustment layer—then Photoshop will force all the layers in the selected area to print with only black ink. Try it; it literally does all the work for you!

There are many more uses for the color channels, and we'll get to some of them in later chapters.

Understanding Spot Channels

Remember when you got your first box of crayons? I'll bet you that it was the standard issue eight-color box from Crayola. I remember mine vividly. I thought it was great— that is, until the rich kid across the street swaggered over and showed me his box. It was the gigantic 64-color model with the built-in sharpener. My box was limited to black, brown, blue, red, purple, orange, yellow, and green, which seemed adequate until I discovered Periwinkle, Prussian Blue, and Raw Sienna in his huge set. Well, you can think of spot channels as a way to get all those colors that don't come in the standard (CMYK) box.

It all comes down to this. If you are planning to print an image using inks other than (or in addition to) cyan, magenta, yellow, and black (such as fluorescent orange), you'll need to use one or more spot channels. These channels will allow you to paint with PANTONE colors (the most popular brand of spot color ink). Spot channels also allow your image to look correct onscreen and print correctly from both Photoshop and your page-layout program. But I should warn you before we get too far into this: If you are not actually purchasing a PANTONE ink, but would just like to simulate the look of PANTONE colors, then stay in RGB or CMYK mode and stay away from spot channels. Instead, just click on your foreground color and then click the Custom button to get to the PANTONE color picker. But beware that simulations are just that—the closest possible approximation—and they'll use a combination of the regular CMYK inks, which will cause those colors to look different from what they look like in a PANTONE swatchbook. But if you are really purchasing a PANTONE ink, then continue, and I'll show you how to get it set up.

No Layers Support

Just because Photoshop has direct support for spot colors doesn't mean it's easy to use them. The information you add to a spot channel will not appear on any layer—not even the background layer (**Figure 10.23**). It's as if the spot color information were sitting on an invisible overlay slapped on top of everything else. In fact, any information you put on a layer will be in the same mode as the document you're working on (RGB, CMYK, grayscale, etc.). That means that you can use layers, but none of the information on the layers will print using a spot color. If you'd like to strictly use PANTONE colors, start with a grayscale image and then choose Image > Mode > Multichannel. Then you can change the grayscale channel into a spot channel by Option-double-clicking (Mac), or Alt-double-clicking (Windows) on its name.

NOTES

Because spot colors will not be reproduced using CMYK ink, you can completely ignore the gamut Warning icon when choosing colors for use with a spot channel.

Figure 10.23 Information contained in a spot channel will not appear in any layer. (©2002 Stockbyte, www.stockbyte.com)

Figure 10.24 Spot Channel Options dialog box.

Figure 10.25 Solidity: 100%

Figure 10.26 Solidity: 40%.

Creating Spot Channels

You'll need to create one spot channel for each PANTONE color you would like to use. To create one, choose New Spot Channel from the side menu of the Channels palette. A dialog box will appear, asking for the specific color you would like to use and its Solidity setting (**Figure 10.24**). To specify the color, click on the color swatch at the left of the dialog box. This will bring up a standard Color Picker dialog box. To get to PANTONE colors, click on the Custom button.

Unlike process colors, which are transparent, many PANTONE inks are almost completely opaque. Certain PANTONE colors (such as the metallic inks) will completely obstruct the view of colors that appear underneath them, while others will allow you to see a hint of the colors that are underneath. The Solidity setting controls how translucent these inks will appear onscreen (**Figures 10.25** and **10.26**). Unfortunately, Photoshop doesn't automatically supply a setting for you, and there is no resource I can think of that will give you great settings. I contacted both Adobe and Pantone and neither of them could supply recommended settings. So, this is a setting you have to guess at unless you have a lot of experience with the inks you are using or have the time and money needed to perform a press check.

After you have created some spot channels, you can view those channels at the same time as the normal color channels by turning on the eyeball icon next to the composite channel as well as the ones next to each spot channel.

Painting with Spot Colors

To paint with a spot color, you must first click on the name of the color you would like to use from the Channels palette. Next, open the Color palette and, from the grayscale slider, choose the percentage of this ink you would like to use (**Figure 10.27**), and then paint away. Photoshop acts as if you are working on a separate grayscale image when you paint in one of the spot channels. So if you attempt to paint with a color chosen from the Color Picker, Photoshop will convert it to a shade of gray when you are painting.

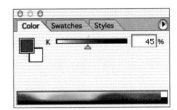

Figure 10.27 Color palette.

When you paint in a spot channel, Photoshop leaves the normal color channels unchanged (also known as overprinting). That means if you don't want the spot color you are painting with to print on top of the CMYK image (that is, if you want it to knock out as opposed to overprint), you'll have to manually switch to the color channels and delete the areas you painted across with the spot color. This can take a tremendous amount of time and isn't always the easiest thing to accomplish.

You can also paste images into the spot channels or apply any filter or adjustment that is available to grayscale images.

Proofing on a Desktop Printer

Most desktop printers aren't capable of printing an image that contains spot colors. The information in spot channels stays separate from the information in the RGB, CMYK, or grayscale channels, which are the ones your desktop printer uses to figure out what to print. That means you'll need to do a few things to get your image to print correctly on a desktop color printer (**Figure 10.28**). To start with, you don't want to mess up the document you've worked so hard to create, so choose Image > Duplicate to work on a duplicate image. Next, choose Image > Mode > RGB Color, click on one of the spot channels, and choose Merge Spot

Channel from the side menu of the Channels palette (**Figure 10.29**). Repeat this process with all of the spot channels in your document. This will make your image printable on a desktop color printer by simulating the look of the spot colors using the normal RGB color channels. After the image has been printed, you can discard this file and go back to editing the original image.

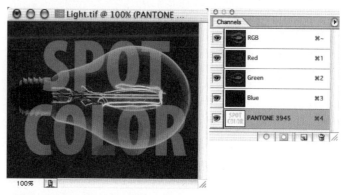

Figure 10.28 Information in the spot channels is difficult to print on desktop color printers.

Figure 10.29 Merging the spot channels will simulate the look of spot colors in RGB mode.

Saving the Image

There are only two file formats that support spot channels: Photoshop and DCS 2.0 (DCS is short for Desktop Color Separations). Since most page-layout programs can't deal with images in the Photoshop file format, you'll have to use DCS 2.0. The DCS file format is really part of the EPS file format, which is supported by most page-layout programs. To be able to save your image in the DCS 2.0 format, the image must be in grayscale or CMYK mode. When saving a DCS 2.0 file, you will be offered a bunch of options; unfortunately, most of them aren't all that straightforward. So let's take a peek at them (**Figure 10.30**).

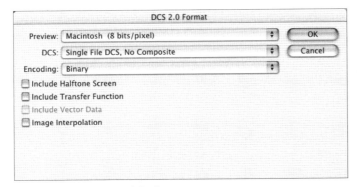

Figure 10.30 DCS 2.0 Save dialog box.

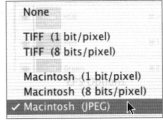

Figure 10.31 The DCS Preview choices (I think JPEG usually produces the best onscreen previews).

The Preview menu (which pops up when you save your file in the DCS 2.0 format) determines what will be seen onscreen in your page-layout program (**Figure 10.31**).

Why can't they use English!? Let's try to decipher these choices. Use the TIFF options when the image will be used on the Windows platform, and use the Macintosh options for a Mac (duh). The option "1 bit/pixel" means pure black and pure white (that looks terrible); "8 bits/pixel" means 256 colors (that looks OK), and "JPEG" means full color (that looks great). See **Figures 10.31a** and **10.31b**. These choices affect only the onscreen image that appears in other programs, not the printed version. No matter which option you choose, the printed version of the image will look great. So, what do I use? I always use the JPEG choice because it looks great and doesn't make the files overly large.

Figure 10.31a An 8-bit preview as seen in a page-layout program. (©2002 PhotoDisc)

The DCS pop-up menu determines how many files you'll end up with (**Figure 10.32**). Unless you really know what you're doing and have a good reason to mess with this (some people can come up with one), leave it set to Single File with Color Composite. I haven't needed to use the other options for any of the files I've output.

Figure 10.31b A JPEG preview as seen in a page-layout program.

The Encoding menu determines how the information that will be printed (as opposed to the onscreen preview) will

Figure 10.32 Single-file DCS documents are the easiest to keep track of.

Figure 10.33 Use Binary for Macs and ASCII for Windows.

be stored. Mac users should use the Binary option, and Windows users should use ASCII (**Figure 10.33**). Binary files are almost half the size of ASCII files, so if your printer can handle them, use them. Some really old Mac programs and printers cannot handle Binary files, so if you run into a problem, resave your image using ASCII encoding. The JPEG choices will degrade the quality of the printed image and deliver a dramatically smaller file. Use JPEG only if the image will not need to be resaved and if quality is not your first concern. (JPEG degrades the image more each time it is saved.)

If you've added spot colors to a grayscale image and find that your printing company dislikes DCS files, you'll need to use CMYK mode in an unusual way. Start by choosing Image > Mode > Multichannel, and add empty channels until you have a total of four channels altogether. Arrange the channels so that Black is at the bottom and the other channels are organized by brightness (of the spot color, not the contents of the channel), darkest on top and lightest toward the bottom (**Figure 10.34**). If you're using a third ink, then put it right below the darkest spot channel. Finally, choose Image > Mode > CMYK Color and save your file (**Figure 10.35**). Now give that file to your printing company; tell them to only output the channels that contain information, and tell them which spot colors to substitute for the CMYK colors.

Figure 10.34 Channels set up for CMYK conversion.

Figure 10.35 Result of CMYK conversion.

Understanding Alpha Channels

Alpha channels are like big storage bins for selections. Whenever you spend more than a few minutes creating a selection and there's the remotest chance that you might need it again, you should transform it into an alpha channel for safekeeping. That way it will be available for you to use again and again. And the great thing about alpha channels is that they're not limited to being just a storage device; the channels are also malleable, like modeling clay, so that you can sculpt and manipulate your selections in ways that are not possible with mere mortal selection tools. Mastering alpha channels is the mark of a true Photoshop virtuoso.

Loading and Saving Selections

If you make a selection, and then choose Select > Save Selection, Photoshop will store the selection at the bottom of the Channels palette (**Figure 10.36**). Go ahead and try it. Make sure the Channels palette is open, so you can see what's going on. An alpha channel is a saved selection—it's that simple (well, almost).

Figure 10.36 Choosing Select > Save Selection will produce a new alpha channel.

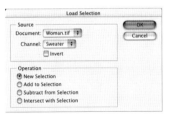

Figure 10.37 Choose Select > Load Selection to reload a saved selection.

Now let's find out how to reload the selection you just saved. But first, choose Select > Deselect (or Command-D on the Mac, Ctrl-D in Windows) to get rid of the selection that is currently active. Good. Now, back to reloading: As long as you saved a selection, you should be able to get it back at any time by choosing Select > Load Selection (**Figure 10.37**). That won't bring the image back to what it looked like when you saved the channel; instead, it will

NOTES

You can also Command-click (Mac) or Ctrl-click (Windows) on the name of a channel to load it as a selection.

just bring back the marching ants as if you created a selection from scratch.

Now let's try the same thing using the Channels palette. To save a selection, Option-click (Mac) or Alt-click (Windows) on the Save Selection icon at the bottom of the Channels palette (it's the second from the left). This accomplishes the same end result as choosing Select > Save Selection—a new channel (**Figure 10.38**). If you click on the Save Selection icon without holding down the Option or Alt key, Photoshop will assign the new channel a generic name such as "Alpha 1."

Figure 10.38 Option-clicking (Mac) or Alt-clicking (Windows) on the Save Selection icon is the same as choosing Select > Save Selection.

To get the selection back, drag the name of the channel onto the far left icon at the bottom of the palette (**Figure 10.39**). That does the exact same thing as choosing Select > Load Selection. The advantage to using the Channels palette is that you get a visual preview of the shape of the selection.

Deleting Alpha Channels

There is no way to delete a saved selection (channel) when using the Select menu. Instead, you need to open the Channels palette and drag the name of a channel onto the rightmost icon (the one that looks like a little trash can).

Viewing Individual Channels

If you would like to see what a channel contains without loading it as a selection, you can simply click on the name of the channel in the Channels palette. This will

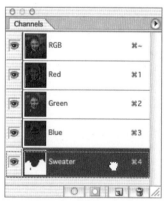

Figure 10.39 Dragging the name of a channel onto the Load Selection icon is the same as choosing Select > Load Selection.

display the channel in the main image window, as seen in **Figure 10.40**. White areas in the channel indicate areas that will be selected, and black areas indicate nonselected areas. After you're done looking at a channel, just click on the composite (topmost) channel to get back to editing all the color channels.

New Channels

So far, all we've been doing is saving and reloading selections that we've made with the normal selection tools. But you can also create a selection by creating a brand-new (empty) channel and editing the channel. Try this: Click on the second icon from the right at the bottom of the Channels palette (the one that looks like a sheet of paper with a folded corner). This action will create a new empty channel and display it in the image window. Now change your foreground color to white, choose the Paintbrush tool and a hard-edged brush, and sign your name in the channel. If you're using a mouse (instead of a graphics tablet), it might not look exactly like your signature, but that's OK. Once you're finished, click on the topmost channel to get back to the main image, drag the name of the channel you were messing with to the Load Selection icon, and bingo! The shape of your signature is selected. Photoshop can't tell the difference between a channel that was created by saving a selection and one that was created from scratch (**Figure 10.41**). That means that you're no longer limited to creating selections with the Marquee, Lasso, and Magic Wand tools.

Feathered Selections

Let's see what a feathered selection looks like when saved as a channel. Make a selection using the Lasso tool, and then save it as a channel. Next, choose Select > Feather and use a setting of 10, and then, again, save the selection as a channel. Now click on the name of the first alpha channel and take a look at it, then click on the name of the second one to see the difference, as demonstrated in **Figures 10.42** and **10.43**. Feathered selections appear with blurry edges in the Channels palette. This happens

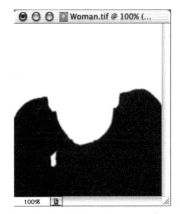

Figure 10.40 Click on the name of a channel to view it in the main image window.

Figure 10.41 Result of painting in a new channel and then loading the channel as a selection.

because shades of gray in a channel indicate an area that is partially selected (50 percent gray means 50 percent selected). You can make the first alpha channel look identical to the second by making it active and then choosing Filter > Blur > Gaussian Blur and using the same setting that was used to feather the other selection (10, in this case).

But when you look at the marching ants that appear after the channel has been loaded as a selection, they show you only where the selection is at least 50 percent selected. That isn't a very accurate picture of what the selection really looks like (**Figure 10.44**). But if you save the same selection as a channel, you can see exactly what is happening on its edge. So if you want to create a feathered selection when editing a channel, just choose a soft-edged brush to paint with.

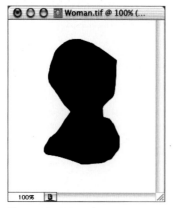

Figure 10.42 Normal.

Figure 10.43 Feathered.

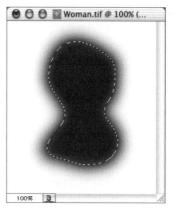

Figure 10.44 The marching ants show up where an area is at least 50 percent selected.

Shades of Gray

Try this out. Create a new channel. Paint in it with 20% gray (choose Window > Color to choose shades of gray), load that as a selection, and paint in the selected area with bright red. Now choose Select > Deselect, lower the opacity of the painting tool to 80%, and paint with bright red. They should look exactly the same. That's how Photoshop makes a selection fade out—by simply lowering the opacity of the tool you are using. The only problem is that the marching ants show up only where an image is at least 50 percent selected (that's 50% gray or brighter in a channel). So, try this one on for size. Create a new channel and paint with 49% gray, and paint in another area with 51% gray. Then load the channel as a selection and paint across the area. Only the areas that are less than 50% gray in the channel show up, but the other areas are still selected (**Figure 10.45**). Try creating a channel and then paint with 55% gray. Now load that one and you'll even get a warning message, pictured in **Figure 10.46**.

We really haven't done anything fancy with channels yet, so let's try something fun. To start with, you have to remember that when you are editing a channel, Photoshop treats it as if it is a grayscale image. That means you can use any tool that is available when working on grayscale images. So give this a try: Select an area using the Marquee tool, and save it in the Channels palette. View the channel, choose Filter > Distort > Ripple, and mess with the settings until you've created something that looks a little kooky (**Figure 10.47**). Finally, click on the composite (topmost) channel and load that channel as a selection. You can create infinite varieties of fascinating selections with this simple technique.

You can also "unfeather" a selection using the Channels palette (**Figure 10.48**). Remember, a feathered edge looks blurry when saved as a channel. Well, all you have to do to remove that blurry look is to save the selection as a channel, and then choose Image > Adjust > Threshold. This will give the channel a very crisp, and therefore unfeathered, edge.

Figure 10.46 When you load a channel that does not contain any shades brighter than 50 percent gray, a Warning will appear.

Figure 10.45 When painting in a channel, only the areas that contain less than 50 percent gray will be visible when the channel is loaded as a selection.

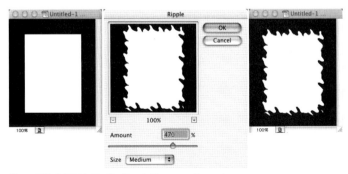

Figure 10.47 Applying the Ripple filter to a channel.

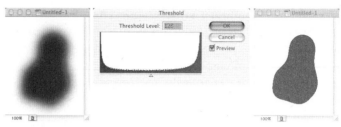

Figure 10.48 Unfeathering a selection using Threshold.

Figure 10.49 Using a selection within a channel to restrict which areas can be edited.

Selections Within Channels

You can even use a selection to isolate a particular area of a channel, as shown in **Figure 10.49**. A selection within a channel can help you create a selection that is distorted only on one side. To accomplish this, open any photograph, then use the Marquee tool to make a selection and then save it as a channel. Next, select half of the channel using the Marquee tool. Now, apply one of the filters that are found in the Filter > Distort menu. Once you're done, switch back to the main image (by clicking on the topmost channel) and load the channel you just created. To see exactly how this selection will affect the image, choose Image > Adjustments > Hue/Saturation and move the Saturation slider all the way to the left.

View with the Image

We've covered some ideal uses for alpha channels, but their usefulness is very limited if you can't see how the channels line up with the main image. At any time, you can overlay a channel onto the main image by simply turning on the eyeball icon next to the composite (topmost) channel while you are editing an alpha channel (**Figure 10.50**). This enables you to see exactly which areas of the image will be selected. When you do this, the dark areas of the alpha channel will be overlaid onto the main image. Photoshop substitutes a color for the shades of gray in a channel to make them easier to see. You can change the color that is used by Option-double-clicking (Mac) or Alt-double-clicking (Windows) on the name of the alpha channel (**Figure 10.51**). This setup is ideal when you create a selection that is feathered in one area and crisp-edged in another. All you have to do is paint

NOTES

Viewing a channel at the same time as the main image is the same as using Quick Mask mode, which we talked about back in Chapter 2: Selection Primer.

with a soft-edged brush for the feathered area, and then switch back to a crisp-edged brush for the rest.

Photoshop also allows you to switch *where* the color shows up. You can specify whether you want the selected or unselected areas to show up. To change this setting, Option-double-click (Mac) or Alt-double-click (Windows) on the name of the alpha channel and change the Color Indicates setting (**Figures 10.52** and **10.53**). Photoshop uses the term Masked Areas to describe areas that are *not* selected. Here's a way to help understand the reasoning of this. If you're painting a room in your house, what do you do to all the trim that you don't want to get paint on? You mask it off, right? Well, in Photoshop, you do the same—you select the areas you want to change, and the nonselected areas are the masked areas.

The Opacity setting determines how much you will be able to see through the overlaid channel. Viewing a channel at the same time as the main image is not a way to colorize your images. The channel that's being overlaid won't print that way; it's just a method for creating a selection, and nothing else. If you'd like to colorize an image, then check out Chapter 13 to find methods that are much easier than anything we're doing here.

WARNING

Keep an eye on the Channel Options dialog box (specifically, the Color Indicates setting). Since the dark areas of a channel are the only parts that show up when overlaying it onto the main image, this setting changes what black means in an alpha channel. When viewing a single channel, just substitute the words "black indicates" where it says "color indicates," and it should make a lot more sense.

Figure 10.50 Viewing a channel at the same time as the main image. (© 2002 PhotoSpin, www.photospin.com)

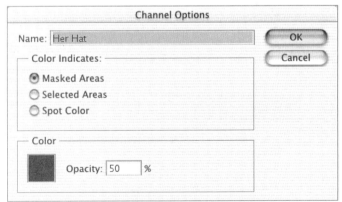

Figure 10.51 Channel Options settings used.

Figure 10.52 The Color Indicates setting changes where the color overlay appears.

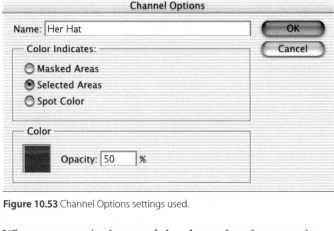

Figure 10.53 Channel Options settings used.

When you are viewing an alpha channel at the same time as the main image, you'll need to keep track of exactly what you are editing. The channel or channels that are highlighted in color are always the ones that you are currently editing, as shown in **Figure 10.54**. Other channels might be visible, but if they aren't highlighted, you won't be able to change them.

Saving Channels with Your Image

If you want to save your spot or alpha channels with your file, you'll have to use a file format that understands them. First of all, the Photoshop file format completely supports all kinds of channels, which makes it a great working file format. Unfortunately, most other programs can't understand images saved in the Photoshop format. The TIFF format also supports alpha channels, but it doesn't know the difference between spot and alpha channels, so it is not usually used for spot channels. The DCS 2.0 format supports spot channels and is compatible with the majority of publishing programs, so it is usually used for spot color work. Most of the other formats do not support alpha or spot channels, so they appear grayed out when you attempt to save an image that contains those types of channels. If you need to save your image using a format that does not support spot or alpha channels, choose File > Save As when saving the file. This dialog box will automatically discard channels if the format you choose does not support them.

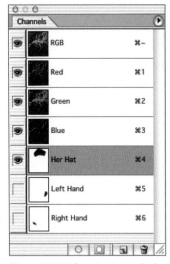

Figure 10.54 When viewing multiple channels, the channel or channels that are highlighted are the only ones being edited.

Use Extract to Select Complex Objects

Before Adobe added the Extract command to Photoshop, you had to isolate complex images by using a complicated technique that involved alpha channels. It was a long and tedious process and involved a lot of guesswork. But now there's a marvelous feature that will save us all those headaches, so you can toss that old, hair-pulling technique in the trash as we explore one of Photoshop's most welcome additions: the Extract command.

Before we start working with the tools in the Extract dialog box, let me give you an overview of what's needed to successfully extract an image from its background. First off, you'll need to highlight all the areas where the subject of the photo is intertwined with the background you'd like to remove. Not only that, but you'll also need to make it all the way around the object with your highlighting, except where the subject bumps into the edge of your document (this is going to show up in green). Next, you'll need to fill (with blue) the area you'd like to keep (**Figure 10.55**). Then Photoshop will do all the work for you. It will keep all of the blue-covered areas, trash those that aren't covered in color, and then try to figure out what to do in the green transition areas, based on where all the highlighting is.

Start with the Highlighter

Go ahead and grab an image of someone with flyaway hair and then choose Filter > Extract (**Figure 10.56**). Next, take a glance at the tools in the upper-left of the dialog box; the Highlighter tool is active by default. Before you start tracing around the edge of your image, you should know that any areas that you cover with the Highlighter have the potential of being deleted, so be sure your highlighting overlaps both the subject and the background. That means if you're going to be sloppy, it's best to overspray onto the background because that area will be deleted anyway. But don't be too careful to avoid overspray on the subject; otherwise you'll end up leaving a tiny one-pixel speck of the background between your highlighting and the subject of the image. That tiny speck has the potential to confuse the Extract

NOTES

In Photoshop 6.0, the Extract command was found under the Image menu instead of the Filter menu.

The Extract command will work on the entire image, unless a selection is active when you choose Filter > Extract. In that case it would work only within the selected area.

Figure 10.55 An image complete with highlighting and a fill. (©2002 Stockbyte, www.stockbyte.com)

command, making it think that things similar to that speck should be kept instead of deleted. So, go forth and highlight the entire edge of the subject to show Photoshop which areas of the image contain a combination of background and subject (**Figure 10.57**).

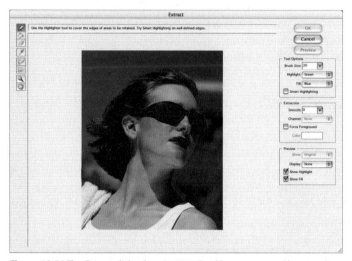

Figure 10.56 The Extract dialog box. (© 2001 Stockbyte, www.stockbyte.com)

The Brush Size setting in the upper right of the Extract dialog box can be changed by pressing the bracket keys (][). If the area you are painting across has a very well-defined (non-blurry) edge, then you can turn on the Smart Highlighting check box to have Photoshop help you limit overspray onto the subject and background (**Figure 10.58**). But be sure that option is turned off when working on areas that have very soft or complex edges. You can also hold the Option key (Mac) or Alt key (Windows) to temporarily transform the Highlighter into an eraser so you can remove overspray from your image. If you're working on a green object and you find that the green highlighting is too hard to see, then you can choose a different color from the Highlight pop-up menu in the upper right of your screen.

Figure 10.57 The edge of the subject has been highlighted. (©2002 Stockbyte, www.stockbyte.com)

Figure 10.58 Smart Highlighting was used for the bottom half of this image.

Fill with the Paint Bucket Tool

Once you've finished highlighting the edge of the image, choose the Paint Bucket tool and click in the middle of the subject of your photo. When you do that, the Paint Bucket tool will completely ignore the photograph you are working on and instead use the highlighting to determine which area should be filled. If, after clicking once with the Paint Bucket tool, the entire subject is not covered in blue, then click on additional areas of the subject that aren't yet covered (**Figure 10.59**). If you find that the entire image (minus the highlighting) is covered with blue, that means that your highlighting didn't make it all the way around the subject of the photograph, so go touch up the high-lighting and then try to fill the subject again. (By the way, the paint bucket's official name is the Fill tool.)

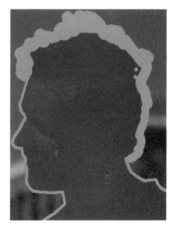

Figure 10.59 The subject has been covered with the blue fill.

Keeping in mind that all areas that are covered with the blue highlighting will not be deleted, take a quick look to make sure no part of the background you are looking to delete is covered in blue. If you've messed up, then fine-tune your highlighting and refill the subject. If you find the blue is too difficult to see, you are welcome to choose another color from the Fill pop-up menu in the upper right of the dialog box. If you think that you have everything set up correctly, then click the Preview button to see what your extraction will look like.

Most of the time, the preview will look rather promising, but that's really deceptive because the checkerboard that appears can hide a lot of problems (**Figure 10.60**). I find it much more effective to replace the checkerboard with a solid color that contrasts with the subject by choosing Other from the Display pop-up menu in the lower right of the dialog box (**Figure 10.61**).

Figure 10.60 The checkerboard can hide many problems.

Figure 10.61 Replacing the checker-board with a solid color will expose most of the problem areas you'll need to fix.

Zoom In and Fine Tune

Now it's time to use that Zoom tool to check things up close. Just remember that any area that's covered with the blue fill will not be deleted. So, scroll around your image and look for remnants of the old background (**Figure 10.62**). If you find any, then turn on the Show Fill check box and see if they become covered with blue (**Figure 10.63**). If they are, then grab the Highlighter tool and cover up those areas. Anytime you use the Highlighter tool, the fill will disappear, so you'll need to use the Paint Bucket tool to refill the sub-ject area and then re-preview the extraction.

After you've made sure that none of the background is vis-ible, then switch gears and look for areas of the subject that might have been unintentionally deleted. You can do that by toggling back and forth between the Extracted and Original choices in the Show pop-up menu. If it looks like areas of the subject were deleted, then choose Original from the Show pop-up menu. Turn on the Show Highlight and Show Fill check boxes, and then search around your image for areas that contain the hints of the subject that aren't covered with highlight or fill (**Figure 10.64**). Remember, areas that do not have any color on them (either highlight or fill) will be deleted. So grab the Highlighter tool and cover up all those areas of the subject that don't have color on top of them. Now you'll need to refill the subject and re-preview the image.

If just a tiny bit of the background is visible after previewing and most of the subject is intact, then start experimenting with the Smooth setting. As you raise the Smooth setting, the transition between the subject and the area that's been extracted should become softer (**Figure 10.65**). To see the effect of changing the Smooth setting, you'll need to re-preview the image.

Figure 10.62 Look for tiny remnants of the old background.

Figure 10.63 The background remnant was covered with the blue fill.

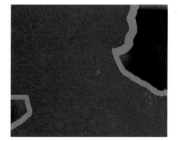

Figure 10.64 Look for areas of the subject that are not covered with color.

Figure 10.65 Left: Smooth=0. Right: Smooth=100.

Figure 10.66 Use the Cleanup tool to rid your image of specks in the background. (©2002 Stockbyte, www.stockbyte.com)

Clean It Up

At this point, you can still refine the result, but let's get away from the Highlighter and Paint Bucket tools and take a look at the Cleanup and Edge Touchup tools. You can drag across your image using the Cleanup tool to slowly lower the opacity of an area. This can be useful when attempting to rid your image of specks that don't quite touch the subject of the photograph (**Figure 10.66**). Or, if you hold down the Option key (Mac) or Alt key (Windows), the Cleanup tool will increase the opacity of an area, which will allow you to bring back areas that should not have been deleted. Then, to make the edge more crisp, use the Edge Touchup tool. If you hold the Command key (Mac) or Control key (Windows), a crosshair will appear in the center of your cursor. Move the crosshair to the place where the subject of the photo should end and Photoshop will create a crisp edge in that position. That can be useful when Photoshop leaves too much leftover information near the edge of your image.

Use Force Foreground for Intricate Images

If the subject of your photo is too small or intricate to trace around and leave space for the fill in the middle (like a chain-link fence), then cover the entire subject with the Highlighter tool (**Figures 10.67** and **10.68**). When it comes time to define the fill, turn on the Force Foreground check box and click on the color of the subject using the Eyedropper tool. That will make Photoshop look through the entire highlight area and attempt to keep things that are similar to the color you clicked on with the Eyedropper.

Once you click OK and exit the Extract dialog box, Photoshop will truly delete the background—as opposed to just selecting it—and will clean up any hint of the old background from the edge (**Figure 10.69**). If you'd rather get a selection out of the Extract command, then Command-click (Mac) or Ctrl-click (Windows) on the layer (after extracting it from its background) and then choose Select > Save Selection. Next, choose Select > Deselect, then View > Show History, and click in the indent to the left of the step listed before the Extract command (**Figure 10.70**). Finally, choose Edit > Fill and choose History from the Use pop-up menu. Now you should have the original image back and a saved selection that you can retrieve at any time by choosing Select > Load Selection.

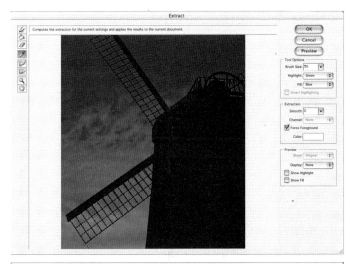

Figure 10.67 Original image. (© 2001 Stockbyte, www.stockbyte.com)

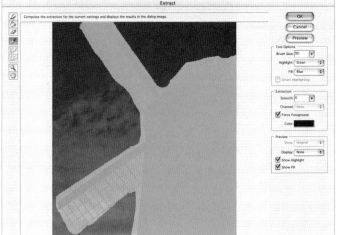

Figure 10.68 Covering the entire subject with a highlight, then checking Force Foreground and clicking the Eyedropper tool to find out what should be kept.

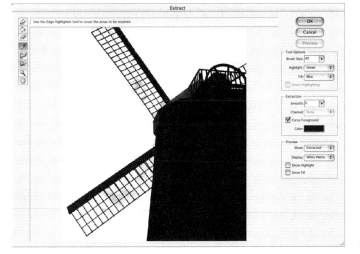

Figure 10.69 The extracted result.

Figure 10.70 Click in the indent to the left of the step listed before the Extract command.

Closing Thoughts

I truly hope that after going through this chapter you've come to terms with channels. They don't really deserve the mind-boggling reputation that seems to follow them. I like to think of them as three friendly little dogs: Spot, Color, and Alpha. They will be loyal to you throughout your lifetime as a Photoshopper and will take care of all sorts of special needs, especially when you're working with color or with complex selections (or, for that matter, *any* selection that you'd like to save for later). Likewise, the Extract command, once mastered, will save you hours of grief when it comes to removing backgrounds from complex images or making complex selections. So if for any reason you're still one of those people who want to throw their hands up in the air when the subject of channels comes up, think twice. It's worth the pain, and believe me when I tell you that the pain will turn into pure pleasure once you've realized what a gem the Channels palette is.

Ben's Techno-babble Decoder Ring

Alpha channel: Alpha channels are basically saved selections. They do not affect how your image will be printed.

Bits: In Photoshop, 256 shades of gray is known as 8 bits. This describes how much memory Photoshop uses to keep track of all those shades. So if you find a setting in your scanning software that is called "8-bit grayscale," it just means a normal 256-shade grayscale scan. If you hear someone say, "I have a 24-bit color image," that means they have an image that is in RGB mode (RGB has three channels; each channel is 8 bits; 8 + 8 + 8 = 24). Or, if you hear about a 32-bit image, that just means the image contains four channels; they are either talking about an image that is in CMYK mode (four channels) or an RGB image (three channels) plus one alpha channel (for a total of four channels).

Color channel: When you edit an image in Photoshop, you are really editing the color channels. These channels break your image into one or more color components.

The mode of the document will determine how many color channels will be present: RGB mode will have three channels (red, green, and blue); CMYK mode will have four channels (cyan, magenta, yellow, and black); and grayscale will contain only one channel (called black).

Composite channel: The composite channel does not contain any information; in fact, it is simply a shortcut to view and edit all the color channels at the same time. This is often used to return the Channels palette back to its "normal" state after isolating a single channel for editing.

DCS: Desktop Color Separation (DCS) is a special version of the EPS file format that comes in two versions, DCS 1.0 and DCS 2.0. You can think of DCS 1.0 as the old version of this file format because prior to Photoshop 5 it was the only version available in Photoshop; and it used to be integrated into the normal EPS save dialog box. DCS 1.0 files allow you to save a CMYK image and get five files total, one for each channel in the image, and one preview image. DCS 2.0 is special because it is the only file format (other than Photoshop's own format) that allows you to save spot channels in addition to the CMYK channels.

EPS: Encapsulated PostScript (EPS) is a file format used to transfer PostScript-language page descriptions between programs and output devices. EPS files should be used only with PostScript-aware printers; otherwise, the resulting images will appear with a low-resolution "jaggy" appearance because they only print the onscreen preview.

Gamut: A term used to describe the entire range of colors that is reproducible using a certain set of inks, dyes, or light. The gamut warning in Photoshop warns you that the currently chosen color is not reproducible using CMYK inks.

Mask: Anytime you view a selection as a grayscale image (as opposed to a "marching ants" selection), it is also called a mask. That means it's OK to call a channel a mask if you'd like. And when you see features like Quick Mask and Layer Masks mentioned in Photoshop, those are things that will also be stored in the Channels palette.

PANTONE: A brand of ink commonly used when printing with fewer than four inks, or when colors are needed that cannot be reproduced using CMYK inks (metallic colors, fluorescent colors, deep blues, and bright greens cannot be accurately simulated using CMYK inks). PANTONE inks are commonly referred to as spot color inks.

Spot channel: Spot channels are a special variety of color channel that allow you to construct your image out of inks other than, or in addition to, cyan, magenta, yellow, and black. Spot channels are usually used when printing with PANTONE inks.

Keyboard Shortcuts

FUNCTION	MACINTOSH	WINDOWS
View Composite	Command-~	Ctrl-~
View Channel	Command-Channel #	Ctrl-Channel #
Load Channel as a Selection	Option-Command-Channel #	Alt-Ctrl-Channel #
Extract	Option-Command-X	Alt-Ctrl-X

PART III

Creative Explorations

Courtesy of Diane Fenster, www.dianefenster.com

11
Shadows

© Bishop Studios, San Francisco

NEW IN 7

There are no new features in 7.0 that would help in the creation of shadows, but I've reorganized this chapter to make things a little easier to digest. The simplest technique now comes first and the most complicated is last.

Between the idea
And the reality
Between the motion
And the act
Falls the Shadow.

— T. S. Eliot, "The Hollow Men," V

Shadows

Go figure. You spend hours creating a great shadow. You sweat over the minutiae. You listen to an entire CD while you fuss over the tiniest details. And when you're done, nobody notices it … Good! You've got the right shadow.

Shadows can make or break an image. It's true. Even though we don't notice them, shadows help create a sense of solidness, of physical existence. Just try this: Close your eyes and think about all the shadows that were present within your field of vision. You probably can't remember a single one. The presence of subtle shadows brings the illusion of substance to your digital images as well; remove the shadows and you remove the realism of the image. Shadowless images seem to float in thin air. On the occasions when anyone does happen to notice a shadow in your image, it's almost surely too dark.

How to Think About Shadows

NOTES

If you combine two images that have radically different light sources, it will be difficult to re-create realistic shadows. The dissimilar lighting of the subjects will not relate in a natural way to the new shadows you're creating, and your mind will know something is not right about the image.

Lay your hand on top of the desk you are sitting at (assuming you're not lounging on the sofa). Notice how dark the shadow below your hand appears. Now, slowly lift your hand above the surface and see what happens to the shadow. It should become lighter, and the edge should become softer. You might also notice that the shadow became larger—it's not always easy to see that happening, but it does. If there is more than one light source above your hand, you will most likely see multiple shadows. If you were to draw a line from one of the light sources to the middle of your hand, and then continue the line through your hand until it hit the desk, the line should be smack dab in the middle of the shadow.

But finding the light source in the real world is much easier than finding the light source in an image. If you can't see the light source in a photo (say there's no lamp or ball of fiery sun), you can instead look at the part of the image that is darker than the rest. This will indicate from which direction the light was coming. Being aware of the source will really help you create natural-looking shadows.

Four Shadow Types

Ideally, when you want a shadowed image, you'd simply remove the background of the image and leave its shadow. This is possible if you happen to have a solid-colored background. But if the background is complicated, you'll have to resort to reconstructing a shadow that resembles the original. The farther you get from the original shadow, the less realistic the image will appear.

There are many techniques for creating great shadows; the complexity of the image will determine which technique you should use. The following four shadow types will cover most all of the shadow situations you might encounter:

▶ **Drop shadow.** Keeps, as a simple offset shadow, the same shape as the object casting it.

▶ **Cast shadow.** Exaggerates the height of an object. A cast shadow is based on the shape of the object that's doing the casting.

▶ **Reconstructed shadow.** Replaces the original shadow with a new one so you can remove a complex background and still retain the basic shape of the original shadow.

▶ **Natural shadow.** Transforms an existing shadow into one that can be overlaid onto another image. Also removes any grays from beyond the edge of the shadow.

NOTES

You can adjust the position of the shadow by clicking on the main image window and dragging the shadow while the Drop Shadow dialog box is still open.

You can also add a drop shadow by choosing that option from the Layer Style pop-up menu at the bottom of the Layers palette (it's the left-most icon).

Simple Shadows

Let's start with the easiest technique, and then we'll progress to more advanced techniques later. If you have a simple subject like a button, coin, or other relatively flat object, you can use Photoshop's Layer Style feature to quickly add a drop shadow, as shown in **Figures 11.1** and **11.2.**

Figure 11.1 Original image.

Figure 11.2 After a drop shadow has been applied.

First you must get the subject of the photo onto its own layer. That way you can create and edit shadows without changing the subject. Do this by selecting the subject with any selection tool and choosing Layer > New > Layer Via Copy (**Figure 11.3**). Now choose Layer > Layer Style > Drop Shadow and adjust the controls until the shadow looks appropriate (**Figure 11.4**).

Figure 11.3 Result of choosing Layer > New >Layer Via Copy to isolate the subject onto its own layer.

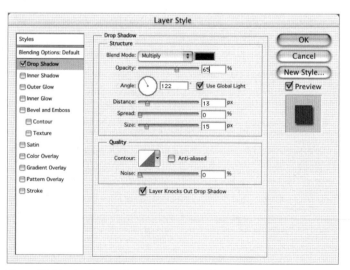

Figure 11.4 Apply a layer style to add a drop shadow.

Sometimes you might need to isolate the shadow onto its own layer so you can distort it using filters or place a layer between the subject and its shadow. You can do that by choosing Layer > Layer Style > Create Layer. After getting the shadow onto an independent layer, I often distort it using the Ripple filter that's found in the Filter > Distort menu.

Cast Shadows

To exaggerate the height of an object, you can create a shadow that falls at an angle away from the subject, also known as a cast shadow. The longer the shadow, the taller the object will appear. This will also make it appear as if the light source that's hitting the subject is coming from a specific direction (**Figures 11.5** and **11.6**).

Figure 11.5 The original file. (© 2002 Stockbyte, www.stockbyte.com)

Figure 11.6 Cast shadow added.

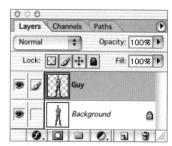

Figure 11.7 Isolate the subject onto its own layer.

Isolate the Subject

To create a cast shadow, you'll first need to get the subject of the photo onto its own layer (**Figure 11.7**). That way you can create a shadow without damaging the subject. Do this by selecting the subject with any selection tool, and then choosing Layer > New > Layer Via Copy.

Fill with a Gradient

Cast shadows are usually based on a blatant copy of the shape of the subject. To create such a shadow, Command-click (Mac) or Ctrl-click (Windows) on the layer in the Layers palette that contains the subject (not the background). This should give you a selection based on the information in that layer (**Figures 11.8** and **11.9**). Now, create a new layer, press D to reset your foreground color to black, click on the Gradient tool, and in the Options bar at the top of your screen, click on the triangle next to the gradient preview to get your drop-down presets palette. Choose Small List from the side menu of that drop-down palette. Now choose the preset that's called Foreground to Transparent (**Figure 11.10**). To fill the selection with a gradient, click on the bottom of the subject and drag to just above the top of the subject and then release the mouse button. Then get rid of the selection by choosing Select > Deselect.

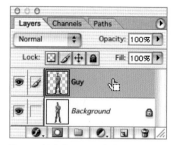

Figure 11.8 Command-click (Mac) or Ctrl-click (Windows) the subject layer.

Figure 11.9 The result of Command-clicking (Mac) or Ctrl-clicking (Windows) on the subject layer.

Figure 11.10 Choose Foreground to Transparent from the gradient drop-down menu in the Options bar.

Distort the Shadow Layer

Now you want to get the shadow to appear beneath the subject, so drag the shadow layer until it is below the subject layer in the Layers palette. To make the shadow fall at an angle, choose Edit > Transform > Distort; the transform bounding box will appear. Move the squares (or handles) on the upper corners of that box around until you have the desired angle, as in **Figure 11.11**.

Blur the Shadow

Now that we've applied a gradient and skewed the shadow layer, our shadow is fading out pretty nicely, but it still has a crisp edge. In the real world, shadows become more blurry as they get farther from the subject of the photograph (or, in my case, the guy's feet). To get a natural-looking fade-out, choose the Marquee tool, then click and drag the selection from the upper-left corner of the image until the bottom of the marching ants slightly overlaps the topmost part of the shadow.

Next, choose Filter > Blur > Gaussian Blur and use a setting just high enough to slightly blur the shadow (**Figure 11.12**). Now move the selection down by pressing Shift–down arrow a few times, and then blur the shadow again, using the same setting. Repeat this process until the selection is all the way at the bottom of the shadow (**Figure 11.13**).

Figure 11.11 Distorting the shadow by using Edit > Transform > Distort.

NOTES

If you can't locate the Foreground to Transparent preset, then choose Reset Gradients from the side menu of the drop-down palette.

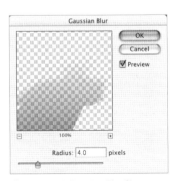

Figure 11.12 Gaussian Blur filter.

Figure 11.13 The placement for the first blur. Move the selection down for each subsequent blur.

NOTES

Instead of going up and choosing Blur each time, you can press Command-F (Mac) or Ctrl-F (Windows) to reapply the last filter you used.

To create a more natural, less refined edge, choose Filter > Stylize > Diffuse and use the default settings. The Diffuse filter will add noise to the edge of the shadow, making it appear less artificial.

Achieve Proper Brightness

To brighten the shadow, adjust the Opacity setting of the shadow layer in the Layers palette (**Figures 11.14** and **11.15**). Make the shadow a little lighter than you think it should be; otherwise, people might notice it.

Figure 11.14 Shadow is too dark.

Figure 11.15 Shadow after lowering Opacity setting to 30%.

Reconstructed Shadows

If the background of an image is complex, then I'd completely remove the background on the image and attempt to re-create new shadows that resemble the originals (**Figures 11.16** to **11.18**).

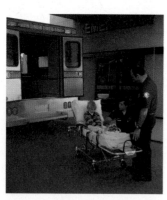

Figure 11.16 Original image. (© 2002 PhotoSpin, www.photospin.com)

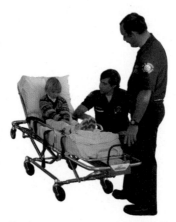

Figure 11.17 Background removed.

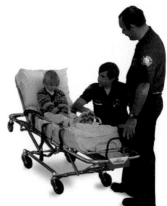

Figure 11.18 Shadows added.

Isolate the Subject

As with cast shadows, the first thing you need to do is to get the subject of the photo onto its own layer, so you can create and edit shadows without changing the subject. Do this by selecting the subject with any selection tool and then choosing Layer > New > Layer Via Copy (**Figure 11.19**).

Trace Shadow Edges

Before removing the layer that contains the shadows, it will be helpful if you trace the shape of the original shadows. That way, any new shadows you create can have the same shape and position. Use the Freeform Pen tool to trace around the edges of each shadow that appears in the image (**Figures 11.20** and **11.21**). Most images contain more than one shadow—maybe a hard-edged shadow on one object and a softer-edged shadow on another. You want to create a new path for each shadow (or small group of shadows) in the image. After you've done that, make a mental note about how soft the edges are and how dark the shadow is. Now you can finally delete the layer that contains the shadows.

Rebuilding the Shadows

To re-create the shadows, first create a new layer below the subject of the image. Now set your foreground color to black and drag the first path in the Paths palette to the first icon in the Paths palette. This should fill the shape of the path with your foreground color, which is black (**Figure 11.22**, where I've added a white background to make it easier to see what the end result will look like). The black shape should appear on the layer you just created. This shape represents one of the shadows. To lighten the shadow, just lower the Opacity setting in the Layers palette (**Figure 11.23**). To make it look more realistic, choose Filter > Blur > Gaussian Blur and move the slider until the edge is as soft as the original, as shown in **Figure 11.24.** Repeat this process for each shadow in the image. It's a good idea to make a new layer for each shadow, so you can control each one separately.

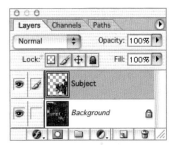

Figure 11.19 Isolate the subject onto its own layer.

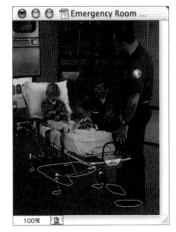

Figure 11.20 Use the Freeform Pen tool to trace the shadows.

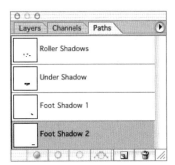

Figure 11.21 Each shadow has its own path.

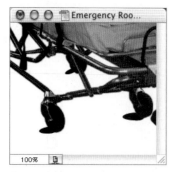

Figure 11.22 Filled with black.

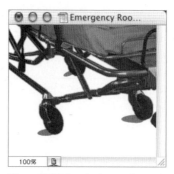

Figure 11.23 Opacity lowered.

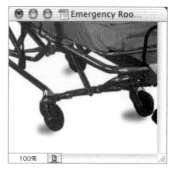

Figure 11.24 Gaussian Blur applied.

NOTES

To quickly change the opacity of a layer, switch to the Move tool and press the number keys on your keyboard (1=10%, 3=30%, 35=35%, and so on).

To make the shadow fade out in a particular direction, drag the name of a path to the selection icon at the bottom of the Paths palette (it looks like a dotted circle). Choose Select > Feather to soften the edge, and then use the Linear Gradient tool (set to Foreground to Transparent) and drag across the selected area (**Figures 11.25** and **11.26**). Or, if you've already filled that area, you can make it fade out by choosing Filter > Blur > Motion Blur.

Once all your shadows look appropriate, link all the shadow layers together and then choose Layer > Merge Linked. This will create a single shadow layer.

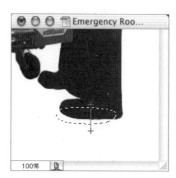

Figure 11.25 Selection.

Figure 11.26 After gradient is applied.

Natural Shadows

Let's finish with my favorite technique. We'll simply (well, not quite simply) slip the background out from beneath the original shadow, leaving just the shadow intact. That way we could feature it on a large poster and you wouldn't be able to tell the difference between the background of the image and the white paper the poster is printed on (**Figure 11.27**). After we've done that, we'll make this original shadow transparent so we can overlay it on any other image within Photoshop. This technique works when your image has a simple, low-contrast background; a white or gray background will give you the best results (**Figure 11.28**).

Figure 11.27 The left side of this image is the original; the right side has be adjusted to blend with the white background.

Figure 11.28 Here the shadow under the flower image was made transparent so it could be overlaid onto the currency. (© 2002 Stockbyte, www.stockbyte.com)

Isolate the Subject

The first thing you need to do is to get the subject of the photo (a flower, in this case) onto its own layer (**Figure 11.29**). (These steps should be starting to sound very familiar by now!) That way you can isolate the shadow from its background without affecting the subject of the image. Do this by selecting the subject with any selection tool and then choosing Layer > New > Layer Via Copy. Or, if you have a complicated object, you can duplicate the layer and then use the Background Eraser or Extract command. This will leave you with two layers: one that contains the flower and the other that contains the flower and its shadow. To avoid confusion, whenever I mention the *subject* of the photo, I'm referring to the top layer (the one that contains only the flower); whenever I talk about the *shadow layer,* I mean the one that is under the subject (which contains both the flower and its shadow).

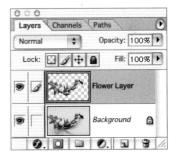

Figure 11.29 Isolate the subject onto its own layer.

It is important to choose Layer Via Copy instead of Layer Via Cut to avoid getting a bright halo around your image. Halos are caused by replacing the underlying image with white, which happens when you cut the subject from its original layer. If you're curious, go ahead and try using Layer > New > Layer Via Cut and then look closely at the edge of the subject.

Now click on the shadow layer (the "Background" layer, in this example). This will allow you to modify the shadow layer of the image without messing up the subject of the image.

Find Edge of Shadow

Next, you'll want to locate the exact edge of the shadow and then force the rest of the background to white, leaving just the shadow visible. To do this, choose Layer > New Adjustment Layer > Threshold and move the slider all the way to the right. A good portion of your screen should now appear black, because the Threshold adjustment is exposing all areas that are darker than white. Now, click on the shadow layer, choose Image > Adjustments > Levels, and move the upper-right slider around until the shadow (which will appear as solid black) is as large as possible without bumping into the edge of the document. The black mass will indicate where the shadow ends and the background begins, as shown in **Figures 11.30** to **11.34**. After you've moved the slider a little, you can use the up arrow and down arrow keys on the keyboard to move the slider in small increments. It's much too difficult to find the edge of a shadow with the naked eye, so you'll always want to use Threshold to help you.

Figure 11.30 Shadow is bumping into the edge of the document.

If the background behind the image is not white or gray, then choose Image > Adjustments > Desaturate before attempting to adjust the Threshold.

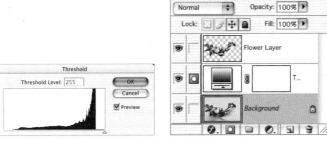

Figure 11.31 Move the Threshold slider all the way to the right.

Figure 11.32 Make sure you are working on the shadow layer before applying Levels.

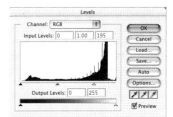

Figure 11.34 Move the upper-right slider to change where the shadow stops fading out.

Figure 11.33 Shadow is as large as possible without bumping into the edge of the document.

Clean Up Unwanted Grays

After getting the proper Levels settings, there might still be some unwanted shades of gray near the edge of the document (they would look like tiny black specks). Not all images will have the extra grays. To remove any specks, click on the shadow layer in the Layers palette and use the Eraser tool to brush over the "dirty" areas (you can see them in **Figures 11.33** and **11.35**). After you've gotten rid of all the extra grays, drag the Threshold adjustment layer to the trash icon at the bottom of the Layers palette.

Figure 11.35 Use the Eraser tool to clean up any stray specks.

Figure 11.36 Original shadow brightness.

Figure 11.37 Lightened by using Levels.

Refine the Result

If you open the Levels dialog box a second time, you'll be able to control many aspects of the shadow's appearance. If you move the lower-left slider, you will lighten the shadow (compare **Figures 11.36** and **11.37**). Remember to make your shadows a little lighter than you think they should be; otherwise, people might notice them, which would ruin the realism of the image. Also, if the image will be printed on a printing press, the image will often appear darker than it does onscreen.

You can also control how the shadow fades out by moving the upper-middle slider. If the shadow isn't dark enough, you can move the upper-left slider over until it touches the beginning of the histogram.

Control the Shadow's Color

After applying Levels, you might notice some color in the shadow. Most of the time, the color will make the shadow appear more realistic. But sometimes the color is too intense. To adjust it, choose Image > Adjustments > Hue/ Saturation and move the Saturation slider (**Figure 11.38**). If you move the slider all the way to the left, there will be no hint of color in the shadow.

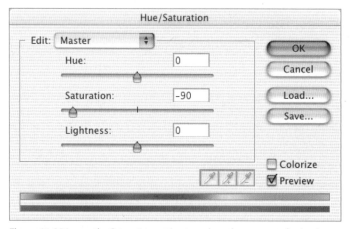

Figure 11.38 Lower the Saturation setting to reduce the amount of color that appears in the shadow.

On the other hand, if you would like to *add* color to the shadow, turn on the Colorize checkbox in the Hue/Saturation dialog box, move the Hue slider to pick the basic color, and adjust the saturation slider to change how intense it appears. This can be useful when you have a shiny object that should reflect some of its color into the shadow area.

Overprint the Shadow

Using the flower and the currency images as an example, we'll overlay the flower's shadow on the money and then make that shadow print on top of the bill as if it were made out of ink. When you place the final image (in this case, the flower) on top of another, you might want its shadow to appear transparent so that the two images look like they belong together. To accomplish this integration, open the image upon which you want to cast the shadow (here, the foreign currency). Now, switch back to the image that contains the shadow (the flower) and link the layer that contains the subject to the layer that contains its shadow by clicking to the left of the layer in the Layers palette. A link symbol should appear, as shown in **Figure 11.39.** Now use the Move tool to drag the flower onto the second document. This should copy both layers into that document, as **Figure 11.40** depicts.

To make the shadow transparent, be sure you are working on the shadow layer. Then, in the Layers palette, set its blending mode menu to Multiply, and bingo!—transparent shadow (**Figure 11.41**).

NOTES

If you can't tell if the shadow has color in it, just choose Image > Adjustments > Desaturate to remove all the color from the shadow. Then choose Edit > Undo to see exactly how much color was in the shadow. Of if you want a shadow that has no hint of color, just choose Image > Adjustments > Desaturate and don't choose Edit > Undo.

You must drag from the image window to copy linked layers from one document to another. If you drag from the Layers palette, only one layer will be copied.

If the edge of the shadow is not soft enough, choose Filter > Blur > Gaussian Blur and use a very low setting, such as 1 or 2.

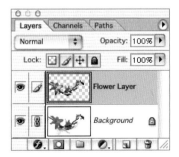

Figure 11.39 Link the layers by clicking to the left of the layer preview icon.

Figure 11.40 Using the Move tool, drag the image on top of another document.

Figure 11.41 Use the Multiply blending mode to make the shadow transparent.

WARNING

Multiply mode works best when your image is RGB. If you use it while in CMYK mode, you can easily get too much ink on the printing press. This happens when the shadow combines with the underlying image and, in effect, darkens it, producing excessive ink coverage. If you use Multiply before converting to CMYK, be sure to choose Flatten Image when converting, or use the black-only shadow technique described at the end of this chapter. For more information about potential CMYK problems, see Chapter 9, "Color Correction."

Creating a Truly Transparent Shadow

Using the Multiply blending mode to print the shadow on top of another image works great when you end up combining your shadow with an underlying image in Photoshop, as we did above. But what if you need to export your image and slide something under it in another program? I wouldn't suggest this for images destined for a printing press (the file formats we are forced to use don't support transparency), but sometimes you might need to do that when working with multimedia applications—for instance, when creating a video. Let's rewind our technique back to the point where we were about to drag the flower on top of the currency.

To get true transparency out of our shadow, it must be the only thing visible. That means you'll have to Option-click (Mac) or Alt-click (Windows) on the eyeball icon for the shadow layer (that's a shortcut for hiding all the other layers). First I'm going to tell you to do a few steps without explaining what's going on behind the scenes. Then, after we get everything to look right, I'll clue you in on what you just did, OK?

Now that you only have one layer visible, press Option-Command-~ on the Mac or Alt-Ctrl-~ in Windows (the tilde ~ key is just to the left of the number 1 key), which should give you an unusual-looking selection (**Figure 11.42**). Choose Select > Inverse, create a new layer, and then fill that selection with black by pressing D and then Option-Delete (Mac) or Alt-Backspace (Windows). Now, to finish the effect, throw away the old shadow layer, click on the flower layer, and choose Layer > Merge Down (**Figure 11.43**). You're done!

Figure 11.42 Option-Command-~ (Mac) or Alt-Ctrl-~ (Windows) will give you an unusual-looking selection.

Figure 11.43 When you're done, you'll have a truly transparent shadow.

Now that you have this wonderful-looking transparent shadow, you might want to know how we accomplished that effect. The whole thing was possible because of that keyboard command we used (Option-Command-~ on the Mac, Alt-Ctrl-~ in Windows). Remember what was on your screen at the time you pressed that command? Weren't you just looking at the shadow layer? Well, that command takes what's visible and selects all the areas that are pure white. It also partially selects shades of gray. For example, if there is an area that is 10 percent gray, it will become 90 percent selected. After we got that selection, we chose Select > Inverse, which gave us what we *really* needed—areas that used to be 10 percent gray became 10 percent selected, and areas that were 40 percent gray became 40 percent selected, etc. Then we created a new layer and filled our selection with black. That effectively took areas that used to be 10 percent gray and made them black with an opacity setting of 10%. This can be a difficult concept to grasp if you've never attempted it before, but actually the concept is simple—you are just translating brightness levels into opacity levels.

RGB Versus CMYK

I usually create all my shadows while I'm in RGB mode, even if the end result will need to be in CMYK mode. Here are a few reasons I prefer to work in RGB mode:

▶ The natural shadow technique described earlier in this chapter will produce shadows that appear slightly brown if applied while in CMYK mode.

▶ The Multiply blending mode can cause problems with too much ink in an area if used in CMYK mode.

▶ File sizes remain smaller with RGB.

▶ All the filters work in RGB mode.

When you convert an image that contains layers to CMYK mode, a dialog box always appears asking if you would like to flatten the image. I usually choose to flatten it when converting; otherwise, I might run into problems with too much ink coverage (because I used the Multiply blending mode). The only time I don't flatten the image is when I'll be creating black-only shadows; there are no problems using the Multiply blending mode on these.

Closing Thoughts

If you feel funny taking so much time to perfect something that will never be noticed, you have two good reasons not to fret. First, shadows are every bit as important as light, but—strangely—the very best shadows are the ones that go undetected. Second, as with everything else in Photoshop, after you've test-driven them a few times, the techniques you learned in this chapter should take only a few minutes to perform. Isn't it worth a few minutes to get those subtle, flawless, ethereal shadows that no one will ever notice?

Keyboard Shortcuts

Function	Macintosh	Windows
New Layer Via Cut	Shift-Command-J	Shift-Ctrl-J
New Layer Via Copy	Command-J	Ctrl-J
Hue/Saturation	Command-U	Ctrl-U
Desaturate	Shift-Command-U	Shift-Ctrl-U
Levels	Command-L	Ctrl-L
Feather	Option-Command-D	Alt-Ctrl-D
Fill Dialog	Shift-Delete	Shift-Backspace
Toggle Preserve Transparency	/	/

12
Collage

© Steve Bronstein

NEW IN 7

The techniques used for creating collages haven't changed with Photoshop 7.0, so you'll find that this chapter is very similar to the one in the last edition of this book. However, I've revised most of the examples, and I will show you the new Layer Mask Hides Effects checkbox.

What you see on these screens up here is a fantasy, a computer-enhanced hallucination!

—Stephen Falken in "WarGames"

Collage

No matter how many times I see them, I'm always in awe of the amazing special effects you see in big-budget Hollywood flicks. I know it's all man-made digital voodoo, but I still get a thrill when the effects are done so well. Consider *Jurassic Park*, where they blended the computer-generated dinos with actors and live-action backgrounds— so incredibly lifelike that you wouldn't be surprised to find yourself standing behind a Velociraptor in the popcorn line.

In Photoshop you can create your own kind of movie magic by blending diverse visual elements into one big picture (the only difference is the picture doesn't move). Some people call this compositing or image blending. This is where Photoshop really gets to strut its stuff, and where you can put your creative agility to the test. The possibilities with compositing are truly boundless. Where else could you create a passionate embrace between an ugly, smelly, wrinkly bulldog and his arch-rival, a prim and proper kitty-cat? (Robert Bowen did it, and the piece won the Gold Lion Award in Cannes! See **Figure 12.1.**) With Photoshop all you need is your imagination and a bag full of good collage techniques.

Four Ways to Blend

In this chapter we'll explore the features that allow you to blend multiple images into one seamless composite. We'll cover grouping layers, blending sliders, layer masks, and Vector Masks. Once you've mastered all four, you'll be able to blend your images together like magic. But before we start to create collages, let's take an introductory look at how these features work.

Figure 12.1 Robert Bowen, working with Howard Berman, created this image for Sony using Photoshop and won a Golden Lion Award. (Courtesy of Robert Bowen Studio, Sony Electronics, Inc., and Lowe & Partners/SMS. Photography by Howard Berman. Art Director: Maria Kostyk-Petro)

Grouping Layers

When two layers are grouped together, the top layer will show up only in those places where there is information on the layer directly below it. This can be useful for simple effects like controlling where shadows fall or placing a photo inside of some text.

Sample Use: You've spent hours creating a big "retro" headline that could have come from the movie poster of *Creature from the Black Lagoon.* Your client—not exactly the king of good taste—calls and says he wants you to put flames inside the headline. You put aside your better judgment and agree to the flames, but only because he pays on time. Then he calls back; he's got some unresolved issues. He doesn't know whether he wants flames or hot lava inside the text, and he's also thinking about changing the headline altogether. He wonders out loud if it will take long or cost much more to do this? "Well," you say, "I think I could wrap this up in about three hours." Greatly relieved, he tells you you're a miracle worker and hangs up. Then you pop open the Layers palette, where you've grouped the headline and flames, and faster than you can say hocus pocus you've tweaked the text and swapped out some lava for the flames and are off to the beach for a three-hour (paid) vacation.

Blending Sliders

The blending sliders allow you to make certain areas of a layer disappear or show up based on how bright or dark they are. For example, it's very easy to make all of the dark parts of an object disappear.

Sample Use: A "big fish" prospect that you've been trying to snag for months finally throws you a bone. She's desperate because the super-swanky design studio she usually uses can't meet her deadline. You know she's just using you, but what the hey, it's a shot at a new client. She's given you some images that you've loaded into Photoshop. One is a photograph of some big, fat, billowy clouds; the other is of a bunch of whales. She wants you to make it look like the whales are swimming around in the clouds. In some places she wants the whales to replace the sky that is behind the clouds, but in other places she wants the whales to actually blend in with the clouds. Very surreal. She impatiently bites her nails and wants to know how many hours it will take to get the effect. You know you can nail this job in a jiffy with the blending sliders, so while your hands are busy with the mouse, you give her a fearless look and reply, "I'll do it while you wait." She frowns, "I can't just sit around here for hours!" You smile, "No problem, it's already done." The look on her face delivers the good news—you've got a client for life.

Layer Masks

I consider layer masks to be the most powerful features for creating collages in Photoshop. With layer masks you can make any part of a layer disappear, and you can control exactly how much you'd like its edge to fade out. What you can do with layer masks is infinite.

Sample Use: You're waiting for your biggest client, a twenty-year-old creative genius with a ring in his nose.

Although this is just a planning meeting, you know from experience that The Genius will want to see some action. Armed with your fastest computer and with Photoshop at the ready, you're not fazed when the kid comes in and starts throwing around madcap ideas like they're going out of style. Blending seems to be the theme of the day. First he wants something that looks like a skyscraper growing out of a pencil. Then he changes his mind and decides he wants to fuse together a hippopotamus and a ballerina. But then he gets a funny look on his face and says, "I know! Let's put Godzilla in an Elvis suit!" Ahhh, you think, a perfect day for layer masks. Without batting an eyelash, you go about the business of giving 'Zilla his new look. Six months later you almost choke on your coffee when you find out that your Elvis-Zilla ad got an award.

Vector Masks

Vector Masks allow you to attach a crisp-edged path to a layer; anything outside of the path will be hidden both on screen and when printed. This feature is special because the edge will remain smooth when printed to a PostScript printer, even if the pixels in the image are so large that the rest of the image appears jaggy.

Sample Use: You're doing a freebie brochure for your non-profit client, Defenders of the Naked Mole Rat. They want the rat to be the most noticeable image on the cover, so you make their logo small and place it in the corner so it doesn't distract from the lovely Rat. But at the last minute (of course!) your penniless client does an about-face and wants you to enlarge the logo to make it almost fill the page. You're tired of doing things for free and fed up with her endless requests, so you tell the client that scaling up the logo that large is a big request when it comes to Photoshop. You even demonstrate your point by scaling one of the photographic elements of the brochure up to a huge size, and of course it looks terrible, very blurry and jaggy. She squeezes out a few tears and gives you her song and dance about the plight of this dear little creature, and how crucial it is to have this brochure just right. You tell her that you'll work on it through the night, and send her on her way. The minute she's out the door, you scale up the logo in a millisecond, and because you used a Vector Mask, the edge remains perfectly crisp and will print that way as well. The job is done. The Naked Mole Rat lives on; unfortunately, since you're so good, the client will never go away.

Now that you have a feeling for the blending options that are available, let's get into the specifics of how this all works.

Grouping Layers

Figure 12.2 Result of grouping a photo with a type layer.

When you group multiple layers together, all the layers within the group will be visible only where there is information in the bottommost layer of the group (see **Figures 12.2 and 12.3**). When you group layers, Photoshop always groups the currently active layer to the one below it. You can group layers together by using any of the following techniques:

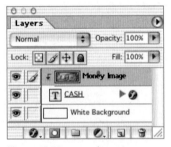

Figure 12.3 Layers palette view.

▶ Option-click (Macintosh) or Alt-click (Windows) between two layers in the Layers palette.

▶ Choose Layer > Group With Previous.

▶ Type Command-G (Macintosh) or Ctrl-G (Windows).

Changing the Stacking Order

Changing the stacking order of the layers may accidentally ungroup some layers, so you'll want to be careful. If you move one of the grouped layers above a layer that is not part of the group, you'll be ungrouping that layer. Or if you move an ungrouped layer between two layers that are grouped, then it will become part of that group. If you move the bottom layer of a group above or below a layer that is not part of the group, all the layers in the group will move with it.

Now that you know how to group your layers, let's take a look at a few of the things you can accomplish by doing that.

Adjustment Layers

Grouping layers can also be helpful when you're using adjustment layers. An adjustment layer allows you to apply an adjustment (like Levels, Curves, etc.) as a layer that affects all the layers that are below it. That's nice, because the change is not permanent—you can always trash that layer and the adjustment is no longer applied. By grouping an adjustment layer, you can force it to affect only the layers that are within the group. This can be extremely helpful when you want to brighten or darken a single layer and you don't want to make the change permanent (**Figures 12.4** to **12.7**).

Figure 12.4 Original image. (Courtesy of Chris Klimek)

Figure 12.5 Adding an adjustment layer at the top of the layers stack affects the entire image.

Figure 12.6 Grouping the adjustment layer makes it apply only to the layers within the group.

Limiting Shadows

I use grouping all the time when I'm creating shadows. Let's say you have a dialog box, and underneath the box is a picture frame, and you want the box to cast a shadow on the frame. Once you create a layer that contains a shadow, all you need to do is group it with the box, and then the shadow will show up only where the picture frame is (**Figures 12.8** to **12.10**).

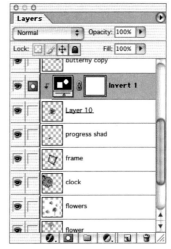

Figure 12.7 Layers palette view.

333

NOTES

If you've created your shadow using a layer style, choose Layer > Layer Style > Create Layer to isolate the shadow onto its own layer. Then you can group it with anything you like.

Figure 12.8 Original image.

Figure 12.9 Grouping the shadow to the picture frame.

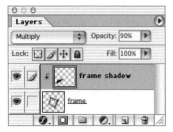

Figure 12.10 Layers palette view.

The Magnifying Glass Trick

I travel all over the country presenting seminars and speaking at conferences, and I know I can always get people to ask questions by showing my magnifying glass trick. I start by opening what looks like a simple image of an ampersand (&). Then, as I move my cursor, a magnifying glass passes over the ampersand and it appears as if it's really magnifying the image! That's not really possible in Photoshop, of course, but I can still trick people into thinking that it's happening for a few seconds. Let's see how the magnifying glass trick works.

Start off by opening any image you'd like to work with. I use a simple one of a black ampersand on a white background. Next, you'll need an image of a magnifying glass or loupe that you can place on a layer above the ampersand (I've included two on the CD at the back of this book). Now select the background and the glass portion of the magnifying glass and press Delete (Macintosh) or Backspace (Windows) to remove those areas (**Figure 12.11**).

Next, drag the name of the image you are using (not the magnifying glass) to the New Layer icon to duplicate it. Use a simple filter like Mosaic (choose Filter > Pixelate > Mosaic) to make an obvious change to the duplicate image (**Figure 12.12**).

Now let's get that modified image to only show up within the glass area of the magnifying glass. Grab the Elliptical Marquee tool and make a selection where the glass should be in the magnifying glass image. Make sure it lines up perfectly on all sides. Next, create a new empty layer and then type Option-Delete (Macintosh) or Alt-Delete

NOTES

When using the Marquee tool, you can press the spacebar to reposition the selection (but don't release the mouse button).

If you're going to remove the background on the magnifying glass before dragging on top of another image, you should be aware that you can't remove a background layer. So, if that's what you have, double-click it to change its name and make it a normal layer.

(Windows) to fill that area with your foreground color and then choose Select > Deselect. Move the layer you just created so that it's positioned directly between the original image and the filtered version in the stacking order of the Layers palette (**Figure 12.13**).

Now, let's get the whole trick to work. Click on the layer directly above the one that contains the circle you just made, and then choose Layer > Group With Previous. Now click on the magnifying glass layer and link it to the circle layer by clicking just to the left of the circle layer's thumbnail image in the Layers palette. That'll make both layers move at the same time (**Figure 12.14**). To see if the trick is working, use the Move tool to drag around your screen. That should make it so the filtered image only shows up in the "magnified" area (**Figure 12.15**).

NOTES

In the Layers palette, the background image is always stuck at the bottom of the palette; you can't move another layer below it in the stack. But you can always double-click on the background image and change its name, which will convert it into a normal layer. Once it's a layer, you can change its stacking order, or drag a layer below it.

To quickly group multiple layers together, link the layers by clicking and dragging in the column just to the left of their preview icons in the Layers palette, and then choose Layer > Group Linked. After you have grouped the layers, you can drag across the link symbols to turn them off.

Figure 12.11 Remove the background of the magnifying glass and place it on top of the image.

Figure 12.12 Make a drastic change to the duplicate layer using a filter.

Figure 12.13 The new layer should be placed between the two image layers.

Figure 12.14 The final setup in the Layers palette.

Figure 12.15 The magnifying glass trick in action.

NOTES

In previous versions of Photoshop you simply double-clicked on a layer to get to the blending sliders (the Option/Alt key wasn't necessary).

Blending Sliders

The blending sliders allow you to quickly make areas of a layer transparent, based on how bright or dark the image appears. You'll find the blending sliders by holding Option (Mac), or Alt (Windows) and then double-clicking the name of a layer (this will open the Layer Style dialog box). The blending sliders are at the bottom of the Layer Style dialog box, shown in **Figure 12.16**. The first thing you'll notice is that there are two sets of sliders. One is labeled "This Layer" and the other is labeled "Underlying." The slider called This Layer will make areas of the active layer disappear. The slider labeled Underlying deals with all the layers underneath the layer that was double-clicked. This slider will make parts of the underlying image show up as if a hole has been punched through the active layer.

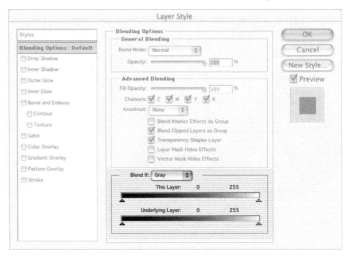

Figure 12.16 The blending sliders.

Figure 12.17 Original unblended image. (both images © 2002 Stockbyte, www.stockbyte.com)

"This Layer" Sliders

First, let's take a look at the topmost sliders. If you move the left slider towards the middle, the dark areas of the image (that is, all the shades that are to the left of the slider) will start to disappear. This slider can be a great help when you're trying to remove the background from fireworks or lightning. The only problem is, once you get the background to disappear, the edges of the lightning will have hard, jagged edges (**Figures 12.17** to **12.19**).

Figure 12.18 Removing the dark sky from the lightning image.

Figure 12.19 Moving the upper left slider makes the dark areas of the current layer disappear.

To remedy this situation, all you have to do is split the slider into two pieces by Option-dragging (Macintosh) or Alt-dragging (Windows) on its right edge. When this slider is split into two parts, the shades of gray that are between the halves will become partially transparent and blend into the underlying image (**Figures 12.20** and **12.21**). The shades close to the left half of the slider will be almost completely transparent, and the shades near the right half will be almost completely opaque.

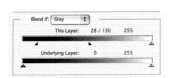

Figure 12.20 The edges of the lightning blend into the underlying image.

Figure 12.21 Splitting a triangle into halves allows the image to smoothly blend into the underlying image.

When you move the right slider, you will be making the bright areas of the image (all the shades of gray to the right of the slider) disappear. This slider can be useful when you come across a multi-colored logo that needs to be removed from its white background. Just like with the upper left slider, you can split this slider into two halves by Option-dragging (Macintosh) or Alt-dragging (Windows) its left edge (**Figures 12.22** to **12.24**).

Figure 12.22 Original image. (© 2002 Stockbyte, www.stockbyte.com)

Figure 12.23 Result of removing all white areas by using the blending sliders.

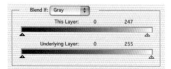

Figure 12.24 Moving the upper right sliders makes the bright areas of this layer disappear.

"Underlying" Sliders

By moving the two sliders on the Underlying bar, you'll be able to make areas of the underlying image show up as if they were creating a hole in the layer you Option (Mac), or Alt (Windows) double-clicked. These sliders are useful when you don't want a layer to completely obstruct the view of the underlying image. I might use this to reveal some of the texture in the underlying image. And, just like the top sliders, you can Option-click (Macintosh) or Alt-click (Windows) to separate the sliders into two parts (**Figures 12.25** to **12.27**).

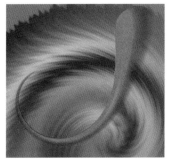

Figure 12.25 Original image.

Figure 12.26 Result of blending in the dark parts of the underlying image.

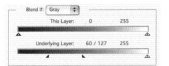

Figure 12.27 Moving the lower left slider makes the dark areas of the underlying image show up as if they are poking a hole in the active layer.

Understanding the Numbers

The numbers that appear above the sliders indicate the exact location of each slider. If you haven't split any of the sliders, then you should see a total of four numbers (one for each slider). When you split one of the sliders into two parts, you'll see one number for each half of the slider. These numbers use the same numbering system as the Levels dialog box (see Chapter 6, "Optimizing Grayscale Images," for a "Percentage to 0–255" conversion table).

If you move the upper left slider until its number changes to 166, for example, you'll have made all the shades darker than 35% gray on that layer disappear. It would be much easier if Adobe would allow us to switch between percentages and the 0–255 numbering system like you can when using the Curves dialog box.

Using Color Channels

If you leave the pop-up menu at the top of the blending slider area set to gray, then Photoshop will ignore the colors in your document and just analyze the brightness of the image (as if the image were in grayscale mode). By changing this menu, you will be telling Photoshop to look at the information in the individual color channels to determine which areas should be visible (**Figure 12.28**). For example, if you have a document that is in CMYK mode and you change the pop-up menu to cyan and move the upper right slider to 26, you'll make all areas of the

Figure 12.28 The Blend If pop-up menu in the Layer Style dialog box determines which channels will be analyzed.

layer that contain 10% or less cyan disappear. This can be useful when you want to remove a background that contains one dominant color.

Choosing the best channel from this pop-up menu usually involves a lot of trial and error. I'll show you how I usually figure out which color would be most effective for different images.

First of all, if the color you would like to work with matches one of the components of your image (red, green, or blue in RGB mode), then the choice is pretty straightforward—to work on someone's blue eyes, just work on the blue channel. But what if you want to work on an area that is yellow and your image is in RGB mode? Well, to find out what to do, I usually hold down the Command key (Macintosh) or Ctrl key (Windows) and press the number keys on my keyboard (1–3 for RGB mode, 1–4 for CMYK mode); this will display the different color channels. You'll want to look for the channel that separates the area you're interested in from the areas surrounding it (**Figures 12.29** to **12.31**). When you find the one that looks best, choose its name from the Blend If pop-up menu in the Layer Style dialog box. Once you've found the best channel, glance up at the top of your document and you'll see the name of the channel you are viewing right next to the name of the document.

Now that you have a general feeling for how the blending sliders work, let's take a look at some of the things we can do with them.

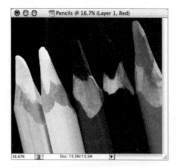

Figure 12.29 Red channel. (© 2002 Stockbyte, www.stockbyte.com)

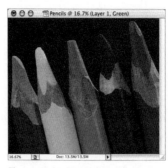

Figure 12.30 Green channel.

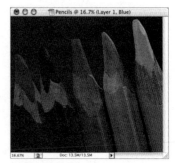

Figure 12.31 Blue channel.

Enhancing Clouds

When you choose Filter > Render > Clouds, you'll get great-looking clouds, but there is one problem—you can't see through them. You'll probably want to see through the dark parts of the clouds, so hold Option (Mac), or Alt (Windows) and double-click the name of the layer your clouds are on. By moving the upper left slider in, you're going to make the dark parts of the clouds disappear so you can see the underlying image. To make the edges of the clouds blend into the underlying image, hold down the Option key (Macintosh) or Alt key (Windows) and split the upper left slider into two parts. Now by experimenting with the halves of the slider, you'll be able to create the look of fog, faint clouds, or dense clouds (**Figures 12.32** to **12.35**). This technique also works great with photos of real clouds. You can even transform Photoshop's Clouds filter into a hurricane by applying the Twirl filter to it (Filter > Distort > Twirl).

WARNING

If you've chosen a color from the pop-up menu before applying the blending sliders, be sure to flatten your image when converting it to another color mode (RGB to CMYK, for example). The appearance of unflattened layers will change because the blending settings will no longer affect the same color channels. If you apply the sliders to the red channel (first choice in the menu) and then convert the image to CMYK mode, the same slider settings will now be applied to the cyan channel (because it's the first choice in the menu). The image will not look the same because the cyan channel doesn't contain the same information that was in the red channel.

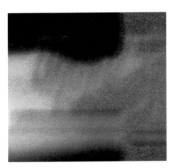

Figure 12.32 Original image.

Figure 12.33 After creating a new layer and applying the Clouds and Twirl filters.

Figure 12.34 Result of discarding the dark area of the clouds by using the blending sliders.

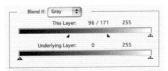

Figure 12.35 Settings used on preceding image.

I'll show you a more customizable version of lightning in Chapter 13: Enhancement.

Homemade Lightning

If you want to play Zeus and create your own lightning, you'll need to start with some clouds; so create a new layer, and then reset your foreground and background colors to their default colors (just press D). Next, choose Filter > Render > Clouds. This will give you clouds, but it won't look anything like lightning, as **Figure 12.36** reveals.

To get closer to something that resembles lightning, choose Filter > Render > Difference Clouds. Then go to the Image menu and choose Adjust > Invert. This should get you a little bit closer to lightning (**Figure 12.37**), but we still have a few steps before it looks electric.

If you remove all the dark information from this image, it might resemble lightning. So hold Option (Mac), or Alt (Windows) and double-click the layer, then pull in the upper left slider. You'll want to hold down the Option key (Macintosh) or Alt key (Windows) to split the slider into two pieces. Move the right half of the slider all the way to the right edge, as far as you can move it. Then grab the left edge of the slider and start moving it to the right until the lightning looks appropriate for the image, as in **Figure 12.38**. You'll have to move it almost all the way across.

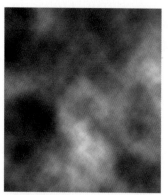

Figure 12.36 The Clouds filter is the starting point for creating artificial lightning.

Figure 12.37 Result of applying Difference Clouds and then inverting.

Figure 12.38 Result of removing all the dark information.

Making the Changes Permanent

The problem with the blending sliders is that they are just settings attached to a layer, and Photoshop doesn't provide an obvious way to permanently apply their effects. Well, if you've used only the top sliders, there is an easy way to get Photoshop to permanently delete the hidden areas. To do this, create a brand-new empty layer, and then move that empty layer underneath the layer that is using the blending sliders. Then all you have to do is merge those two layers. To do that, click on the layer that is using the blending sliders, go to the side menu on the Layers palette, and choose Merge Down. By doing this, Photoshop will permanently delete the areas that were transparent. This can be nice if your client requested the layered file, but you don't want them to know how you did it! (See **Figures 12.39** and **12.40**.)

Figure 12.39 To permanently apply blending slider settings, merge the layer with an empty one.

Layer Masks

Now let's take a look at my favorite method for creating collages, layer masks. By adding a layer mask to a layer, you can control exactly where that layer is transparent and where it's opaque. You'll find that layer masks are used to create most high-end images—this feature really separates the beginners from the pros. But there's no reason why you can't be as adept at layer masks as the most seasoned veteran. It just takes a little time and sweat.

Figure 12.40 Result.

Creating a Layer Mask

You can add a layer mask to the active layer by clicking on the icon second from the left at the bottom of the Layers palette (it looks like a rectangle with a circle inside it). Once you click this icon, you'll notice that the layer you're working on contains two thumbnail images in the palette. The one on the left is its normal preview thumbnail; the one on the right is the layer mask thumbnail. The layer mask is not empty (empty looks like a checkerboard, right?); instead, it's full of white. After adding a layer mask, you can edit it by painting across the image window with any painting tool. Even though this would usually change the image, you're really just editing the layer mask; it just isn't visible on the main screen. The color you paint with (which is really a shade of gray) determines what happens to the image. Painting with black will make areas disappear and painting with white will bring back the areas again. And remember, because you are using a painting tool you can choose a hard- or soft-edged brush to control what the edge looks like (**Figures 12.41** and **12.42**).

Figure 12.41 Layers palette view.

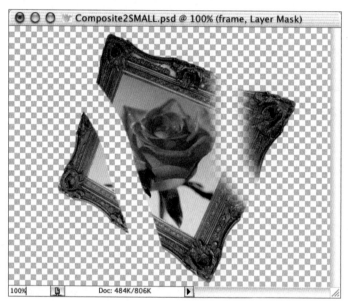

Figure 12.42 The softness of your brush determines how soft the edge of the image will appear. (original image © 2002 Stockbyte, www.stockbyte.com)

What's nice about a layer mask is that it doesn't permanently delete areas; it just makes them temporarily disappear. If you paint with white, you'll be able to bring back areas that are transparent. This can be helpful if you're doing a very quick job for a client who wants to see a general concept. You can do just a very crude job of getting rid of the backgrounds of images, and then later on go back in and refine that layer mask to get it to look just right.

Hiding Selected Areas

If a selection is present when adding a layer mask, Photoshop will automatically fill the nonselected areas of the layer mask with black so the image is visible in the selected area only (**Figures 12.43** and **12.44**). Or, if you'd like to hide the selected area and show the rest of the image, hold the Option key (Macintosh) or Alt key (Windows) when you click the layer mask icon. You can see exactly what Photoshop has done by glancing at the layer mask thumbnail in the Layers palette (**Figure 12.45**).

Figure 12.45 Layers palette view.

Figure 12.43 Make a selection before adding a layer mask. (© 2002 Stockbyte, www.stockbyte.com)

Figure 12.44 Result of adding a layer mask.

If you choose Add Layer Mask from the Layer menu instead of just using the icon in the palette, you will be offered some choices:

▶ **Reveal Selection**—Hides the nonselected areas, giving you the same result as using the layer mask icon in the Layers palette.

▶ **Hide Selection**—Hides only the areas that are currently selected, leaving the non-selected areas visible.

▶ **Reveal All**—Does not hide any areas of the layer.

▶ **Hide All**—Hides the entire layer.

NOTES

The only layer (active or otherwise) that you can't add a layer mask to is the background image. But you can change its name to make it become a regular layer (double-click to do this), and then add a layer mask.

When a selection is present, you can Option-click (Macintosh) or Alt-click (Windows) the layer mask icon in the Layers palette to add a layer mask and hide the selected areas. If no selection is present, Option-click (Macintosh) or Alt-click (Windows) the icon to hide the entire image.

Paste Into

If there is a selection present when you're pasting an image into your document, you can choose Edit > Paste Into (instead of Edit > Paste) to automatically create a layer mask. This layer mask will make the image show up only in the area that was selected. You can also hold down the Option key (Macintosh) or Alt key (Windows) and choose Edit > Paste Into to hide the selected areas. If you choose Select > All before choosing Paste Into, Photoshop will create a layer mask and reveal the entire image. You can also hold down the Option key (Macintosh) or Alt key (Windows) and choose Paste Into to hide the entire image.

Disabling a Layer Mask

After you've created a layer mask, you can temporarily disable it by Shift-clicking its thumbnail in the Layers palette (**Figures 12.46** to **12.48**). With each click you will toggle the layer mask on or off. This is a great help when you want to see what the layer would look like if you didn't have a layer mask restricting where it shows up.

Figure 12.46 Layer mask active.

Figure 12.47 Layer mask disabled.

Figure 12.48 Layers palette view.

Switching Between the Layer Mask and the Image

Now that you have two thumbnails attached to a layer, you have to be able to determine if you are working on the layer mask or the main image. If you look at the layer mask icon right after you've created one, you'll notice an extra outline around its edge (**Figures 12.49** and **12.50**). That border indicates what you're working on. If you want to work on the main image instead of the layer mask, click the image thumbnail in the Layers palette. The outline will appear around the image thumbnail indicating that you are editing the main image instead of the layer mask. To work on the layer mask again, just click its icon and the outline will move.

There is another way to get a visual indication of whether you're working on the main image or the layer mask. If you look just to the left of the image thumbnail, you'll see a paintbrush icon if you are working on the main image, or the layer mask thumbnail image if you're working on a layer mask.

Viewing a Layer Mask

You can also view the layer mask in the main image window. To do this, hold down the Option key (Macintosh) or Alt key (Windows) and click on the layer mask thumbnail (**Figure 12.51**). You'll see it looks just like a grayscale image, and you can actually paint right on this image. I use this a lot when I get someone else's document, or when I open an old document I worked on months ago and can't remember exactly what I did in the layer mask. To stop viewing the layer mask, just Option-click (Macintosh) or Alt-click (Windows) its icon a second time.

Shades of Gray

Photoshop treats a layer mask as if it were a grayscale document. That means that you can use any editing tool that is available to a grayscale image. Areas that are full of pure black will become transparent, pure white areas will be completely opaque, and areas that contain shades of gray will become partially transparent. Painting with 20% gray

NOTES

To quickly switch between editing the layer mask and editing the main image, use the following keyboard commands.

▸ Command-~ (Macintosh) or Ctrl-~ (Windows) to work on the image
▸ Command-\ (Macintosh) or Ctrl-\ (Windows) to work on the layer mask

Figure 12.49 Editing the main image.

Figure 12.50 Editing the layer mask.

Figure 12.51 Viewing the layer mask in the main image window.

You can view a layer mask as a color overlay (just like Quick Mask mode) by Shift-Option-clicking (Macintosh) or Shift-Alt-clicking (Windows) on the layer mask icon, or by just typing \ (backslash).

in a layer mask will lower the opacity of that area to 80%. So using a painting tool with an opacity setting of 80% will produce the same result as painting with 100% opacity and then adding a layer mask that is full of 20% gray.

Filling Areas

Because Photoshop treats layer masks as if they are grayscale documents, you can create selections and fill those areas with white or black to hide or show the contents of a layer. To fill a selected area with the current foreground color (which is black by default), press Option-Delete (Macintosh) or Alt-Backspace (Windows). To fill a selected area with the current background color (white by default), press Command-Delete (Macintosh) or Ctrl-Backspace (Windows). This is nice because it frees you from having to use the painting tools.

Using Gradients

The most common way to make one image fade into another is to add a layer mask and then use the Gradient tool. In a layer mask, areas that are pure black become completely transparent and areas that are pure white are completely opaque. Shades of gray in a layer mask will make the image become partially transparent. So, if you would like one image to fade into another, apply a gradient to a layer mask with the Gradient tool set to Black, White (**Figures 12.52** to **12.54**).

Figure 12.52 Image before adding a layer mask. (both images © 2002 Stockbyte, www.stockbyte.com)

If you try to apply the gradient a second time, you might run into a few problems. If you apply the gradient from right to left one time, and then immediately after that you apply a second gradient in the other direction, the second gradient will completely obstruct the first one. To combine two gradients, set the Gradient tool to Foreground To Transparent and make sure the foreground color is set to black. Then you should be able to apply the Gradient tool as many times as you want within a layer mask, and it simply adds to what was already in the layer mask (**Figures 12.55** to **12.58**).

Figure 12.53 Result of applying a gradient to a layer mask.

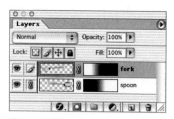

Figure 12.54 Layers palette view.

Figure 12.55 First gradient.

Figure 12.56 Second gradient using Foreground To Background setting.

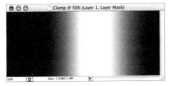

Figure 12.57 Second gradient using Foreground To Transparent setting.

Figure 12.58 Both ends of the ruler image blend into the underlying image (the C-clamp) because two gradients were used.

Applying Filters

After painting in a layer mask, you can enhance the result by applying filters to it (**Figures 12.59** to **12.62**). Choose Filter > Distort, and then select something like Ripple. Then, instead of having a really smooth transition, there will be some texture in it.

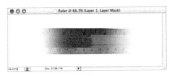

Figure 12.59 Original image.

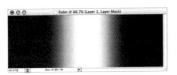

Figure 12.60 Original layer mask.

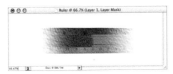

Figure 12.61 Result of applying the Ripple filter to the layer mask.

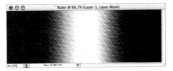

Figure 12.62 Modified layer mask.

If you want the edge of an image to fade out slowly, you can choose Filter > Blur > Gaussian Blur. You can blur a layer mask as many times as you'd like; each time you blur it, the edge will become softer (**Figures 12.63** to **12.65**).

Figure 12.63 Dartboard image contains a pure black and pure white layer mask. (© 2002 Stockbyte, www.stockbyte.com)

Figure 12.64 Apply the Gaussian Blur filter to a layer mask to give it softer edges.

Figure 12.65 Result of blurring the layer mask.

You can also expand or contract the areas that are transparent by choosing Minimum or Maximum from the Filter > Other menu (**Figures 12.66** to **12.68**). The Minimum filter will make more areas transparent, while the Maximum filter will make fewer areas transparent.

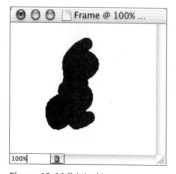

Figure 12.66 Original image.

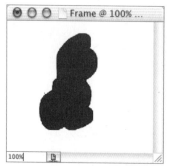

Figure 12.67 Result of applying the Minimum filter.

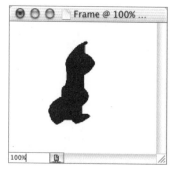

Figure 12.68 Result of applying the Maximum filter.

Interesting Edges

To create a rippled-edge effect on your mask, try this out. Open the photograph you want to apply the effect to, and make a selection with the Marquee tool. Make sure your selection is a little inside the edge of the photograph (so there's room for our effect). To get the photograph to show up only where the rectangular selection is, click the layer mask icon at the bottom of the Layers palette.

Now you can distort the edge of the photo by using any filter you'd like (**Figures 12.69** to **12.71**). For now, just use one of the filters under the Filter > Distort menu, such as Ripple, Twirl, or Polar Coordinates.

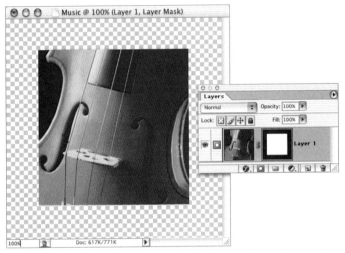

Figure 12.69 Result of adding a layer mask to limit where the photo shows up. (© 2002 Stockbyte, www.stockbyte.com)

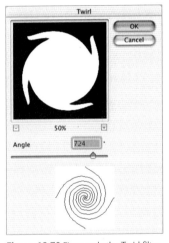

Figure 12.70 First apply the Twirl filter.

Once you're happy with how the edge looks, you might want to add some other effects, such as a black border around our shape. There's a trick for that, too. Choose Layer > Layer Style > Inner Glow (**Figures 12.72** and **12.73**). Now click on the color swatch to pick the color you would like to use and set the Mode pop-up menu to Normal. To get the color to appear around the edge of the image only, be sure Edge is chosen at the bottom of the dialog box. Now you can experiment with the Opacity, Size, and Choke settings to fine-tune the result. If you are having trouble getting the edge to completely show up, try increasing the Opacity and Choke settings. You don't have to restrict yourself to the Inner Glow effect, so experiment with the other layer styles until you find your favorite.

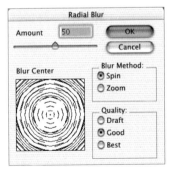

Figure 12.71 Then apply the Radial Blur filter.

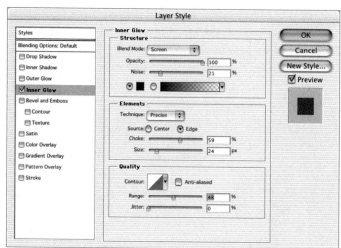

Figure 12.72 Result of adding an Inner Glow layer effect.

Figure 12.73 Inner Glow settings used to create the border.

Adjusting with Levels

You can also adjust the appearance of a layer mask (as long as it contains shades of gray) by choosing Image > Adjust > Levels. The sliders in the Levels dialog box (**Figure 12.74**) will do the following to your image:

▶ **Upper left slider**—Forces the darkest shades of gray to black, which will make more areas transparent.

▶ **Upper right slider**—Forces the brightest shades of gray to white, which will make more areas opaque.

▶ **Middle slider**—Changes the transition from black to white and therefore changes the transition from opaque to transparent.

▶ **Lower left slider**—Lightens the dark shades of gray, which will make transparent areas appear more opaque.

▶ **Lower right slider**—Darkens the bright shades of gray, which will make opaque areas appear more transparent.

Image as Layer Mask

You can achieve interesting transition effects by pasting scanned images into a layer mask (**Figures 12.75** and **12.76**). I like to run off to the art supply store, purchase

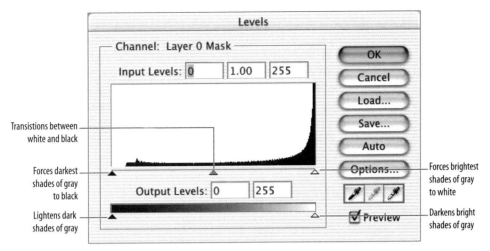

Transitions between white and black

Forces darkest shades of gray to black

Lightens dark shades of gray

Forces brightest shades of gray to white

Darkens bright shades of gray

Figure 12.74 The Levels dialog box.

interesting handmade papers, and spatter a bunch of ink on them using paintbrushes. Then, to get the image into a layer mask, I scan the paper, select the entire image by choosing Select > Select All, and then copy the image by choosing Edit > Copy. After I've done that, I close the scanned image and switch over to the image I would like to use it in. Next, I click on the layer I would like to work on and add a layer mask. In order to paste something into a layer mask, you must be viewing the layer mask. That means you must Option-click (Macintosh) or Alt-click (Windows) the layer mask before pasting something into it. To stop viewing the layer mask, just Option-click (Macintosh) or Alt-click (Windows) its thumbnail again.

NOTES

To quickly paste something into a layer mask, press the \ key to view the layer mask, type Command-V (Macintosh) or Ctrl-V (Windows) to paste the image, and finally type \ again to stop viewing the layer mask. This technique does not view the layer mask as it would normally appear; it shows up as a color overlay.

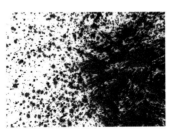

Figure 12.75 Scanned image to be used as a layer mask.

Figure 12.76 Two images blended together using scanned image as layer mask. (© 2002 Stockbyte, www.stockbyte.com)

Using the Move Tool

After you have created the perfect layer mask, you might want to start rearranging your document by using the Move tool. You have three choices: you can move just the layer, just the layer mask, or both at the same time. The link symbol between the layer mask and image thumbnails determines what the Move tool will actually move. If the link symbol is present (that's the default), the layer and layer mask will move together (**Figures 12.77 to 12.79**).

Figure 12.77 Original image. (images © 2002 Stockbyte, www.stockbyte.com)

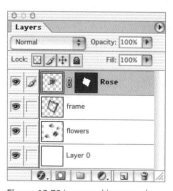

Figure 12.78 Layer and layer mask thumbnails linked together.

Figure 12.79 Rose layer and layer mask moved together.

If you turn off the link symbol (by clicking it), then you'll only be moving whatever has the extra-outline border around it. That means if the layer mask has it, you'll just be moving that around the screen. And if the main image has it, you'll move just the main image around the screen, leaving the layer mask in its original position (**Figures 12.80** and **12.81**). If part of the layer mask lines up with another part of the image, you'll want to move just the layer and not the layer mask (**Figures 12.82** and **12.83**).

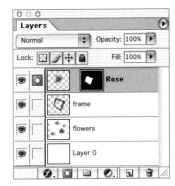

Figure 12.81 When the link symbol is missing, the outlined border (layer mask) determines what will get moved.

Figure 12.80 Moving just the layer mask, leaving the main image stationary.

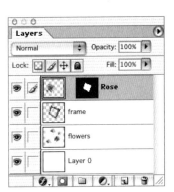

Figure 12.83 When the link symbol is missing, the outlined border (layer) determines what will get moved.

Figure 12.82 Moving the main image, leaving the layer mask stationary.

355

Load as Selection

Once you have perfected a layer mask, you might need to select the areas that are visible in order to add a border or perform another effect. You can do this in many ways. The fastest method is to Command-click (Macintosh) or Ctrl-click (Windows) the layer mask thumbnail, as demonstrated in **Figures 12.84** and **12.85**. If there is already a selection present, you can Shift-Command-click (Macintosh) or Shift-Ctrl-click (Windows) to add to the selection; Option-Command-click (Macintosh) or Alt-Ctrl-click (Windows) to subtract from it; or Shift-Option-Command-click (Macintosh) or Shift-Alt-Ctrl-click (Windows) to intersect the selection. Or, if you are not very good at remembering a bunch of keyboard commands, you can Control-click (Mac) or right-click (Windows) the layer mask thumbnail to get a menu of options.

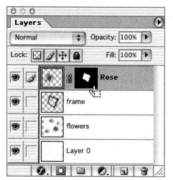

Figure 12.84 Command-click (Macintosh) or Ctrl-click (Windows) the layer mask thumbnail to select the areas that are visible.

Figure 12.85 Result of Command-clicking (Macintosh) or Ctrl-clicking (Windows) on the "x" layer's layer mask thumbnail.

Masking Layer Styles

If you have a layer style (like bevel and emboss) applied to a layer that contains a layer mask, you'll find that the mask changes where the style shows up (see **Figures 12.86** and **12.87**). If you'd rather have the layer mask hide the style instead of changing where it shows up, then hold Option (Mac), or Alt (Windows) and double-click on the layer to access the Layer Style dialog box (**Figure 12.88**). Turning on Photoshop 7.0's new Layer Mask Hides Effects check box will cause the layer mask to hide the original style position instead of changing where it shows up (**Figure 12.89**).

Figure 12.86 The original image included a layer style.

Figure 12.87 Applying a layer mask changes where the style appears.

Figure 12.89 Using the Layer Mask Hides Effect check box causes the layer mask to hide the layer style.

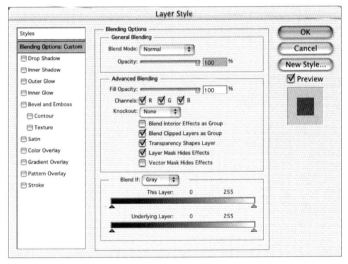

Figure 12.88 The Layer styles dialog box.

NOTES

In previous versions of Photoshop, you had to unlink the mask from the layer in order to have it mask the effects. If you wanted to reposition the mask without moving the layer and didn't want it to mask the effects, then you'd have to leave the layer mask linked to the layer and then choose Select > Select All before using the move tool to move the mask.

Converting the Blending Sliders into a Layer Mask

Earlier in this chapter we talked about making areas of a layer transparent using the blending sliders in the Layer Style dialog box. Occasionally, you might need to turn off the sliders and create a layer mask that produces the same result. (Why? You might want to be able to edit the layer mask using painting tools and filters instead of just the blending sliders.) To accomplish this, you'll need to go through a multi-step process.

First, create a new empty layer below the layer that is using the blending sliders. Next, click the layer above it (the one that uses the blending sliders) and type Option-Command-E (Macintosh) or Alt-Ctrl-E (Windows). This deposits information into the layer that does not use the blending sliders, but produces the same results (permanently deleting the transparent areas).

Now you can hold Option (Mac), or Alt (Windows) and double-click the layer that uses the blending sliders, then set all the sliders back to default positions so they are no longer affecting the layer. Then, to add a layer mask that produces the same result, Command-click (Macintosh) or Ctrl-click (Windows) the layer directly below the one that was using the sliders (to select the non-transparent areas of the layer), and finally click the layer mask icon on the layer that used the sliders to add a layer mask based on that selection (**Figures 12.90** and **12.91**).

Figure 12.90 Result of typing Option-Command-E (Macintosh) or Alt-Ctrl-E (Windows) with an empty layer.

Figure 12.91 Layer mask added after Command-clicking (Mac) or Ctrl-clicking (Windows) the merged layer.

NOTES

A quick way to remove a layer mask is to drag its thumbnail to the trash can icon that appears in the Layers palette.

Remove Layer Mask

If you know you will no longer need to edit a layer mask and would like to permanently delete the areas that are transparent, you can choose one of the options from the Layer > Remove Layer Mask menu (**Figures 12.92** and **12.93**). When you do this, you will be presented with two choices.

▶ **Apply**—Removes the layer mask and deletes all transparent areas.

▶ **Discard**—Removes the layer mask and brings the image back into full view.

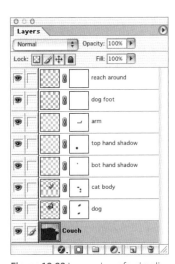

Figure 12.92 Layers view of a simplified version of the "Dog & Cat" image shown at the beginning of this chapter. I removed over a dozen adjustment layers, all of which had layer masks attached to them.

Figure 12.93 Final "Dog & Cat" image. (Original image courtesy of Robert Bowen Studio, Sony Electronics, Inc., and Lowe & Partners/SMS. Photography by Howard Berman)

Vector Masks

Vector Masks allow you to control which area of a layer will be visible, by using an easily editable, smooth-shaped, crisp-edged path. This capability was first added in Photoshop 6.0 and it represented a rather radical shift from what was possible in the past. Before 6.0, everything created in Photoshop was made out of pixels, where the resolution of the file determined how large the pixels would be when printed. If those pixels were large enough, then the image would appear jaggy when printed. But with Vector Masks, you can create a very low resolution (read: jaggy) image and still get a smooth-shaped, crisp-edged transition between the content of a layer and the underlying image.

Adding a Vector Mask

The simplest way to add a Vector Mask is to choose Layer > Add Vector Mask > Reveal All. After you choose that option, the layer that is active will have two thumbnail

NOTES

Vector Masks were known as Layer Clipping Paths in previous versions of Photoshop.

To change the options for a shape, click on the shape with the solid-arrow tool and then change the settings that appear in the Options bar.

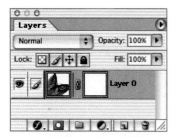

Figure 12.94 After adding a Vector Mask, you will see two thumbnail images in the Layers palette.

images in the Layers palette (**Figure 12.94**). It should look like you just added a layer mask. The only difference is that with a layer mask, you paint with shades of gray to control which areas of a layer will be hidden or visible, whereas with a Vector Mask, you define the area that will be visible using a path.

The easiest way to define where the image should be visible is to use one of the shape tools. Before you start creating shapes, be sure to take a peek at the settings in the Options bar. You should find four options available on the left side of the Options bar when a layer that contains a Vector Mask is active. The leftmost choice allows you to create a shape to define where the image should be visible (**Figure 12.95**). The second choice will allow you to define a shape where the image should be hidden (**Figure 12.96**). The third choice will limit the areas that are already visible, so they only show up within the shape you draw (**Figure 12.97**). And the last choice will invert the visibility of the area inside the shape you draw, making visible areas hidden and hidden areas visible (**Figure 12.98**).

You can also use any of the Pen tools to create and modify a Vector Mask. If you're not already familiar with the Pen tools, then start out with the Freeform Pen tool because it allows you to create a path by drawing a freeform shape, much like the Lasso tool allows you to create a selection.

Figure 12.95 This shape defines where the image is visible.

Figure 12.96 The shape that was added is being used to hide part of the image.

Figure 12.97 The shape that was added is being used to limit where the image is visible.

Figure 12.98 The shape that was added is being used to invert the visibility of the image.

Using the Pen Tool

The Pen tool can be a bit tricky to learn because it doesn't work like anything else in Photoshop. Instead of creating shapes out of a grid of solid-colored squares (pixels), the Pen tool creates shapes from a collection of points and directional handles (**Figure 12.99**). If you've used Adobe Illustrator, then you might be familiar with paths, but just in case you're not, let's take a look at how they work.

First off, you'll need to think of the shape that you'd like to create as being made of a series of curves and straight lines that connect to one another. Visualize tracing around the shape and looking for transitions where one curve connects with another. That might be in an area where a very tight curve starts to become more gradual, like on some coffee cup handles (**Figure 12.100**). At each of these transitions, you'll want to click with the Pen tool to add a point.

When adding a point you'll need to click and drag if you are looking to create a smooth curve. If you don't drag, you'll end up with a sharp corner instead of a curve. When you click and drag, you'll add a point and pull a set of directional handles out of that point. The angle of the directional handles determines what direction the path will go when it leaves that handle, so make sure it points in the direction you want the curve to go in (**Figure 12.101**). I think of it as if you were walking around the edge of the shape using baby steps. Just think of what direction would you take for your first step—that's the same direction the directional handle should point when entering and exiting a point. When you first pull out a set of handles, they will both move at the same time and act a bit like a seesaw in that their angles will create a straight line that goes all the way through the point.

The lengths of the directional handles determine the overall shape of the curve (**Figure 12.102**). Getting the length of the handles to be just right is difficult, because the curve won't show up until the next handle is made, and its

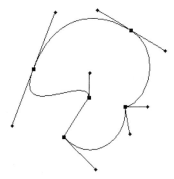

Figure 12.99 A path is made from many points and directional handles.

Figure 12.100 The curve of the handle changes from a tight curve to a more gradual one right where a point would be needed. (© 2002 Stockbyte, www.stockbyte.com)

handles will also influence the shape of the curve—so for now, keep your handles short.

Once you've added the next point and got the angle of the handle that points towards the last point positioned correctly, it'll be time to adjust the length of the handles. I find it easiest to adjust the handle lengths by holding the Command key (Macintosh) or Ctrl key (Windows) and dragging the middle of the curve that appears between the two points you just created (**Figure 12.103**). It's a little tricky, but by pulling on the middle of the curve, you should be able to get the curve to fit the shape you were attempting to create. If you find that you just can't get it to become what you need, then one of the directional handles must be pointing in the wrong direction. If you continue to hold down the Command key (Macintosh) or Ctrl key (Windows), then you should be able to reposition the directional handles as well.

On occasion, you'll find that you need one curve to abruptly change direction instead of smoothly flow into another curve. When that happens, remember that the directional handles determine which direction your path will go when it leaves a point. That means you'll need the two handles that come out of a point to be at radically different angles. You can accomplish that by holding the Option key (Macintosh) or Alt key (Windows) and dragging one of the handles that protrude from the point you just created (**Figure 12.104**).

Figure 12.101 Click and drag to create a smooth curve.

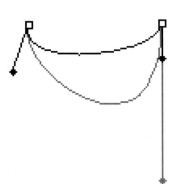

Figure 12.102 The length of the directional handles determines the overall shape of the curve.

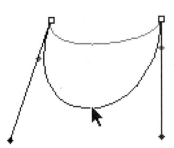

Figure 12.103 Hold Command or Ctrl and drag the curve to adjust the length of the directional handles.

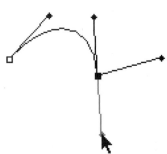

Figure 12.104 Hold Option or Alt to change the angle of one directional handle without affecting the other handle connected to that point.

Sometimes you will need to have a curve end at an abrupt corner, where the next portion of the shape will be a straight line. In that case, you'll need a handle on the side of the point that points towards the curve, and no handle on the side of the straight line. To accomplish that, right after adding the point and pulling out the handles, Option-click (Macintosh) or Alt-click (Windows) the point and Photoshop will retract the handle on the open end of the path (**Figure 12.105**).

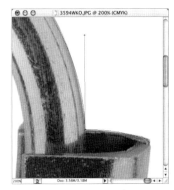

Figure 12.105 A curve ending in an abrupt corner.

By combining these ideas you should be able to create just about any smooth shape you can think of. But since it's not an overly natural process, it might take you a while to master using the Pen tool. If you don't feel like tackling it right now, then stick with the shape tools and the Freeform Pen tool.

If you already have a path saved in your file (it will show up in the Paths palette), you can use it as a Vector Mask. Just make sure the layer you'd like to apply it to is active (you can't add one to the background layer), click on the name of the path in the Paths palette, and then choose Layer > Add Vector Mask > Current Path. That will allow you to use any paths that are included with stock photos you have purchased.

Disabling the Vector Mask

After you have created a Vector Mask, you can temporarily disable it by Shift-clicking its thumbnail in the Layers palette (**Figures 12.106** and **12.107**). With each click you will toggle the Vector Mask on and off. This is a great help when you want to see what a layer would look like if you didn't have a Vector Mask restricting where it shows up.

Figure 12.106 Vector Mask active.

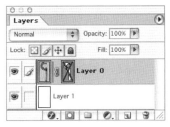

Figure 12.107 Vector Mask disabled.

Using the Move Tool

When you use the Move tool to reposition a layer, you'll notice that the layer and the Vector Mask move together (**Figures 12.108** to **12.110**). If you turn off the link symbol (by clicking it), you'll leave the Vector Mask alone and just move the image (**Figure 12.111**).

If you'd like to move the Vector Mask and leave the image stationary, use the solid arrow tool that appears directly above the Pen tools (**Figure 12.112**).

Transforming the Vector Mask

The Edit > Transform commands are very useful when working on a Vector Mask. Since the path is made from a collection of points and directional handles (instead of pixels), scaling, rotating and other transformations will not degrade the quality of the shape. All you have to do is make sure the path is visible before you choose Transform Path from the Edit menu. You can toggle the visibility of a Vector Mask by clicking its thumbnail in the Layers palette.

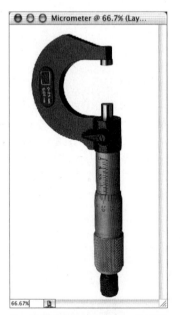

Figure 12.108 Original Image. (© 2002 Stockbyte, www.stockbyte.com)

Figure 12.109 Layer and Vector Mask moved together.

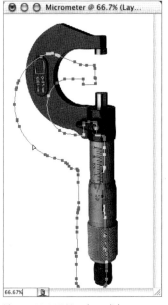

Figure 12.110 Layer and Vector Mask linked together

Figure 12.111 Vector Mask left stationary while the layer is repositioned.

Figure 12.112 Use the solid arrow tool to reposition a Vector Mask.

Removing the Vector Mask

If you find that you'd like to remove the Vector Mask from your image, just choose Layer > Delete Vector Mask, or drag its thumbnail to the trash can that appears at the bottom of the Layers palette. You can also convert a Vector Mask into a layer mask by choosing Layer > Rasterize > Vector Mask. But be aware that you'll lose the crisp-edged, smooth look of the path, and any transformations applied to the layer mask will cause it to appear blurry.

Saving Vector Data

If you plan on saving your image and using it in a page layout program (instead of using it for a Web site), then you'll need to be careful about how you save it; otherwise, the crisp edge of your path may be lost. Remember when I said that a path is different than pixels in that it's made out of points and directional handles? Well, technically, that's known as vector information, whereas images made from pixels are known as raster information. In order to

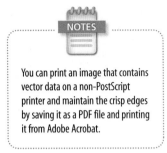

You can print an image that contains vector data on a non-PostScript printer and maintain the crisp edges by saving it as a PDF file and printing it from Adobe Acrobat.

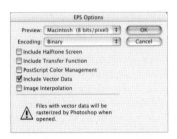

Figure 12.113 Turn on the Include Vector Data check box when saving an image for print-based publishing.

maintain the crisp edges of your paths, you'll need to save your image in the EPS or PDF file formats (which support vector data). Not only that, but you'll have to turn on the Include Vector Data check box (**Figure 12.113**) when saving your file (this option only shows up *after* you click the Save button). There's one last thing: your paths will only print with crisp edges if you print to a PostScript output device like a $500+ laser printer. Most inkjet printers don't understand PostScript, so your image has the potential of appearing jaggy on those.

Clipping Paths

You can also assign a path to a document, as opposed to a single layer. A clipping path will limit which areas of an image will show up and print in a page layout program (**Figures 12.114** and **12.115**). These paths are simply known as clipping paths. To create one, use the Pen or a shape tool to create a path, and then choose Window > Show Paths to open the Paths palette. Next, double-click the name of the path and assign it a name. Then choose Clipping Path from the side menu of the Paths palette (**Figure 12.116**). When prompted, be sure to enter a Flatness setting. When the image is printed, it will be converted into a polygon made out of straight lines of identical length. The Flatness setting will determine the length of those lines. Low settings product short lines, which require more memory and processing time to output. If you use too low of a setting, then your printer might run out of memory when attempting to output your image. The more complex your path is (lots of points and directional handles), the higher a flatness setting is necessary to avoid printing problems. In general, I use a setting between 3 and 10 depending on the complexity of the path I'm using. After you've assigned a clipping path to an image, you'll need to save it in the TIFF or EPS file format in order for it to be understood by a page layout program.

Figure 12.116 Choose Clipping Path from the side menu of the Paths palette.

Figure 12.114 Image imported into a page layout program without a clipping path. (© 2002 Stockbyte, www.stockbyte.com)

Figure 12.115 Image imported into a page layout program with clipping path.

Closing Thoughts

I hope that you get as much of a kick out of creating collages as I do. It's one of those things that never get old; I can always count on another surprise waiting for me around the corner. We always have bets going on in our office about whether or not certain images have been "Photo-shopped." I'm often surprised to find out that what looks like a still frame from *America's Funniest Home Videos* is really a studio shot collaged in Photoshop.

I also hope that you'll devote some serious time to playing around with the three methods for collaging (grouping layers, blending sliders, and layer masks), as well as learning how to use the Vector Masks. Both separately and together, they will give you enormous amounts of freedom to do wondrous and strange things with your images. And besides all that, it can impress the heck out of your boss or next client.

Keyboard Shortcuts

Function	Macintosh	Windows
Activate Layer instead of mask	Command-~	Ctrl-~
Activate Layer Mask instead of image	Command-\	Ctrl-\
Group Active layer to underlying layer	Command-G	Ctrl-G

Computer Graphics: Robert Bowen; Photography: Plamen Petkov

Computer Graphics: Robert Bowen; Photography: Steve Bronstein; A.D. James Rothwell

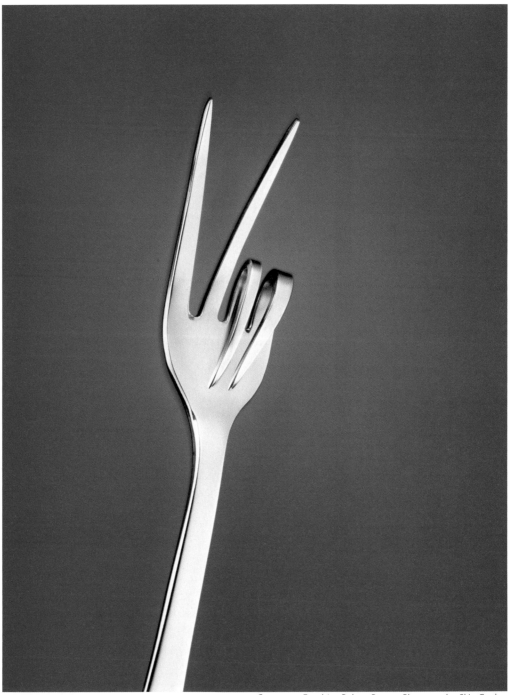

Computer Graphics: Robert Bowen; Photography: Skip Caplan

Courtesy of Gregg Lauer, www.gregglauer.com

13

Enhancement

© Steve Bronstein

NEW IN 7

We'll cover the five new blending modes and look at how the menu in which they reside has been reorganized. We'll also explore a bunch of techniques that are new to this version of the book.

I'm trying to free your mind, Neo. But I can only show you the door. You're the one that has to walk through it.

—Morpheus, from *The Matrix*

Enhancement

In this chapter we're going to explore a tantalizing variety of enhancement techniques. The truth is that you can't put a measuring stick on the many ways there are to enhance your image. The possibilities in Photoshop are beyond the horizon and only limited by your willingness to experiment. But I think I can get you off to a good start so that you can feel comfortable tackling most jobs.

In an effort to impose some order on this somewhat random collection of techniques, I've structured this chapter around Photoshop's blending modes. They are what you find at the top of the Layers palette and in many other areas. Blending modes comprise one of the most powerful features in Photoshop—and one of my personal favorites.

Since the Blending Modes menu draws the map for this chapter, let's just start at the top and work our way down the list. We'll take a detour or two on our way, but at least we'll know where we're headed.

With the release of Photoshop 7.0, Adobe has added five new blending modes and has reorganized the menu on which they reside. Let's start by taking a look at how they are organized; then we can jump in and start using them. The blending modes are divided into six categories (see **Figure 13.1**).

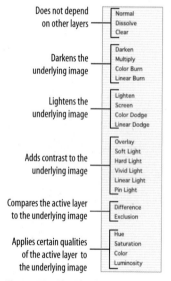

Figure 13.1 The Blending Modes menu is organized into six sections.

The Battalion of Blending Modes

Dissolve Mode

The first blending mode is called Dissolve, and while it might be useful to some, it's the one that I use the least out of the whole collection. It only affects areas that are partially transparent. All it does it take areas that are partially transparent and transform them into a scattered spray of solid pixels. As a result, those areas end up looking noisy (see **Figures 13.2.** and **13.3**). I do see the Dissolve blending mode used on occasion for product packaging, usually to create a noisy-looking shadow or glow around some text. You can accomplish this quite easily by adding a Drop Shadow or an Outer Glow layer style to a layer and setting its blending mode (in the Layer Style dialog box) to Dissolve (see **Figure 13.4**). It's not very often that I need this kind of a look, so let's move on and see what the other blending modes can do.

Figure 13.2 A drop shadow created in Photoshop's default blending mode.

Figure 13.3 The same drop shadow created in Dissolve mode.

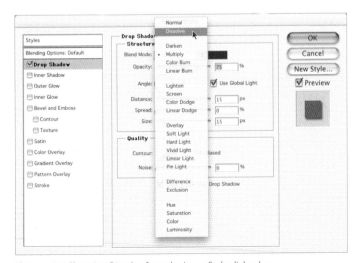

Figure 13.4 Choosing Dissolve from the Layer Style dialog box.

Darken Blending Modes

The blending modes on the second section of the menu are grouped together because they can only darken the underlying image. In all of these modes, white simply disappears, and in most of them, anything darker than white will darken the underlying image. Each mode has its own personality, so let's look at them one at a time.

Darken Mode

Darken compares the active layer to the underlying image and allows only those areas that are darker than that image to show up (**Figures 13.5, 13.6** and **13.7**). It's that simple when you're working on grayscale images, but if you try the same mode out on a color image, you might be surprised by the result.

Figure 13.5 The top layer. (© 2002 Stockbyte, www.stockbyte.com)

Figure 13.6 The bottom layer. (© 2002 Stockbyte, www.stockbyte.com)

Figure 13.7 Result of using Darken mode on the top layer.

Color images are usually made up of three components: Red, Green and Blue. Darken mode compares two layers by looking at red, green and blue individually. So, let's say you have a layer with some red in it that's made out of 230 Red, 50 Green and 30 Blue, and you have a layer above it that contains a blue color made from 50 Red, 55 Green and 200 Blue. The blue in the top layer would usually completely cover up the color below (**Figure 13.8**), but when you set the top layer to Darken mode, Photoshop will compare the red, green and blue components of each layer and use the darkest of each. In this case, it would see that the red information on the top layer is darker (50 versus 230, lower numbers mean less light). When comparing the green components, it would see that the bottom layer is darker, and it would see that the blue component is darkest on the bottom layer. So, once it picked the darkest of each, it would end up with 50 Red, 50 Green and 30 Blue, which would result in a dark yellow color (**Figure 13.9**). I don't usually think about the red, green and blue components of each layer when I'm using Darken mode, but I occasionally blame them when I don't get the result I am looking for.

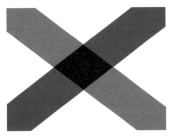

Figure 13.8 In Normal mode, the top layer obstructs your view of the underlying image.

Figure 13.9 In Darken mode, Photoshop uses the darkest of the red, green and blue components.

I mainly use Darken mode when I'm retouching an image, which we'll talk about in the next chapter, but for now, let's see how we might use it with Photoshop's filters. Let's say you've chosen Filter > Pixelate > Pointillize, but you don't like all the white areas that show up (**Figure 13.10**). If that's the case, you can choose Edit>Fade Pointillize immediately after applying the filter, and then you can tell Photoshop how to apply that filter to the original. If you choose Darken, Photoshop will compare the filtered result with the original and only allow the filter to darken the original, which should in effect get rid of the white areas (unless the original contained white) (**Figure 13.11**). I often use this technique after applying the Sharpen filter, because the bright halos it produces are oftentimes distracting. By using Darken mode, I can limit that filter so that it will create only dark halos.

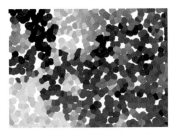

Figure 13.10 Result of applying the Pointillize filter.

Figure 13.11 Result of fading the Pointillize filter in Darken mode.

Multiply Mode

Of all the Darken blending modes, the one I use the most is Multiply. Multiply acts just like ink. To see what I mean, just imagine taking **Figure 13.12** and printing it on an inkjet printer. Then, imagine sending the sheet back through the printer and printing a second image on top of the first (**Figure 13.13**). All the second printing can do is darken the first because all an inkjet printer can do is add ink to the page (see **Figure 13.14**). Or, if you're a photographer, think about what happens when you sandwich two 35mm slides together. The second can only darken the first, right…? Well, it's the same concept. In this mode, white simply disappears. After all, how do you print white with an inkjet printer? You don't. Instead you just leave the paper alone. It's the same way in Multiply mode; white simply disappears. But anything darker than white will darken the underlying image.

This is a simple way to make text or graphics "overprint" on the underlying image instead of just covering it up (see **Figures 13.15** and **13.16**). In essence, using Multiply mode causes one layer to act like a Magic Marker on the layer

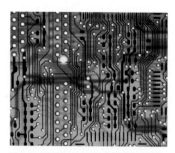

Figure 13.12 The first image to be printed. (© 2002 Stockbyte, www.stockbyte.com)

Figure 13.13 Image to be printed on the second pass. (© 2002 Stockbyte, www.stockbyte.com)

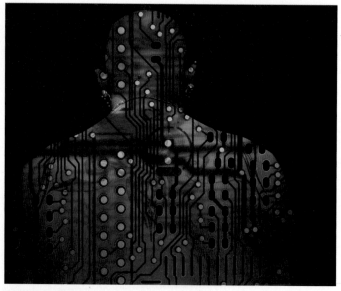

Figure 13.14 Result of combining the two images.

below. I find this mode to be extremely useful when working with images that contain natural shadows. Back in Chapter 11, we used this mode to make an existing shadow print on top of a new image (see **Figures 13.17** through **13.19**). You can also use it anytime you have scanned text or other graphics that you'd like to print on something else. The main thing you'll have to look out for is areas that are not completely white. Any area that is darker than white will darken the underlying image. This means that you'll occasionally need to choose Image > Adjustments > Levels and move the upper-right slider to make sure the background is pure white. As an example, let's say that I'd like to take the tattoo from **Figure 13.20** and make it look as if it were on **Figure 13.21** instead. I'd go about that by placing the tattoo on a layer above the second image, setting the blending mode of that layer to Multiply (**Figure 13.22**), choosing Image > Adjustments > Desaturate, and then adjusting the image using Levels until only the tattoo appeared and the background surrounding it disappeared (see **Figure 13.23**). If there ended up being a few areas that simply didn't disappear, then I'd switch to the Eraser tool to eradicate those trouble areas.

Figure 13.15 Top layer set to Normal mode. (© 2002 Stockbyte, www.stockbyte.com)

Figure 13.16 Top layer set to Multiply mode.

Figure 13.17 Image that contains two layers: subject and shadow. (© 2002 Stockbyte, www.stockbyte.com)

Figure 13.18 Image to overlay the shadow onto. (© 2002 Stockbyte, www.stockbyte.com)

Figure 13.19 Result of combining two images and setting the shadow layer to Multiply.

Figure 13.20 Tattoo to be transplanted to another image. (© 2002 Stockbyte, www.stockbyte.com)

Figure 13.21 Image that the tattoo will be applied to. (© 2002 Stockbyte, www.stockbyte.com)

Figure 13.22 Result of setting the tattoo layer to Multiply mode.

Figure 13.23 Result of desaturating and then adjusting the image Levels mode.

During my seminars, I usually end up talking about how both your screen and printer simulate a wide range of colors using just Red, Green and Blue light, or Cyan, Magenta and Yellow ink. To demonstrate this, I usually create an image that contains three circles—one per layer: one Cyan, one Magenta, and the third Yellow. The problem is that they don't act like ink when they overlap (**Figure 13.24**). So I simply set the blending mode for each layer to Multiply, and then everything works the way I want it to (**Figure 13.25**).

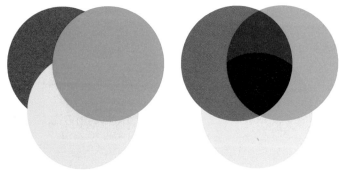

Figure 13.24 In Normal mode, the three circles don't interact with each other.

Figure 13.25 Result of setting each layer to Multiply mode.

Now let's see how we might be able to use Multiply in a project where you need to create a contour drawing out of a photograph (see **Figure 13.26**). To start out, open any image. (Faces work rather well.) Since we're going to end up with black lines and no color information, let's choose Image > Mode > Grayscale. Now let's start playing with Photoshop's filters to get our contours. Choose Filter > Stylize > Trace Contour, and move the slider around a bit just to see what happens (**Figure 13.27**). You'll see that Trace Contour puts a black line around the edge of a particular shade of gray. There are just two problems: First, the contours aren't usually smooth, and second, there's only one contour for the entire image. To fix the first problem, just smooth out your image by applying either the Gaussian Blur or the Median filter. The latter will require a little more effort, and that's where we can start

Figure 13.26 Left: The original image. Right: Result of conversion to a contour drawing. (© 2002 Stockbyte, www.stockbyte.com)

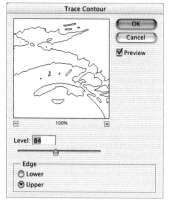

Figure 13.27 The Tract Contour dialog box.

putting the Multiply blending mode to work. Duplicate the layer enough times so that you end up with one layer for each contour that you'd like to end up with. (I want to end up with six, so I'll press Command-J (Macintosh), or Ctrl-J (Windows) five times to end up with six layers total.) Then apply the Trace Contour filter to each layer, using a different level setting each time. The level setting can be found in the Trace Contour dialog box. You'll end up with six layers, each containing a different contour (**Figure 13.28**). Now to combine those images into one, set the blending mode of each layer to Multiply so they print on top of each other, which will make the white areas disappear (**Figure 13.29**).

Here's another way of using blending modes with filters. Let's say you've opened an image and then chosen Filter > Stylize > Find Edges. After doing that, you'd end up with a bunch of black lines that represent the edges of all the objects that were in your photo (**Figure 13.30**). But what if you wanted those black lines to print on top of the original image? Well, immediately after applying the filter, you could choose Edit > Fade Fine Edges and set the blending mode menu to Multiply. Photoshop would then apply the filtered image to the original as if you had printed on top of it (**Figure 13.31**).

Figure 13.28 All the layers that are needed to create the drawing.

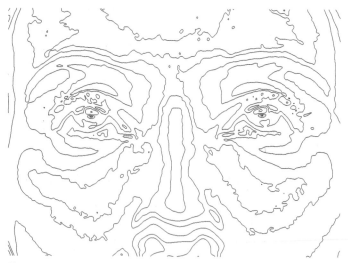

Figure 13.29 Result of combining all the layers in Multiply mode.

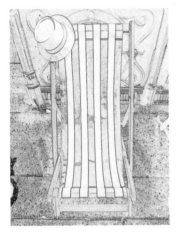

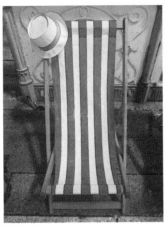

Figure 13.30 Result of applying the Find Edges filter. (original image © 2002 Stockbyte, www.stockbyte.com)

Figure 13.31 Result of Fading the edges in Multiply mode.

You'll find that Multiply mode is used quite a bit in Photoshop's Layer Styles. This occasionally messes me up when I'm trying to do something unusual. Here's an example. Let's say I have some black text on a red background, and I'd like to add a drop shadow. So, with the text layer active, I choose Layer > Layer Style > Drop Shadow. But a black drop shadow with black text makes the text hard to see (**Figure 13.32**), so I decide to change the shadow color to white. When I do this, however, the shadow simply disappears! That's because its mode is automatically set to Multiply (in the Layer Style dialog box), and white disappears in Multiply mode. To get things to work the way I want them to, I simply change the mode from Multiply to Normal, and everything works fine (**Figure 13.33**).

Figure 13.32 The black drop shadow does not contribute to the legibility of the text.

Figure 13.33 A white shadow isn't possible in Multiply mode, so the mode has been changed to Normal.

Color Burn Mode

This mode is not easy to describe or understand, but can be very useful nonetheless. Just as with all the Darken blending modes, white doesn't do anything in Color Burn mode. Black will leave any red, green or blue numbers that are 255 alone and force all others to zero. When you paint with a primary color (pure red, green or blue), you'll end up with the amount of that primary color that was in the underlying image and nothing else. When you paint with a color that's made out of two primaries, then Photoshop will strip the third primary color out of the underlying image. Here's where the goodies come in. Paint with shades of gray to darken and intensify the colors that are in the underlying image. This can work wonders for darkening bland-looking skies, making them more colorful while at the same time maintaining the bright white clouds (see **Figures 13.34** and **13.35**). I sometimes like the way shadows look when I use Color Burn. If a shadow is falling on a textured background, then more of the texture will come through because it will maintain more of the highlights (**Figures 13.36** and **13.37**). I also use this mode to colorize grayscale images. If you're going to try it, just make sure to change the mode of your image from grayscale to RGB or CMYK. You'll most likely want to lower the opacity of the painting tool you use; otherwise you'll end up with a rather dark result. I'll talk more about using the mode for colorizing once we've had a chance to cover some of the other modes that are also used for that purpose.

Figure 13.34 The original image. (© 2002 Stockbyte, www.stockbyte.com)

Figure 13.35 Result of painting gray across the sky in Color Burn mode.

Linear Burn Mode

This mode acts much like Multiply mode, but has a greater tendency to make areas pure black. It also seems to maintain more of the color from the underlying image. Use it anytime you'd think about using Multiply mode, but when you'd like a higher-contrast result. If you ever find that standard shadows (which usually use Multiply mode) look a little too gray, then try Linear Burn; you might like the result better (**Figures 13.38** and **13.39**), although you will need to lower the opacity setting to avoid getting an overly dark result. So, anytime you'd usually use Multiply mode, be sure to also try Linear Burn mode—especially if you're looking for a darker, more saturated result (**Figures 13.40** and **13.41**).

Figure 13.36 Shadow applied in the default blending mode: Multiply mode.

Figure 13.37 Shadow applied in Color Burn mode.

Figure 13.38 Shadow corrected in Multiply mode.

Figure 13.39 Shadow corrected in Linear Burn mode.

Figure 13.40 Two images combined in Multiply mode.

Figure 13.41 Two images combined in Linear Burn mode.

Lighten Blending Modes

For each of the darken blending modes (Darken, Multiply, Color Burn and Linear Burn), there is an equally useful opposite mode. With all the lighten blending modes, black simply disappears, and anything brighter than black has the potential to brighten the underlying image.

Lighten Mode

This mode compares the active layer to the underlying image, and allows the areas of the active layer to show up that are brighter than the underlying image. But again, it looks at the red, green, and blue components of the image separately, which makes for some unpredictable results. Lighten mode was a lifesaver the last time I visited my brother in New York. He's an artist who has no sense for normal sleeping hours. Right when I was getting ready to call it a night, my brother decided to work on a computer project. The problem was that his computer was in the guest room, so I knew he was going to keep me up until he finished his project. Knowing that, I took a keen interest in the project. It turned out that he was attempting to create a photo-realistic 3D rendering of a lamp that he was thinking of making. The only problem was that he could either get the glass part of the bulb to show up, or the glowing filament, but he couldn't get both (**Figures 13.42** and **13.43**). It looked as if it was going to take him hours to figure it out, so in the interest of a good night's sleep, I volunteered to help. After looking at the two images he had created, I thought that if Photoshop could only compare them and let one image lighten the other, then I could get to sleep. So I loaded both images into Photoshop, one atop the other, and set the blending mode of the top layer to Lighten and—bingo, I could call it a night (**Figure 13.44**).

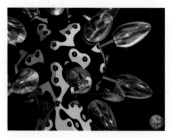

Figure 13.42 Image with bulbs visible. (Courtesy Nik Willmore, www.e-dot.com)

Figure 13.43 Image with filament visible.

Figure 13.44 Result of combining two images in Lighten mode.

I use Lighten mode a lot when I'm experimenting with filters. For instance, choosing Filter > Stylize > Glowing Edges will create bright lines where the edges of an object were in your image (**Figure 13.45**). I sometimes use this filter to add extra interest to an image by choosing Edit > Fade Glowing Edges, and then setting the mode menu to Lighten immediately after applying the filter (**Figure 13.46**). That way I can get the bright edge effect while maintaining the overall look of the original image. The same concept works great when you're using the Lighting Effects filter, which usually brightens or darkens an image. In Lighten mode, you can force that filter to only brighten the image (**Figures 13.47, 13.48 and 13.49**). I like to use it after applying the Blur filter to add a soft-focus look (**Figure 13.50**). It can also be wonderful when sharpening an image. You can duplicate the layer twice, set the top layer to Lighten and the middle layer to Darken, and then sharpen the top two layers. Then you can control the dark and bright halos separately by lowering the opacity of each of those two layers. (This mode will be helpful in the next chapter when we talk about retouching.)

Figure 13.45 The colors shift when the Glowing Edges filter is applied. (original image © 2002 Stockbyte, www.stockbyte.com)

Figure 13.46 More of the original image is visible after Lighten mode is used. (The original contained mostly red.)

Figure 13.47 The original Image.
(© 2002 Stockbyte, www.stockbyte.com)

Figure 13.48 The Lighting Effects filter both brightens and darkens the image.

Figure 13.49 Result of fading the Lighting Effects filter in Lighten mode.

Figure 13.50 Top: The original image Bottom: A soft-focus look. (© 2002 Stockbyte, www.stockbyte.com)

Screen Mode

If Multiply mode acts like ink, then Screen mode is its opposite, acting like light instead. In this mode, black simply disappears, while anything brighter than black will brighten the underlying image. Screen mode is useful when you have an image with a black background, or anything that resembles light. I like to use it with fireworks and lightning. I just put the lightning on a layer above another image, set the layer mode to Screen, and then choose Image > Adjust > Levels and pull the upper-left slider in until the background of the lightning disappears (**Figures 13.51** and **13.52**).

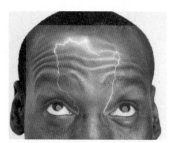

Figure 13.51 Result of using Screen mode to combine images (© 2002 Stockbyte, www.stockbyte.com)

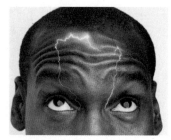

Figure 13.52 Result of applying Levels to darken the background of the lightning to black.

Screen mode is used in many of Photoshop's Layer Styles. Let's say you have some text and you add a glow around it by choosing Layer > Layer Style > Outer Glow. That will work fine as long as you choose a color that is bright like white or yellow, but it won't look so good if you use a dark color like navy blue (**Figure 13.53**). This is because Photoshop uses Screen mode as the default method for applying the glow to the underlying image, and shining a dark blue light at something isn't going to change it much. To remedy the situation, just change the blending mode (in the Layer Style dialog box) to either Normal or Multiply (**Figure 13.54**).

Figure 13.53 A deep blue outer glow created in the default blending mode: Screen mode.

Figure 13.54 Result of switching from Screen mode to Normal mode.

In my Photoshop seminars, I usually talk about how red, green and blue light interact to create all the colors that a computer monitor can display. To demonstrate this, I start with a document that has a black background layer. Then I create three layers: one with a red circle, one with a blue one, and the third using green. But when I move these circles so they overlap, they don't interact like they would if they were made by shining a flashlight at a dark wall (**Figure 13.55**). By setting each of the layers to Screen mode, I can get the circles to interact with each other as if they were circles of light (**Figure 13.56**).

Color Dodge Mode

This mode will usually brighten the underlying image while at the same time making the colors more saturated. It's very useful because it doesn't change the darkest part of your image much, which allows you to brighten an area while still maintaining good contrast. I usually just use the Paintbrush

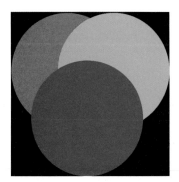

Figure 13.55 In Normal mode, the three circles don't interact with each other.

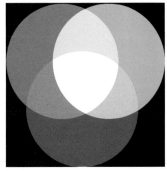

Figure 13.56 Result of switching each layer to Screen mode.

tool and paint with a dark shade of gray on a layer set to Color Dodge mode (**Figures 13.57** and **13.58**). It's sometimes useful for adding more interest to otherwise dull-looking hair. (Photographers often use a separate light source just to add highlights to hair.) I often use Color Dodge mode as a replacement for Screen mode when I'm adding an outer glow layer style to text (see **Figures 13.59** and **13.60**).

Figure 13.57 The original image. (© 2002 Andy Katz)

Figure 13.59 Yellow glow created in Screen mode. (original image © 2002 Stockbyte, www.stockbyte.com)

Figure 13.60 The same yellow glow created in Color Dodge mode.

Figure 13.58 The trees on the left were brightened with gray paint in Color Dodge mode.

Linear Dodge

This mode works much like Screen mode but it has a greater tendency to make areas pure white. Use it any time you're considering Screen mode but would like a higher-contrast result (**Figures 13.61** and **13.62**).

Figure 13.61 A simple glow created in Screen mode. (original image © 2002 Stockbyte, www.stockbyte.com)

Figure 13.62 The same glow created in Linear Dodge mode.

Contrast Blending Modes

The majority of blending modes available on the next section of the menu combine the ideas we've used in the Darken and Lighten blending modes. In all of these modes, 50% gray simply disappears, and anything darker than 50% has the potential of darkening the underlying image, while areas brighter than 50% have the potential to brighten the underlying image. In essence, these modes increase the contrast of the underlying image by brightening one area while darkening another.

Overlay Mode

In Overlay mode, the information on the underlying image is used to brighten or darken the active layer. Any areas that are darker than 50% gray will act like ink (or Multiply mode), while any areas brighter than 50% gray will act like light (or Screen mode). Overlay mode is useful when you want to add color to the underlying image while maintaining its highlights and shadows (**Figures 13.63** and **13.64**). I also use this mode a lot when I'm working with Layer Styles. If I use both a pattern fill and a color overlay, then the color overlay always completely covers up the pattern that is underneath it. But if I apply the color using the Overlay

Figure 13.63 The original image. (© 2002 Stockbyte, www.stockbyte.com)

Figure 13.64 Result of placing solid red on a layer set to Overlay mode.

Figure 13.65 When you use color overlay and a pattern fill, the color obstructs your view of the pattern.

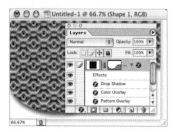

Figure 13.66 Applying the color overlay in Overlay mode allows it to combine with the underlying pattern.

blending mode (in the Layer Style dialog box), it allows the highlights and shadows from the texture to brighten and darken the color that I'm applying (**Figures 13.65** and **13.66**). This allows me to create many grayscale patterns and then colorize them with the Color Overlay layer style.

Soft Light Mode

As with the other modes in this category, Soft Light mode makes 50% gray disappear while making brighter areas brighten and darker areas darken the underlying image. It usually does this with more subtle results than those you get in either Overlay or Hard Light mode. I primarily use this mode for applying textures to photographs. I'll show you a bunch of texture techniques in Chapter 15, "Type and Background Effects," but for now let's create just one. Open any photographic image and create a new, empty layer above that image. Next, type "D" to reset your foreground and background colors, and then choose Filter > Render Clouds. Now choose Filter > Stylize > Find Edges, and then Filter > Stylize > Emboss. Set the angle to −45°, the height to 1, and the amount as high as it can go. If you've done everything right, you should end up with a texture that resembles most refrigerators. To apply that texture to the underlying image, set its blending mode to Soft Light at the top of the Layers palette (**Figure 13.67**).

Figure 13.67 A texture applied in Soft Light mode. (© 2002 Stockbyte, www.stockbyte.com)

Soft Light mode is also useful when you're attempting to add a reflection to a metallic image. Just place the image you want to reflect on a layer above the metallic object, and set its blending mode to Soft Light (**Figures 13.68, 13.69**).

Figure 13.68 Two layers, both set to Normal mode. (© 2002 Stockbyte, www.stockbyte.com)

Figure 13.69 Result of switching the top layer to Soft Light mode.

Hard Light Mode

This has got to be one of my absolute favorite blending modes. In essence, it's a combination of Multiply mode (which acts like ink) and Screen mode (which acts like light). In Hard Light mode, any areas that are 50% gray will disappear, areas darker than 50% will darken the underlying image, and areas brighter than 50% will brighten the underlying image. You'll find me using this mode anytime I use the Emboss filter. When I choose Filter > Stylize > Emboss, I end up with a gray image that has almost no hint of the colors from the original image (**Figures 13.70** and **13.71**). But the gray gunk I do end up with happens to be exactly 50% gray, which means that I can choose Edit > Fade Emboss and set the mode to Hard Light, and bingo...the gray is gone! (**Figure 13.72**). So Hard Light mode allows me to emboss an image while maintaining its color qualities. You can go one better by duplicating the layer before you emboss it. Then, choose Image > Adjustments > Desaturate to ensure there won't be any color shifts (**Figures 13.73** and **13.74**). Next, set the duplicate layer to Hard Light mode, and then apply the

Emboss filter. This way you'll get a real-time preview instead of staring at a bunch of gray stuff while you're applying the filter.

Figure 13.70 The original image. (© 2002 Andy Katz)

Figure 13.71 The Emboss filter delivers a gray result.

Figure 13.72 Result of applying the Emboss filter in Hard Light mode.

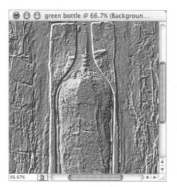

Figure 13.73 Embossing a color image produces color residue.

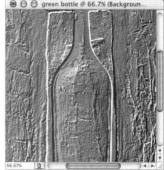

Figure 13.74 Desaturating the image prevents color residue.

Vivid Light

This mode is a combination of Color Dodge and Color Burn. In Vivid Light mode, areas darker than 50% darken and the colors become more saturated; areas brighter than 50% brighten and the colors become more saturated. This mode is great when an image really needs some kick. Just duplicate the layer and set it to Vivid Light mode. You'll most likely need to turn down the opacity setting in order to get an acceptable result (**Figures 13.75** and **13.76**). I also use Vivid Light when I want to apply a texture to an image and I'm concerned that Overlay, Soft Light, or Hard Light mode will make the colors look a little too dull. For example, you can create a new layer above the image you want to texturize. Next, choose Filter > Render > Clouds, then apply Filter > Sharpen > Unsharp Mask with settings of 500, 1.5 and 0, and finish by applying Filter > Stylize > Emboss with settings of 145, 1 and 500. Now if you set the texture layer to Vivid Light mode, you'll be adding texture and enhancing the colors in the image (**Figures 13.77** and **13.78**).

Figure 13.75 The original image could use a little contrast and saturation. (© 2002 Andy Katz)

Figure 13.76 Result of duplicating the layer and setting it to Vivid Light mode.

Figure 13.77 The original image. (© 2002 Stockbyte, www.stockbyte.com)

Figure 13.78 Texture applied in Vivid Light mode.

Linear Light

This mode is a combination of Linear Dodge and Linear Burn. I try this mode anytime I'm considering using Hard Light mode. It produces a higher contrast result where more areas will become pure black and pure white. This is another mode that is great with textures. I mainly use it when I want the highlights and shadow areas of a texture to become pure white and pure black, which usually makes the texture look extra crisp. If you'd like to give it a try, just create a new layer above the image you want to enhance, then fill that layer with white. Now, to make the texture, choose Filter > Artistic > Sponge and use settings of 2, 12, and 5, to pull out some contrast; then choose Image > Adjustments > Auto Levels and finish it off with Filter > Stylize Emboss with settings of 135, 1 and 65. Once you set the blending mode to Linear Light, you should see what I'm talking about (See **Figures 13.79** and **13.80**). If you find that the colors become too vivid, then duplicate the original image, place it on top of the layers stack, and set its blending mode to Color. (We'll talk about Color mode in a bit.) (See **Figures 13.81** and **13.82.**) I often use this technique to create a high-contrast, soft-focus look. I'll end up with three versions of the original image, the bottom one being normal, the middle one being blurred and set to Linear Light mode, and the top one being set to Color mode and not blurred (**Figures 13.83, 13.84,** and **13.85**).

Figure 13.79 The texture that will be applied to a photo.

Figure 13.80 Applying the texture in Linear Light mode produces more saturated colors. (© 2002 Andy Katz)

Figure 13.81 Place a duplicate of the original image on top, and set the mode to Color.

Figure 13.82 Result of applying a duplicate of the original in Color mode.

Figure 13.83 The original image.
(© 2002 Stockbyte, www.stockbyte.com)

Figure 13.84 Blurring a duplicate layer set to Linear Light mode produces saturated colors.

Figure 13.85 Result of applying the original image in Color mode.

Pin Light

This mode is a combination of Lighten and Darken modes. I find that I use this mode mainly when I'm experimenting with filters. I'll end up trying all the contrast modes, and on occasion Pin Light will be the most effective. But it's not very often that I think of a technique that is created specifically with Pin Light in mind. Here's an example of a situation where I ended up liking what Pin Light gave me. I duplicated the original layer, set the top layer to Pin Light, and left the bottom layer set to Normal. Then, with the top layer active, I chose Filter > Sketch > Note Paper and used settings of 25, 5 and 2. That created 3D highlights, but too much of the gray background was showing up (**Figure 13.86**). To finish it off, I chose Image > Adjustments > Levels and moved the middle slider until the background disappeared (**Figure 13.87**).

Figure 13.86 The Note Paper filter delivers a result that contains large areas of gray.

Figure 13.87 Applying the filter in Pin Light mode and adjusting the image with Levels. (© 2002 Stockbyte, www.stockbyte.com)

How to Tell Them Apart

Here's my general thinking when using the contrast blending modes. Overlay mode will make the underlying image more prominent than the active layer. Hard Light mode does the opposite, making the active layer more prominent. Soft Light mode usually makes both layers equally prominent. Vivid Light acts a lot like Hard Light, but will increase the saturation of the colors while preserving more of the highlights and shadows from the underlying image. Linear Light is also like Hard Light, but it has a greater tendency to make areas pure black and pure white. Finally, Pin Light is the loner of the group. It compares the two layers, brightens the underlying image in the highlight areas of the active layer, and darkens the underlying image where there are shadows in the active layer (in a rather unpredictable way).

Comparative Blending Modes

The next two modes are very similar to each other. In general, they compare the active layer to the underlying image, looking for areas that are identical in both. Those areas appear as black, while all non-matching areas show up as shades of gray or color. The closer the non-matching areas are to being black in the end result, the more similar the areas are to the underlying image. In these modes, white on the active layer will invert whatever appears on the underlying image, but black on the active layer will not change the underlying image.

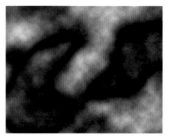

Figure 13.88 Painting on a layer below some clouds that are set to Difference mode.

Difference Mode

This mode works exactly as described above. Let's use it to create some homemade lightning. Start with a new document that contains a white background. Next, create a new layer, and reset your foreground and background colors by typing "D"; then choose Filter > Render Clouds, and set the layer containing the clouds to Difference mode. Now choose a large, soft-edged brush, and paint with black on the bottom layer. You should end up with a cloudy-looking image that has black areas around the edges of the area where you've painted (**Figure 13.88**). Now it's time to transform those black areas into lightning. We'll start the process by inverting the image to make black areas white. Do this by clicking on the top-most layer and then choosing Layer > New Adjustment Layer > Invert (**Figure 13.89**). Finally, choose Layer > New Adjustment Layer > Levels and move the upper-left slider until all you can see is the white "lightning" (**Figure 13.90**). Now you

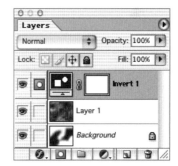

Figure 13.89 Adding an Invert adjustment layer above the clouds.

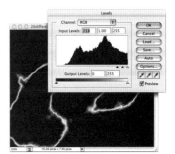

Figure 13.90 Pulling in the upper-left slider in Levels isolates the "lightning."

Figure 13.91 Result of applying the Clouds filter.

Figure 13.92 Smoothing out the clouds by using the Median filter.

Figure 13.93 Fading the Chrome filter in Exclusion mode.

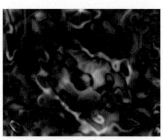

Figure 13.94 The end result after application of a gradient map.

can continue painting on the bottom-most layer to create more and more lightning. When you're all done, choose Layer > Merge Visible to combine the layers. You can apply the lightning to another image at any time by placing your lightning on a layer above and then setting the blending mode of the layer to Screen, so it acts like light. There are a number of other neat things to do with the Difference mode, which we'll explore again in Chapter 15, "Type and Backgrounds."

Exclusion Mode

I'm sorry to say that this mode, along with Diffuse mode, usually just sits around collecting dust. It's just not very often that I have an image that will benefit from Exclusion mode, unless I'm going for a psychedelic, tripped-out '60s look. Let's see what I came up with when randomly experimenting with filters. I started by typing "D" to reset my foreground and background colors; then I chose Filter > Render Clouds (**Figure 13.91**). Next, I chose Filter > Noise > Median and used a setting somewhere around 10 (**Figure 13.92**). Then to spice things up, I chose Filter > Sketch > Chrome with settings of 4 and 7. I chose Edit > Fade Chrome and tried both Difference and Exclusion modes (**Figure 13.93**). I preferred the look of Exclusion mode, so I clicked OK. I then chose Layer > New Adjustment Layer > Gradient Map and used the Color Burn blending mode. I created a gradient that went from orange to yellow, experimenting until I liked what I ended up with (**Figure 13.94**).

Hue/Saturation/Brightness Blending Modes

The next set of modes divides the colors of your image into three components: hue, saturation, and brightness. Photoshop applies only one or two of these qualities to the underlying image. These are wonderfully helpful modes, and the ones that I feel have the most practical and obvious uses.

Hue Mode

This mode looks at the basic colors contained on the active layer and applies them to the brightness and saturation information on the underlying layers. You can think of *hue* as the pure form of a color. In order to get to the pure form of a color, you have to ignore how dark the color is, and how vivid it is, so you can concentrate just on its basic color. It's kind of like when you were a kid and only knew about a dozen words to describe color. Back then, you might have thought of a maroon car, or a pink dress, as being red.

Figure 13.95 Changing the color of an image in Hue mode. (© 2002 Stockbyte, www.stockbyte.com)

That's because you were limited to describing things by their hue. This mode is great for changing the colors of objects that are already in color. All you have to do is create a new layer above the image, set it to Hue mode, and then paint away (**Figure 13.95**). I like to use the Gradient tool to create a two-tone look (**Figure 13.96**). You can even set the Gradient tool to Foreground to Transparent in order to shift one area and have it slowly fade out to the original color of the image (**Figures 13.97** and **13.98**). And then, after painting on the layer, you can really refine things by using the Eraser tool to bring areas back to normal (**Figure 13.99**). Be careful, though, because there are a few things that might mess you up when you're using Hue mode. First off, this mode cannot introduce color into an area that does not already contain color. (In order to do this, it would need to change the saturation of the area.) Secondly, it will not change the saturation of the underlying image. This means that if an area has just a hint of color in it, it will still have just as much color when you're done, because you will have only shifted that color to a different hue. It also can't change how bright areas are. This means that painting across a white area will not change the image, because there is no way to introduce color into a white area without darkening it. You should use this mode when you need to shift the color of something that already contains color.

Figure 13.96 A car with two-tone coloring created by applying the Gradient tool in Hue mode. (© 2002 PhotoSpin, www.photospin.com)

Figure 13.97 Adding a gradient set to Foreground to Transparent

Figure 13.99 Final result after the Eraser tool was used to remove the color change from a few spots.

Figure 13.98 Result of applying the gradient in Hue mode.

Saturation Mode

As a seminar speaker, I often find myself in a room filled with Photoshop users, and I'm fond of getting them to think in new ways that will help them understand what's really going on with their pixels. When I talk about Saturation mode, I usually ask the participants to close their eyes and visualize what fluorescent…gray looks like! That usually sends them for a spin, because there is no such thing as fluorescent gray. However, the attempt to visualize it forces their brains to think completely about saturation and nothing else. Saturation determines how much color shows up in your image. If there is no saturation, then there is no color at all, which just leaves brightness (grays). As things become more saturated, the color in that area becomes more vivid. When you get everything completely saturated, you end up with almost fluorescent colors. Now, with that in mind, let's see how Photoshop's Saturation mode works. First off, it completely ignores what colors (red, green, yellow, orange, etc.) are on a layer. It also ignores how bright those colors are and just concentrates on how *vivid* they are. Then it changes the colors in the underlying image until they become just as saturated as those on the active layer. If you paint with the most vivid green you can find, the colors in the underlying image will become just as vivid—BUT bear in mind that the only areas that will end up as green will be those areas that were green to begin with (**Figures 13.100** and **13.101**). Saturation mode simply can't shift any of the basic colors; reds stay red, blues stay blue, etc. They just become more or less vivid to match the quality of the active layer.

Figure 13.100 The original image. (© 2002 Stockbyte, www.stockbyte.com)

Figure 13.101 Applying a vivid green color to half the image in Saturation mode.

One of the most common uses for this mode is to force areas of an image to appear in black and white. All you have to do is create a new layer, set its blending mode to Saturation, and then paint with any shade of gray. Since grays don't contain any color (they are pure brightness information), they will change the underlying image to grayscale (**Figure 13.102**). If you don't want to take the image all the way to grayscale, then just lower the opacity setting of the painting tool you are using (**Figures 13.103** and **13.104**). You can even use the Gradient tool to make the transition fade out. Just set it to Foreground to Transparent, and drag across the layer that is set to Saturation mode (**Figure 13.105**).

Figure 13.102 Painting with black on a layer set to Saturation mode changes the painted areas to grayscale. (© 2002 Stockbyte, www.stockbyte.com)

Figure 13.103 The original image.
(© 2002 Andy Katz)

Figure 13.104 The area surrounding
the bottle was painted in Saturation
mode with a medium opacity setting.

Figure 13.105 Applying a gradient causes the color to slowly fade out. (© 2002
Stockbyte, www.stockbyte.com)

Color Mode

This mode applies both the Hue (basic color) and Saturation (vividness) of the active layer to the underlying image, leaving its brightness intact. In essence, it applies the color of the active layer to the brightness information of the underlying image. It's almost the same as Hue mode, with the exception that it can change the saturation of an area and therefore introduce color into an area that did not have it to begin with.

The most common (and most fun) use for this mode is to colorize grayscale photographs. All you have to do is change the mode of the image from grayscale to RGB or CMYK, create a new layer, set it to Color, and then paint away (**Figure 13.106**). If you feel the color you're adding is just too vivid, then lower the opacity of your brush (**Figure 13.107**). Or, if you just can't get enough color into an area, then you might want to try using Color Burn mode instead (**Figure 13.108**). If the highlights and shadows of the underlying image don't quite look right, then try using Overlay mode (**Figure 13.109**).

Figure 13.106 Color applied in Color mode at 100% opacity. (© 2002 Stockbyte, www.stockbyte.com)

Figure 13.107 Lowering the opacity reduces the amount of color applied.

Figure 13.108 Color applied in Color Burn mode with a medium opacity setting.

Figure 13.109 Color applied in Overlay mode.

Luminosity Mode

This mode applies the brightness information of the active layer to the color in the underlying image. It can't shift colors or change how saturated those colors are. All it can do is change how bright they are.

I'm connected at the hip to Luminosity mode, because it seems that no matter what I'm doing, this mode is equipped to help out. Here are a few examples: Immediately after sharpening an image, I choose Edit > Fade Unsharp Mask and set the mode to Luminosity. This prevents the sharpening from adding odd colors to the edges of objects (**Figures 13.110** and **13.111**). A lot of people sharpen their images after converting them to Lab mode, but you can achieve the same result using the technique I just mentioned. Any time I adjust the brightness or contrast of an image using Levels, Curves or anything else, I'll end up choosing Edit > Fade and setting the mode to Luminosity; otherwise the colors might become too vivid (**Figure 13.112**). If you're using an adjustment layer instead of applying the adjustment directly to the image, just set the blending mode of the adjustment layer to Luminosity instead of using the fade feature. If you apply a filter and you notice it shifting the color of the image (**Figures 13.113, 13.114,** and **13.115**), then choose Edit > Fade, and then use Luminosity mode to limit the filter so that it changes only the brightness of the image.

Figure 13.110 The Unsharp Mask filter produces vividly colored halos. (original image © 2002 Stockbyte, www.stockbyte.com)

Figure 13.111 Fading the filter in Luminosity mode prevents the overly saturated halos.

Figure 13.112 Left. The original image. Middle: A Curves adjustment designed to darken the image. Right: Result of fading the Curves adjustment in Luminosity mode. (© 2002 Andy Katz)

Figure 13.113 The original image. (© 2002 Andy Katz)

Figure 13.114 The Plaster filter.

Figure 13.115 Fading the filter in Luminosity mode prevents the filter from shifting colors.

Using Hue/Saturation as a Substitute

You can perform the same types of changes we made when we used the last set of modes by choosing Image > Adjustments > Hue/Saturation. The Hue/Saturation dialog box divides your image into three components (again, hue, saturation and brightness), but it allows you to do some more interesting things.

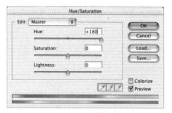

Figure 13.118 The color bars at the bottom of the Hue/Saturation dialog box indicate how the changes will affect the image.

To get a feeling for how the Hue/Saturation options work, open a colorful image and then choose Image > Adjustments > Hue/Saturation. Move the Hue slider around and see what happens to the image (**Figures 13.116** and **13.117**). You'll notice that *all* the colors in the image are shifting. Move the slider back to the middle, and this time concentrate on what happens to the two color bars at the bottom of the dialog box. The top bar shows all the hues you could possibly have in your image. The bottom bar indicates what they will shift to once you apply the adjustment (**Figure 13.118**). Since all the colors shift, you'll need to make a selection of the area that you want to change before you start adjusting the image.

Figure 13.116 The original image. (© 2002 Stockbyte, www.stockbyte.com)

Figure 13.117 Moving the Hue slider shifts all the colors in the image.

Figure 13.119 Leaving a little saturation leaves a hint of color. (© 2002 Stockbyte, www.stockbyte.com)

You can also make areas black and white using this dialog box. All you have to do is select the area you want to change, choose Image > Adjustments > Hue/Saturation, and then move the Saturation slider all the way to the left. I usually don't move it all the way to the left because I like to keep a hint of color in every area of the image (**Figure 13.119**).

I use the Saturation slider on about 90% of the images that I scan. I find that raw scans just feel a little flat, and that even after color correction and contrast adjustments, they still need a bit more saturation. When this is the case, I choose Hue/Saturation and then bump up the colors by moving the Saturation slider toward the right (**Figures 13.120** and **13.121**).

Figure 13.120 The Image after color correction has been performed. (© 2002 Andy Katz)

NOTES

Some saturated colors are difficult to reproduce on a commercial printing press. I suggest you choose View > Proof Colors to preview what your image will look like when it's converted to CMYK mode before increasing the saturation setting.

Figure 13.121 Result of boosting the saturation of the image.

It's not very often that I use the Lightness slider in the Hue/Saturation dialog box. That is, I don't use it all by itself because it's rather crude; I prefer to use more sophisticated tools such as Levels and Curves. However, I do use it on occasion after I've shifted the color of an object if some color just seems too bright and vivid.

You can colorize black-and-white photographs using Hue/Saturation. All you need to do is convert from grayscale to

RGB or CMYK mode and then choose Image > Adjustments > Hue/Saturation. You'll find that the Hue and Saturation sliders don't do anything on a grayscale image. In order to add color, you'll need to check the Colorize checkbox. I often make a selection and then create a new Hue/Saturation adjustment layer to colorize an area. Then I repeat the process until I've added color to the entire image (**Figures 13.122** and **13.123**).

Figure 13.123 Result of creating a bunch of Hue/Saturation layers to colorize the image.

Figure 13.122 The Colorize checkbox (found in Image > Adjustments > Hue/Saturation) will introduce color into a grayscale image that has been converted to RGB mode. (© 2002 Stockbyte, www.stockbyte.com)

So far, the Hue/Saturation dialog box sounds like an easy shortcut to changing the color of your image, but as you toy with it, you'll realize that it's changing all of the colors of your image, and most times that's not what you'll want. Instead, you'll want to be able to control exactly where and how the color is changing. To do this, you have to make some pretty surgical selections, which can be painstaking and time-consuming. But you'll be happy to know that you can avoid having to make those icky selections by practicing with Hue/Saturation until you can use it to isolate areas of your image based on color.

Let's see how it works: You can isolate a range of colors to work on by choosing a color from the Edit pop-up menu at the top of the Hue/Saturation dialog box. Once you've done that, you should see a few slider bars showing up between the two color bars at the bottom of the dialog box (**Figure 13.124**). These bars allow you to change only the colors that appear between them. The problem, however, is that the range of colors you'll be changing will be too wide for most uses. To remedy the situation, grab the small triangle that makes up one end of the slider and move it towards the others until they all smash together into a single mass (**Figure 13.125**). After you've done this, the sliders will probably no longer be below the color you were looking to change, so move the cursor onto your image and click on the area you'd like to change. This will precisely center the sliders on the color you've selected (**Figure 13.126**). Next, make a radical change to the hue or saturation of that area (maybe shifting a red area to green) **Figure 13.127**. Now hold down the Shift key and click on other areas until all of the areas you want to change shift in color (**Figure 13.128**). If you accidentally click on an area that shouldn't shift, then press down Option (Macintosh) or Alt (Windows) and click on that area again to remove it from the range of colors being changed. Once you've isolated the range of colors you want to change, then experiment with the hue and saturation sliders until you get the effect you're looking for (**Figure 13.129**).

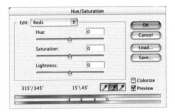

Figure 13.124 Choosing a color from the pop-up menu at the top of the dialog box causes sliders to appear between the color bars.

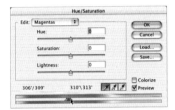

Figure 13.125 Smashing the sliders together limits the range of colors that you can change.

Figure 13.126 Clicking on the image will center the sliders on the color you've selected. (original image © 2002 Stockbyte, www.stockbyte.com)

Figure 13.127 Make a radical shift to the image so you can see which areas are changing.

Figure 13.128 Shift-click on additional areas to expand the range of colors that change.

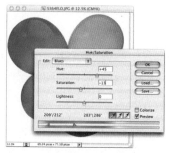

Figure 13.129 Once you've isolated the range of colors you'd like to change, then fine-tune the Hue and Saturation settings to get the color you desire.

You can use this technique to shift the colors of objects (using Hue) and to make areas black and white (using Saturation). I've also used it to pull all the color out of all but one color in an image. I usually do this by manually moving the sliders so they are under all the colors except for the one that I want to keep; then I bring the Saturation setting all the way to the left (**Figures 13.130** and **13.131**).

Figure 13.130 The original image. (© 2002 Andy Katz)

Figure 13.131 Result of desaturating all colors except green.

Liquify

Filter > Liquify will allow you to pull and push on your image as if it were printed on Silly Putty. When you choose Filter > Liquify, you'll see a dialog box that dominates your screen (**Figure 13.132**).

NOTES

The Liquify command was located under the Image menu in previous versions of Photoshop.

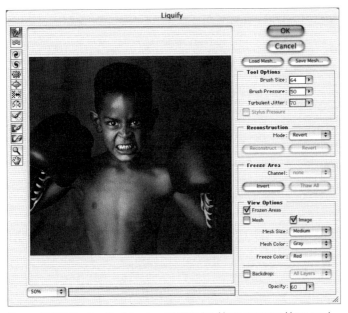

Figure 13.132 The Liquify dialog box. (© 2002 Stockbyte, www.stockbyte.com)

Let's run down the tools that appear in the upper left of the dialog box.

At the top you'll find the Warp tool, which allows you to push the image in the direction that you drag (**Figure 13.133**). Next comes the Turbulence tool, which is new in Photoshop 7.0. It allows you to push and pull on your image, much like the Warp tool, but it will add more of a wavy look, which can be useful when you're attempting to create water ripples and smoke (**Figure 13.134**). Next are the Twirl Clockwise and Twirl Counterclockwise tools, which slowly rotate the area inside your cursor (**Figure 13.135**). Under that you'll find the Pucker tool, which allows you to pull the image in towards the center of

Figure 13.133 Result of applying the Warp tool. (© 2002 Stockbyte, www.stockbyte.com)

your brush (**Figure 13.136**). Or, you can do the opposite of that by using the Bloat tool, as shown in **Figure 13.137.** Below the Bloat tool is the Shift Pixels tool, which acts as though the line you draw is a bulldozer, and pushes the image away from it on the left side. (Press down Option on the Mac or Alt in Windows to move the image on the right side instead.) See **Figure 13.138.** After that you'll find the Reflection tool, which will flip a portion of the image horizontally or vertically, depending on the direction you drag. If you drag downward, then you'll be reflecting the area to the left of the cursor. Drag up and you'll reflect what's to the right (**Figure 13.139**). Drag right and you'll reflect the area below the cursor, and drag left to reflect the area above.

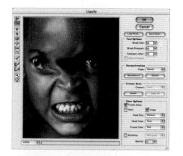

Figure 13.134 Result of applying the Turbulence tool.

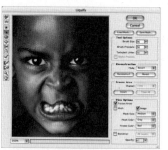

Figure 13.135 Result of applying the Twirl tool.

Figure 13.136 Result of applying the Pucker tool.

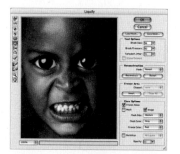

Figure 13.137 Result of applying the Bloat tool.

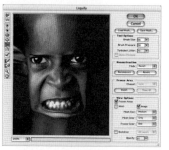

Figure 13.138 Result of applying the Shift Pixels tool.

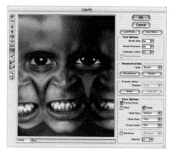

Figure 13.139 Result of applying the Reflect tool.

There is no Brushes palette available to change the size of your brush in the Liquify dialog box. The size of the brush is determined by the number entered in the Brush Size field in the upper right of the dialog box. You can use the bracket keys (][) to change this setting in increments of one, or press Shift with them to change the size in increments of 10. Photoshop 7.0 also adds the ability to zoom in on your image; simply press Command-+ or Command- – (Mac), or Ctrl-+, Ctrl- – (Windows). 7.0 also gives you the ability to access multiple undos by pressing Shift-Command-Z (Mac) or Shift-Ctrl-Z (Windows) multiple times.

For all of these tools, the Brush Pressure setting will determine how radical a change you'll make when you paint across the image. If you have a pressure-sensitive graphics tablet, then you can turn on the Stylus Pressure checkbox to make Photoshop pay attention to how much pressure you're using with the pen. With this option turned on, the Brush Pressure setting will be determined by how hard you press down on your graphics tablet.

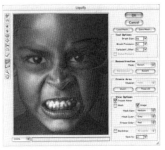

Figure 13.140 The red overlay indicates an area that has been frozen.

If you find that you end up changing too much of the image, you can freeze an area to prevent it from changing. The Freeze tool will apply a red overlay on your image to indicate which areas have been frozen (**Figure 13.140**). The Freeze tool also uses the Brush Pressure setting, which means that you can partially freeze an area to make it change less than the unfrozen areas. (For example, 50% frozen areas will change half as much as unfrozen areas when they're painted across.) Areas that are partially frozen will appear with a more transparent red overlay. If you'd rather not see the overlay, click to uncheck the Show Frozen Areas checkbox. If you'd like to unfreeze an area, use the Thaw tool to remove some of the red overlay, or click Thaw All to unfreeze the entire image. The Freeze and Thaw options are great when used with Photoshop 7.0's new Backdrop setting, which allows you to see through the transparent areas of a layer to the underlying layers. This way you can see exactly how your image lines up with the rest of the document (**Figure 13.141**).

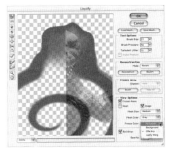

Figure 13.141 The left side indicates what you see when the Backdrop checkbox is unchecked. The right side shows what you see when an underlying layer is visible.

Once you're done manipulating your image, you might find that you've gone a little too far in a few areas. If that's the case, grab the Reconstruct tool and paint across the area that you'd like to take back to normal (**Figure 13.142**). The more you paint across an area, the closer it will become to what the image looked like before you applied the Liquify command.

After you play around in this dialog box, it's often difficult to determine the exact areas in your image that have changed. You can see a different view of the changes you've made by checking the Show Mesh checkbox (**Figure 13.143**). You might also want to uncheck the Show Image checkbox so you can get a clear view of the mesh (**Figure 13.144**). You can still use all the Liquify tools while the mesh is visible.

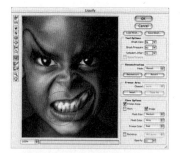

Figure 13.142 The Reconstruct tool will bring areas back to what they looked like before you used the Liquify command.

Figure 13.143 An image with the mesh visible.

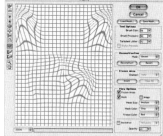

Figure 13.144 Viewing the mesh with the image hidden.

Closing Thoughts

If someone were to actually publish all of the great enhancement techniques out there, you'd be wading through a book ten times the size of *War and Peace*. With this chapter, I've tried to give you some nice, tasty samples that will inspire you to go forth and try some more on your own. I hope you've enjoyed it. This part of Photoshop is always a pure pleasure for me—I could do this stuff every day. (Wait a minute—I do!) The more you work with Photoshop, the more you'll be able to add to your own personal cookbook of enhancement recipes. The trick is to find the time to experiment. I used to stay at work until rush-hour traffic died down just so I could have more time to play with Photoshop. When I went to college, there weren't any Photoshop classes, so I'm self-taught, thanks to a lot of midnight jam sessions with the tunes cranked up and Photoshop glowing on my computer screen. And look at me...I got to write this book!

Ben's Techno-babble Decoder Ring

Blending modes: A function in Photoshop that alters the behavior of a layer or tool, allowing it to interact with the underlying image.

Snapshot: A user-created record of the current state of a document (content and order of layers, adjustment settings, and so forth).

Scratch disk: The virtual memory scheme used by Photoshop. It allows Photoshop to create an invisible file on your hard drive that is used as a substitute for actual physical memory (RAM). This way Photoshop can manipulate files larger than could be opened in RAM.

RAM: Random Access Memory. The physical memory chips that are installed in your computer. (64MB of memory in your computer is called 64MB of RAM.)

Keyboard Shortcuts

The following keyboard commands change the blending mode of the current tool (if it supports blending modes); otherwise, they will change the blending mode of the currently active layer.

FUNCTION	MACINTOSH	WINDOWS
Previous blending mode	Shift-– (minus sign)	Shift-–
Next blending mode	Shift-+ (plus sign)	Shift-+
Normal	Shift-Option-N	Shift-Alt-N
Dissolve	Shift-Option-I	Shift-Alt-I
Clear	Shift-Option-R	Shift-Alt-R
Darken	Shift-Option-K	Shift-Alt-K
Multiply	Shift-Option-M	Shift-Alt-M
Color Burn	Shift-Option-B	Shift-Alt-B
Linear Burn	Shift-Option-A	Shift-Alt-A
Lighten	Shift-Option-G	Shift-Alt-G
Screen	Shift-Option-S	Shift-Alt-S
Color Dodge	Shift-Option-D	Shift-Alt-D
Linear Dodge	Shift-Option-W	Shift-Alt-W
Overlay	Shift-Option-O	Shift-Alt-O
Soft Light	Shift-Option-F	Shift-Alt-F
Hard Light	Shift-Option-H	Shift-Alt-H
Vivid Light	Shift-Option-V	Shift-Alt-V
Linear Light	Shift-Option-J	Shift-Alt-J
Pin Light	Shift-Option-Z	Shift-Alt-Z
Color Dodge	Shift-Option-D	Shift-Alt-D
Difference	Shift-Option-E	Shift-Alt-E
Exclusion	Shift-Option-X	Shift-Alt-X
Hue	Shift-Option-U	Shift-Alt-U
Saturation	Shift-Option-T	Shift-Alt-T
Color	Shift-Option-C	Shift-Alt-C
Luminosity	Shift-Option-Y	Shift-Alt-Y

© 2002 Jim DiVitale, www.divitalephoto.com

© 2002 Jim DiVitale, www.divitalephoto.com

Courtesy of Diane Fenster, www.dianefenster.com

Courtesy of Diane Fenster, www.dianefenster.com

14

Retouching

Courtesy of Nick Koudis, www.koudis.com

NEW IN 7

In this chapter, you'll learn how to use Photoshop 7.0's new Patch and Healing Brush tools.

A doctor can bury his mistakes, but an architect can only advise his clients to plant vines.

–Frank Lloyd Wright

Retouching

The doctoring of photographs didn't begin with the advent of computers in magazine production departments. One of history's most notorious photograph "doctors" was Joseph Stalin, who used photo retouching as a way to manipulate the masses. People who vanished in real life, whether banished to the farthest reaches of the Soviet Union or eliminated by the secret police, vanished from photos as well, and even from paintings. In many cases, they were airbrushed out completely; in others, their faces were clumsily blacked out with ink.

And then there were the Hollywood photo doctors. They didn't want to get *rid* of anyone; they just wanted to make them look better. I think they actually coined the term "too good to be true." Think about it—have you ever seen a photograph of a starlet with a blemish, or a wart, or bags under her eyes, or even the slightest indication that her skin actually had pores? Of course not!

If you look at it from these two extremes, you can appreciate why the subject of retouching is something of a, well, touchy subject. If you're brave enough to bring it up at a photographer's convention, you're likely to spark a pretty lively debate. A purist might tell you that every aspect of a photograph (including the flaws) is a perfect reflection of reality and should never be tampered with. Then again, a graphic artist, who makes a living from altering images, might tell you that an original photograph is just the foundation of an image, and that the so-called tampering is, in fact, a means of enhancing and improving upon it. Either way you look at it, you can't deny the fact that retouching photographs has become an everyday necessity for almost anyone who deals with graphic images. And when it comes to retouching, hands down, nothing does it better than Photoshop.

Photoshop packs an awesome arsenal of retouching tools. These include the Dodge and Burn tools, Blur and Sharpen tools, Patch tool and Healing Brush, as well as the Clone Stamp tool. We'll get to play with all of them, and for each one I'll also give you a little bag of tricks. You'll learn how to do all sorts of neat things, including retouching old ripped photos, getting rid of those shiny spots on foreheads, and adjusting the saturation of small areas. Or, you can put yourself in the doctor's seat and give someone instant plastic surgery. Remove a few wrinkles, perform an eye lift, reduce those dark rings around the eyes, and poof!—you've taken off ten years. So let's look at these tools one at a time, starting with what I consider to be the most important one.

Patch Tool

The Patch tool is one of the most innovative yet simple tools I've ever seen Adobe come up with. The general concept is simple. You select an area of your image that needs to be touched up (maybe a blemish on skin), and then you click in the middle of the selection and drag it to an area of your image that has similar texture but with no blemishes. Then Photoshop does an amazing job of blending the second area into the first. It makes sure that the brightness and color is consistent with what was on the edge of the original selection and it blends the texture from the second area with that color. You simply have to try it to see what I mean (**Figure 14.1**).

Figure 14.1 Left: Original image. Right: After applying the Patch tool. (© 2002 Stockbyte, www.stockbyte.com)

NOTES

When editing an image that is in 16-bit mode, the Patch tool will always use the source setting and the options usually found in the Options bar will be unavailable (grayed out).

Just because this tool is rather sophisticated in the way it blends with the image, that doesn't mean you shouldn't be careful when making the selection. I always try to make the smallest selection that will completely encompass the defect I'm trying to retouch (**Figure 14.2**). The larger the area being patched, the less likely it will look good (**Figure 14.3**).

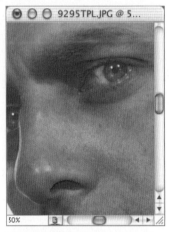 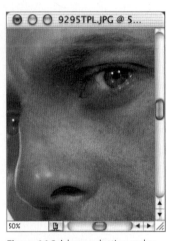

Figure 14.2 A small selection produces a nice blend. (© 2002 Stockbyte, www.stockbyte.com)

Figure 14.3 A large selection makes things look artificial.

There aren't many options to deal with when using this tool (**Figure 14.4**). The main choice is to patch the source or destination. With the Patch option set to Source, Photoshop will replace the area that was originally selected with a combination of the brightness and color values from its edge, along with the texture from the area you drag the selection to (**Figure 14.5**). Using the Destination setting does the opposite, letting you pick from a clean area of the original and then dragging it over the area that needs to be patched (**Figure 14.6**).

Figure 14.4 The Options bar for the Patch tool.

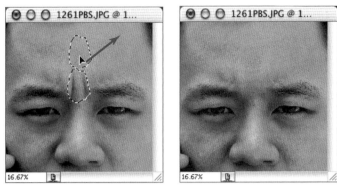

Figure 14.5 Left: Original image. Right: Result of using the Source setting.
(© 2002 Stockbyte, www.stockbyte.com)

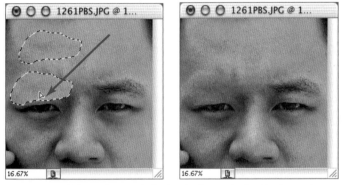

Figure 14.6 Left: Original image. Right: Result of using the Destination setting.

If you can't find a clean area from which to steal texture, then you can select a pattern by clicking on the down-pointing arrow in the Options bar (**Figure 14.7**) and then clicking the Use Pattern button. You'll find that patching with a pattern isn't all that effective unless you've created a custom pattern for this specific purpose. Be sure to check out Chapter 15: "Type and Background Efffects," for details on how to create your own patterns.

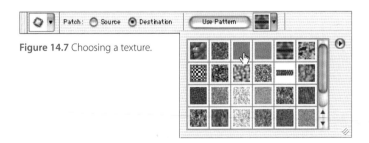

Figure 14.7 Choosing a texture.

I find that the Patch tool is best for those situations where you have scratches, blemishes, or other defects in an area that should otherwise be relatively consistent in color (such as skin). It can even maintain some of the three-dimensionality of the surface with its blending capabilities (**Figure 14.8**). But you'll find that it's not very useful when you have an area that has multiple colors bordering it that shouldn't blend together. That's because Photoshop will attempt to blend the patched area into all the surrounding colors. In that case you should either switch to the new Healing Brush or try out the Clone Stamp tool.

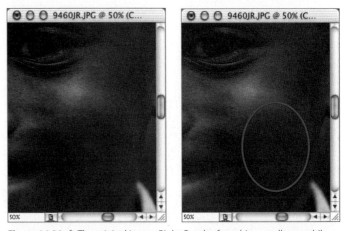

Figure 14.8 Left: The original image. Right: Result of patching small area while keeping the dimensionality of the skin. (© 2002 Stockbyte, www.stockbyte.com)

Figure 14.9 The Fade dialog box.

If you find that the end result of using the Patch tool looks a little dark, then you'll want to choose Edit > Fade immediately after applying a patch (**Figure 14.9**). Simply lower the Opacity setting.

Healing Brush Tool

The Healing Brush works using the same general concepts as the Patch tool. It attempts to patch a defect in your image using the texture from another area while blending all the edges with the surrounding colors. The main difference is that the Patch tool works by moving a selection, while the Healing Brush allows you to paint over the area that needs to be repaired. To use it, you'll first have to Option-click (Mac) or Alt-click (Windows) on the area you would like to use to fix an area and then click and drag across the area that needs fixing. When you do that, be sure to cover the entire area without releasing the mouse button. Once you let go, Photoshop will check out the edges of the area you covered to make sure your "patch" blends with the color and brightness that is in the surrounding area (see **Figures 14.10** and **14.11**). You'll have to use a soft-edged brush to get a good blend (**Figures 14.12** and **14.13**). Just make sure that you choose your brush from the Brush drop-down menu in the Options bar. This tool will ignore the stand-alone Brushes palette because it doesn't work with Photoshop 7.0's new Brush Dynamics settings.

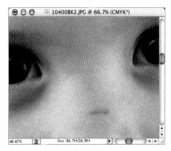

Figure 14.10 Original image. (© 2002 Stockbyte, www.stockbyte.com)

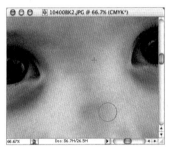 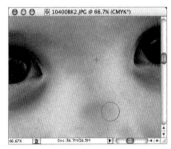

Figure 14.11 Left: While applying the Healing Brush, things don't blend in. Right: After releasing the mouse button, the retouched area blends in to its surroundings.

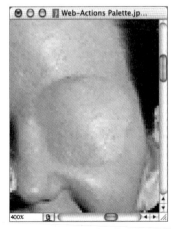 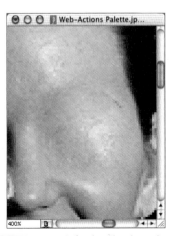

Figure 14.12 Hard-edged brush used. **Figure 14.13** Soft-edged brush used.

If you'd rather completely replace an area instead of attempt to blend the brightness and color of the edges with the texture of another area, set the Mode pop-up menu in the Options bar to Replace and go at it. In that case, Photoshop will copy the area on which you Option-click (Mac) or Alt-click (Windows) and completely cover up the area you patch; then it will attempt to have the edges smoothly fade into the surrounding area without trying to maintain its brightness and color (**Figure 14.14**). This is the same principle that the Clone Stamp Tool uses. The only difference is that the Clone Stamp tool doesn't attempt to blend the result with the underlying image.

There are a few blending modes available in the Options bar, but you'll find out that they work a little differently from what you might be used to. Most tools would apply their general effect, and then once everything is done, they would apply the blending mode. But in this tool, the blending mode is applied *before* Photoshop does the work needed to blend the patched area with the surrounding image (**Figures 14.15** and **14.16**).

If neither the Patch tool nor the Healing Brush delivers the results you are looking for, then you'll have to switch over to the trusty old standby—the Clone Stamp tool.

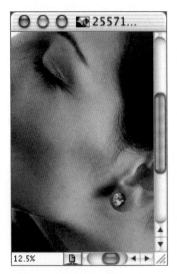  

Figure 14.14 Left: The original image. Middle: Result of using Normal mode (source point was an area of skin). Right: Result of using Replace mode. (© 2002 Stockbyte, www.stockbyte.com)

Figure 14.15 How Multiply mode would usually look. (© 2002 Stockbyte, www.stockbyte.com)

Figure 14.16 How Multiply mode looks in the Healing Brush.

Clone Stamp Tool

The Clone Stamp tool copies information from one area of your image and applies it somewhere else. Before applying the Clone Stamp tool, there is one thing you should know: All retouching tools use the Brushes palette, shown in **Figure 14.17.** The brush that you use with the Healing Brush isn't all that important since it will end up blending your retouching into the surrounding image, but the brush you choose is critical when using the Clone Stamp tool because it doesn't have those blending capabilities. So you have to decide if you want what you're about to apply to fade into the image or to have a distinct edge. For most applications it helps to have a soft edge on your brush so you can't see the exact edge of where you've stopped.

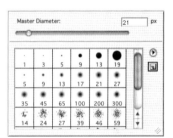

Figure 14.17 The brush that you choose determines how much your retouching work will blend into the underlying image.

I find that the default soft-edged brushes are often too soft, which can cause the area you retouch to look blurry compared with the rest of the image. To prevent that from happening, click on the brush preview in the Options bar and increase the Hardness setting. The default brushes have a hardness of either 100% (for hard-edged brushes) or 0% (for soft ones). I find a Hardness somewhere between 30% and 60% to be ideal for retouching with soft-edged brushes.

Figure 14.18 The Clone Stamp tool copies from under the crosshair and pastes into the circle. (© 2002 Stockbyte, www.stockbyte.com)

Cloning Around

After you've chosen your brush, you'll need to tell Photoshop exactly where you'd like to copy from. Do this by holding down the Option key (Mac) or Alt key (Windows) and clicking the mouse button. Then move to a different part of the image and click and drag the mouse. When you do, you'll notice two cursors (**Figure 14.18**). The first one is in the shape of a crosshair; it shows you the source of Photoshop's cloning. When you apply the Clone Stamp tool, there will be a second cursor—a circle showing you exactly where it's being applied (if the Caps Lock key is pressed, you may get a crosshair cursor). When you move your mouse around you'll notice both of the cursors moving in the same direction. As you drag, Photoshop is constantly copying from the crosshair and pasting into the circle.

Clone Aligned

The Clone Stamp tool operates in two different modes: Aligned and Non-aligned (it's just a simple check box in the Options bar). In Aligned mode, when you apply the Clone Stamp tool, it doesn't matter if you let go of the mouse button and click again. Each time you let go and click again, the pieces that you're applying line up (**Figure 14.19**). It's as if you're putting together a puzzle: Once you have all of the pieces together, it looks like a complete image.

Clone Non-Aligned

But if you turn off the Aligned checkbox, it's a different story. Then if you apply the tool and let go of the mouse button, the next time you click the mouse button it will reset itself, starting back at the original point from where it was cloning (**Figure 14.20**). So if you click in the middle of someone's nose, go up to the forehead, click and drag, you'll be planting a nose in the middle of the forehead. Then if you let go, move over a little bit, and click again, you'll add a second nose. But that would happen only if you have the Aligned check box off. For most retouching, leave the check box on (assume you'll need to have it turned on to follow the techniques I cover here, unless I specifically tell you to turn it off). That way you don't have to be careful with letting go of the mouse button.

Figure 14.19 You can release the mouse button as many times as you want with the Aligned check box turned on because the pieces of the cloned image will line up to create a continuous image. (© 2002 Stockbyte, www.stockbyte.com)

Figure 14.20 When the Aligned checkbox is turned off, the Clone Stamp tool resets itself to the original starting point each time you release the mouse button.

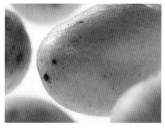

Figure 14.21 You might want to play down some recognizable feature. (© 2002 Stockbyte, www.stockbyte.com)

Opacity Settings

Sometimes you don't want to completely cover something up; you may just want to lessen its impact (**Figure 14.21**). For example, you might not want to completely wipe out a recognizable feature (such as Gorbachev's birthmark) for fear that it'll be obvious the image was enhanced. To do this, lower the opacity on the Clone Stamp tool (**Figure 14.22**). You can also press the number keys on your keyboard; pressing 1 will give you 10%, 2 will give you 20%, and so on. To get it all the way up to 100%, just type 0 (zero). This will allow you to paint over an area and partially replace it, so that the area you're applying blends with what used to be in that area.

Figure 14.22 By lowering the opacity of the Clone Stamp tool, you can reduce the impact of undesirable features.

Straight Lines

Have you ever seen a carpenter "snap a chalk line" to get a straight line over an area? There are occasions when I've been grateful to know how to do something similar in Photoshop. Let's say you have an image with someone holding a surfboard. You want to remove the arm that is draped over the board. That means you're going to have to replace it with a new chunk of surfboard. For it to look realistic, of course, the new chunk of surfboard will have to align perfectly with the rest of the board. When you get into this kind of situation, try this: Move your cursor until it's touching the original line (or edge of the surfboard, in this case). When it's perfectly touching it, Option-click (Mac) or Alt-click (Windows), as shown in **Figure 14.23**. Then go to the area where you want the new piece of surfboard to appear and click where you think it would naturally line up with the other part of the board. Then when you drag, your two cursors will line up just right, making the line look continuous and straight, as in **Figure 14.24**. You can even Shift-click in two spots and Photoshop will trace a straight line with the Clone Stamp between those two areas. Other examples would be stairs, or a lamppost, or any object with straight lines that has been obstructed by another object.

Figure 14.23 When retouching straight lines, Option-click or Alt-click when your cursor touches the line, then click in another area that also touches the line. (© 2002 Stockbyte, www.stockbyte.com)

Figure 14.24 If the cursors align, lines will remain nice and straight.

Layers

If you are using layers in your document, the Clone Stamp tool will work on one layer at a time unless you turn on the Use All Layers checkbox located on the Options bar. With this option turned on, Photoshop will act as if your document has no layers at all. In other words, it will be able to take from any layer that is below your cursor, as if they were all combined. However, it will apply, or deposit, the information you are cloning only onto the currently active layer. That way, you can create a new empty layer, turn on the Use All Layers checkbox, and retouch your image (**Figure 14.25**). Don't worry if you mess up, because the information is sitting on its own layer, while the unretouched image is directly below it (**Figures 14.26 and 14.27**). This allows you to switch over to the Eraser tool and erase small areas of that layer, or do other things such as lower the opacity of the layer.

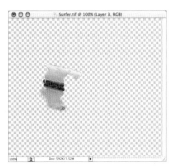

Figure 14.25 You can place your retouching on a new layer so it is isolated from the underlying image.

Figure 14.26 The underlying image will be untouched under the retouching layer.

Figure 14.27 When the layers are viewed at the same time, you can see the complete retouched image.

Patchwork

Sampling from one area and applying it all over the place will make it look pretty obvious that you've cloned something. You'll start seeing repeated shapes. For instance, if there happens to be a little dark area in the image you were cloning from, you will see that same dark area in the image you've applied it to. And if you look at it closely enough, you will see the shape repeat itself, which can start to look like a pattern. (You've just been busted cloning!) Sometimes, though, you might want to do this just to fill in an area, but then go back and fix up the places that appear patterned. You can do this by Option-clicking (Mac) or Alt-clicking (Windows) a random area around the place you've retouched, and then applying it on top of one of the patterned areas. But watch out—Photoshop's round brushes can be a dead giveaway, because you can easily pick out the areas that you're trying to disguise. This is a great time to use one of the odd-shaped brushes that appear at the bottom of the Brushes palette. These will provide better cover for areas that look obviously cloned. Another trick is to apply some noise to the entire image, which will make any retouching you've performed blend right into the image. To accomplish that, choose Filter > Noise > Add Noise, use an amount somewhere around 3, set the Distribution to Uniform, and turn off the Monochromatic checkbox.

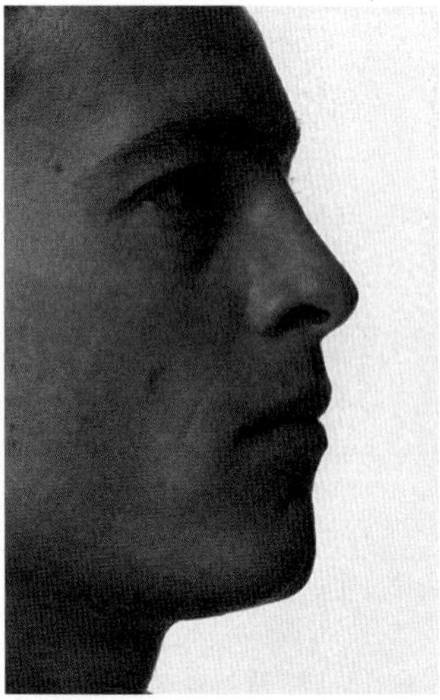

Let's see how this works in action. I'll show you how I reconstructed a forehead using the Clone Stamp tool. **Figure 14.28** displays a photo of a man's face. I copied one side of his face and chose Edit > Transform > Flip Horizontal to make it appear as a mirror image (**Figure 14.29**). However, the top of his head was cut off in the photograph, so I decided to put in a new one (forehead, that is). The first thing I did was clone the area directly below the part of his forehead that was missing (**Figure 14.30**). With the cloned forehead material, I filled in the missing part of his forehead, doing my best to make it even. After I applied several doses of forehead, it was obvious to me that I had cloned from one large area. So, I went in and touched up any repeated shapes to make it look more natural (**Figure 14.31**).

Figure 14.28 Original image. (© 2002 Stockbyte, www.stockbyte.com)

Now, however, if you look at the top of his head, there is a highlight on each edge that suddenly stops in the area I retouched. When I was filling up his forehead by clicking back and forth, I didn't get any of the highlights. So to add the highlight on the edge of his head, I grabbed from very small areas on other highlighted parts of his forehead and applied it right on the new edge (**Figure 14.32**).

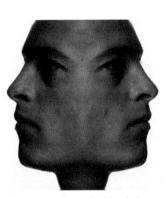

Figure 14.29 Two sides blended together, but missing a forehead.

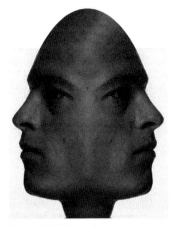

Figure 14.30 Basic cloning to reconstruct forehead.

Figure 14.31 Repeated patterns retouched.

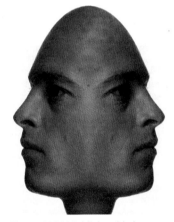

Figure 14.32 Highlight added to edge of forehead.

Lighten/Darken

It's easy to remove small scratches or little imperfections that are much brighter or much darker than the image that surrounds them; all you have to do is know a few little tricks. Let's say you have a background that has a scratch that is much brighter than the area around it. Naturally, you'll want to clone from the surrounding area; but before you do, you'll need to mess with the blending mode settings from the Options bar. (We talked about blending modes in

Chapter 13, "Enhancement," so here we'll just look at what we need for the Clone Stamp tool.) The blending mode pop-up menu in the Options bar is labeled Mode. The Lighten and Darken options are both very useful when retouching. If you set that menu to Darken, it will compare what you're about to apply to what the image looks like underneath, and it will only allow you to darken things. So let's say you had a light-colored scratch in the background of your image (**Figure 14.33**). You could clone from an area directly around it that is the correct brightness. But before you apply the cloned material to the scratch, you might want to set the blending mode to Darken (**Figure 14.34**). In Darken, all Photoshop can do is darken your picture. Under no circumstances will it be able to lighten it.

The blending mode menu can also be useful when you have a background with little bitty dark specks in it (**Figure 14.35**). To remove them, choose the Clone Stamp tool and set the blending mode to Lighten (**Figure 14.36**). Then clone from the areas around the specks and cover up the dark specks. This will allow the retouched areas to blend into the image more so you don't see a big gob where you retouched the image.

Automatic Sharpening

The automatic sharpening function that's built into some scanners makes retouching much more difficult. If possible, turn off any sharpening settings in your scanning software (**Figures 14.37** and **14.38**).

Figure 14.33 Original image.

Figure 14.34 Scratch retouched by using the Clone Stamp tool set to Darken.

Figure 14.35 Image contains dark blotches in the background.

Figure 14.36 Blotches removed by using the Clone Stamp tool set to Lighten.

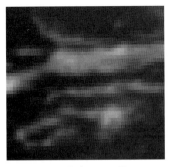

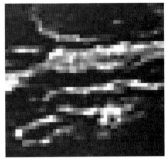

WARNING

To clone between two documents, both documents need to be in the same color mode. If one of the documents is in RGB and the other is in CMYK, Photoshop won't allow you to cross-clone.

Figure 14.37 Unsharpened image.

Figure 14.38 Image sharpened during scan.

Cloning Between Documents

With the Clone Stamp tool, you're not limited to just cloning from what's in the active document. You can open a second image and clone from that image as well (**Figure 14.39**). All you have to do is move your cursor outside the current image window and on top of another open document. Now you can Option-click (Mac) or Alt-click (Windows) anywhere in that second document and apply it within the document you are working on. It will copy from one document and paste into another.

Figure 14.39 Cloning between two documents. (© 2002 Stockbyte, www.stockbyte.com)

The Dodge and Burn Tools

Now that we've had some fun with the Clone Stamp tool, let's take a look at the Dodge and Burn tools. The words *dodge* and *burn* are taken from a traditional photographic darkroom. In a darkroom, an enlarger projects an image onto a sheet of photographic paper. While the image is being projected, you could put something in the way of the light source, which would obstruct the light in such a way that it would hit certain areas more than others—a technique known as *dodging the light*. Or you could intensify the light by cupping your hands together, creating just a small hole in between them, and allowing the light to concentrate on a certain area more than others—a technique known as *burning*. Using a combination of these two methods, you can brighten or darken your image. Photoshop reproduces these techniques with two tools: Dodge and Burn. If you look at the icons for these tools, you'll see that one of them looks like a hand; that would be for burning, allowing the light to go through the opening of your hand. The other one looks like (at least I think it looks like) a lollipop, which you can use for obstructing, or dodging, the light.

The Dodge Tool

Let's take a closer look at the Dodge tool. Because it can lighten your image, the Dodge tool comes in handy when you are working on people with dark shadows under their eyes. But before we get into cosmetic surgery, I'll introduce you to a very important pop-up menu, called the Range menu, which is associated with this tool. You'll find it in the Options bar at the top of your screen (**Figure 14.40**). The pop-up menu has three choices: Shadows, Midtones, and Highlights. This menu tells Photoshop which shades of gray it should concentrate on when you pan across your image.

NOTES

The Spacing setting of your brush will also affect how much the image is changed when using the Dodge and Burn tools. Higher Spacing settings will affect the image less.

Figure 14.40 Dodge tool Options bar.

If you use the Shadows setting, you will change mainly the dark part of your image. As you paint across your image, your brush will brighten the areas it touches. But as you get into the midtones of the image, it will apply it less and less. And if you paint over the light parts of the image, it won't change them much, if at all. The second choice is Midtones. If you use this setting, you will affect mainly the middle shades of gray in your image, or those areas that are about 25 to 75 percent gray. It shouldn't change the shadows or highlights very much. They may change a little bit, but only so they can blend into those areas. The third choice is Highlights. Highlights will mainly affect the lightest parts of your image and slowly blend into the middle tones of your image. You can see the effects of all of these settings in **Figure 14.41**.

Figure 14.41 Top: Shadows. Middle: Midtones. Bottom: Highlights.

Obviously, you'll need to decide exactly which setting would work best for your situation. If you don't do this before using the Dodge tool, you might cause yourself some grief. Let's say you're trying to fix dark areas around someone's eyes, but the Dodge tool doesn't seem to be doing the job (**Figure 14.42**). Then, after dozens of tries, you finally realize that the Range pop-up menu is set to Highlights instead of Midtones (look at the eyes in **Figures 14.43** and **14.44**).

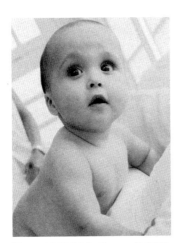

Figure 14.42 Original image. (© 2002 Stockbyte, www.stockbyte.com)

Figure 14.43 Dodge tool set to Highlights.

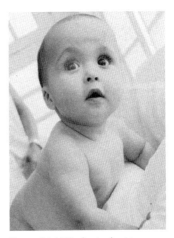

Figure 14.44 Dodge tool set to Midtones.

You also have an Exposure setting on the Options bar that controls how much brighter the image will become. As with most Photoshop tools, you can use the number keys on your keyboard to change this setting.

Color Images

The Dodge tool works exceptionally well on grayscale images. All you have to do is choose which part of the image you want to work on—Shadows, Midtones, or Highlights—and paint across an area. Unfortunately, it's not as slick with color images. If you use the Dodge tool on color, you'll find that it tends to wash out some of the colors and in some cases even change them (**Figures 14.45 and 14.46**).

One good solution is to duplicate the layer you're working on and set the blending mode of the duplicate to Luminosity before using the Dodge tool. That should maintain the original colors and limit your changes to the brightness of the image. Or, you can forgo the Dodge tool and just use the Paintbrush tool. You can set your Paintbrush tool's blending mode to Color Dodge and choose white to paint with. But just going ahead and painting across an image will look rather ridiculous, because all it's doing is blowing out the detail (**Figure 14.47**).

Figure 14.45 Original image. (© 2002 Stockbyte, www.stockbyte.com)

Figure 14.46 Eyes lightened by using the Dodge tool.

To get it to work correctly, just lower the Opacity setting on the tool to about 20% (**Figure 14.48**). This will allow you to create highlights or to brighten areas. Sometimes this works a little bit better than the Dodge tool.

Figure 14.47 Painting with white by using the Color Dodge mode.

Figure 14.48 Eyes lightened by painting with white by using the Color Dodge blending mode and a low Opacity setting.

The Burn Tool

The Burn tool is designed for darkening areas of an image. Like the Dodge tool, it has Range options in its palette for Highlights, Midtones, and Shadows, as well as an Exposure setting. It, too, works great with grayscale images. So if you are ever dealing with a shiny spot on someone's (grayscale) forehead or nose because the light is reflecting off it, you can go ahead and try to fix it with the Burn tool (compare **Figures 14.49** and **14.50**).

Color Fixes

Just as with the Dodge tool, you'll start having problems when you use the Burn tool with a color image. Flesh tones are the worst—they just seem to look sunburned or they turn black (**Figures 14.51** and **14.52**).

Figure 14.49 Original image. (© 2002 Stockbyte, www.stockbyte.com)

Figure 14.50 Forehead darkened (subtly) by using the Burn tool.

Figure 14.51 Face darkened by using the Burn tool set to Midtones. (© 2002 Stockbyte, www.stockbyte.com)

Figure 14.52 Face darkened by using the Burn tool set to Highlights.

Let's say you're in CMYK mode. When you use the Burn tool, it's going to darken all of the different channels in your image (**Figure 14.53**). Remember, a CMYK image is made out of cyan, magenta, yellow, and black. Think about a face. Do you want very much black? Probably not. Do you want very much cyan? Maybe only a tiny bit. For the most part, Caucasian faces are mainly made up of magenta and yellow. (Black, Asian, and Hispanic faces might need a wee bit extra cyan; it makes the skin look tan.) Using the Burn tool, if you try to get rid of a bright spot on somebody's forehead and you're in CMYK mode, it's just going to make that forehead get darker and darker and, of course, look terrible. To overcome this, start out by setting the Range pop-up menu in the Options bar to Highlights, because you want to work on the light part of the image. Then isolate just the magenta and yellow channels by opening the Channels palette and clicking on the magenta channel and Shift-clicking on the yellow channel (**Figures 14.54** and **14.55**).

Figure 14.53 Burning all the color channels.

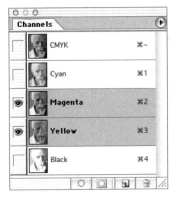

Figure 14.54 Magenta and yellow channels visible.

Figure 14.55 Editing the magenta and yellow channels.

There's one more thing you might want to do, for your own convenience. If you look at the main image window, it will appear as if your entire image is made from just magenta and yellow. That makes it a little difficult to work with. Ideally, you'd want to view the image in full color, but still only work on magenta and yellow. To do this, turn on the eyeball on the topmost channel, which is the Composite channel (**Figure 14.56**). That will make it so you see all four channels of the image but you're still editing magenta and yellow only.

Now you can go in and try to get rid of those bright spots on foreheads and noses (**Figure 14.57**). This should work quite nicely. If you are working in RGB mode, you can accomplish the same thing; you just want to work on the green and blue channels. You don't have to remember which specific channels to work on—instead, just click through the channels, look for where the problem area shows up, and fix only those channels.

One Last Step

OK, you've retouched your image; now you have one very important bit of housekeeping to take care of. Remember when you clicked on the specific channels to isolate the colors? Well, if you leave the Channels palette as is, everything you do from now on will affect only those two channels. To remedy this, click the topmost channel in the Channels palette so that all the channels are highlighted and all the channels are visible for editing, as shown in **Figure 14.58**. Now you're ready to go.

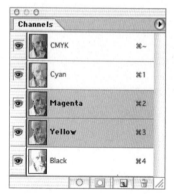

Figure 14.56 Editing the magenta and yellow channels while viewing all the color channels.

Figure 14.57 Using the Burn tool on the magenta and yellow channels.

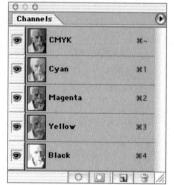

Figure 14.58 When you're finished, be sure to click the topmost channel to make all channels active for editing.

The Sponge Tool

Hiding in with the Dodge and Burn tools is the Sponge tool. It works as if you have a sponge full of bleach, where you can paint across your image and soak up the color. Or you can do the opposite and intensify the colors—it's all determined by what you choose from the Mode menu in the Options bar. If you choose Desaturate, then the Sponge tool will tone down the colors in the area you are painting. The more you paint across an area, the closer it will become to being grayscale. This can be useful when you'd like to make a product stand out from an otherwise distracting background (**Figure 14.59**). I also use it (with a very low Pressure setting) to minimize the yellow/orange colorcast that usually shows up in the teeth of people who smoke or drink coffee a lot.

The Saturate setting will intensify the colors as you paint over them, which is great for giving people rosy cheeks (**Figure 14.60**). This can also be great for adding a bit more color to people's lips.

The Sharpen and Blur Tools

When you need to blur or sharpen an area, you have two choices: Select an area and apply a filter, or use the Blur and Sharpen tools. Using filters to blur and sharpen your image has a few advantages over using the tools. These include getting a preview of the image before you commit to the settings being used and having the ability to apply the filter effect evenly to the area you are changing. But occasionally the Blur and Sharpen tools can really help when working on small areas, so let's take a look at how they work and when to use them.

The Blur Tool

The Blur tool is pretty straightforward. You can paint across any part of your image and blur everything that your cursor passes over. In the Blur tool Options bar, you will find a Pressure setting that determines how much you will blur the image; higher settings blur the image more.

Figure 14.59 Front and rear apples were desaturated to make the central one stand out. (© 2001 Stockbyte, www.stockbyte.com)

Figure 14.60 The woman's left cheek was enhanced using the Sponge tool set to Saturate. (© 2001 Stockbyte, www.stockbyte.com)

WARNING

Don't go over the image once with the Blur tool set to Lighten and then switch over to Darken and go over it again. That would be the same as leaving it set to Normal, and you would be back to Vaseline face. So use it just once, with it set to either Lighten or Darken. Just think about what is most prominent in a wrinkle. Is it the light area of the wrinkle, or the dark area? That will indicate which setting you should use.

This can be useful if there are little, itty-bitty areas of detail obstructing your image. I generally prefer to use the Gaussian Blur filter instead of this Blur tool because it does a better job of evenly blurring an area.

I like to use the Blur tool instead for reducing—not removing—wrinkles (**Figure 14.61**). If you turn the pressure way up on this tool and paint across a wrinkle a few times, you'll see it begin to disappear. But you'll also notice that it doesn't look very realistic. It might look as if you had smeared some Vaseline on the face. To really do a wrinkle justice, you have to take a closer look. Wrinkles are made out of two parts, a highlight and a shadow (light part and dark part). If you paint across that with the Blur tool, the darker part of the wrinkle will be lightened, while the lightest part will be darkened, so that they become more similar in shade (**Figure 14.62**).

To reduce the impact of a wrinkle without completely getting rid of it (if I wanted to get rid of it, I would use the Clone Stamp tool), turn the Pressure setting all the way up. Then change the blending mode to either Darken or Lighten. If the part that makes that wrinkle most prominent is the dark area, then set the blending mode menu to Lighten (**Figure 14.63**). Then when you paint across the area, the only thing it will be able to do is lighten that wrinkle. But because you are using the Blur tool, it's not going to completely lighten it and make it disappear. Instead, it will reduce the impact of it. You really have to try this to see how it looks.

Figure 14.61 Original image. (© 2002 Stockbyte, www.stockbyte.com)

Figure 14.62 Wrinkles around eye blurred.

Figure 14.63 Wrinkles around eye lessened by using the Blur tool with a blending mode of Lighten.

Layers

When I'm retouching wrinkles, I usually create a brand-new, empty layer (**Figure 14.64**). Then, in order to be able to use the Blur tool, I have to turn on the Use All Layers checkbox in the Options bar (**Figure 14.65**). Otherwise, Photoshop can look at only one layer at a time, and it won't have any information to blur. By doing all these steps, I can easily delete areas or redo them without having to worry about permanently changing the original image. If you're attempting the wrinkle technique I mentioned earlier, then you'll need to set the blending mode of the layer to Lighten, and you might need to lower the Pressure setting of the Blur tool.

Figure 14.64 By creating a new layer before using the Blur tool, you can isolate the unretouched image.

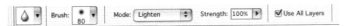

Figure 14.65 The Blur tool will not be able to use information on other layers unless you turn on the Use All Layers checkbox.

The Sharpen Tool

The Sharpen tool works in a fashion similar to that of its relative the Sharpen filter. But with this tool you have to adjust the Pressure setting in the Options bar to determine how much you want to sharpen the image. And you have to be careful: If you turn the Pressure setting up too high or paint across an area too many times, you're going to get some really weird effects (**Figures 14.66** to **14.68**).

Figure 14.66 Original image. (© 2002 Stockbyte, www.stockbyte.com)

Figure 14.67 Sharpened using the Sharpen tool with a medium Pressure setting.

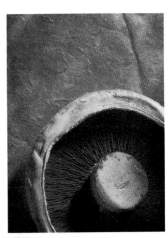

Figure 14.68 Sharpened using the Sharpen tool with a high Pressure setting.

Figure 14.69 Original image. (© 2001 Stockbyte, www.stockbyte.com)

Figure 14.70 Metallic highlights sharpened.

Reflected Highlights

When you run across an image that contains glass, metal, or other shiny objects, it usually contains extremely bright highlights (known as specular highlights). This usually happens when light reflects off one of those very shiny areas, such as the edge of a glass. These extra-bright highlights often look rather flat and lifeless after being adjusted. This happens because whenever we adjust an image to perform color correction, or prepare it for printing or multimedia, the brightest areas of the image usually become 3 or 4 percent gray (instead of white). But if you sharpen those areas, you're going to brighten them and make them pure white. This will make them stand out and look more realistic. So this means any time you have jewelry, glassware, or reflected light in people's eyes, you'll want to use the Sharpen tool, bring down the pressure to about 30%, and go over those areas once. That will make them almost pure white; when you print them, they will almost jump off the page, as they should (**Figures 14.69** and **14.70**).

Closing Thoughts

We've covered all the tools you'll need to become a bona fide "photo doctor." Bear in mind that you don't need to limit yourself to just photographs; the tools and techniques we've covered in this chapter can be used for non-photographic images as well. And, as with everything else in Photoshop, once you've gone around the block with these tools a few times, you'll probably think of a dozen other things you can do with them.

So, whether you're giving someone a face-lift, removing your former boy- or girlfriend from a photograph, or clear-cutting telephone poles from an otherwise perfect Kodak moment, just promise me that you won't do anything underhanded for some ethically challenged dictator.

Ben's Techno-babble Decoder Ring

Specular highlight: An area that shines light directly into the camera lens, usually caused by a light source reflecting off the reflective surface of glass, metal, or other shiny objects. Specular highlights do not contain any detail and should be reproduced as solid white to maintain realism.

Keyboard Shortcuts

FUNCTION	MACINTOSH	WINDOWS
Next Brush	>	>
Previous Brush	<	<
First Brush	Shift-<	Shift-<
Last Brush	Shift->	Shift->
Tool Opacity	0 through 9	0 through 9
Toning Tool	O	O
CYCLE THROUGH TONING TOOLS	SHIFT-O	SHIFT-O
Blur/Sharpen Tools	R	R
Switch between Blur and Sharpen	Shift-R	Shift-R
Use Shadows	Shift-Option-S	Shift-Alt-S
Use Midtones	Shift-Option-M	Shift-Alt-M
Use Highlights	Shift-Option-H	Shift-Alt-H

Computer Graphics: Robert Bowen; Photography: Howard Berman

Computer Graphics: Robert Bowen; Photography: Howard Berman

Courtesy of Nick Koudis, www.koudis.com

15

Type and Background Effects

© Don Barnett, Nekton Inc., www.donbarnett.com

When ideas fail, words come in very handy.

—Goethe

NEW IN 7

There haven't been all that many changes to text in Photoshop 7.0, so we just created a bunch of new type effects and background patterns. We also cover the new Pattern Maker filter.

Type and Background Effects

For me, coming up with the ideal text and background to complement an image is a thoroughly enjoyable process. It's like putting the icing on the cake and then being able to stand back and admire the final creation. I can't help you with your design, but I can help you master the tools you'll need to create some awesome type and background effects.

Figure 15.1 Photoshop 5.5's text was pixel-based, which could cause it to appear jaggy.

No More Jaggy Text

Jaggy text is an unsightly blemish that we've all experienced and wished we could make go away. The unwanted jaggies appear when the pixels in an image are big enough that you can easily see them when printed (**Figure 15.1**). They show up as rough, jagged edges on your printouts, and they are the cause of much hair-pulling and sudden bursts of profanity in the graphic arts industry.

Pixel-based text is great for the Web, but was less than ideal when you had to save the text in a file, use it in a page layout program, and send it off to the printer. Invariably you would get some degree of jagginess, which is why so many professional designers would bypass Photoshop (pre 6.0, that is) and create text in their page layout program, or in Adobe Illustrator, where it would be object-based (also known as vector-based).

Stick with me on this. In the graphic arts industry, the distinction between object-based and pixel-based is an extremely important one, and understanding it will serve you well. Object-based simply means that text is no longer made up of pixels; it's a single element that can be scaled up or down without losing the integrity of its shape. For example, if you import a photograph of a circular object into your page layout program and then try to scale it up, it doesn't make more pixels to accommodate the larger size.

Instead, it simply makes each pixel larger to fill the space. Thus the jaggy look. Not so with object-based shapes! If you created that same circle in Adobe Illustrator (which creates strictly object-based images), you could do anything you want to that circle (make it bigger, smaller, oval, etc.), and it will always retain its smooth edge. That's why most logos are created in Illustrator. But with Photoshop 6.0 and above, we can have object-based text (**Figure 15.2**).

But not everything is roses and chocolate. The one stipulation about the new object-based text is that it must be printed on a *PostScript printer*. Otherwise it will revert to being plain old pixel-based text again, and the jaggies you love to hate will be back staring you in the face. So if you have a $200 inkjet printer, you're really no further ahead when it comes to the jaggies, unless your printer happens to have a PostScript RIP, which is usually a software accessory you can add to a low-end inkjet printer.

Entering Text

This is going to be a short section, because all you have to do to lay down some text is click with the Type tool and start typing directly on your image. Photoshop will automatically create a new Type layer. If you want Photoshop to act like an old Smith Corona typewriter—that is, where you have to press Return (Macintosh) or Enter (Windows) to create a new line—just click the mouse button without dragging, and begin typing. This is known as point text and is useful for creating headlines that you don't want to wrap onto multiple lines. But if you'd rather have Photoshop automatically wrap your text into a multi-line paragraph, then click and drag to create a rectangular box that will contain your text. Then you can enter your text and press Return (Macintosh) or Enter (Windows) whenever you need to create a new paragraph. Photoshop will do the rest, wrapping your text onto multiple lines based on the column width you define. While you are in the Type tool, you can always change the column width by dragging one of the side handles, and then the text will reflow.

NOTES

You can achieve crisp text on a non-PostScript printer by saving your image as a PDF file and printing it from Adobe Acrobat.

Figure 15.2 In Photoshop 6.0, text became object-based, which allows it to stay crisp as long as it is printed on a PostScript printer.

Figure 15.3 The Character and Paragraph palettes.

Editing Text

The Character and Paragraph palettes offer a wide range of choices for editing text (**Figure 15.3**). But before you start messing with these settings, you'll need to highlight the text you would like to edit. You can do this by dragging across a range of text or by typing Command-A (Macintosh) or Ctrl-A (Windows) to select all the text. The Character palette will work exclusively on the text that is highlighted, whereas the Paragraph palette will work on entire paragraphs regardless of whether all the text is selected.

Some of you Photoshoppers may not have been steeped in desktop publishing, so here's a basic rundown of the typographical controls you're going to know and love.

Font—I like to click on the Font field and then use the up and down arrow keys to cycle through all the choices that appear in the list. You can also click on the Font field and start typing a font name, and Photoshop will move you to the first font that starts with those letters. Or, if you want to do it the traditional way, just click on the arrow to the right of the Font field and you'll be presented with a full font menu. If you have more than one version of the same font installed, then Photoshop will add (T1) next to the PostScript Type 1 version of the font, (TT) next to the TrueType version, or (OT) for an OpenType font.

Style—Once you've chosen the font family you'd like to use, you can find out which styles (bold, italic, etc.) are available by clicking on the Style menu. If you find that the font you want to use doesn't contain a bold or italic style, you can experiment with the Faux Bold and Faux Italic icons near the bottom of the Character palette to have Photoshop thicken or slant the typeface.

Size—You can specify the measurement system that will be used to determine the size of your type by choosing Edit > Preferences > Units & Rulers. There are three ways to measure your text: in pixels, in millimeters, or in points. The pixels option is resolution-independent, meaning that the height of the text in pixels will be the same regardless of the resolution of your image. The only time I use the pixels option is when I need to match the height of some existing text that has already been measured in pixels. More often than not, I prefer to measure text in points because I can use the same setting in multiple documents and know that the text will appear the same size when printed regardless of the resolution of the file it is used in. It's also a system that's consistent with most publishing programs. I have never used the millimeters option because I don't know of any other program that uses that system to measure type.

To be honest, it isn't very often that I pay attention to the actual type-size settings. Instead, I eyeball it and compare the size of my text to the rest of the image. To quickly adjust the size of the text in increments of two, highlight the text and type Shift-Command-> or Shift-Command-< (Macintosh) or Shift-Ctrl-> or Shift-Ctrl-< (Windows). To change the size in increments of ten, just add the Option key (Macintosh) or the Alt key (Windows) to these keyboard commands. Also, you can scale text up or down using the Edit > Transform > Scale option; it won't harm your text.

Leading—To change the vertical space between lines of text, you'll need to change the leading setting. If you leave it set to (Auto), then Photoshop will automatically calculate its own setting and keep it hidden from you (**Figure 15.4**). It does this by multiplying the size of the text by the percentage specified in the Justification dialog box that appears in the side menu of the Paragraph palette; the default setting is 120%. So 100-point text, for example, would have an automatic leading setting of 120. The Auto setting is useful if you know you'll be changing the size of the text later on, because the leading setting will change as you change the size of the text. If you don't like the Auto setting, you can type in your own setting (**Figure 15.5**). To quickly change the leading in increments of two, highlight the text, then type Option-up arrow and Option-down arrow (Macintosh) or Alt-up arrow and Alt-down arrow (Windows). To set the leading to Auto, either type (Auto) into the Leading field, or type Shift-Option-Command-A (Macintosh) or Shift-Alt-Ctrl-A (Windows).

NOTES

You can double-click to select a word, triple-click to select a line, quadruple-click to select a paragraph, and quintuple-click to select all.

You can type Command-H (Macintosh) or Ctrl-H (Windows) to hide the highlighting that indicates a range of text is selected. If you type that shortcut a second time, the highlighting will become visible again.

Graphic Savage

Figure 15.4 Leading setting determined by Photoshop (auto).

Graphic Savage

Figure 15.5 Leading setting adjusted manually.

Kerning—If you need to tighten up or loosen the space between two letters, click between the letters, then change the Kerning setting to increase (positive numbers) or decrease (negative numbers) the amount of space between those letters (**Figures 15.6** and **15.7**). Kerning is essential when working with numbers, because they are designed to line up in a spreadsheet program, which means the number 1 will always have a bunch of space around it to force it to take up as much space as the other numbers. To quickly change the Kerning setting in increments of 20, type Option-right arrow and Option-left arrow (Macintosh) or Alt-right arrow and Alt-left arrow (Windows). You can also add the Command key (Macintosh) or the Ctrl key (Windows) to these keyboard commands to increase the Kerning setting in increments of 100. If you use the Metrics setting, then Photoshop will use the kerning settings that are built into the typeface.

Figure 15.6 Text entered with the Metrics kerning setting selected.

Figure 15.7 Manually kerned text.

Tracking—To add or remove space between all the letters in a range of text, highlight the text, and then change the tracking setting (compare **Figures 15.8** and **15.9**). Or type Option-right arrow (Macintosh) and Option-left arrow (Macintosh) or Alt-right arrow (Windows) and Alt-left arrow (Windows) to change the Tracking in increments of 20. To change the Tracking setting in increments of 100, just add the Command key (Macintosh) or Ctrl key (Windows) to these keyboard commands. To set the tracking to zero, just leave the Tracking field empty, or type Shift-Command-Q (Macintosh) or Shift-Ctrl-Q (Windows). I often use a negative tracking setting for headlines where I like the text to be nice and tight. I use positive tracking any time I have ALLCAPS text because it seems to make it easier to read.

Figure 15.8 Tracking: 0.

Figure 15.9 Tracking: 260.

Vertical Scale—This setting allows you to stretch your text vertically without changing its width. I often do this when I want to create a raised capital at the beginning of a paragraph. I just set both the vertical and horizontal scale settings to an equal number, and then, when I change the size of the text, the raised cap will change along with it, as long as all the text is selected (**Figure 15.10**). To set the Vertical Scale to 100%, type Shift-Option-Command-X (Macintosh) or Shift-Alt-Ctrl-X (Windows).

Horizontal Scale—This setting allows you to stretch or compress your text horizontally without changing its height. I often lower this setting a small amount (like by 1%) to make a line of text take up less space and prevent it from overflowing the space I have allotted. The alternative would be to use tracking, which leaves the shape of the characters intact, and simply removes an equal amount of space between each letter. To set the Horizontal Scale to 100%, type Shift-Command-X (Macintosh) or Shift-Ctrl-X (Windows).

Baseline Shift—To shift one or more letters up or down, highlight the letters, and then change the Baseline Shift setting (**Figures 15.11** and **15.12**). This is very useful when working with symbols, where a parenthesis might appear to be too low compared to the text, or an equal sign needs to be shifted to make it look better. To change this setting in increments of two, type Shift-Option-up arrow and Shift-Option-down arrow (Macintosh) or Shift-Alt-up arrow and Shift-Alt-down arrow (Windows).

Color—To change the color of the text, click on the color swatch to bring up the standard Color Picker. To use your foreground color, type Option-Delete (Macintosh) or Alt-Backspace (Windows). To use your background color, type Command-Delete (Macintosh) or Ctrl-Backspace (Windows).

Anti-aliased—You'll find five options in this pop-up menu; None, Sharp, Crisp, Strong, and Smooth (**Figure 15.13**). Using anything other than None will cause the pixels on the edge of the text to blend into the image and create a

A solid foundation of knowledge is essential before attempting to understand Photoshop's more advanced features.

Figure 15.10 The initial capital in this paragraph was created by setting the Vertical and Horizontal Scale settings to 200%.

Figure 15.11 No baseline shift.

Figure 15.12 Equal sign and small 2 baseline shifted.

smooth edge. Sharp will make the edges appear the sharpest, while Crisp will come in a close second in sharpness. Strong will make the text look a little bolder, and Smooth will make the edges appear softer. These options are great when creating small text that will be used on the Web. I suggest experimenting with each setting until you think the text looks its best. You can also use the Strong setting when creating text that will be printed, because it can help disguise the jaggies that appear on non-PostScript printers.

Anti-aliased
Anti-aliased
Anti-aliased
Anti-aliased
Anti-aliased
Anti-aliased

Figure 15.13 Anti-aliased settings from top to bottom: None, Sharp, Crisp, Strong, Smooth.

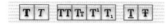

Figure 15.14 From left to right; Faux Bold, Faux Italic, All Caps, Small Caps, Superscript, Subscript, Underline, and Strikethrough.

Next, let's take a look at what the tiny icons are for near the bottom of the Characters palette (**Figure 15.14**).

All Caps—Changes your text to all capital letters. This can be useful if, for example, you decide to make a few subheads uppercase after the text has been entered. (Remember that all-capped text is more difficult to read, so you may want to add some tracking, which can make reading a bit easier.) Type Shift-Command-K (Macintosh) or Shift-Ctrl-K (Windows) to specify All Caps type.

Small Caps—Changes all lowercase letters into smaller capital letters while the capital letters you entered remain full size. This is useful for headings (**Figure15.15**), but is not as good as using a typeface that is specifically designed as a small caps font (the smaller letters don't have the same thickness when using this feature). Type Shift-Command-H (Macintosh) or Shift-Ctrl-H (Windows) to specify Small Caps type.

The Small Caps style will convert your text into all capital letters, where the characters that were created using the shift key will be larger than the characters that were previously lowercase.

THE SMALL CAPS STYLE WILL CONVERT YOUR TEXT INTO ALL CAPITAL LETTERS, WHERE THE CHARACTERS THAT WERE CREATED USING THE SHIFT KEY WILL BE LARGER THAN THE CHARACTERS THAT WERE PREVI-OUSLY LOWERCASE.

Figure 15.15 Top: type entered without formatting. Bottom: Small Caps style applied.

Superscript—This will reduce the size of the selected text and move the characters above the baseline of the rest of the text. I use this all the time when I'm typesetting prices—I remove the decimal and then use this option for the dollar sign and cents (**Figure 15.16**). Type Shift-Command-+ (Macintosh) or Shift-Ctrl-+ (Windows) to specify Superscript type.

Subscript—This option will also make your text smaller, but will shift things downward. It's useful when entering scientific and chemical formulas (**Figure 15.17**). Type Shift-Option-Command-+ (Macintosh) or Shift-Alt-Ctrl-+ (Windows) to specify Subscript type.

Underline—This option will place a line under each letter of your text in the same color as the type. (You cannot control the placement or thickness of the underline.) This feature can be useful when you want to make a selection of text stand out, like a link on a Web page, or the cents in a price (**Figure 15.18**). Type Shift-Command-U (Mac) or Shift-Ctrl-U (Windows) to specify underlined type.

20^{00}

Figure 15.16 The dollar sign and last two numbers were set using the Superscript style.

H_2O

Figure 15.17 The 2 was set using the Subscript style.

$371^{\underline{50}}$

Figure 15.18 The last two digits were set with both the Superscript and Underline styles.

On a Macintosh, type Option-8 to create a bullet; in Windows, type Alt-0149 on your numeric keypad.

Photoshop has keyboard shortcuts for just about everything. The key is to remember and use what's important to your particular workflow.

Photoshop has keyboard shortcuts for just about everything. The key is to remember and use what's important to your particular workflow.

Photoshop has keyboard shortcuts for just about everything. The key is to remember and use what's important to your particular workflow.

Photoshop has keyboard shortcuts for just about everything. The key is to remember and use

Figure 15.19 Paragraph alignment settings from top to bottom: Centered, Flush Left, Flush Right, Justified.

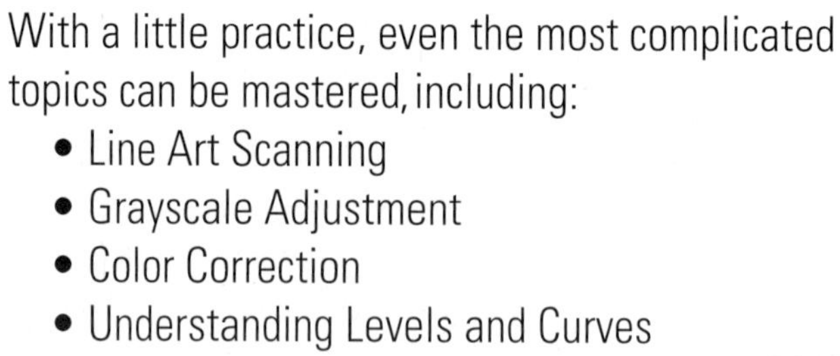

Strikethrough—This option will place a line through the center of the text using the same color as the type. (You cannot control the size or placement of the line.) This can be useful when advertising prices; you can cross out the old price and place the new one right next to it. Type Shift-Command-/ (Macintosh) or Shift-Ctrl-/ (Windows) to specify Strikethrough type. I find that the Underline and Strikethrough options are usually too thin and often appear as semi-transparent lines on small text.

Now let's move on to the Paragraphs palette and see what's in store for us.

Alignment—The Alignment choices determine the method used to align multiple lines of text (**Figure 15.19**). Most of the time I use the flush left option because it seems to be the easiest to read. Type Shift-Command-L (Macintosh) or Shift-Ctrl-L (Windows) to specify flush left text. Centered is good for headlines; type Shift-Command-C (Macintosh) or Shift-Ctrl-C (Windows) to specify centered text. Flush right is often useful for numbers, because it will line up the decimal points. Type Shift-Command-R (Macintosh) or Shift-Ctrl-R (Windows) to specify flush right text. I only use the justified option when I'm using a rather long column width; otherwise it causes huge spaces between words. Type Shift-Command-J (Macintosh) or Shift-Ctrl-J (Windows) to specify justified text.

Left Indent—This setting is useful when you have a bulleted list that you want to set off from the main flow of text (**Figure 15.20**).

With a little practice, even the most complicated topics can be mastered, including:
- Line Art Scanning
- Grayscale Adjustment
- Color Correction
- Understanding Levels and Curves

Figure 15.20 Bulleted list was set using a left indent of 12 pts.

Right Indent—I often use this setting along with the left indent setting to make a long quotation stand out from the rest of the text (**Figure 15.21**). You can also make the quotation marks extend beyond the margins by choosing Hanging Roman Punctuation from the side menu of the Paragraph palette.

It can be more pleasing when the flow of text is interrupted by other elements such as quotes and bullet points

> "This is a mighty fine example of a spiffy looking quote that is set off from the rest of the text."

Figure 15.21 Quote was set using a left indent of 24pts and a right indent of 30pts.

First Line Indent—This function indents the first line of each paragraph as if you pressed the Tab key on your keyboard. I also find this useful when I have a list of bulleted items that have more than one line each. I'll end up setting the Left Indent setting to something like 20pt and the First Line Indent setting to –20pt. That will force all the lines after the bulleted line to be indented (you may need to put some spaces after the bullet on the first line to make the text there line up with the lines below). Compare **Figures 15.22** and **15.23**. This technique is also useful when you want the first letter of a paragraph to extend into the margin.

Bulleted lists can pose many problems unless you are thoughtful when using Photoshop's settings.
- Some bulleted lists might extend to more than a single line, which can make them less than ideal for a simple left indent.
- That's when you might want to consider using a negative first line indent setting along with a simple left indent to control the rest of the lines.

Figure 15.22 Bulleted list was set using a left indent of 12 points.

NOTES

Did you know that the proper quote characters used by typography professionals are the curly ones, and not the straight ones (which are really inch and feet marks)? Previous versions of Photoshop gave you inch and feet marks, but Photoshop 7.0 creates quotes like a pro (the Use Smart Quotes option must be turned on in the General Preferences dialog box). If you're using an older version of Photoshop, then you'll need to use the following key combinations:

▸ Macintosh: For a single opening quote, type Option-], and for a single closing quote use Shift-Option-]. For a double opening quote, type Option-[, and for a closing double quote use Shift-Option-[.

▸ Windows: For a single opening quote, type Alt-0145, and for a single closing quote, type Alt-0146. For a double opening quote, type Alt-0147, and for a double closing quote type Alt-0148. Use your numeric keypad, and make sure your NumLock key is on.

Unfortunately, the Hanging Roman Punctuation option did not recognize proper curly quotes in previous versions of Photoshop.

Bulleted lists can pose many problems unless you are thoughtful when using Photoshop's settings.

- Some bulleted lists might extend to more than a single line, which can make them less than ideal for a simple left indent.
- That's when you might want to consider using a negative first line indent setting along with a simple left indent to control the rest of the lines.

Figure 15.23 Bulleted list was set with a left indent of 32pt and a first line indent of –20pts.

Space Above and Space Below—These settings are exactly what their names indicate. They control the space above and below your paragraph. I use Space Above as a substitute for indenting the first line of every paragraph (like all the paragraphs in this book). It is also useful when you have a bulleted list that contains more than one line per bullet point. I use Space Below to add a bit of extra space below the last line of a bulleted list so it doesn't look like it has melded with the paragraphs below it.

Hyphenate—This setting will use the settings in the Hyphenation dialog box (from the side menu of the Paragraph palette) to determine which words should break onto the next line of the text (**Figure 15.24**). Type Shift-Option-Command-H (Macintosh) or Shift-Alt-Ctrl-H (Windows) to toggle Hyphenation on and off. If you want to prevent a word from breaking, select the letters you'd like to keep together and then choose No Break from the side menu of the Character palette. The No Break feature is useful when you have initials, Web addresses, or company names that don't read well when broken onto multiple lines.

You'll also find other useful options in the side menu of the Character and Paragraph palettes. Let's take a look at the choices in these side menus that we haven't covered already.

Figure 15.24 The Hyphenation dialog box.

Ligatures—This option only works with OpenType fonts. It allows Photoshop to automatically replace certain combinations of characters (like "fi" and "fl") with a specially designed character that is a combination of those two, which makes them look more aesthetically pleasing (**Figure 15.25**).

fitness flex fitness flex

Figure 15.25 Left: text as entered with no formatting applied. Right: text with ligatures applied.

Old Style—This option only works with OpenType fonts. It tells Photoshop to use an alternative set of numerals that are smaller than the standard ones (**Figure 15.26**).

2929 2929

Figure 15.26 Left: text entered with no formatting applied. Right: text with Old Style applied (it only affects the numerals).

Fractional Widths—When this option is turned off, it forces Photoshop to use full pixels for spacing between words. This is useful for Web graphics where your text can be extra small and you want to prevent your text from smashing together (**Figure 15.27**).

1111111   1111111

Figure 15.27 Left: Fractional Widths turned on. Right: Fractional Widths turned off.

Reset Character—This option will reset all the Character palette settings to their defaults. This can be useful when you've just finished messing with a bunch of options and need to get back to setting some normal type.

Adobe Single-line Composer—This option is best when you want to "massage" type by hand and want to precisely control character and word spacing by manually kerning and tracking the characters.

Adobe Every-line Composer—This option will evaluate an entire paragraph to determine where each line of text should break. That means that the upper lines in a paragraph might suddenly change as you continue to add text to the bottom of a paragraph. This option usually gives you the best-looking text, but makes it a bit more difficult to manually tweak everything. Type Shift-Option-Command-T (Macintosh) or Shift-Alt-Ctrl-T (Windows) to toggle between the Single-Line and Every-Line Composer settings.

Reset Paragraph—This option will reset all the Paragraph palette settings back to their defaults. But be careful using it, because it will also reset all the settings in the Hyphenation and Justification dialog boxes.

The Options bar at the top of your screen contains the most commonly used choices from the Character and Paragraph palettes, along with a few options that can't be found in the other palettes. Let's take look at the options that are exclusive to this palette (**Figure 15.28**).

Figure 15.28 Photoshop Options bar for typographical controls.

If you click and hold on the Type tool in Photoshop 7.0, you'll notice a few extra choices. Let's see what these can do, then we'll see if there's anything unique in the Options Bar.

Type Mask—This option will deliver a selection shaped like text, instead of an actual Type layer. While you are entering your text, you will see a colored overlay that represents the bounds of the text. Once you finalize the text, it will create a selection. Just be aware that you will not be able to edit the text after it has become a selection. If you're worried that you might find a typo later, then use the normal Type tool, and once you're done editing the text, Command-click (Macintosh) or Ctrl-click (Windows) on the name of the layer to get a selection.

Vertical Type—This option will allow your text to run vertically, with each letter appearing below the previous one. This can be useful when setting type for the spine of a book, or when using Asian typefaces (**Figure 15.29**).

Now we're on to the choices that appear in the Options bar at the top of your screen. Most of these choices are available in the Character and Paragraph palettes, but there are a few that are unique to the Options bar.

Warp—This option is simply a shortcut for choosing Layer > Type > Warp Text. Either one will bring up the Type Warp dialog box, which we will cover later in this chapter.

C
O
O
L

Figure 15.29 Text set using the Vertical Type option.

NOTES

The Type Mask setting was removed from the Options bar in 7.0. You will now find it hiding out in your tool palette along with the normal type tool.

Palettes—The Palettes icon button will open the Character and Paragraph palettes. This allows you to close those two palettes (which I usually have stacked together as shown in Chapter 1) to avoid screen clutter and then quickly make them available with a single click.

There are some sparkling new additions to the Edit menu of Photoshop 7.0—Spell checking and Find and Replace Text. Being the abysmal speller I am, I used to enter text into a word processor just so I could get it spell checked before pasting into Photoshop. Pathetic and *very* cumbersome. You can imagine my delight when these new features came along and I loudly welcome them with gratitude and relief.

Spell Checker—The spell checker is pretty easy to use (**Figure 15.30**). It will indicate any words that it thinks are misspelled and then display a list of suggested alternatives at the bottom. Double-clicking on one of the alternatives will substitute that word and move on to the next questionable word. If Photoshop isn't able to come up with the correct alternative, then you can enter your own in the Change To field and then click the Change button. I just wish it could spell check the words that you manually enter. Clicking the Add button will add the highlighted word to Photoshop's dictionary so that it won't flag that word as a misspelling in the future. That's useful for company names and other unusual words that aren't in Photoshop's default dictionary. The Check All Layers check box will force Photoshop to spell check every Type layer that is available in the currently open document.

Figure 15.30 The Check Spelling dialog box.

Find and Replace Text—This allows you to search all the Type layers in the active document and replace the specified string of characters (**Figure 15.31**). If you've clicked within the text of a Type layer, then Photoshop will start searching from that point. This is useful when you find out that you've been misspelling someone's name for the entire length of a project, or when someone suddenly decides to change the name of a product.

Figure 15.31 The Find and Replace Text dialog box.

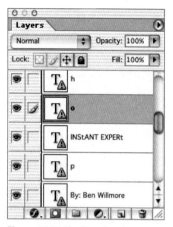

Figure 15.32 The Type layer's warning triangles.

Type Layers

After you add text to your image, the text will appear on a Type layer (indicated by a T where there would usually be a preview thumbnail in the Layers palette). This layer is special because you can edit the text at any time by using the Type tool and clicking within the text. If a yellow warning triangle appears along with the T that designates a Type layer, that's an indication that the typeface you've chosen is not currently installed in your operating system (**Figure 15.32**). When a font is missing, you will not be able to edit the text without having Photoshop substitute a different typeface. You might also run into a gray warning triangle on a Type layer. That's an indication that the text will be reflowed if it is edited; that might change the way the paragraph breaks into multiple lines. You'll get that symbol any time you open an image that was created in a version of Photoshop prior to 6.0.

A Type layer is also special because when you print your image on a PostScript printer, your text will appear crisp, even if the pixels in your image are large enough to make the rest of the image appear jaggy. That's because the text is object-based, instead of being made out of pixels. Photoshop will not convert the text to pixels unless you choose Layer > Rasterize > Type or merge a Type layer with another layer. Not only that, but Photoshop allows you to do a whole bunch of stuff to the Type layers without having to permanently convert them to pixels. Let's take a quick look at your choices. You can:

▶ Apply any of the choices in the Layer > Type > Warp Text dialog box.

▶ Apply most of the Edit > Transform functions.

▶ Add layer styles.

▶ Add a layer mask.

Before you can apply a filter or perform adjustments to the text, you have to convert the Type layer into a normal layer by choosing Layer > Rasterize > Type. That will convert the text from being object-based to being pixel-based. Once you've done that, you'll no longer be able to edit the text

NOTES

If you double-click the T that appears in the Layers palette for a Type layer, Photoshop will switch you to the Type tool and select the full range of text.

(Photoshop will treat it as a scanned image instead) and the text will no longer print with an absolutely crisp edge. If you don't rasterize, and you attempt to apply a filter to your text, Photoshop will warn you and then offer to rasterize the text for you.

Now that you've seen the options that are available when creating text, let's get into the juicy stuff and start creating type effects. I'll break the effects into two sections: effects that use type warping; and layer styles (which are especially wonderful because they are the only effects that allow the text to be edited). So without further ado, let's get started.

NOTES

In order to add a layer style to the Background image, you must first change its name (by double-clicking on it) to convert it into a normal layer.

Type Warping

Let's begin by choosing Layer > Type > Warp Text. You'll find 15 different warping effects you can use to contort your text into numerous shapes (**Figure 15.33**). Remember, this is a layer-based feature, so you can't warp only a part of a layer, or just a few words on a layer.

The Bend setting determines how dramatically your text will change (**Figure 15.34**). The Horizontal and Vertical Distortion settings can make it look as if your text is being viewed from different 3D angles (**Figure 15.35**).

After you've warped your type, you'll notice that a curve has been added below the T in the Layers palette. That signifies that the layer is a Type layer with warping applied, but you can still edit the text by using the Type tool and clicking within the text. The warp function is also great for creating animations in ImageReady, which we'll explore in a later chapter.

Figure 15.33 The Warp Text dialog box and the styles available on its drop-down menu.

Layer Styles

Okay, you've got your text formatted just the way you want it—you've typed and kerned and aligned and warped into wildness. Now you can rub your hands together and get ready for a thrill, because it's time to explore the Type Style dialog box (which is ground zero for creating type effects). Why the excitement? Because you'll be able to add a multitude of effects and still be able to edit your

WARNING

If you find that the Warp option is grayed out, then you most likely have used the Faux Bold style from the side menu of the Character palette. Unfortunately, warping doesn't work when that style is applied.

Figure 15.34 Bend settings from top to bottom: -50%, -25%, 0, +25, +50 (with the Arc effect).

Figure 15.35 Top: Horizontal and Vertical Distortion set to zero. Bottom: Horizontal Distortion of 85% and Vertical Distortion of 50%.

text! And because the effects are made by using layer styles, they won't require much memory (they are just simple settings applied to a layer) and should not increase the file size of your image too much. That means you can go crazy creating some great effects such as edge embossing, extruded or indented type, shadows, and beveled type, and you don't have to worry about bloating your file size. There are four ways to access the Layer Style dialog box:

▶ Option-Double-click (Macintosh), or Alt-Double-click (Windows) any layer name in the Layers palette.

▶ Choose one of the options from the Layer > Layer Style menu.

▶ Choose one of the options from the Layer Style menu at the bottom of the Layers palette (it's the black circle with the "f" inside).

▶ Choose Blending Options from the side menu of the Layers palette.

Once you've made it into the Layer Style dialog box, you can click on the name of any style listed on the left side of the dialog box to turn on that style and view its options. If you just click the check box next to a style's name, you will toggle that style on or off, but you will not view its settings—you have to click its name for that.

Layer styles determine their shape based on the contents of the layer that they are applied to. Typically, the entire content of a layer is fully visible, and an effect adds dimension on top of, or a shadow underneath, that content. It doesn't have to be that way. Sometimes you might want just the *effect* to be in the shape of a letter or word, but you don't want the original solid text to be visible. In that case, you have the option of tricking Photoshop into hiding the solid text that's in the Type layer. That will allow you to just use the shape of the text to figure out where to apply the layer style. To accomplish that, either change the Fill setting at the top of the Layers palette to zero, or click on the Blending Options choice in the upper left of the Layer Style dialog box, and then set the Fill Opacity (in the

Advanced Blending section) to zero (**Figure 15.36**). That should make the contents of the layer disappear, but will not affect any of the layer styles applied to the layer.

Beveled Edge Type

Now let's make our text disappear and then add some effects around its edge. Start by changing the Fill setting to zero at the top of the Layers palette. That should make the text completely disappear. Now let's get its outline to show up by adding a 10-pixel stroke on the outside of the text. Then to add a little more interest to that edge, add a Bevel and Emboss with the Style set to Stroke Emboss, the Technique set to Chisel Hard and the Size set to 10. Add a Contour to the Bevel and Emboss and click on the Contour preview and experiment with different shapes until you like the result (mine looked a little like a shark's fin). The final touch would be to add both a drop shadow and an inner shadow (**Figure 15.37**).

Textured Type

Let's make a type effect that has some texture to it and an interesting beveled edge. Start by adding a Pattern Overlay with the fourth preset pattern (it looks a little like brown cloth). Next, add a Bevel and Emboss, set the Style to Inner Bevel, the Technique to Chisel Hard, the Size to 10 and experiment with the other settings until you like the general look. To add a little more interesting texture, click the Texture choice just below the Bevel and Emboss choice on the left side of the Layer Style dialog box. Use the same pattern we used for the Bevel Overlay and experiment with the Depth setting until you get some good dimension to your text. Then to finish it off, add a nice drop shadow (**Figure 15.38**).

Jelly Type

Now let's create something a bit more complex. Let's make the style that Apple made famous that is often called Aqua, but just in case they copyrighted that name, we'll

Figure 15.36 Top: Fill Opacity 100%. Bottom: Fill Opacity 0% (background © 2002 Stockbyte, www.stockbyte.com)

Figure 15.37 Result of applying a stroke, stroke emboss, and both a drop and inner shadow. (background © 2002 Stockbyte, www.stockbyte.com)

Figure 15.38 Result of applying pattern overlay, bevel and emboss (using texture) and drop shadow. (background © 2002 Stockbyte, www.stockbyte.com)

Figure 15.39 Result of creating Jelly Type. (background © 2002 Stockbyte, www.stockbyte.com)

call it Jelly Type. Start by setting the Fill setting at the top of the Layers palette to zero, then add a Color Overlay with a color mode from H: 200°, S: 70%, and B: 80% and an Opacity of 80%. Now, add a Bevel and Emboss setting the Style to Inner Bevel, the Technique to Smooth, the Size to 10 pixels, an Altitude of 70 and set both Opacity settings to 100%. While you're at it, set the Shadow Mode to Color Burn.

Well, that's a start, but we still have a lot to do if we really want this to look good. Add an Inner Glow with the Blend Mode set to Multiply, the Opacity at 75%, set the color to H: 225, S: 70, B:60, set the Choke to 35% and the Size to 7 pixels. That should add a nice dark blue edge to the text. Now let's add a drop shadow with a color made from H: 200, S: 50, B: 60, set the Opacity to 70%, the Distance to 7 and the Size to 5. Then to really make it look like light can pass through the text, let's add an Outer Glow using an Opacity of 30%, a color made from H: 200, S: 60, B: 50, and a Size of 10 pixels.

One more thing to finish it off: Add an Inner Shadow using H: 200, S: 50%, B: 60%, an Opacity of 50%, a Distance of 5 pixels, a 5 pixel Choke and a Size of 10 pixels (**Figure 15.39**). After doing all that work, you might find that the beveled edge is either too large or small. If that's the case, then choose Layer > Layer Style > Scale Effects and move the slider around until the effect looks appropriate for your type size.

Figure 15.40 An example of what can be accomplished by combining many layer styles. (background © 2002 Stockbyte, www.stockbyte.com)

Wild Type

We've created some pretty cool effects, but we've really only scratched the surface of what's possible. What's exciting is that you can combine as many of these layer styles as you'd like to create some truly eye-popping effects. In **Figure 15.40**, I've used the following styles: Pattern Overlay, Gradient Overlay (set to Hard Light), Stroke (with the Gradient setting), Bevel and Emboss (using the Stroke Emboss option), Inner Shadow, Drop Shadow, and an Inner Glow!

The Styles Palette

Figure 15.41 The Layer Styles palette (with a lot of my own styles added).

If it feels like it took too darn much time to create these effects, then you can take comfort in knowing that Photoshop's Styles palette allows you to store a collection of layer styles so they can be applied over and over again. To save a style, just make sure the layer with the style(s) applied is active and then click the New Style icon at the bottom of the Styles palette (**Figure 15.41**). Your style should appear at the bottom of the palette. To apply that style to another layer, just make that layer active and then click on the style you created in the Styles palette. (Or you can choose Layer > Layer Style > Copy Style, click on the layer you'd like to apply it to, and then choose Paste Style from the same menu.) That's all there is to it! You can also remove all the styles applied to a layer by clicking on the No Style icon at the bottom of the Styles palette. The styles that appear in this palette will stay there (available in any document) until you decide to change them.

Now, this is significant, so please pay close attention. *With all the effects we just created, you have the freedom to edit the text and the effects will update.* That's a giant stride towards creative freedom. But not *all* effects out there in Photoshop allow you to edit the text. With the next technique we'll be converting our text into a *shape;* after you've done that, you'll no longer be able to edit it as text.

Intertwined Type

All of the effects we've just tried out can be a little more interesting if you make the letters of your type interact with each other. To do that, right after entering your text, choose Layer > Type > Convert To Shape. Next, grab the solid arrow tool that appears directly above the Pen tool and drag the individual letters around your screen. (You can drag a box around multiple adjacent letters to move them as a group.) To create holes where the letters overlap, click on the rightmost icon of the four that appear in the Options bar (**Figure 15.42**). You'll need to do that to each letter in order to get all of them to work that way. I used this technique to create the art that appears in **Figure 15.43**.

Figure 15.42 Solid Arrow options.

Figure 15.43 Image created using the right-most solid arrow option.

Backgrounds & Textures

Backgrounds and textures might not be something that you'd think you want to spend a lot of time learning about. But if you look around at what's considered "high art" in the world of print, and especially on the Web, you'll notice that a skilled hand with backgrounds and textures can make the difference between elegance and clunkiness. In this section I'll show you how to create some background effects that I find interesting, and in the making you should be able to gain the skills you need to create your own elegant inventions. The first ones will be simple black and white textures that can be applied to photographs or colorized using the techniques described in Chapter 13, "Enhancement."

In general, we'll be starting with some raw material and then we'll enhance it to turn it into a texture. Most of Photoshop's filters require a detailed image in order to produce a noticeable result, but there is a select group of filters that can create something out of nothing.

Filters That Can Create Something out of Nothing

▶ Artistic > Sponge

▶ Noise > Add Noise

▶ Pixelate > Mezzotint

▶ Pixelate > Pointillize

▶ Render > Clouds

▶ Sketch > Halftone Pattern

▶ Sketch > Note Paper

▶ Sketch > Reticulation

▶ Stylize > Extrude

▶ Stylize > Tiles

▶ All filters in the Texturize submenu

NOTES

Not all of the raw material filters are capable of working on an empty layer. If you get an error message while attempting to apply one of these filters, then fill the active layer with white and then try again.

We'll walk through a few of these raw-material filters to give you some ideas. Then you'll be free to go off and play with your new filter toys and come up with your own uniquely wonderful backgrounds.

A Simple Texture

Let's start with an easy texture. Start by typing "D" to reset your foreground/background colors and then choosing Filter > Render > Clouds. Next, choose Filter > Artistic > Dry Brush and move all three sliders all the way to the right. Apply that filter a total of three times in a row and then choose Filter > Stylize > Emboss, set the Angle to 135°, the Height to 2 pixels and the Amount to 100% (**Figure 15.44**).

Figure 15.44 The simple texture.

Moon Texture

We'll start this one the same as the last by applying the clouds filter. Then choose Filter > Artistic Paint Daubs, set the Brush Size to 15, the Sharpness to 7 and use a Brush Type of Simple. To finish things off, choose Filter > Stylize > Emboss, set the Angle to 135°, the Height to 2 pixels and the Amount to 500% (**Figure 15.45**).

Figure 15.45 The moon texture.

Figure 15.46 The stucco wall texture.

Stucco Wall

Our base texture will be clouds again, so go ahead and apply it. Then follow that with three applications of the Difference Clouds filter. Then to shake things up a bit, choose Filter > Stylize > Find Edges and then immediately choose Edit > Fade > Find Edges and set the Mode to Linear Burn. Then, as usual, the last step is to choose Filter > Stylize > Emboss. This time set the Angle to 135°, the Height to 1 pixel and the Amount to 500% (**Figure 15.46**).

Figure 15.47 The painterly wall texture.

Painterly Wall

I'm sure you'll get sick of this, but, we're going to start this one with the Clouds filter—again. Follow that with three passes of the Artistic > Dry Brush filter using a Brush Size of 3, Brush Detail of 9, and a Texture of 2. Next, choose Filter > Stylize > Find Edges, then choose Image > Adjustments > Auto Levels. Finally, choose Filter > Other > High Pass, use a Radius of 3.3 and then apply the Emboss filter with whatever settings you'd like (you've used that one enough already). See **Figure 15.47**.

Figure 15.48 The sponged stuff texture.

Sponged Stuff

OK, I think we've used the Clouds filter enough for a base, so let's try something else now. Start by choosing Filter > Artistic > Sponge and use settings of 2, 12 and 5. To get a little more contrast, choose Image > Adjustments > Auto Levels. Next, choose Filter > Stylize > Solorize and then finish it off with the usual—Emboss (**Figure 15.48**).

Figure 15.49 The artificial map texture.

Artificial Map

This time we're going to make a map of some fake countries. Start by applying the Clouds filter, then get good contrast with auto levels. Then to get your countries, choose Filter > Sketch > Plaster and use settings of 38, 7 and Top Left (**Figure 15.49**).

Patchy Paint

So far, we've used clouds and sponge, so now let's see what we get with the Noise > Add Noise filter. Apply that with an Amount of 330, using uniform distribution and turn on the Monochrome check box. Next, choose Filter > Noise > Median, use a setting of 21 and then apply auto levels. Next, choose Filter > Brush Strokes > Spatter, set the Spray Radius to 25 and the Smoothness to 15, then emboss it using settings of 45°, 1 pixel and 146%. Finally, choose Edit > Fade > Emboss and set the Mode to Hardlight. If you'd like to add some color, then either go back to the Enhancement chapter and read away, or paint with your brush set to Overlay mode (**Figure 15.50**).

Figure 15.50 The patchy paint texture.

All the textures we've created to far have been grayscale. That makes them ideal as raw material to texturize photographs. All you have to do is place the texture above a photograph and then try any one of the contrast blending modes that we talked about in the Enhancement chapter.

Brown Reeds

OK, it's time to get fancy. No more grayscale textures. This one will be photo-realistic. We'll start by choosing Filter > Sketch > Halftone Pattern and use a Size of 7, a Contrast of 23 and a Dot Pattern Type. Now choose Filter > Distort > Ripple, use an Amount of 110% and a Size of Medium. Next, Choose Filter > Sketch > Chrome, set the Detail to 2 and the Smoothness to 7, then Choose Edit > Fade and set the Mode to Difference. Now it's time to choose Filter > Blur > Motion Blur, set the angle to zero and use a Distance of 14. Now to add some color (it's about time we got to color, huh?), choose Layer > New Adjustment Layer > Gradient Map and set the Mode to Overlay. When the gradient Map dialog box appears, click the gradient preview and then double-click on the left-most color and choose a nice orange, then change the right color to yellow and click OK. Finally, choose Layer > Merge Down and we're done (**Figure 15.51**)!

Figure 15.51 The brown reeds texture.

Repeating Patterns

Try this out: choose Edit > Fill and set the Use pop-up menu to Pattern. Then take a look at the preset custom patterns. These patterns are actually tiny images repeated over and over (like tiles on a bathroom wall). If you stood back, they would appear to be one large image instead of what they were—a bunch of small repeating images with their edges lined up with each other. These default patterns are all right for adding interest to simple shapes; but this is Photoshop, which means we're not stuck using plain old vanilla defaults. We can create our own exquisitely unique patterns! They can be used in many situations, especially when it comes to producing graphics for the Web. So, let's dive in and see what we can come up with.

There are two general methods I use to create a seamless pattern. The first one involves using filters that produce tileable results. Then, after using a combination of filters, we'll find the smallest tileable area and turn that into a pattern. The second method is to take an image that is not tileable and to retouch the areas that would appear as seams.

Using Tileable Filters

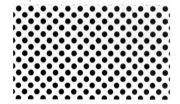

Figure 15.52 Result of applying the Color Halftone filter.

Figure 15.53 Result of applying the Emboss filter.

Let's start with a pattern that is tileable from the beginning. We can use that small image to fill a larger area without it looking like the simple repeating image that it really is. First, create a new document in grayscale mode. Next, choose a light shade of gray and then type Option-Delete (Macintosh) or Alt-Backspace (Windows) to fill the image with that color. Now, choose Filter > Pixelate > Color Halftone, set the Max. Radius to 14, and set all the angles to 45. That should produce a bunch of circles on a grid (**Figure 15.52**). Next, let's add some dimension by choosing Filter > Stylize > Emboss; set the Angle to 135, the Height to 1, and the Amount to 75 (**Figure 15.53**).

Now that we've got something that is seamless, let's find the smallest area that can be tiled. That way, the pattern won't take up memory and our file size can stay small when we apply the pattern using layer styles and pattern layers. Use the Marquee tool to select a relatively small but wide selection near the top of the image. Next, choose View > Show Rulers, click on the top ruler and drag down a guide until it snaps to the top of the selection you just made (**Figure 15.54**).

Now you want to find out whether the information you just selected is used elsewhere in the image, and if so, where. We use an odd little technique to do that. Choose Layer > New > Layer Via Copy to place a copy of the currently selected area onto a brand-spankin'-new layer. Next, change the blending mode of that layer (at the top of the Layers palette) to Difference. That mode will compare the layer that is active to the one below it, and will show you where the two layers are different. Since both layers are identical in that area, it should appear black. Now change to the Move tool and use the down-arrow key to nudge the layer one pixel at a time. As you move it down, the black area should change to indicate that the information no longer lines up with what's underneath it. You'll want to continue to nudge it down until that area becomes black again. Once that happens, drag out another guide and let it snap to the top edge of that layer (**Figure 15.55**).

Now you'll want to trash the layer you've been working with and repeat the exact same process using a vertical selection. So, make a tall, skinny selection, pull out a guide, and snap it to the left side of the marching ants. Then choose Layer > New > Layer Via Copy, set the blending mode to Difference, and then nudge that layer (using the Move tool) until it becomes black again. Finally, pull out another guide, snap it to the left edge of that layer, and then trash the layer (**Figure 15.56**).

You should end up with a total of four guides that define the smallest tileable area of the image. To turn that area into a pattern, use the Marquee tool to select the area defined by the guides, and then choose Edit > Define Pattern. Finally, test your pattern by creating a new document, choosing Edit > Fill, and selecting Pattern from the Use pop-up menu. You should find your pattern listed at the bottom of the pattern pop-up list.

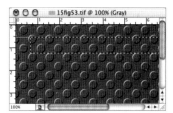

Figure 15.54 Drag a guide down until it snaps to the edge of your selection.

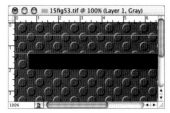

Figure 15.55 When the layer turns black again, add a guide that lines up with the top of that layer.

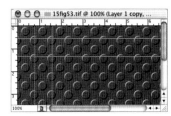

Figure 15.56 Repeat the process using a vertical selection.

The process of finding the smallest tileable area can be difficult if you are working on a very low-contrast pattern. If that's the case, choose Layer > Duplicate Layer and then choose Image > Adjust > Auto Levels to exaggerate the contrast in that new layer. Then go through the exact steps mentioned earlier for finding the smallest tileable area. Once you have all four guides placed, just trash the high-contrast layer so you'll end up with your original image and the four guides you need to create a pattern.

Create Your Own Pattern

Figure 15.57 Cropping the image down to the area you'd like to use.

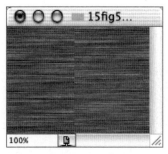

Figure 15.58 The Offset filter will expose the seams in your pattern as a pattern.

Now that you've seen how to create a tileable pattern from scratch, let's see how we can produce one from an existing image (like a photograph or one of the textures we created earlier). Since we are striving for "seamless," we will first expose the seams of our image, and then retouch them to make them disappear. For this example, let's create a brushed-metal effect and transform it into a seamless tile. To create the metal look, create a new grayscale image and then choose Filter > Noise > Add Noise (I used Amount=400%, Distribution=Uniform, and I turned on the Monochromatic `). Now choose Filter > Blur > Motion Blur (I used Angle=0 and Distance=60). You can see the resulting brushed-metal look in **Figure 15.57**. Once you have the texture made (or you have the photo you'd like to work with), choose Select > All, and then Edit > Copy (though you won't be pasting for a while). Use the Crop tool to select the area you'd like to use for your pattern and then press Return or Enter to crop it. Now let's expose the seams that would show up if we used that image as a pattern. To accomplish that, choose Filter > Other > Offset and set the Vertical and Horizontal offset settings to approximately half the width of your image (**Figure 15.58**).

Now that we can see the seams that prevent our image from being a seamless tile, all we have to do is retouch them to make them disappear. If you are working with a photographic image, you'll most likely want to use the

Rubber Stamp tool, but since we copied our full-size original to start with, we can take advantage of a different approach. Choose Edit > Paste to create a new layer (assuming you haven't copied something else in the meantime) and fill it with part of the original image. Next, choose Layer > Add Layer Mask > Hide All. Now you should notice two thumbnail images for the currently active layer (**Figure 15.59**). Next, choose the Paintbrush tool, choose white to paint with, and choose a very large, soft-edged brush (one that's about 1/3 of the width of your image). Use that large brush to cover up the seam by painting over it vertically. That should make the pasted image show up over the seam and blend into the rest of the image, resulting in a seamless pattern. To define your pattern, choose Layer > Merge Down, then Select > All, and then Edit > Define Pattern. Now you should be able to create a new, large document and choose Edit > Fill to apply your pattern (**Figure 15.60**).

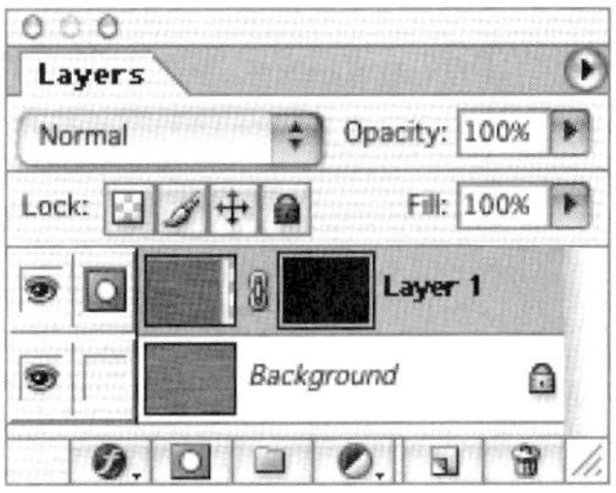

Figure 15.59 After adding a layer mask, the layer should contain two thumbnail images.

Figure 15.60 The pattern applied to a large area.

Using the Pattern Maker Filter

The new Pattern Maker filter is designed for creating seamless patterns. It's no substitute for using the manual tiling techniques we discussed earlier in this chapter, but it can do a decent job of generating textures that tile.

The general concept is to find an image where you like the colors and overall texture, then choose Filter > Pattern Maker. Once the dialog box appears (**Figure 15.61**), you make a selection of the area you'd like to use to create a pattern, then click the Generate button multiple times until you like the result you are presented with (**Figure 15.62**). If you find that the seams in the repeating pattern are too obvious, try increasing the smoothness setting, which will lower the contrast of the next pattern you generate. If Pattern Maker chops up a photo's objects beyond recognition, then bring the sample detail setting up a bit and regenerate the pattern. I've found that the Pattern Maker works best on images with a lot of sharp-edged detail, because it seems to literally rip your image to

NOTES

I've found that the new Healing Brush and Patch tool work great for patching the seams on organic textures (like the ones we created earlier in this chapter).

shreds and then reassemble the pieces in a random way. Once you've achieved the look you desire, click the disk icon that appears in the lower right area to save the pattern. Saved patterns can be used with the Layer Styles that we talked about earlier in this chapter.

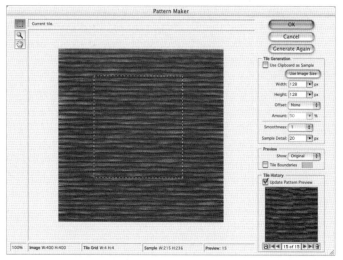

Figure 15.61 The Pattern Maker dialog box before generating a pattern.

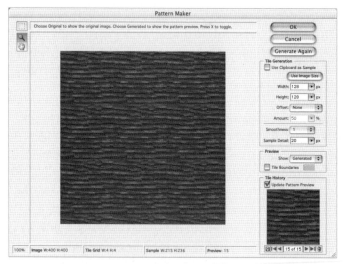

Figure 15.62 A seamless pattern created from the image shown in figure 15.61.

Closing Thoughts

With almost 100 filters, and the idea that you can throw them together in any combination, it's probably safe to say that you will be well into retirement before you could exhaust the supply of unique text and background effects that can be produced in Photoshop. That makes your job both challenging and exhilarating. Never stop testing the limits; never stop playing. And if you run out of ideas, do what I do—read through your favorite magazines for interesting looking text and backgrounds, rip out the pages with the best ones, and then try to reproduce them on your own.

Ben's Techno-babble Decoder Ring

Point: A unit of measurement, used in the publishing industry, that is $\frac{1}{72}$ of an inch (there are 12 points to a pica, and 6 picas per inch). Most programs measure text in point sizes because it is much more friendly than using fractions of an inch. But there is very little consistency in the size of text. For example, 12-point Times is taller than 12-point Helvetica, so you can think of the point size as a general (not exact) measure of the size of your text.

Baseline: The invisible rule that a line of text sits on. Letters that drop below the baseline (such as lowercase j, g, q, and y) are known as descenders.

Leading: The line spacing of a paragraph of text measured from one baseline to the next. It's named after the strips of lead that were used to increase line spacing in hot metal typography. In order to make sure the lines of text don't overlap, you'll usually want to use a leading setting larger than the point size of the text.

Kerning: The art (lost art, really) of removing space between letters to create consistent letter spacing. In Photoshop, the kerning increases (positive setting) or decreases (negative setting) the space between two letters.

Tracking: The act of increasing or reducing the space between all the letters in a range of text. Often used with uppercase text to increase readability.

PART IV

Web Graphics

Courtesy of Michael Slack, www.slackart.com

16

Interface Design

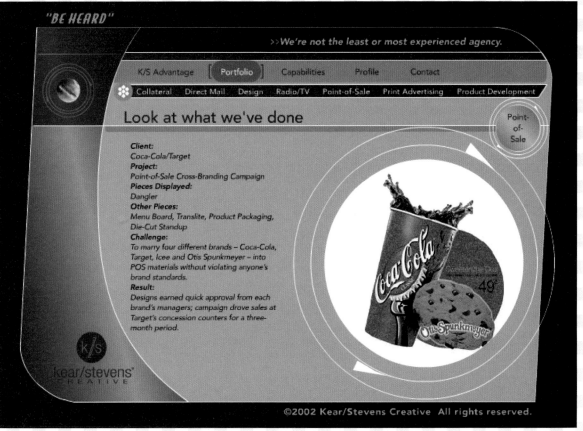

©2002 Kear/Stevens Creative, www.kscreative.com

Buckle your seatbelt, Dorothy, 'cause Kansas is going bye-bye.

—Cypher, from *The Matrix*

Interface Design

Like the tornado that spirited Dorothy away to the land of Oz, the Web is taking us by force and launching us into new orbits of digital reality. But this time around, *we* get to be the little man with the big mustache who hides behind the green curtain. If L. Frank Baum had been born in 2002, his Oz story might have more closely resembled *The Matrix*, and his wizard would have been an insomniac with an ergonomic chair, a high-speed data line, and a clutter of monitors and keyboards at his or her fingertips. In other words, someone just like you or me.

So, with Web-wizardry being a regular 9-to-5 job, and the competition between wizards becoming fierce, we are naturally motivated to keep up with the latest techniques that will keep our clients and bosses dazzled and bewitched. This chapter will help you toward that goal. It's where you can develop the understanding and skills needed to create highly professional-looking interface elements for your Web site. For those of you who are new to the process of putting together a Web site, this chapter isn't about constructing your site or about special effects such as animation and sound. Instead, it's about creating the essential elements that help users navigate through your site.

The good news is that it doesn't matter whether you're the world's highest-paid designer doing graphics for BMW or you're just starting out with your first Web site on your home computer. You both use Photoshop, and there's nothing stopping you from creating stunning, Web-perfect interface elements that are worthy of any Fortune 500 company. This chapter will give you what you need to create your basic navigational elements, and once you've mastered that, you'll be ready to advance to the next chapters where you'll learn about optimizing your images and creating rollovers and animation.

Consistent Design Principles

This chapter isn't about "design," in the aesthetic sense, but there are some basic standards that are smart to follow to make it easy for all those people who are viewing your site on a variety of computer monitors. To get an idea of what I'm talking about, the next time you're browsing the Web, be sure to visit a few major corporate sites (such as www.amazon.com and www.barnesandnoble.com) to see if you find any consistency between them. For instance, if you visit a bunch of major computer manufacturers' sites, you might notice that they don't use the full width of your screen. On the day I wrote this chapter, the majority of people browsing the Web (54 percent) were using a monitor that displays 800 by 600 pixels. If you look at **Figure 16.1**, you'll notice that www.gateway.com limits the width of their site to what is visible on an 800-pixel-wide screen. They were even smart enough to leave space for the scroll bar that would usually appear on the right edge of the screen.

Although 800 by 600 might be the norm, currently 4 percent of viewers browse the Web using 640-by-480 screens. Sites designed for the widest audiences will often keep the most essential content within the width visible on this

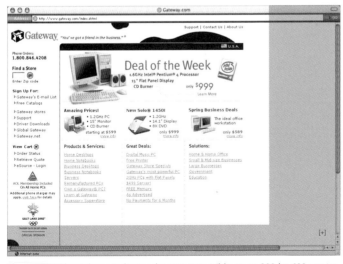

Figure 16.1 The red area indicates the area not visible on an 800-by-600 screen.

small screen (**Figure 16.2**). You might not think that 4 percent of viewers is a lot of people, but think of it this way: There are more than 544 million users worldwide, with more than 181 million users in the United States and Canada alone. I know—counting Internet users is an inexact science at best, but even so, do the sloppy math, and you'll get an idea of the number of people who just might be browsing on a 640-by-480 screen (7.24 million in the United States and Canada, 21.8 million worldwide).

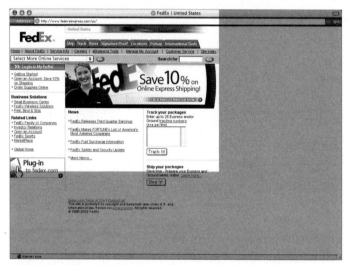

Figure 16.2 The Federal Express Web site (www.federalexpress.com) keeps the most essential information within the area visible on a 640-by-480 screen. The red area indicates the viewing area of 640-by-480 screens.

In browsing the Web, people are accustomed to scrolling vertically to see an entire site, but you still might want to keep the most important interface elements within the first screenful that would be visible on a small monitor. It's kind of like the fold in a newspaper—all the major story headlines always appear above the fold.

Your View of This Small World

If you're working on a large monitor, you'll most likely want to set up a special document that will remind you of what people with smaller screens will be able to view. To accomplish that, start by launching your browser. Turn on all the features that most people use (button bar, address bar, favorites bar, status bar), and then visit a popular site and expand your browser window to fill your screen. Now take a screen shot by pressing Shift-Command-Control-3 (Mac) or Alt-Print Scrn (Windows). Open Photoshop and choose File > New (use the default settings, which are based on whatever was copied last, which in this case is your screen shot). Next, choose Edit > Paste and then Layer > Merge Down. Now you'll want to add some guides that represent how much of your browser would be visible on 640-by-480 and 800-by-600 screens. You'll need to choose View > New Guide a total of four times. First create a vertical guide at 640 pixels (be sure to type the "pixels" part, otherwise it might assume inches), and then create another at 800 pixels. Finally, create two horizontal guides at 480 pixels and 600 pixels (**Figure 16.3**).

If you create all the graphics for your site within this document, you'll constantly be reminded of what the majority of your viewers will be able to see in one screenful. Try to keep all major navigation elements within the 640-by-480 space, and limit most of your content to what is visible in the width of an 800-by-600 screen.

NOTES

To choose a resolution in Windows, go to the Display control panel, choose the Settings tab, and then drag the Screen Area slider.

Did you know that the user interface that makes up most computer operating systems—icons, menu bars, dialog boxes, and so on—is completely designed using a special set of 256 colors (known as the system palette)? That's so everyone has a consistent experience using the computer, no matter if their computer can display millions of colors or only 256.

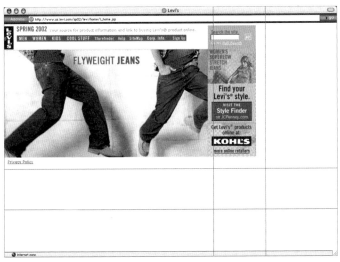

Figure 16.3 A screen shot of a Web browser with guides placed to represent the viewing area of 640-by-480 screens.

Figure 16.4 The system-level control panels that determine how many pixels will be displayed onscreen and therefore how large the pixels will appear.

Resolution and the Web

All documents that you work with in Photoshop have a resolution setting attached to them. That setting determines how large the pixels in the image will be (measured in pixels per inch, or ppi) if the image is printed. But when it comes to a Web browser, that setting is completely ignored. Why? Because your Web browser is not capable of changing the size of the pixels that make up your screen. In fact, you are the only one who is in control of that. The Monitors control panel setting (Mac) or Display control panel setting (Windows) determines how many pixels are displayed on your screen and therefore their size (**Figure 16.4**).

Since your browser can't change the size of the pixels, it simply uses as many screen pixels as your image requires, determined by its width and height in pixels. Most 15-inch monitors can display somewhere around 800 by 600 pixels total. There is no way a browser could display your images at a resolution of 300 ppi (the most popular scanning resolution)—that is, not unless you have a 15-inch monitor that's capable of displaying 3,600 by 2,700 pixels!

So if your Web browser ignores the resolution setting, does it matter what setting you use when scanning an image? Yes! Your browser might ignore that setting, but your scanner uses it to determine how many pixels to create out of each inch of your original image. If you have a 3-inch-wide original and you scan with a resolution of 100 ppi, you'll end up with 300 pixels in the width (3 inches x 100 pixels per inch = 300 pixels total). Scan the same image with a resolution of 72 ppi and you'll end up with only 216 pixels total in the width (3 x 72 = 216). Since your browser will ignore the resolution setting and just look at the width and height in pixels, the higher the resolution the image is scanned at, the larger it will appear in a browser (you simply get more pixels when you scan at higher resolutions). If you were to measure how many pixels fit in each inch of a typical computer monitor, you'd find that it's somewhere around 85. That means if you scan an image with a resolution of 85 ppi, it should appear close to actual size in the majority of Web browsers.

But don't worry about scanning images with high-resolution settings, because you can always scale them down later. If you want to see how large an image will appear in a Web browser, choose View > Actual Pixels when you're in Photoshop. If you find that's too big, open the Navigator palette (View > Show Navigator) and move the slider at the bottom of the palette until the image is the size you'd like it to be in a browser. Next, choose Image > Image Size, turn on the Resample Image checkbox, change the Width pop-up menu to Percent, and then enter the percentage that shows up in the lower-left corner of your image. Now, if you choose View > Actual Pixels again, your image should appear at the size you'd like it to be in the browser.

Color on the Web

If you've already been creating graphics for the Web, you've probably had the painful experience of seeing one of your brilliantly colored images end up with a shade of color when view online that doesn't even come close to your original creation. Getting your colors consistent is another important step toward achieving a professional-looking Web site.

Most graphic designers have monitors that are capable of displaying millions of colors, but you might be surprised to learn that there are still some people out there who browse the Web using only 256 colors. That's right—4 percent of all your viewers will be using only 256 colors to browse your site (more than all the Mac users out there). Even those people who have a computer capable of displaying millions of colors might, under certain conditions, end up seeing your site with only 256 colors. Just think about it for a moment. What if you start up your computer, then launch Photoshop, ImageReady, and GoLive so you are all set to create some Web graphics. Then you launch your email program and decide you need to make a phone call, so you launch your contact-management program. Then when you're on the phone, you have to check your calendar (another program) and then your buddy mentions a Web site for you to check out. With a total of six programs already running, do you think your Web browser will have much memory to work with? Well, when your browser is running out of memory, it takes some "conservation" measures to ration its use of

NOTES

The concept of Web-safe colors is really simple, but the execution gets a little bit complicated. A Web-safe color is any color that is composed of red, green, and blue values in increments of 20%. That means if you have 0, 20, 40, 60, 80, or 100% of red, green or blue, you'd have a Web-safe color. But the RGB numbers in Photoshop are not measured in percentages. They range from 0–255. In that numbering system, 20% = 51. So as long as all your RGB numbers are divisible by 51, you have Web-safe colors.

memory. One of those measures might be to display all sites using only 256 colors. That means that even people with high-end computers might sometimes end up seeing your site with only 256 colors.

So, what's your site going to look like with 256 colors? Well, any color used that isn't from that special set used for your computer interface will be simulated using two colors from the system palette. That means that a big blue logo might suddenly appear as blue with cyan specks sprinkled throughout it (the technical term for these specks is known as dithering). That's your browser's way of being able to simulate more than 256 colors. It's a good thing it can do that; otherwise photographs would look rather terrible (**Figure 16.5**). The only problem is that large areas of solid color don't look so hot when they are contaminated with specks of another color (**Figure 16.6**).

You can prevent areas from becoming dithered when viewed with 256 colors by creating your interface elements using the colors used in your system palette. That's easy enough to do, but (of course) there's a catch: The Mac and Windows operating systems use different system palettes. But if you were to compare the colors used in both operating systems, you'd find that there are 216 colors that are common to both. I call these the dither-free colors because they are the only ones I can use that guarantee I won't get specks showing up in areas that should be solid.

Figure 16.5 Left: A photo without dithering. Right: The photo with dithering. (© Chris Klimek)

But just because I like to call them dither-free colors doesn't mean everyone else uses that name. In fact, most people call them Web-safe colors. I hate that name, because many people think they must use those colors for *everything*, when they are really only useful in areas that should appear as a solid color. Dithering is not always a bad thing—it really helps on photographs and in graphics that contain gradients (**Figure 16.7**). You'll also find these special colors being called colors that are "within the color cube," which is what Photoshop uses as an icon to describe them (**Figure 16.8**).

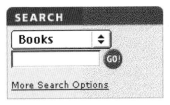

Figure 16.6 The left half of this image doesn't have dithering; the right half does.

Figure 16.7 From top to bottom: Image viewed with millions of colors, 256 colors, and 256 colors with dithering. (© Chris Klimek)

Figure 16.8 The cube icon is used to create dither-free colors.

Now that we know why these colors are so special, let's figure out how to use them in Photoshop. First off, when you're in the Color Picker dialog box, you could type in RGB numbers that are in increments of 51 and you'd be all set. But most people don't like having to think of those numbers. So, to make it easy, Photoshop provided us with a color cube icon that you can use to get your dither-free colors. After you've chosen a color, be sure to click that icon if you plan to use the color to fill a large solid area. Or, if you are picking a bunch of colors at once, you might want to turn on the Only Web Colors checkbox; then Photoshop will display only the dither-free colors (**Figure 16.9**).

If you prefer to use the Color palette, you'll want to choose Web Color Sliders from the side menu of that palette. After you've chosen that feature, you'll find tick marks where the dither-free colors are (**Figure 16.10**). To have a Web-safe color, you have to get all three (RGB) sliders to point at those marks, but that's pretty easy, because the sliders snap

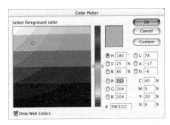

Figure 16.9 Turning on the Only Web Colors checkbox will limit the colors shown to the 216 dither-free colors.

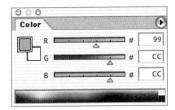

Figure 16.10 When using the Web Color Sliders, the tick marks indicate dither-free colors.

to them. If you don't want a dither-free color, hold the Option key (Mac) or Alt key (Windows) to prevent the sliders from snapping to the tick marks.

You can also pick colors from the color bar that appears at the bottom of the Color palette. But be careful, because those colors aren't dither-free. If you choose Make Ramp Web Safe from the side menu of the Color palette, all the colors within that color bar will be Web-safe.

Take a look at **Figure 16.11** and you'll see what a major news site looks like when viewed using 256 colors. Notice that most of the large areas of color are free from specks (dithering). As I've said before, dithering is useful on photographs, and you'll see it in all the photos on that site.

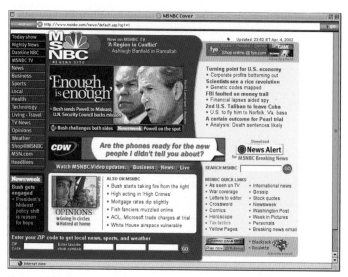

Figure 16.11 The www.msnbc.com site viewed with 256 colors.

Photoshop vs. the Browser: Getting Consistent Color Between the Two

You're probably champing at the bit and ready to start creating, but before we get down to business, we have to look at one more color issue that just can't be ignored. Often you'll find that the colors in your image will change (sometimes radically) when they are displayed in a Web browser. That's usually because Photoshop is taking steps to make sure the color in your image is accurate, but your browser is not taking those steps. To avoid this disparity between Photoshop and your browser, you can set up Photoshop to display things the way they will appear for the majority of people who browse the Web. Start by choosing Edit > Color Settings and choose Web Graphics Defaults from the pop-up menu at the top of the dialog box (**Figure 16.12**). That turns off most of Photoshop's color-management features, which is a good thing, because your browser doesn't use that kind of stuff to display your images. Next, choose View > Proof Colors (to enable that feature) and then choose View > Proof Setup > Windows RGB. (Windows monitors display images darker than Macintosh monitors, and when the Windows RGB option is checked, a Macintosh will display images as if viewed on a Windows machine.) Then, if I'm working on a critical area of the site, I'll switch Proof Setup back and forth between the Macintosh RGB and Windows RGB settings to make sure it will look good on both systems.

NOTES

More than 91 percent of the people browsing the Web are using the Windows operating system, so I use the Windows RGB setting in Proof Setup when designing my graphics.

Instead of switching between Proof Setups, you can leave the original at Windows RGB, choose New View, and set the new view's Proof Setup to Macintosh RGB. That way, when you make adjustments (such as a Curves adjustment layer), you can view Mac and Windows previews side by side.

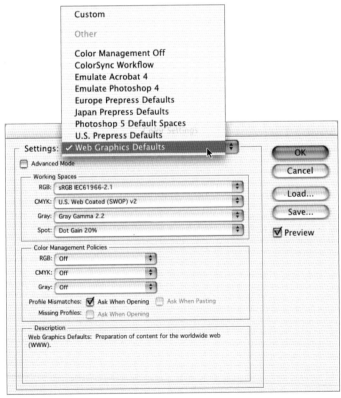

Figure 16.12 Choose Web Graphics Defaults from the pop-up menu at the top of the Color Settings dialog box.

Creating Interface Elements

OK, you have a veritable treasure trove of knowledge. You understand monitor size and screen resolution and how to deal with color. Now, using what we know, it's time to start learning how to create user interface elements. Bear in mind that there are literally hundreds of interface elements that can be created (as evidenced by a 5-minute surf on the Web), and that this book can dedicate only so many pages to this subject. You can consider this chapter your starter kit. Try out my techniques, and then go off-leash and create your own interface masterpieces.

The Shape Tools

Photoshop 7.0's shape tools are perfect for creating interface elements because you can make changes to the elements later without lowering the quality of your imagery. We took a brief look at the shape tools in Chapter 1, but there's a lot more to know that will serve you well when creating interface elements. Before using the shape tools, be sure to check out the settings in the Options bar. You should see three choices in the far left of the bar (**Figure 16.13**). The leftmost choice is what you want; it's the one that creates a shape layer. Shape layers are special because you can scale, rotate, and manipulate them without degrading the quality of your image. If you find that the shape layer choice isn't available, then you are most likely already working on a shape layer, and Photoshop is assuming you would like to add to that layer. If that's the case, press Return (Mac) or Enter (Windows) to tell Photoshop that you are done working on that shape layer and would like to start another one.

After you've created a shape layer, you'll see a new set of choices in the Options bar (**Figure 16.14**). The first choice will cause the shape tool to create a new shape layer instead of adding to an existing one. The second choice will allow you to add more shapes to the currently active layer. This choice is great when you want to create shapes that can be made from a combination of the shape tools (**Figure 16.15**). The third choice allows you to take away from the current shape using any shape tool (**Figure 16.16**). The fifth choice (I know I skipped one) inverts what you have (**Figure 16.17**). And the fourth choice gives you just the areas where your next shape overlaps the current ones (**Figure 16.18**).

Figure 16.13 When you see three choices on the far left of the Options bar, choose the leftmost one to create a shape layer.

Figure 16.14 The Options bar offers different choices when you're already working on a shape layer.

Figure 16.15 The second choice allows you to add to the current shape layer.

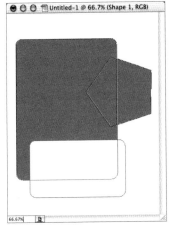

Figure 16.16 The third choice allows you to take away from the current shape layer.

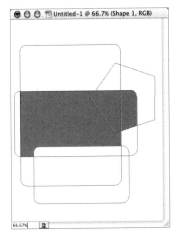

Figure 16.17 The fifth choice inverts what you have.

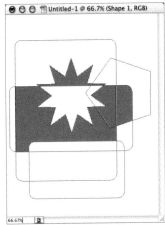

Figure 16.18 The fourth choice gives you the intersection between the current shape layer and the new shape you are creating.

Using a combination of these features, you can create some rather sophisticated shapes. But you might find that once you've gotten the shape you'd like, your screen is littered with shapes that overlap each other (**Figure 16.19**). You can simplify the end result by switching to the solid arrow tool that's to the left of the Type tool in your Tools palette, and then clicking on the Combine button in the Options bar (**Figure 16.20**). This simplifies your shape down to a single outline instead of one that's created using a combination of shapes.

Figure 16.19 A sophisticated shape can be made from multiple shapes that overlap each other.

Figure 16.20 The Combine button will simplify a compound shape into a single element.

If you think you'll need to use that shape over and over, be sure to choose Edit > Define Custom Shape. That will make it available as a choice when you're using the Custom Shape tool (the rightmost of the shape tools in the Options bar). After you've chosen that tool, click on the shape preview in the Options bar and you should find your new shape (**Figure 16.21**).

Sometimes you'll find that you'd like to break an interesting shape into multiple pieces so they can be repositioned individually or so they can be used as buttons on your Web site. You can accomplish that by adding shape layers on top of the shape you already have (remember to press Return or Enter to finish off each shape before attempting to add more shapes).

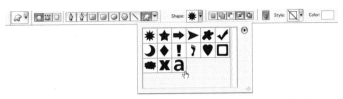

Figure 16.21 After you define a custom shape, it should show up at the bottom of the Shape Picker.

In **Figure 16.22** you'll see an example where I created a bunch of horizontal bars that cover an interesting shape; each bar is on its own layer. To divide the bottom shape into multiple pieces based on the other layers, I clicked on the shape thumbnail image in the bottom layer and chose Edit > Copy. Then, I clicked on one of the shape layers that define the horizontal bars and chose Edit > Paste. That added a path to that layer that is shaped like the bottom layer (**Figure 16.23**). (If you'd like to find out more about paths, check out the "Vector Mask" section of Chapter 12.) Next, I clicked on the fourth choice from the left in the Options bar, which instructed Photoshop to use the shape I just pasted to transform this layer so that only the areas where the two shapes overlap are visible (**Figure 16.24**). Finally, I clicked on the solid arrow tool and then clicked the Combine button in the Options bar to simplify the shape. After repeating this process for each of the horizontal bars, I deleted the bottom layer and ended up with its shape divided into separate pieces that I could move around independently of each other (**Figure 16.25**).

NOTES

To reposition the shape while you're creating it, just press the spacebar (without releasing the mouse button) and then drag.

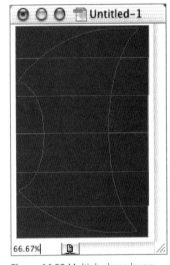

Figure 16.22 Multiple shape layers overlapping a central shape.

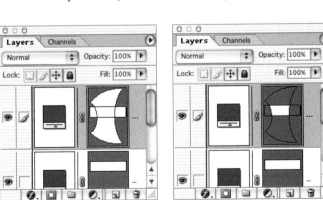

Figure 16.23 After pasting, you'll have two shapes on that layer

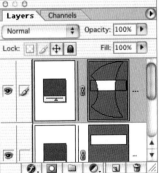

Figure 16.24 Clicking the third choice in the Options bar will use the pasted shape to limit where the other shape shows up.

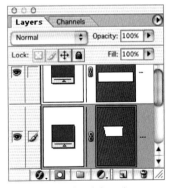

Figure 16.25 After clicking the Combine button, you will end up with a simplified shape.

After you've created the shapes you need, you can scale and rotate them using a command from the Edit > Transform menu. Applying these commands (Scale, Rotate, etc.) will not lower the quality of the result at all.

If you have multiple shape layers that you need to align (**Figure 16.26**), click on the layer you'd like to align them with and then link all the other layers you'd like to work with (**Figure 16.27**). Then grab the Move tool and click on one of the alignment icons that appear in the Options bar (**Figures 16.28** and **16.29**)

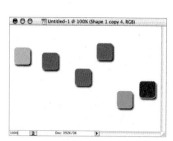

Figure 16.26 Shape layers that need to be aligned.

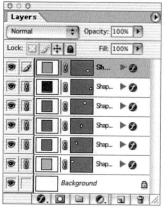

Figure 16.27 All the layers that will be aligned are linked together.

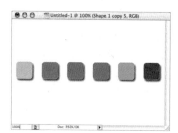

Figure 16.28 Result of centering the layers vertically and distributing them horizontally.

Figure 16.29 The alignment icons in the Options bar.

Layer Styles

At this point, your button will look rather flat and boring, but we can quickly spice it up using a Layer Style. Make sure the layer you just created is active in the Layers palette and then choose Bevel And Emboss from the Layer Style pop-up menu (it looks like a black circle with an "f" in it) at the bottom of the Layers palette (**Figure 16.30**).

In the Layer Style dialog box, you'll see a lot of choices. But don't worry; we're just going to start with an easy one that'll work well with simple buttons: the Inner Bevel style.

(You choose a style from the topmost drop-down menu.) The first decision you'll have to make for your Inner Bevel is what type of edge you'd like. The Smooth setting will give your button a rounded top look; Chisel Hard will give you a straight and sharp edge (**Figure 16.31**). Next, go to the Size setting and use the up and down arrow keys to adjust that setting until you think your button looks appropriate.

You can get much fancier than this by applying additional styles to your button. I occasionally use a drop shadow to simulate additional depth; a gradient fill can also give your buttons some extra life. I also like to vary the shape of the buttons; I might have rectangular ones in the middle and rounded corner buttons on the end of the button bar (**Figure 16.32**). It may seem like "perfecting" your button is taking a lot of time, but there's a payoff—you can save the style you're creating and easily apply it to other objects.

Once you have your button style complete, take a look in the Layers palette, where you'll find a list of the styles you used. You can experiment by turning on and off the eyeballs next to each style. Once you're sure it's what you want, just collapse the style by clicking on the arrow that appears within that layer. Now, let's save your style into the Styles palette, so we can easily apply it to other buttons. To accomplish that, click on the New Style icon (it looks like a sheet of paper) in the Styles palette, pictured in **Figure 16.33**. (You may have to choose Window > Show Styles to see the palette.) Now you should see a preview of your style at the bottom of the Styles palette. You can double-click on it to rename it.

With your style saved for future use, go back to the shape tool and look up at the Options bar. You should notice an area where you can specify a style, so choose the one you just created (**Figure 16.34**) and then continue making buttons until you have what you need. If the Style area isn't available, then press the Return (Mac) or Enter (Windows) key to make sure Photoshop knows you don't want to add to the shape layer that is currently active. You'll have to press Return or Enter after each button you create, because you'll want each button to appear on its own layer—that will make

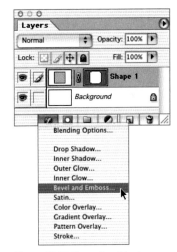

Figure 16.30 Chose Bevel And Emboss from the Layer Style pop-up menu at the bottom of the Layers palette to add a 3D look to your newly created button.

Figure 16.31 From left to right: Original image, Inner Bevel with Chisel Hard style, Inner Bevel with Smooth style.

Figure 16.32 These buttons have the following styles: Stroke, Bevel And Emboss, Gradient Overlay, Drop Shadow.

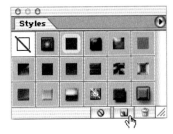

Figure 16.33 Click the New Style icon to save that collection of styles for later use.

it easier to add rollovers later. Now that you have everything set up, each time you create a button, Photoshop should automatically use the style you created. If you have trouble getting the buttons to line up, turn on your rulers and pull out some guides. The guides will snap to the edges of the first button you created, which will make it easier to position future buttons. (Or, if each button is on its own layer, you could use the Alignment options that we talked about a few paragraphs ago.)

Figure 16.34 The Style drop-down menu in the Options bar.

Sophisticated Designs Start with Simple Shapes

You can create complicated design solutions (**Figure 16.35**) by combining Photoshop basic shape tools and Layer Styles. By stacking multiple layers, you can create more sophisticated designs (**Figure 16.36**). It's just a matter of getting used to the settings available with layer styles and learning to combine the basic shape tools to combine more complex elements.

Figure 16.35 Example of a complex design.

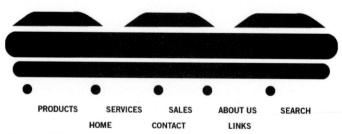

Figure 16.36 The elements used to create a complicated design.

Text for the Web

Once you have your buttons looking good, you can add some text to them. To accomplish that, first click on your foreground color and choose a Web-safe color, and then click in the center of your newly created button with the Type tool. If you have trouble finding the center of the button, try pressing Command-T (Mac) or Ctrl-T (Windows), which should place a crosshair in the center of the button. Once you have your cursor positioned just right, press the Escape key (Mac), or Esc (Windows) to get rid of the crosshair and then click with the Type tool. Next, click on the centered text icon in the Options bar and then enter the label for this button. After you've gotten the text entered, press Command-A (Mac) or Ctrl-A (Windows) to select the full range of text, and then adjust its size by clicking on the size setting and using the up and down arrow keys on your keyboard. (Adding Shift to the arrow keys jumps the value up or down by 10.)

If you'd like to experiment with different typefaces, click on the name of the font in the Options bar and then use the up and down arrow keys to cycle through all the available fonts. If you need to kern any of the letters (change the spacing between individual pairs of letters), click an insertion point between two letters, click the Palettes button in the Options bar, click in the Kern option, and tweak away. Once everything fits the space and looks just about right, experiment with the Anti-aliased setting in the Options bar (it's the icon that looks like two lowercase A's). When you adjust this setting, make sure you are viewing your image at 100% (Actual Pixels) because that's how the people viewing your Web site will see the text. You can do that by double-clicking on the Zoom tool or by choosing View > Actual Pixels. If you need to fine-tune the positioning of the entire text layer, switch to the Move tool and use the arrow keys to nudge the text one pixel at a time.

If you need to create very small text, you might want to abandon anti-aliasing and instead rely on fonts that are designed to be used at small sizes. There are many choices available and a simple search for "pixel fonts" on www.google.com will

Arachnid

Atomic

Bionika

Bylinear

Cellular

GENETICA

Joystik

MICROSCOPIC

MONOCULE

QUANTA

Remote

Scriptometer

W1RED

Figure 16.37 These pixel-based fonts are from www.atomicmedia.net.

usually send you in the right direction. Pixel-based fonts are designed specifically for onscreen use and are best used with anti-aliasing turned off.

Striped Graphics

I browse the Web every day, and I see a lot of graphics that contain really cool-looking horizontal stripes. This effect is rather easy, and the GIF file format will make it so it your file size doesn't get much larger. Let's take a look at what it takes to make the striped look (**Figure 16.38**).

Figure 16.38 When I wrote this chapter, www.ibm.com featured a striped look.

Start by creating a new document that is one pixel wide, two pixels tall, and contains a transparent background. Next, grab the Pencil tool and fill in only the topmost pixel, leaving the bottom one empty. Choose Select > All and then Edit > Define Pattern. Photoshop will prompt you for a name, so use something like "horizontal stripes." Now open the image you would like to apply the stripes to, create a new layer, and then choose Edit > Fill. Set the Use pop-up menu to Pattern, click on the pattern square, and choose the pattern you just defined (you can use a selection if you don't want it to fill the entire screen). If you'd like the stripes to apply only to the layer below, choose Layer > Group With Previous. Finally, if you'd like to use a different color for the stripes, turn on the Preserve Transparency checkbox at the top of the Layers palette (it looks like a checkerboard) and then paint away or use the Gradient tool.

Screw Heads

This should be pretty simple. Go ahead and create a new document in RGB mode with a white background. Change your foreground color to a medium shade of gray, create a new layer, and then Shift-drag with the Ellipse shape tool (not the Marquee tool) to create a round object (have it set to the rightmost setting so it doesn't create a path), and choose Layer > Layer Style > Clear Style if a layer style is automatically applied (due to settings in the Options bar). Now add dimension to the image by choosing Layer > Layer Style > Bevel And Emboss. Use the Smooth setting and experiment with the Size setting until the gray circle starts to resemble the head of a screw (a drop shadow can be another good addition to that layer). Now we just need to add the slot in the top and we'll be just about done. Create a new layer and use the Line tool (it's hidden in with the shape tools) and make a straight line across the screw head, making it extend beyond both edges. Press Command-G (Mac) or Ctrl-G (Windows) to group it with the image below, which should make it show up only where the screw head is. Change to the Move tool and link those two layers together by clicking the box at the left of the screw head layer in the Layers palette. Now click the Align Vertical Center and Align Horizontal Center buttons in the Options bar.

Our screw head is shaping up now, but that slot should look indented, right? So choose Layer > Layer Style > Bevel And Emboss, change the Technique to Chisel Hard, and click the Down radio button. You might also need to adjust the size setting until things look just right. If you think the result looks just a little too perfect, click on the screw head layer (not the slot layer) and choose Filter > Texture > Texturizer. When Photoshop asks if you would like to rasterize the layer, click the OK button. Use the Sandstone texture and turn the Relief setting way down (**Figure 16.39**).

Figure 16.39 The progression from simple circle to finished screw.

Drill Holes

Let's make some cool-looking indents that look like you drilled into a metal surface. Start by clicking on the New Layer icon at the bottom of the Layers palette. Using the Elliptical marquee tool, go to one of the corners of the image, and click and drag to create a circular selection about the size of the tip of your pinky (hold Shift to constrain it to a circle).

Figure 16.40 Set the Radial Blur filter to at least 35.

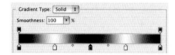

Figure 16.41 The finished gradient.

Figure 16.42 The progression from simple noise to a finished drill hole.

Now let's start to turn it into a drill hole. Choose Edit > Fill and select White from the Use pop-up menu (make sure the Preserve Transparency checkbox is turned off(you might end up with a white circle on a white background, but don't worry, we'll change that in a second). Next, we'll need random information to distort, so choose Filter > Noise > Add Noise and use a setting around 400% with the Monochromatic checkbox turned on. Now, choose Filter > Blur > Radial Blur, set the amount to at least 35, and use the Spin setting (**Figure 16.40**).

Next we'll add a special gradient to help simulate lighting. Click on the Gradient tool and choose the third kind of gradient from the Options bar (known as the Angle gradient). After you've done that, choose Black, White from the gradient drop-down menu in the Options bar. Click directly on the gradient preview to edit the gradient and do the following: Click on the white square on the far right of the gradient bar and then type 25% into the Location text field. Now hold down the Option key (Mac) or Alt key (Windows) and drag the white square toward the right—this will create a duplicate. To position this square in the correct location, type 75% in the Location field. Now Option-drag (Mac) or Alt-drag (Windows) the black square to duplicate it and then type 100% into the Location field, and then make one more black square for the 50% location. You should end up with something that looks like the dialog box in **Figure 16.41**.

Now create a new layer above the layer that contains the circular object you made earlier. Choose Select > Deselect and then click in the center of the circle and drag until your cursor is at the upper-right edge of the circle. Now you'll combine the gradient with the circle by choosing Layer > Group With Previous. Change the pop-up menu at the top of the Layers palette to Hard Light. You can also lower the opacity to let more of the circle texture show through (**Figure 16.42**).

One final touch: Let's add an edge that will make the circle appear to be indented from the surface of the background. Click on the layer that contains the circle, choose

Layer > Layer Style > Bevel And Emboss, and then choose Inner Bevel from the Style pop-up menu. To get the effect I have here, use the following settings: Depth 70, Direction Down, Size 5, Angle 138, Highlight opacity 40%, and Shadow opacity 87%.

Closing Thoughts

Your interface design choices are truly unlimited when working in Photoshop. Once you're comfortable with the techniques covered in this chapter, you can start building your own inventory of fresh and fascinating interface elements. One good way to start is to go to your favorite Web site, look closely at the interface elements, and try to re-create them on your own. I'm not suggesting you steal ideas, but this is a great way to test out your skills.

Ben's Techno-babble Decoder Ring

Anti-aliasing: A technique that blurs lines slightly by mixing together the colors on both sides of a curved or a diagonal line (which may look jagged on your computer monitor, since it's made up of a grid of square pixels). Viewed from a distance, the anti-aliased line appears smooth.

Dithering: The simulation (by placing small dots of color next to each other) of a greater range of colors than a given monitor can correctly display.

8-bit color: A technical term used to describe an image or computer that is displaying only 256 colors.

System palette: A special set of colors that are used to create all the interface elements used in a computer operating system.

Web-safe colors: A special set of 216 colors common to both the Macintosh and Windows operating systems that will not become dithered when viewed using 256-color displays.

17

Slicing and Rollovers

Courtesy www.factmonster.com

I invented the Internet.
—Al Gore

If Al Gore invented the Internet, I invented Spellcheck.
—Dan Quayle

NEW IN 7

I'll show you the completely revamped Rollovers palette, the new Selected State feature, the new Hide Auto Slices button, and the Propagate Frame 1 Changes option.

Slicing and Rollovers

In the last chapter we learned how to create the basic ingredients for your Web site, but now it's time to breathe some life into your design. So let's find out how to add interactivity to our images, or how to get our images to "do something" when the user clicks his or her mouse, or rolls over a certain area on a Web page (this is known as a *rollover*). But first, we must take a few moments to get familiar with some Web terms—stare them in the face, understand their purpose, and realize that they're really not so terribly complicated. I'm referring to slices and image maps.

If you're a regular Web trotter, you're probably visiting sites everyday that use slices and image maps. You can't see them, but they are making it possible for you to do things like rolling your mouse over an image and seeing it change, clicking on a button or tab to move to a different part of the site, or clicking on a state in a map of the U.S. to get information specific to that state.

First I'll tell you what a slice is, then what an image map is, and finally I'll explain the difference between the two and why you might choose one over the other, or sometimes use both at the same time. Once we get this worked out, we can get on with the business of energizing our Web graphics.

Think of a birthday cake. You know the flat ones you can get at the grocery store that are usually rectangular and already have "Happy Birthday" written on them with soccer balls or Barbies made out of thick frosting? Well, slicing an image is much like slicing up that birthday cake. You take an entire image and slice it up into small, rectangular shaped images called slices. Once you've created your slices (which end up as individual files), you can tell each piece how you want it to behave: you can choose the most efficient file format, prepare the image for a rollover, add HTML links, etc. And unlike cake, you can reassemble your slices and the final result will be that the end user will see one big seamless image (or Web page).

One of the greatest features of slicing is the ability to assign each slice a different file format. We'll get into the detailed pros and cons of these file formats in Chapter 19, but suffice it to say that a .jpg file format is designed for photographs, and the .gif file format is designed for graphics. If you use the wrong format for your image element, you'll end up with a much larger file size than you actually need for the image to look its best. Being able to assign different file formats within one image means that you can use the most efficient combination of formats in your Web page.

An image map is similar in that it allows you to dictate functionality to various parts of an image, but instead of chopping it up into rectangular slices, you can take one large image and designate certain areas of the image to behave in certain ways. Some people call these areas *hot spots*. Unlike the cake slices, which result in multiple files, an image map just produces one big chunk of a file. The best example of this is the often-used map of the United States. For example, many hotel Web sites have a U.S. map that lets you click on any state to find their hotels located in that state. Now how do they do that? They can't use slices, because slices are always rectangular and you can't make the shape of the state of Texas out of a rectangle. But you can get pretty darn close to making the shape of Texas with the Image Map tool. That's because the Image Map tool can create shapes not just from rectangles, but from circles and polygons as well. So you could take a map of the United States, create 50 image maps each in the shape of each different state, and make it so that each image map will send the user to the place on your site that is specific to the state they clicked on.

So, besides the obvious rectangle versus circle and polygon characteristics of the two, what's the difference between slicing and using image maps? And how do you decide whether you should slice your image, or use an image map, or use both? One answer is speed.

The problem with image maps is that you're stuck with one file format, so if your image contains both photos and graphics, it might end up being a little bloated in size. It can take a long time for that one big fat file to show up in someone's Web browser. Whereas if you took that same image of the United States and created it from *slices*—each slice saved in its most efficient file format—it would load faster, and hopefully keep your user engaged long enough to stick around your site.

In the instance of a rollover, where you want your image to change when the mouse is going over it, an image map has to swap out the *entire* file, literally doubling its size to create the effect. In contrast, to do the same thing a slice only needs to swap out areas on a slice-by-slice basis, and doesn't have to load the entire picture.

Sometimes you'll have a situation that can benefit from both slicing and image mapping. Perhaps 75 percent of your Web page is suitable for slicing (which allows you to assign different file formats, making that part of your page load faster), but there's a part of your page that really needs the versatility of the Image Map tool, and so you'll sacrifice the file size for just that 25 percent of the page. ImageReady lets you do all of this in the Rollovers palette, which is where you go to tell each slice and image map what you want it to do.

If these concepts are still confusing to you, they shouldn't be after you've gone through this chapter and created a few slices and image maps of your own. So, let's get on with it!

The Slice Tool

Photoshop's Slice tool (it's just below the Magic Wand tool) allows you to slice your image into rectangular areas that will each get special treatment when you save your image. To create a slice, just grab the Slice tool and click and drag across your image. There are two types of slices:

user slices and auto slices. A user slice is one that you've made; it appears with a blue background behind the slice number. Auto slices are the ones that are necessary to complete the rest of the image (and therefore are filled in automatically), and appear with a gray background behind the slice number, as shown in **Figure 17.1**.

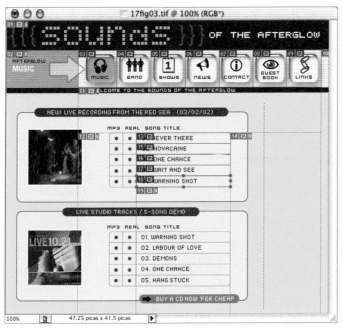

Figure 17.1 Slices show up as numbered rectangular boxes in Photoshop.

Once you have a few slices defined, you can click and hold on the Slice tool in the Tools palette to access the Slice Select tool (or just hold down the Command key on the Mac or the Ctrl key in Windows to temporarily access it while the Slice tool is active). The Slice Select tool allows you to resize and move slices that you've already created. If you find that your screen is just a clutter of slice outlines, then you just might want to click on Photoshop 7.0's new Hide Auto Slices button in the Options bar. Once you've done that, you'll only see the User Slices (**Figure 17.2**). Once you've finessed the size and position of a slice, it's time to turn that slice into a HTML link that will send your viewer to another Web page. You can accomplish that by double-clicking on the slice with the Slice Select tool and changing the options for that slice (**Figure 17.3**).

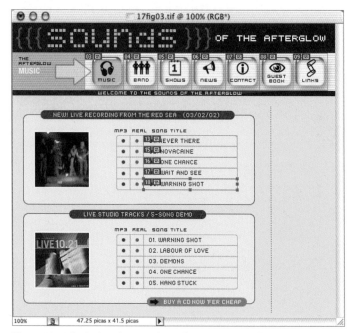

Figure 17.2 After hiding the auto slices, all you will see are the slices that you have made.

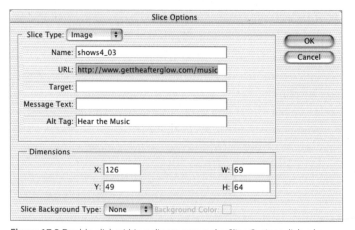

Figure 17.3 Double-click within a slice to access the Slice Options dialog box.

Let's take a look at the choices in the Slice Options dialog box. We'll start at the top and work our way down.

▶ The Name field determines the file name for the slice. Each slice name is based on the name of your Photoshop file and consists of the document name followed by an underscore and the slice number. Because of that, it's best to save your file so it's no longer called Untitled; that way, all your slices won't end up with really unhelpful names like "Untitled_02."

▶ The URL field allows you to link to another Web page. You'll need to start the URL with http:// and then you can enter any Web address (for example, my site at www.digitalmastery.com). Once you have a URL assigned, clicking on that slice in a Web browser will send you to the Web site you entered in that field.

▶ The Target field is only used if you are using frames on your Web site. With frames, you can have multiple Web pages loaded into a single browser window that is divided into panes (also known as frames). The Target setting tells the Web browser which one of these panes you want to load for the Web page that you've listed in the URL field. If you've never dealt with frames before, then just leave that field empty.

▶ If you enter anything into the Message Text field, then that information will be displayed in the status bar at the bottom of a browser window when a user moves his or her cursor over this slice. (Note that the user's browser must support JavaScript for this feature to work correctly.) If you leave the Message Text field empty, then the status bar in the Web browser will just list the URL you're linking to (**Figure 17.4**).

▶ Finally, any text you put in the Alt Tag field will be displayed within a slice before the slice image loads. I usually enter a very short description (because it has to fit within the slice) of what the slice looks like. So if one of your slices contains your company logo, you might want to say something like "Digital Mastery Logo" in the Alt tag. That way people with slow Internet connections won't have to wait for the entire page to load before they have an idea of what's to come. (Plus, people who use text-only browsers will be able to see what the slice connects to, if it's a button.) If you have any button bars, I'd suggest you enter the text of each button into its Alt Tag field; that way, people can click on those buttons before the images load (**Figure 17.5**).

Figure 17.4 The Message Text field determines what will be shown in the Status bar of a Web browser.

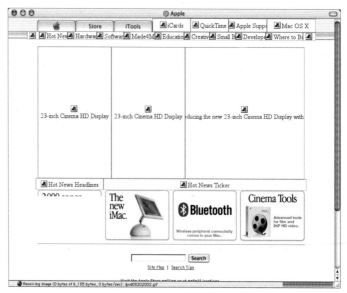

Figure 17.5 The Alt tags will appear within each slice before the images have had a chance to load.

You'll need one slice for each button that contains a roll-over, and one slice for each graphic that contains a link or that is to be saved with different compression settings (we'll talk about compression settings in Chapter 19). If you have a button bar that contains equally sized buttons, then you can save some time using Photoshop 7.0's new Divide Slice feature. To use it, first make a slice that encompasses the entire length of the button bar and then, with the Slice Selection tool active, click the Divide Slice button in the Options bar. That will bring up the Divide Slice dialog box, where you'll be able to split what used to be a single slice into multiple slices of equal size (**Figure 17.6**).

When you're adding slices to your image, you might have a clear vision of how those slices relate to the underlying image, but Photoshop isn't quite so smart. If you reposition a layer after you've put a slice around it, the slice won't know that it should move as well. This can create lots of problems if you suddenly want to make changes at the last minute (**Figure 17.7**), but there's a way to get around that.

In ImageReady, you can transform a single slice into multiple ones by choosing Slices > Divide Slice.

Figure 17.6 The Divide Slice dialog box.

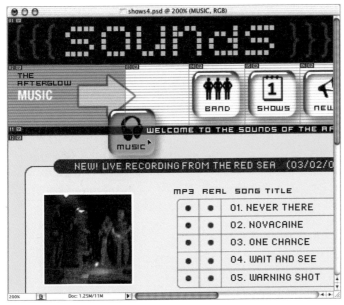

Figure 17.7 The slices you create won't move when you reposition a layer.

Layer-based slices can solve this problem. They give you the flexibility to rearrange, move, or edit buttons without having to redo any of your slicing. To create a layer-based slice, make sure the layer you are thinking about is active and then choose Layer > New Layer Based Slice. By doing that, Photoshop will create a slice that includes the entire contents of that layer (that way, if you move or resize that layer, the slice will update).

Layer-based slices are great when you create simple buttons, one per layer. You can even add a layer style (like a drop shadow) and the slice will expand to include the style. This makes slicing your images very quick and easy.

If all you wanted to do is slice your image so that you can use different file formats for different areas of your image, then at this point, you can choose File > Save for Web. Once you get there, you'll want to use the Slice Selection tool (there's a copy right there in the dialog box) to highlight a slice, and then head to Chapter 19 where you'll learn how to save your image.

If you're still with me, then I'm guessing that you'd rather add some spice to your images by adding rollovers. But before we jump into the fun of rollovers, we'll need to take a quick look at one more feature. Slices are fine and dandy when you have an image that can easily be divided into rectangular areas, but you'll have to move on to Image Maps to get odd-sized areas that you'd like to turn into links or rollovers triggers.

To create image maps, you'll need to switch over to ImageReady, because Photoshop isn't capable of creating an image map. ImageReady is loaded on your hard drive when you install Photoshop, so even if you didn't know it existed, it's there for you. ImageReady can create three things that Photoshop can't: image maps, rollovers and animation. To jump from Photoshop to ImageReady, click on the icon at the very bottom of Photoshop's Tools palette (it looks like two icons with an arrow between them).

ImageReady contains a lot of the same tools that are available in Photoshop, but if you take a good look, you'll find that ImageReady just isn't as powerful. I do most of my interface design in Photoshop and then switch to Image-Ready when I need to do things Photoshop can't. If you ever need to make a change to a slice while you're in ImageReady, click on the slice with the Slice Select tool (just like you did in Photoshop). Change the options in the Slice palette, which should be visible at the bottom of your screen (**Figure 17.8**).

Now that you know a little about what ImageReady is used for, let's see what it takes to create Image Maps.

The Slice palette contains additional options (like Message Text and the Alt tag). To access them, click on the small arrows on the palette's name tab.

Figure 17.8 ImageReady's Slice palette.

The Image Map Tools

Once you've played with slices for a while, moving on to Image Maps is pretty darn easy. You'll find the Image Map tools just to the left of the Slice tools in ImageReady's tool palette. And unlike Photoshop, you can click and hold on the Image Map icon and then mouse down to the tiny down-pointing arrow that appears under those tools to pop them into their own floating palette (**Figure 17.9**).

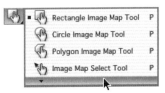

Figure 17.9 Release your mouse at the bottom of the Image Map tool pop-out menu to transform it into its own floating palette.

You can create three different shapes of Image Maps: rectangles, ovals or polygons. You'll find a tool for each in your tool palette along with an Image Map selection tool. Just like with slices, you draw a shape on your image and then turn it into a link by changing the settings that appear at the bottom of your screen (in the Image Map palette in this case). See **Figure 17.10**. That's where you'll find the same general options that we had when we were talking about slices. You can even create an Image Map based on the contents of a layer by choosing Layer > New Layer Based Image Map Area. Then, be sure to experiment with the Shape pop-up menu that appears in the

Image Map palette (**Figure 17.11**); otherwise you'll end up using a simple rectangle and you'll be no better off than using a slice.

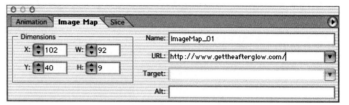

Figure 17.10 The Image Map palette.

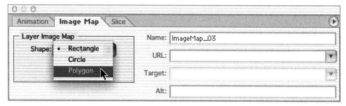

Figure 17.11 The Shape pop-up menu in the Image Map palette.

That's really all there is to Image Maps. If all you need are a few odd-shaped links, then you're welcome to go check out Chapter 19 where you'll learn how to pick the proper file format for your image. If you'd rather use your Image Map to cause part of your image to change when someone interacts with it, then you'll want to know all about our next subject—Rollovers!

Creating Rollovers

Now that your image is sliced, diced and image mapped, it's time to make part of your image change when someone moves his or her cursor over those areas. All that is going to happen in ImageReady's Rollovers palette.

The Rollovers palette is rather boring when you have an image that hasn't been sliced or image mapped (**Figure 17.12**). That's because those features are the triggers that allow a rollover to happen and without them, the only thing left to work with is the entire image. But once you have a few slices or image maps, you'll find the palette comes alive (**Figure 17.13**).

By default, the palette will list anything that has the potential of triggering a rollover. The icons in the upper-left of each item indicate what is being referenced (**Figure 17.14**). A hand indicates an image map and a knife indicates a slice. You can hide those icons by Control-clicking (Mac), or right-clicking (Windows) within an empty area of the palette and turning off Show Thumbnail Icon Badges (**Figure 17.15**). If a layer-based slice or image map was used, then you'll see a layer symbol on the left side of the item. You can even click between the items and select those elements of your image, just as if you were using the Slice Selection or Image Map Selection tool. To make the image change when you move over it, you'll need to add a *rollover state* to it. To do that, click the New Rollover State icon (it looks like a piece of paper with the corner turned over) and double-click on the rollover state that appears to change its options (**Figure 17.16**).

NOTES

ImageReady's Rollovers palette has been completely revamped in version 7.0. So, even if you're a seasoned rollover veteran, you'll want to pay close attention to this section.

Figure 17.12 The rollovers palette with no triggers available.

Figure 17.13 The rollovers palette with many triggers available.

Figure 17.14 The thumbnail icon badges.

You can automate the process of creating a layer-based slice and adding a rollover state to it by clicking the Layer-based rollover icon at the bottom of the Rollovers palette (it looks like an arrow with a spark on top of it).

Figure 17.15 Result of hiding the icon badges.

Figure 17.16 Double-click on a state in the Rollovers palette to define the type of rollover you are creating.

Here's what the rollover states do:

▶ **Over**—controls what happens when the viewer moves the cursor over the slice, but does not press the mouse button.

▶ **Down**—controls what happens when the viewer presses the mouse button within the slice.

▶ **Click**—controls what happens when the mouse button is released after clicking on a slice.

▶ **Out**—controls what happens when the viewer moves the cursor outside of the slice (if an Out rollover state has not been defined, then the image will return to the Normal state).

▶ **Up**—controls what happens when the viewer releases the mouse button over the slice.

▶ **Selected**—just like the Click state, but it stays active until another selected state is triggered, even if other non-selected states are triggered within the document.

▶ **Custom**—used by people who know how to use the programming language JavaScript and therefore outside the scope of this book.

▶ **None**—doesn't do anything except keep track of what your image looks like at this stage, so you could change it to another state in the future.

Each slice can have multiple rollover states attached to it. For example, you might have an image of a grayscale balloon. When you move your cursor over it (the Over state), it becomes a full-color balloon. When you press your mouse button over the image (the Down state), the balloon gets blown even more full of air (like it's about to burst). Then when you release the mouse button (the Click state), the balloon bursts and becomes a shriveled mess. Finally, when you move your mouse outside of the slice (the Out state), the re-inflated balloon becomes grayscale again.

You can also make one rollover state stay active after you stop interacting with the trigger that caused the image to change. You do that by using the Selected state. It's special because, unlike the other states, it can stay active even while you mouse over other areas of your image that contain rollovers—in effect, you have two rollovers active at once. The only time it will change is when someone clicks within a trigger that has another selected state specified. For example, you might have a car site where you can mouse over samples of colors that a car is available in. When you do, you see a swatch of the "moused-over" color near the car. Then, when you click on the color sample, the car actually changes color (the selected state). After that, you could still mouse over other color choices and the color swatch would still appear near the car, but the car would stay in the color that the selected state caused until you clicked on another color choice. I think of it as a sticky click state, meaning a click state that stays on until another one of those special states is triggered.

Once you've created a new rollover state and have chosen the type of rollover you want, it's up to you to change the look of your image. When you're working with rollovers, you have to limit yourself to changing a simple setting that's attached to a layer. If you paint, run a filter, or do anything else that isn't a simple setting attached to a layer, then that change will happen in *all* of your rollover states (including the normal state). You can change the position, opacity, layer style settings, and visibility of individual layers to create different rollovers.

Each trigger that has a rollover state attached to it will have a gray arrow next to it in the Rollovers palette. Clicking that arrow either hides or shows the list of rollover states that are attached to the trigger (**Figure 17.17**).

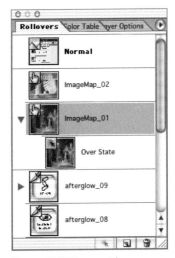

Figure 17.17 Triggers with an arrow next to them indicate a rollover is present.

To work with layer styles in ImageReady (not the presets in the Style palette), choose an individual effect from the Layer Effects pop-up menu at the bottom of the Layers palette (it looks like a circle with the letter "f" in it). A Layer Options palette for that effect will appear.

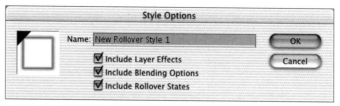

Figure 17.18 Left: image in the Normal state. Right: the same image in the Over state. This is an example of an ImageReady layer style that includes a rollover.

Simple Rollover Effects

The easiest way to create an interesting rollover is to click on one of ImageReady's preset styles (in the Styles palette) that contain a black triangle in the upper left corner; the triangle indicates that it contains a rollover (**Figure 17.18**). Or, you can choose one of the other styles, manually add a rollover, and modify the style settings on your own.

After you've made a change while one of the rollover states was active, you can preview the effect by clicking the Preview Document icon near the bottom of ImageReady's tool palette (it looks like a hand with a spark under it). When that mode is turned on, you can move your cursor over the slice in the image window to see exactly what the rollover looks like. I usually find the slice borders to be too distracting to get a good sense for what my rollover looks like. You can type Q to toggle the visibility of the slices. Once you're sure everything looks good, just click that Preview Document icon a second time and you'll be back to normal.

If you manually created this rollover using the layer style feature, then you can now save it in the ImageReady Styles palette for later use. All you have to do is make sure that the correct layer is active, and then click the New Style button at the bottom of the Styles palette. When you do, you'll be prompted for exactly what you'd like to save in the style (**Figure 17.19**). Just make sure the Include Rollover States check box is turned on. The next time you'd like to apply that rollover style, just click on the layer you'd like to apply it to, and then click the style in the Styles palette. That's all there is to it!

Figure 17.19 ImageReady's Style Options dialog box.

Sophisticated Rollover Effects

Our first rollover was pretty simple, so now let's create something that's a little more compelling. You can overcome the limitations I mentioned earlier (using only position, opacity, layer styles, etc.) by swapping the visibility of two layers that have been enhanced using filters or other effects. Here's how it works.

First, click on the layer you'd like to work with to make it active. Next, choose Layer > New > Layer Via Copy, which should give you an exact duplicate of that layer. Hide the original layer, and then apply a filter to the duplicate layer. Finally, create a trigger (slice or image map) and a rollover state for that area and then, in the Over rollover state, hide the dupe and show the original (**Figure 17.20**). You can use this technique to create just about any kind of rollover effect that you can imagine, because you're not limited to any particular tool.

NOTES

The Styles palette in ImageReady is independent of the one in Photoshop. Just because a style appears in Photoshop doesn't mean it will also appear in ImageReady. Also, ImageReady's Styles palette includes rollover information, which is not available in Photoshop.

Figure 17.20 Left: the Normal rollover state. Right: the Over rollover state.

The changes made to your image with a rollover don't have to be limited to the boundaries of the slice that triggers the rollover. The change can be anywhere in the image. That means you can have a rollover prompt a change in the central area of a Web page (**Figure 17.21**). You can even make a rollover trigger an animation, which we'll learn about in the next chapter.

NOTES

If you've made it this far through the chapter and you're starting to feel like you miss the old version of ImageReady's Animation palette, then you just might want to try this: Control-click (Mac), or right-click (Windows) within an empty area of the Rollovers palette and turn off the Include Slices and Image Maps option. That way you'll only see the rollovers that are attached to the currently active slice or image map, which is very close to how the last version of ImageReady was set up.

WARNING

The unify icons also affect the settings for the active layer across all the frames of an animation, so be careful that you don't mess up an animation when you're just trying to fix a rollover.

Figure 17.22 The Unify icons from left to right: Position, Visibility, Style.

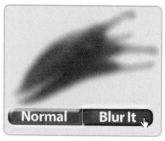

Figure 17.21 Left: the Normal state. Right: what happens when your cursor passes over one of the buttons at the bottom of the Web page. (© 2002 Stockbyte, www.stockbyte.com)

You have to be careful after you've created a rollover state; any changes to the position, opacity, layer style, or visibility will only affect that state, and not the others in the image. If you don't want to screw things up, then make sure that any global changes are made when the Normal item is active at the top of the Rollovers palette. All of the rollovers are based on that normal state, so changes to it will affect all the states. That means you can move a layer while the normal item is active and that layer will move the same distance in all the rollovers. If you'd rather not have that happen, then turn off the Propagate Frame 1 Changes from the side menu of the Layers palette.

There's one exception to this, and that's when you're working with a layer that has a layer-based slice or image map. In that case, it always acts as if that funky-sounding Propagate Frame 1 Changes feature is turned on. If you've changed a layer while one of the rollover states was active, then click on that layer in the Layers palette and use one of the icons that appear at the top of the layers palette (**Figure 17.22**). They will cause that layer's position, visibility or style settings to be consistent across all the rollover states.

Saving Your Image with Slices

Once you're done slicing your image and adding image maps and rollovers, you'll need to save your image in a special way so that the slices become individual images, and so that the HTML code needed to make the image maps and rollovers is generated. You do that by choosing Save Optimized As from the File menu in ImageReady. In the Save dialog box, choose HTML And Images from the Format pop-up menu (**Figure 17.23**). After you save the file, you should end up with an HTML file and a folder full of images (**Figure 17.24**). If you look in the Images folder, you'll find one image for each slice that was in your image (both user and auto slices). You'll also find one image for each rollover you created.

Figure 17.23 Choose HTML And Images from the Format pop-up menu in the Save dialog box.

Figure 17.24 An example folder of images created from slices and rollovers.

Closing Thoughts

The majority of popular Web sites use slicing to make sure that graphics are optimized using the correct file formats (which we'll learn about in Chapter 19). They use image maps for odd-shaped links and rollovers to enhance the user's navigational experience. If you work regularly with Web graphics, these techniques will become second nature to you. And even though this may not be the "fun" part of designing, the skills you gain from this chapter should be included in your inventory of essential tools for your Web work.

Ben's Techno-babble Decoder Ring

Slice: A rectangular area of an image that will be saved as a separate file and that can have special properties attached to it (HTML links, rollovers, etc.).

Image map: An area of an image that has been designated to be used as an HTML link or as a trigger for a rollover.

Rollover: A feature of JavaScript that allows a different image to be substituted for the original image when a user interacts with a slice.

JavaScript: A special programming language used to add features that make the Web page more interactive.

Frames: A method for loading multiple Web pages into a single browser window.

URL: An acronym that stands for Universal Resource Locator. Most URLs begin with either "http" or "ftp" and they direct a Web browser to a resource on the Internet (like a Web page or file server). Example: http://www.digitalmastery.com is the URL for the companion site to this book.

HTTP: An acronym that stands for HyperText Transfer Protocol. Web browsers and the servers that house Web sites communicate using the http protocol.

FTP: An acronym that stands for File Transfer Protocol. FTP is a very common method for transferring files over the Internet.

HTML: An acronym that stands for HyperText Markup Language. HTML is the programming language used to create Web pages.

18
Animation

Courtesy of Michael Slack, www.slackart.com

NEW IN 7

You'll see ImageReady 7.0's new Propagate Frame 1 Changes command and you'll learn how to overcome the limitations of the tween command.

A successful tool is one that was used to do something undreamed of by its author.

–S. C. Johnson

Animation

In the last chapter we found out how to breathe life into our interface elements by adding HTML links and JavaScript rollovers. Now let's find out how to add even more energy to our graphics by exploring ImageReady's animation capabilities. (In case you didn't read the last chapter, ImageReady is a companion program that installs with Photoshop; it focuses on Web functions like rollovers and animation.)

But first, a personal comment. Animation is fun and cool and can make for an exciting Web site. But this is one area where you really need to think about whether the animation adds or takes away from a good Web experience. In other words, will it slow your site down to the point that it's frustrating for users who have slower connections, or will it truly enhance the experience for your Web visitors? I think the trick is to always be able to answer this question honestly, and proceed accordingly. So, enough of my wet blanket, let's get on with the fun stuff.

ImageReady allows you to easily create layer-based animations. What do I mean by layer-based? I mean that you are limited to changing the position, opacity, visibility, or layer styles for a layer. If you paint, or apply a filter to, a layer, that effect will apply to the entire animation.

Once you have your animation created, you can save it as a GIF file that can be used on any Web page. You'll learn all about the GIF file format in the next chapter, but there's one thing you should know about it before you start creating your animations. GIF files are limited to 256 colors total. That means that photographic images will look less than ideal, and solid-colored graphics will look great.

Simple Animations

Let's start off with a simple example. Let's say you have a document that contains two layers; one contains a striped background and the other contains some text. You want to make it look like the text is moving from left to right and slowly becoming more opaque. With the document open in ImageReady, you'd need to lower the opacity of the text layer and make sure it's at the left edge of the document. Then you can click on the New Frame icon (**Figure 18.1**) and use the Move tool to reposition the text and increase the opacity setting a little bit. Now repeat that about a dozen times until you've completed the path that you'd like the text to follow. Then, to preview your animation, click the Play button at the bottom of the Animation palette.

But what if you later decide to move the striped layer? Well, if the first frame of the animation is active, then ImageReady will move the layer the same amount in each frame of the animation. But, if any other frame is active, then it only records the movement in the currently active frame of the animation (**Figure 18.2**). All the other frames still contain the original positioning of the striped layer. To change the position of the striped layer across all frames while any frame is active, you need to make sure the striped layer is active and then click the Unify Layer Position icon at the top of ImageReady's Layers palette (**Figure 18.3**).

NOTES

You can prevent ImageReady from treating the first frame of the animation differently than the others, by turning off the Propagate Frame 1 changes from the side menu of the layers palette.

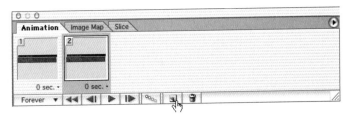

Figure 18.1 Use the Animation palette to create and manipulate the frames of an animation.

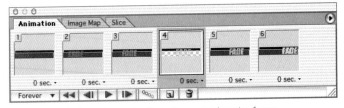

Figure 18.2 Moving a layer only affects the currently active frame.

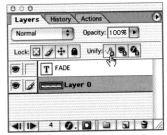

Figure 18.3 Clicking the Unify Layer Position icon will make the currently active layer consistent across all the frames of the animation.

Tweening

The animation we just looked at could have been created much faster if we took advantage of ImageReady's Tween command. All you need to do is create the critical frames of the animation (called keyframes), and then Tween makes all the intermediate frames for you. So, in our example, you could create one frame with the text at the left of the image with an opacity of zero, and a second with the text at the right of the image with an opacity of 100% (**Figure 18.4**).

Once you have the two keyframes, you can instruct ImageReady to create everything else. Start by clicking on the second frame. Then choose Tween from the side menu of the Animation palette and specify how many frames you'd like to have in the transition between the first two keyframes (**Figures 18.5** and **18.6**).

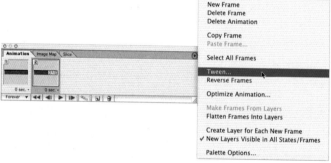

Figure 18.4 First create all the keyframes that you'll need, then choose Tween from the side menu of the Animation palette to instruct Photoshop to create all the frames needed for a transition.

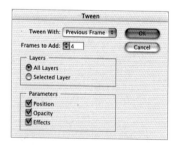

Figure 18.5 The Tween options let you control how tweening happens.

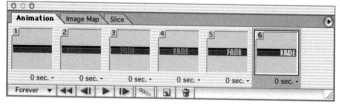

Figure 18.6 After creating the in-between frames with tweening, you should have a full animation.

Oops, I spoke too soon. If you actually played this animation, you'd notice that the text starts on the left, and smoothly moves to the right. That's fine, but once it's made that trip, then the animation starts over again—and the text suddenly pops back to its original position. What we really need is to be able add a smooth transition from the end of the animation back to the beginning.

Let's start by choosing Select All Frames from the side menu of the Animation palette. Next, choose Copy Frames, and then Paste Frames, from that same menu. When prompted, choose Paste After Selection so those frames will appear at the end of the animation (**Figure 18.7**). After doing that, you should end up with twice as many frames in your animation, and the frames you just pasted should appear at the end of the animation. You might need to use the scroll bar at the bottom of the Animation palette to see the new frames. Now all we have to do is choose Reverse Frames from the side menu of the palette to get all the frames in the correct order for a smoothly looping animation.

NOTES

You can click through your animation one frame at a time using the Next Frame and Previous Frame button at the bottom of the palette. This is an easy method to search through your animation to look for duplicate frames.

It's best if you experiment to find out the fewest frames that will create the illusion of fluid motion. The more frames you use, the larger your file size will become, and the longer your animation will take to download on a Web page.

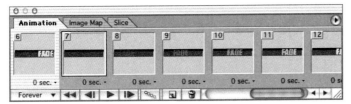

Figure 18.7 When you use Paste After Selection, all of the copied frames will be added into the palette, effectively duplicating your animation.

There's one final step. When we duplicated those frames and then reversed the order of the second half of the animation, we ended up with two frames that aren't needed. The starting and ending frame of our animation are identical, as are the middle two frames. So click on the last frame and then click the Delete button (trashcan), and get rid of one of the middle ones as well, and then everything should be perfect.

For more information about rollovers, check out Chapter 17, "Slicing and Rollovers."

Text Warping

You can create some very interesting animations using Photoshop's Text Warping feature (which we talked about back in Chapter 15). Start with some text that has warping applied (you can do this in Photoshop or ImageReady). In ImageReady, create a new keyframe and adjust the warping settings by choosing Layer > Type > Warp Text (**Figure 18.8**). Then let ImageReady do all the work by tweening between those two frames! (See **Figure 18.9**.)

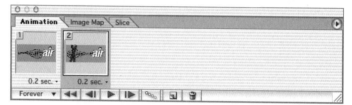

Figure 18.8 Start with two keyframes of warped text.

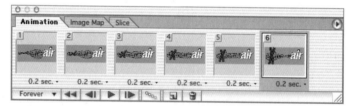

Figure 18.9 Use tweening to create the in-between frames.

Other Text Transformations

If you want your text to rotate and get larger or smaller as the animation progresses, you'll need to create a bunch of layers. But you have to remember that any change to the pixels in a layer (such as scaling) will affect all the frames of the animation. That means you'll need one layer for each frame!

You can make this process go much faster by using the Actions palette (and remember—in case you've been switching back and forth between programs—you need to record this one in ImageReady). You'll want your action to contain the following steps (**Figure 18.10**):

1. Create a new frame in the Animation palette.

2. Hide the layer you want to transform.

3. Duplicate that layer.

4. Make the duplicate layer visible.

5. Transform the layer using Edit > Transform > Numeric.

The Actions feature is actually very easy to use. Just go to the Window menu to activate (show) the Actions palette, and then you can use it to record the steps you take in Photoshop, and save them for later use.

When you do any scaling or other transformations, be sure to use percentages instead of exact measurements when you duplicate the layer. Otherwise the scaling will make all the scaled layers the same size, instead of progressively bigger. When you duplicate the layer, be sure to use the side menu of the Layers palette, so Photoshop doesn't keep track of the layer name (like it would if you just dragged that layer name to the duplicate icon). After you've created the action, just apply it over and over until you have the right number of frames for your animation.

If you'd like to rotate a layer, then divide 360 by the number of frames you plan to use. That way you can create a looping animation that smoothly repeats without any shakiness. I use this all the time for rotation gears, planets and car wheels. It just takes a little practice, but once you're used to it, it becomes quite easy.

After you've created all the frames you want, you can fine-tune the timing by changing the delay setting that appears below each frame. If you want to adjust the delay setting for more than one frame, just hold down the Shift key and click on more than one frame before changing the setting (**Figure 18.11**).

Once you've got the timing just right, you should click in the lower left of the Animation palette to specify how many times the animation should repeat (**Figure 18.12**).

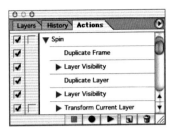

Figure 18.10 Use the Actions palette to automate the creation of rotational and zooming effects.

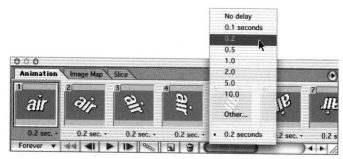

Figure 18.11 Select the frames you'd like to change and then click below one of the frames to specify the delay between frames.

Figure 18.12 Click in the lower left of the Animation palette to choose how many times your animation will repeat itself.

One-Shot Features

ImageReady's Animations palette is really designed for overly simple animations where you end up changing the opacity, position, visibility or layer styles of a layer. If you'd like to go beyond those limitations, then you'll have to start thinking a little differently about your animations. Let's say you want to use Photoshop's Liquify command. The problem is that the tween command is not able to slowly change the Liquify settings, it simply changes from the original image to the liquified result halfway through the animation.

Let's figure out an alternative that will give us the result we're looking for. Start by typing Command-J (Macintosh), or Ctrl-J (Windows) to duplicate the current layer. Next, choose Filter > Liquify and make a slight change to the image. Then repeat the process (duplicate, liquify) multiple times until you get the change you were looking for (**Figure 18.13**). Once you've gotten enough layers accumulated to make the transition between the original image and the liquified result, choose Make Frames From Layers from the side menu of the Animation palette. Once you're done, you should end up with an animation that is a simple slide show of the contents of the Layers palette, which should make the transitions you were looking for. This can be used for filters, rotations and scale effects that aren't usually possible using the tween command in ImageReady.

Rollover Animations

Earlier in this chapter, we learned how to create a basic animation. You can go one step further and use a rollover to trigger an animation. All you have to do is create a rollover state in the Rollover palette, and then, when that state is active, create an animation. That will make it so the animation will play only when your cursor is over the slice that has the rollover assigned to it. Fun, yes?

Closing Thoughts

Animation can add quite a bit of spice to your Web site, but be careful, because animations can also distract your viewers from important content on your site. So use this powerful tool with caution. Otherwise, you might find people thinking your site looks cool, but they won't even know about the product or service you might be attempting to promote because the animation distracted them from your message. Or, if they suffer with (and from) a slow connection, they might have given up and gone looking for a faster site. So have your fun, but use your good judgment!

Ben's Techno-babble Decoder Ring

Keyframes: The essential frames of an animation that are used to determine the important changes within the animation before using tweening to create intermediate, transitional frames.

Tweening: Creating a transition between two keyframes by making a number of intermediate keyframes, and automatically adjusting their settings so that the transition is smooth.

Figure 18.13 Create a new layer for each slight change you make to the image.

19

Optimization

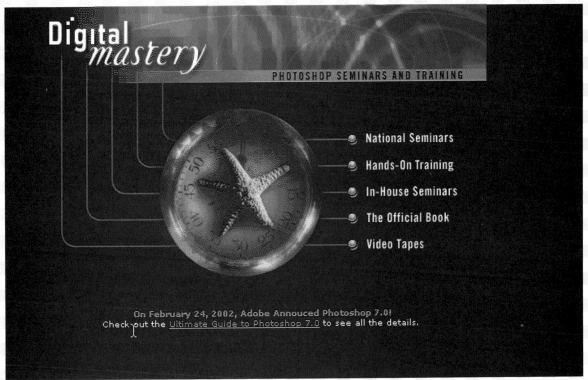

Digital *mastery*

PHOTOSHOP SEMINARS AND TRAINING

- National Seminars
- Hands-On Training
- In-House Seminars
- The Official Book
- Video Tapes

On February 24, 2002, Adobe Annouced Photoshop 7.0!
Check out the Ultimate Guide to Photoshop 7.0 to see all the details.

www.digitalmastery.com

NEW IN 7

We'll explore Photoshop 7.0's new dithered transparency and talk about all the files you end up with after optimizing a sliced image.

Perfection is achieved, not when there is nothing left to add, but when there is nothing left to take away.
—Antoine de Saint-Exupéry

Optimization

Have you ever stumbled onto some Web site where you felt like you could have gotten a haircut in the time it took for some huge image to appear on your screen? Did it make you want to do the primal scream? Well, if you want to do your part to keep the rest of the world sane, and make sure that your Web graphics look great but are nimble and fleet of foot, you'll want to learn everything there is to know about optimizing your images. What does "optimizing" mean? Simple: It's all about effectively managing the balance between image quality and file size. That means understanding how to reduce the size, colors, and quality of the image to the exact point where the image still looks good but the file size is as small as possible.

A big part of optimizing is using the right compression methods. To do that, we have to know about the most commonly used Web file formats, how they compress your image, and which is optimal for your kind of image. We'll also venture into an exciting new feature known as *weighted optimization,* which allows you to set different optimization levels for various parts of your image. Once you've run your image through its "optimization paces," you'll be ready to incorporate all your graphics along with text in an HTML editing program such as Adobe GoLive. But first, let's get down to the serious business of optimizing. There are two major methods for reducing the file size of an image: JPEG and GIF.

JPEG Compression

JPEG is an acronym that stands for Joint Photographic Experts Group. It's a file format that was designed to reduce the file size of photographic images. Let's take a look at the general idea behind it. First off, JPEG is known as a *lossy* file format because it degrades the quality of the image each time it is saved. So what exactly does JPEG do? It separates your image into color and brightness information, and then degrades the quality of the color information while maintaining the quality of the brightness information.

To get a sense for how this affects an image, open any full-color photograph and then choose Filter > Blur > Gaussian Blur. Move the slider around and see how much you can blur (read: degrade) the image before you really notice it. It doesn't take much blurring before you can see a huge change in the image (**Figure 19.1**).

Now, click Cancel to get back to the original image. Duplicate the layer that contains the photo by dragging its name onto the new layer icon (it looks like a piece of paper with the corner folded over). Next, choose Luminosity (another word for brightness) from the pop-up menu that appears at the top of the Layers palette (also known as the blending mode menu). That will make it so any changes you make to this layer will change only the brightness of the image and won't shift the colors. Now try your blur test again, seeing how much you can get away with before you really notice it (but ignore the preview window in the filter's dialog box and just look at the document window). It shouldn't be much different from our first try (**Figure 19.1**). Click Cancel again to return to the nonblurred version of the image.

 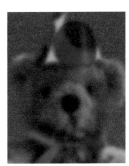  

Figure 19.1 From left to right: Original image, full image blur = 5, blur = 5 on luminosity, blur = 5 on color. (original image © 2002 Stockbyte, www.stockbyte.com)

So how is this going to show us how Photoshop can get away with making such small file sizes? Now you'll see: Set the blending mode menu to Color and then try the blur test one last time. You should notice that you can blur the image like crazy and you won't see a large change in the image (**Figure 19.1**). The only areas that usually start to look terrible are the ones where you have large areas of solid colors touching each other (what I would call graphics, as opposed to photos). That's how JPEG gets away with compressing an image—it mainly degrades the quality of the color transitions, which are not very discernible to the human eye. That's why it's the preferred format for compressing photographic images.

GIF Compression

GIF is an acronym that stands for Graphics Interchange Format. It's a file format designed for saving images that contain large areas of solid color (what I call graphics). GIF achieves a small file size by dividing the image into one-pixel-tall horizontal strips. Then it analyzes those strips and looks to see if any adjacent colors are exactly the same. If it finds same-colored areas, it can compress them by describing them in a more efficient way. So, instead of describing every single pixel (red pixel, red pixel, red pixel, red pixel, red pixel), it can describe it as a solid-colored line (red pixel x 5). This can save considerable space on your hard drive as long as there are a lot of solid-colored areas in the image. To guarantee some file size savings, GIF limits your images to 256 colors or fewer (also known as indexed color mode). If you want to get a sense for how GIF thinks about your image, open the same image you blurred earlier, choose Image > Adjust > Posterize, and use a low number like 2 (**Figure 19.2**). This will reduce the number of colors in your image, and you should notice that more areas of solid color appear. You should also notice that photographic areas don't look so good, but graphical areas (logos, text, bar charts, etc.) generally look fine. So now you should be able to see why GIF is mainly used to compress graphics.

Figure 19.2 Left: Original image. Right: Posterized with a setting of 2.

Optimize in Photoshop or ImageReady?

In general, Photoshop is fine if all you want to do is slice and optimize a few images, but you'll need to optimize in ImageReady if you're working with rollovers or animation. The optimization features are almost identical between the two, but you'll find that they present the information differently. Let's take a tour and see what kind of options we have for optimizing our images.

To optimize an image in Photoshop, choose File > Save For Web. This will bring up a huge dialog box that will pretty much take over your screen (**Figure 19.3**). At the top, you can choose to view the original, the optimized version, or a combination of both. At the bottom of the image window, you'll find information about how small the file size has become and how long the image should take to download. To tell Photoshop what type of connection to think about when calculating file size, click on the small arrow in the upper right of the preview image window (**Figure 19.4**).

Next, let's look at the optimization settings in this dialog box. The first step to optimizing an image is to click the 2-Up tab so you can compare the optimized version of the image to the original, then click within the right image so

NOTES

If your image is large enough that you can't see the whole thing at once, press the spacebar to temporarily access the Hand tool (or just grab it from the Tools palette) and then scroll around.

that a bold border appears, indicating that's the area we'll be working on. Next you'll need to choose the file format you'd like to use (GIF for graphics and JPEG for photos). When you change file formats, the options in the optimization area will change to reflect what the selected format offers. If you'd like to use some preset optimization settings, choose one from the Settings pop-up menu.

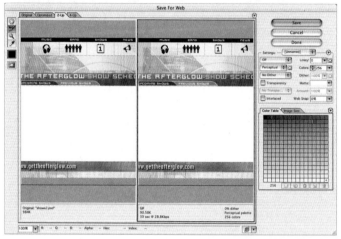

Figure 19.3 The Save For Web dialog box, set to view both the original and the optimized images. (Web site courtesy of www.gettheafterglow.com)

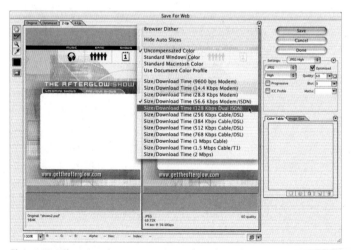

Figure 19.4 Changing the connection speed used to calculate download times.

Below the optimization area, you will find the Color Table (which works for GIF files only) and Image Size tabs. The Image Size area often comes in handy once you can see what your image will look like when it's optimized, because even a small reduction in dimensions can make a noticeable difference in the file size. (**Figure 19.5**). If you need to scale an image down, just change the width (assuming the Constrain Proportions checkbox is on) and then click Apply.

That's how easy it is in Photoshop. Now let's look at how ImageReady organizes these same features into a collection of floating palettes (**Figure 19.6**).

At the top of the document window, you'll find the familiar tabs to determine what you'd like to view. The file size information is at the bottom as in Photoshop, but now you can also choose the connection speed from a pop-up menu at the bottom of the document window (**Figure 19.7**). The Optimization palette is in the upper right and the Color Table palette is directly below that. The Slice palette replaces Photoshop's Slice Options dialog box, and the slice tools are in the main Tools palette. So, as you can see, Photoshop and ImageReady are very similar. I use Photoshop if all I want is to slice and optimize a few images; I switch to ImageReady anytime I need rollovers or animation.

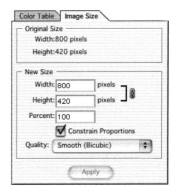

Figure 19.5 The Image Size area of the Save For Web dialog box.

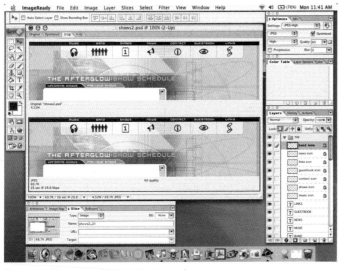

Figure 19.6 ImageReady's optimization tools.

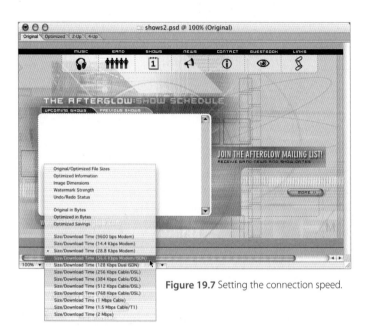

Figure 19.7 Setting the connection speed.

Optimizing Photographs

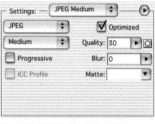

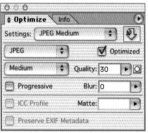

Figure 19.8 Top: Photoshop's JPEG compression options. Bottom: ImageReady's JPEG compression options.

Let's take a tour of the features needed to optimize a photographic image. (Remember, if you're in Photoshop, you're still in the Save For Web dialog box—this is "where it all happens" in terms of optimization.) First you'll need to set the Format pop-up menu to JPEG. Next, try to determine the best optimization setting (**Figure 19.8**). You can do that by watching the optimized view of your image while you choose a general setting from the Quality pop-up menu. After you've done that, you can fine-tune the setting by moving the Quality slider around (click on the triangle that appears next to the Quality number). I find that settings below 30 work only for images that don't contain much detail. I always leave the Optimized checkbox turned on because it will deliver a slightly smaller file size.

The Progressive option makes it so that your image will display a low-resolution preview that slowly becomes more detailed as more of its data is downloaded to the Web browser (**Figure 19.9**). That's essential for large images in today's fast-paced world, where a 5-second wait could mean the difference between someone who browses your site and one who leaves in a fit of impatience. If you have an image that is more than 20 Kbytes in size, you might want to consider using the Progressive checkbox in an attempt to entice viewers to wait for your graphic to load before moving on.

I do not suggest you use the ICC Profile feature unless you're producing a site that sells expensive clothing. An ICC profile will attempt to make the colors in your image appear to be more accurate in a Web browser. That sounds like a great thing, but the profile is often much larger than the file you are attempting to optimize and will therefore increase download times. Not only that, but the only people who will see an accurate image are those who have calibrated monitors and have a browser that understands profiles (not many do).

If you'd like to squeeze a few extra kilobytes out of your image, consider using the Blur feature. Use very low settings, otherwise your image will look ridiculous. Blurry images usually achieve better compression than overly sharp ones. Likewise, applying the Sharpen filter to any image saved as a JPEG file will increase its file size.

The JPEG file format doesn't support transparency, but if your Web page has a single background color, you can use the Matte option (**Figure 19.10**) to create the illusion of transparency in the exported JPEG version of the file. It does this by replacing all transparent (checkerboard) areas of the Photoshop file with your Matte color, so set it to the same as the background color of your Web page.

Figure 19.9 From top to bottom: The progression of an image being downloaded using the Progressive option. (original image © 2002 Stockbyte, www.stockbyte.com)

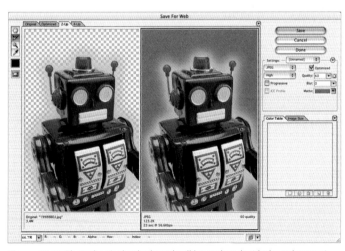

Figure 19.10 Photoshop's checkerboard will be replaced with the color specified in the Matte field. (© 2002 Stockbyte, www.stockbyte.com)

Optimizing Graphics

Graphics present a whole different set of challenges. The first thing you'll need to do is change the Format pop-up menu to GIF and then clear out any unusual settings (**Figure 19.11**). I always start with Lossy, Web Snap, and Dither set to 0. Then you can experiment with the Colors setting. I usually click on the pop-up menu just to the right of this setting (it looks like a tiny arrow pointing down), start with the lowest setting, and then increase it until the image has acceptable quality. Each time you change this setting, the program will double the number of colors used. Once the quality seems to be OK, try reducing the number of colors even more by clicking the down-pointing arrow directly to the left of the Colors setting, which will reduce the number of colors in increments of one. You can also click on that number and then use the up and down arrow keys on your keyboard (hold Shift to change them in increments of 10). Next, try each of the choices in the pop-up menu that appears to the left of the Colors setting. This setting determines exactly which colors will be used.

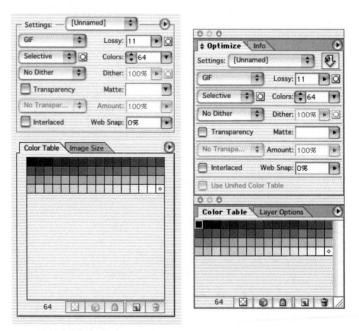

Figure 19.11 Left: Photoshop's GIF compression options. Right: ImageReady's GIF compression options.

Finally, if the colors in your image slowly fade out (like a gradient), you might want to experiment with the Dither setting as well (**Figure 19.12**). But be careful, because you can often get better results by leaving that feature off and just giving the image more colors instead. As you work through these options to figure what's going to work best for your image, keep your eye on the file size, which is displayed below the optimized image.

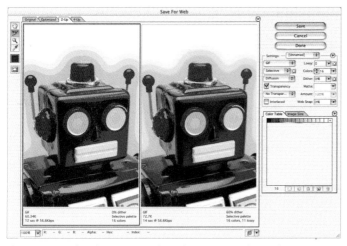

Figure 19.12 Left: Dither set to 0. Right: Dither set to 60%. (original image © 2002 Stockbyte, www.stockbyte.com)

The Interlaced checkbox allows your image to download a little at a time in a striped pattern (**Figure 19.13**). This allows someone to get a general sense of what the image looks like before the entire image loads. I usually reserve this feature for large images, where I need to supply a preview to entice viewers into waiting for the image to load. I also avoid it on normal-sized images because it will increase their file size. Interlacing a GIF image is the same concept as creating a progressive JPEG image, but the result looks a little different.

GIF supports transparency, but that doesn't mean that it can reproduce exactly what you see onscreen. You know that in Photoshop, an image can contain very soft, subtle edges (like a drop shadow), but GIF supports only one level of transparency. That means an area can be either 100% transparent or 100% opaque, but nothing in between. It's almost as if you are using a pair of scissors to cut out your image—and I don't have to tell you it's impossible to make soft edges using scissors. To enable transparency in a GIF image, just turn on the checkbox in the Optimization palette. The Matte color listed in the Optimization palette will be used to fill any partially transparent areas, so pick one that matches the background color of your Web page (**Figure 19.14**).

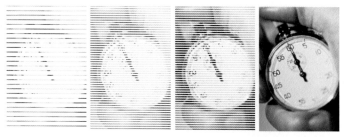

Figure 19.13 From left to right: The progression of an image downloaded using the Interlaced option. (original image © 2002 Stockbyte, www.stockbyte.com)

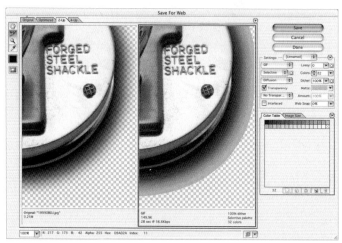

Figure 19.14 Partially transparent areas are filled with the Matte color. (original image © 2002 Stockbyte, www.stockbyte.com)

If you have an image with a soft edge and you'd rather not have the Matte color show up behind it, set the menu that appears below the Transparency checkbox to Diffusion Transparency Dither so the edge fades out using a pattern of noise (**Figure 19.15**). Once you've got that turned on, then experiment with the Amount setting that appears to the right of the pop-up menu. Lower settings will usually reduce the file size. You can also try Pattern and Noise Transparency Dither, but they don't involve an amount setting (**Figure 19.16**). These settings are a great help when you need to save an image that includes a soft-edged shadow that will need to be placed on top of a multicolored background.

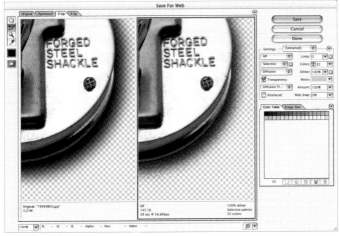

Figure 19.15 On the left is an image without dithered transparency. The right one is using 100% dithered transparency.

Figure 19.16 From left to right: Diffusion, pattern, and noise transparency.

Figure 19.17 Top: Image as shown using GIF compression. Bottom: Image shown with Browser Dither preview turned on. (original image © 2002 Stockbyte, www.stockbyte.com)

Figure 19.18 The color cube icon will convert the currently highlighted color to a Web-safe color so it won't dither.

Figure 19.19 When the Lossy option is set too high, you'll see noisy-looking artifacts.

Once you think you have your image perfected, you'll want to start thinking about what it will look like on monitors that display only 256 colors. (At the time I wrote this chapter, only 6.7 percent of all the people browsing the Web were using computers limited to 256 colors. But 6.7 percent of the 544 million people browsing the Web worldwide is still more than 36 million people.) You can do that by choosing Browser Dither from the View menu in ImageReady or by clicking the triangle that appears in the upper right of Photoshop's Save For Web dialog box. When you turn on Browser Dither, you'll suddenly start to see random specks in many areas of your image (**Figure 19.17**). This is also known as dithering. These dithered areas usually look good where one color fades into another but not so good in areas that should appear as solid colors (such as logos and text). But you can get rid of the dithered look. Look at your image with the Browser Dither feature turned on and note which areas need to be changed. Then turn off the Browser Dither feature. Now, grab the Eyedropper tool and click on an area that was dithered (when the preview was on) but should now be filled with a solid color, and then click the cube icon at the bottom of the Color Table (**Figure 19.18**). If you find that the color used doesn't look good in the image, double-click the color in the Swatches area and choose an alternative color (just make sure it's a Web-safe color). Continue to do that with the rest of your image until you've fixed all the areas that didn't look good when the Browser Dither preview was on. Once that's set up, you can turn Browser Dither on again to check your work.

At this point you've taken advantage of a lot of GIF optimization features. But there is one more way to squeeze more out of your image. Click on the Lossy setting and play around with the up and down arrow keys while you stare at the image. Keep increasing the setting until you notice some noisy-looking artifacts showing up (**Figure 19.19**), and then back off just enough to make the artifacts disappear. This feature will attempt to create more areas that contain solid color, but it does it in a very unusual way that often produces noise. It's kind of weird to find a Lossy option when saving a GIF file, because GIF is known as a lossless file format. Photoshop hasn't changed the way GIF files are saved; instead, Adobe has just added a special feature that degrades the look of your image *before* it's saved.

Weighted Optimization

Weighted optimization allows you to make one area of an image look better than the rest without slicing the image into multiple files. Here's how it works: You start by making a selection of the area that is most important to you. You can choose Select > Feather if you want to have the quality slowly change over an area. Once you have a selection in place, choose Select > Save Selection and assign it a memorable name. Then, when you go to optimize your image, look for a small dotted-circle symbol (**Figure 19.20**) that will appear next to many of the optimization settings (Lossy, Dither, and Color for GIF files and Quality for JPEG). If you click on that symbol, you'll get to a special dialog box where you can specify how you'd like Photoshop to use your selection (**Figure 19.21**). The white slider determines the setting for the area that was selected; the black slider determines which will be used in the area that was not selected. If the selection was feathered, then the settings will slowly change across the area that was feathered.

You've now learned how to use weighted optimization to influence where Photoshop will apply the highest Quality settings without slicing your image into multiple documents (**Figures 19.22** and **19.23**).

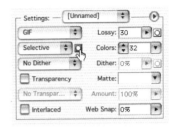

Figure 19.20 Clicking this symbol will allow you to use weighted optimization settings

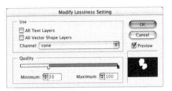

Figure 19.21 The Weighted Optimization dialog box. Depending on which feature you chose, it will reflect a different name, but it's always about modifying a setting.

Figure 19.22 Image before applying weighted optimization. (© 2002 Stockbyte, www.stockbyte.com)

Figure 19.23 The result of using weighted optimization.

Combo Images

So far, we've separated our images into two categories—graphics and photographs—but you'll often have an image that contains a combination of both. When that's the case, you'll have to make a compromise and decide which area is most important to the image. If it's the solid areas of color, save it as a GIF file (**Figure 19.24**). On the other hand, if the photographic areas are more important, use the JPEG file format (**Figure 19.25**). This can also be a great time to use the new weighted optimization feature that we just talked about, so you can use different settings for each area of the image (**Figure 19.26**). Or, if the image can be easily divided into multiple rectangular areas of graphic and photo, then consider slicing the image. No matter what you choose, part of the combo image will look less than ideal, but that's the nature of combination images.

Slice Tricks

If your interface design contains many same-colored buttons, you might want to use the same optimization settings for all those buttons. You can accomplish that in Image-Ready by Shift-clicking on each one of the slices when you're using the Slice Select tool. Next, choose Link Slices from the Slice menu. That will force all the buttons to use the same compression settings (**Figures 19.27** and **19.28**).

Figure 19.24 A combo image saved as a GIF file. (© 2002 Stockbyte, www.stockbyte.com)

Figure 19.25 A combo image saved in the JPEG file format.

Figure 19.26 A combo image saved as a GIF file with weighted optimization.

Optimizing Rollovers

If you have created rollovers in ImageReady, be sure to look at the optimized view of both rollover states. You can do that by turning on the Rollover Preview button in ImageReady, which looks like a hand with lines radiating from the fingers (it's near the bottom of the main Tools palette in ImageReady). With the preview turned on, you should be able to move your cursor around the screen and see how the optimization settings affect the look of the rollovers. Also, be sure to turn on the Browser Dither preview again to make sure your rollovers will look good in 256 colors. If you're in a multipane view (2-Up, 4-Up) this works only when the pane you're trying to preview is active. If you find that solid-colored areas are shifting between the different rollover states, then turn on the Use Unified Color Table option, so ImageReady uses a consistent set of colors for all the rollover states.

Figure 19.27 Buttons with inconsistent optimization settings.

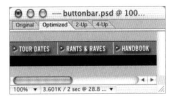

Figure 19.28 Buttons that are linked and therefore use the same optimization settings.

Optimizing Animations

The JPEG format does not support animation, so you'll have to use GIF, even if your animation contains photographs. When optimizing an animation, be sure to click through all the frames of the animation, because some frames might contain more colors than others. And be extra careful when attempting to optimize an animation; it's really easy for an animation's file size to get out of hand. I often lower my image-quality standards when working with animations, just so they load fast in a Web browser.

Saving Your Images

After you've chosen the optimization settings for each area of your image, it's time to save the resulting file. In Photoshop, that's a pretty simple affair. All you have to do is click the Save button in the Save For Web dialog box and assign a name to your image. (If you want, you can confirm the settings in the Format menu and the Settings and Slices menu at the bottom of that dialog box, but the default settings should be fine.) In ImageReady, however, you'll have to choose File > Save Optimized As and then,

NOTES

You can change the file naming convention that is used by clicking the Edit Output Settings button in Photoshop's Save For Web dialog box or by choosing File > Output Settings in ImageReady.

from the pop-up menu near the bottom of that dialog box, choose HTML And Images, for sliced images, or Images Only, for nonsliced images. Animations will be saved as a single GIF file.

If your image contains slices, you'll end up with a folder that contains one image for each slice and another for each rollover (**Figure 19.29**). The filenames will be based on what you entered as a filename in the Save dialog box. Each image will contain that name, then an underscore and then the number of the slice it represents. Rollovers will have the same name followed by *over* or other name depending on what type of rollover it is. All these files are simple GIF and JPEG images that you can open in Photoshop or a Web browser. You'll also get an HTML file with a sliced image that contains the code needed to reassemble all those images into a seamless composite and the JavaScript code to make the rollovers work. You can load the HTML file into a Web browser to test your work or load it into an HTML editing program to integrate your work into a more complex Web site.

It's very easy to mess up the files that you get from a sliced image. Simply moving the HTML file will make all the images appear with a broken image icon. Because of that, it's best to load the HTML file into a sophisticated HTML editing program such as Adobe GoLive, which can keep track of the files and can keep everything up-to-date when you move the files around your hard drive.

Name	Size
home.html	12 KB
▼ images	--
home_01.jpg	20 KB
home_02.jpg	16 KB
home_03.gif	4 KB
home_03-over.gif	4 KB
home_04.jpg	4 KB
home_05.jpg	4 KB
home_06.jpg	4 KB
home_07.gif	4 KB
home_07-over.gif	4 KB
home_08.jpg	4 KB
home_09.jpg	4 KB
home_10.gif	4 KB
home_10-over.gif	4 KB
home_11.jpg	4 KB
home_12.jpg	4 KB
home_13.gif	4 KB
home_13-over.gif	4 KB
home_14.jpg	4 KB
home_15.jpg	4 KB
spacer.gif	4 KB

Figure 19.29 An example of the files you might get when saving a sliced image.

Closing Thoughts

When you save your graphics in the correct file format, and with appropriate settings, they will look better and load faster than what you'd get from any other file format. In fact, optimizing your images can often result in a Web site that loads twice as fast as most other sites. And you now know how to do all that, so you're all ready to load your images and that HTML file into an HTML editing program such as Adobe GoLive. So, go forth and optimize your Web world, so everyone has a chance to see and enjoy it.

Ben's Techno-babble Decoder Ring

GIF: An acronym that stands for Graphics Interchange Format. This lossless file format is limited to a maximum of 256 colors and is ideal for imagery that contains large areas of solid color.

JPEG: An acronym that stands for Joint Photographic Experts Group. This lossy file format achieves great levels of compression by generalizing the color information in the image, while maintaining most of the brightness information. It's ideal for images containing soft edges, gradations, or a wide range of color, such as photographs.

Lossy compression: Any kind of compression that results in a lower-quality image when compared with the original.

Lossless compression: Any kind of compression that delivers an identical image when reopened.

Index

8-bit color, 511
16-bit images, 181–182
16-bit mode, 145, 426
24-bit scanners, 180, 187
30-bit scanners, 180, 187
35mm slides, 138

A

Absolute Colorimetric, 245
Acrobat, 48, 366, 457
Actions feature, 538–539
Actions palette, 538–539, 540
Actual Pixels option, 18
Add Layer Mask command, 345
adjustment layers, 112–113, 156–158, 333
Adobe Acrobat, 48, 366, 457
Adobe GoLive, 560
Adobe Illustrator, 456, 457
Adobe ImageReady. See ImageReady
Adobe Photoshop. See Photoshop
Adobe RGB working space, 225, 240
Airbrush option, 28
alignment
    layers, 504
    text, 464
All Layers option, 116
alpha channels, 287–294. See also channels
    creating, 289
    deleting, 288
    described, 271–272, 287, 302
    editing, 289
    illustrated, 270
    loading selections, 287–288
    saving selections, 287–288
    saving with image, 294
    uses for, 272
    viewing, 288–289
    viewing with image, 292–294
Amount setting, 183–186
Angle gradient, 510
animation, 533–541
    GIF format, 534, 559
    JPEG format, 559
    optimizing, 559
    rollovers. See rollovers
    saving, 560
    simple, 535–537
    text transformations, 538–541
    text warping, 538
    tweening, 536–537
    Web sites and, 534, 541
Animation palette, 535
annotations, 47–48
Annotations tool, 47
Anti-aliased option, 62

anti-aliasing
    described, 52, 511
    text, 461–462, 507
Apple calibration utility, 229–232
Apple RGB working space, 225
arrow keys, 14
artifacts, 556
ASCII files, 286
audio annotations, 47, 48
Auto Color feature, 258–259
Auto Kern checkbox, 460
auto slices, 517

B

Background Eraser tool, 29–31
background images, 99–100, 335, 345
background layers, 99–100
backgrounds
    color, 18–19, 46
    deleting, 300–301, 316, 334
    erasing, 29–31
    repeating patterns, 480–484
    textured, 476–479
    transparent, 30, 155
balance, 253–259
banding, 52, 181. See also dithering
bar charts, 194–197
baseline, 485
baseline shift, 461
beveled edges, 473, 504–505, 511
big data, 91, 104
binary files, 286
bitmap mode, 150, 154
bitmaps, 161–162, 163
bits, 302
black-and-white images
    bitmap mode, 150
    colorizing, 405, 409–410
    forcing grayscale images to, 279–280
    photographs, 409–410
Blending Mode menu, 114–115
blending modes, 373–422
    Clone Stamp tool and, 438
    Color Burn mode, 384
    Color Dodge mode, 389–390
    Color mode, 397, 405
    comparative blending modes, 399–400
    contrast blending modes, 391–399
    Darken mode, 376–377
    darken modes, 376–385
    described, 374, 417
    Difference mode, 399–400
    Dissolve mode, 375
    Exclusion mode, 400
    Hard Light mode, 393–394, 398

Hue mode, 401–402
hue/saturation/brightness modes, 400–412
keyboard shortcuts, 418
Lighten mode, 386–388
lighten modes, 386–391
Linear Burn mode, 385
Linear Dodge mode, 391
Linear Light mode, 396–397
Luminosity mode, 406–407
Multiply mode, 378–383
Overlay mode, 391–392, 398
overview, 28–29
Pin Light mode, 398
Saturation mode, 402–404
Screen mode, 388–389
Soft Light mode, 392–393, 398–399
types of, 375–412
Vivid Light mode, 394–395, 398
Blending Modes menu, 374
blending sliders, 330, 336–343, 357–358
Bloat tool, 414
Blur tool, 447–449. *See also* blurring
blurring
compression and, 545–546, 551
layer masks, 350
layers, 449
selectively, 447–449
shadows, 315, 316, 318, 323
BMP format, 163
Border command, 79
brightness
adjusting, 205, 213, 262
brushes, 37–38
color, 20–21, 37, 202
described, 53
grayscale images, 174
highlights, 450
Lab mode and, 274–275
Luminosity mode, 406–407
selecting colors by, 20–21
shadows, 316, 322
Brightness/Contrast dialog box, 166–167, 173
Brightness setting, 37–38
Browser Dither preview, 556, 559
browsers. See Web browsers
Brush Pressure setting, 415
Brush Size setting, 296, 415
Brush Tip Shape settings, 33–35
brushes
activating, 31
Clone Stamp tool and, 431
opacity, 39
presets, 31, 32, 39, 40
resetting defaults, 39
round, 32
sampled, 32–33
saturation, 37, 38
saving, 39
settings, 33–39
shape of, 33–36

size of, 31
Spacing setting, 440
texture, 36–37
Brushes palette, 31, 32–40
Brushes Presets palette, 31, 32
Burn tool, 159, 443–446
burning photographs/images, 440, 443–446
buttons, navigational
adding text to, 507–508
creating, 503–506

C

calibration utility, 229–232
cameras, digital, 141–142, 278–279
cast shadows, 311, 313–316
CD, included with book, xii
Channel Options dialog box, 293–294
channels, 267–304.
activating, 272–273
alpha. *See* alpha channels
applying filters to, 278–279
changing stacking order, 273
CMYK, 274
color. *See* color channels
composite, 276
creating, 273, 289
deleting, 273
editing, 277–278, 289, 291
grayscale, 290–292
isolating areas of, 292
keyboard shortcuts, 304
Lab, 275
layers and, 275
loading, 289, 291
multiple, 277–278
noise, 271
painting in, 289, 291
renaming, 273
retouching and, 445–446
RGB, 274
sharpening, 278–279
spot, 270, 271, 280–286
types of, 270–272
uses for, 268–269
viewing, 276–277, 294
Channels palette, 272–273
Character palette, 458, 462–464, 469
Cleanup tool, 300
clipping paths, 366–367
Clone Stamp tool, 431–439
cloning, 431–439
clouds, 341, 399–400
Clouds filter, 399–400
CMYK channels, 274
CMYK color
color management and, 221–224
Custom Color Picker and, 21
described, 53
purpose of, 19, 25

reproducibility of, 19
thermal-wax devices, 148
CMYK images, 204
CMYK inks, 53, 304
CMYK mode
    Burn tool and, 444–445
    CMYK Spectrum option, 22
    converting images to, 237–238, 243–244, 263
    shadows and, 324–325
    uses for, 274
    vs. RGB mode, 275
CMYK working space, 237–238, 243
collage, 327–372
    blending sliders, 330, 336–343
    grouping layers, 229–330, 332–335
    keyboard shortcuts, 347, 368
    layer masks, 330–331, 343–359
    methods for, 328–332
    vector masks, 331–332, 359–367
color, 18–26
    8-bit, 511
    adjusting with curves, 201–203, 212
    backgrounds, 18–19, 46
    balance, 253–259
    brightness, 20–21, 37, 202
    choosing, 19–25
    CMYK. See CMYK color
    custom, 21
    dithered, 496–498
    foreground, 18–19, 27, 46
    gamut, 224, 225, 246, 264, 303
    gradients, 22, 45, 46
    HSB, 53
    hue. See hue
    indexed, 546
    Lab, 54, 203
    layers, 120
    Matte, 554–555
    measuring, 25
    monitors and, 491–492, 495, 556
    out-of-gamut, 19, 224, 263
    PANTONE, 21, 281–282, 304
    previewing, 19–20
    Quick Mask mode and, 90–91
    resolution, 132–142
    RGB. See RGB color
    samples, 25–26
    saturation. See saturation
    selecting, 81, 90–91
    shadows, 322–323
    skin tones, 259–262
    spot, 280–286
    text, 461
    toning down, 447
    TruMatch, 21
    Web browsers, 498–499
    Web graphics, 495–498
    Web-safe. See Web-safe colors
color bar, 22

Color blending mode, 397, 405
Color Burn mode, 384
color channels, 270–271. See also channels
    collage, 339–340
    described, 302–303
    illustrated, 270
    overview, 273–280
    uses for, 270–271
color correction, 247–266
    Auto Color feature, 258–259
    described, 248
    gray areas, 249–259
    highlights, 253–259
    process for, 252–262
    professional, 252–262
    refinements, 262–264
    RGB, 249–252
    shadows, 253–259
Color Dodge mode, 389–390
Color field, 20
Color Halftone filter, 480
color management, 217–246
    calibration utility, 229–232
    described, 246
    implementing, 223–239
    overview, 218–223
    profiles. See ICC profiles
    RCB working spaces, 224–227
    uses for, 239–245
color modes, 274–275, 439
color overlays, 348, 392
Color palette, 21–22, 196, 497
Color Picker, 19–21, 253, 497
Color Range command, 76–78
Color Sampler tool, 25–26, 256, 260
color samples, 253
color swatches, 46, 47
Color Table, 549
colorimeter, 233, 235
Colorize checkbox, 410
colorizing images, 293, 405, 409–410
ColorMatch RGB working space, 226
Colors setting, 552
ColorSync control panel, 232
composite channels, 276, 303
compositing. See collage
compression
    blurring and, 545–546, 551
    GIF, 546, 552, 556
    JPEG, 544–546, 550
    lossless, 561
    lossy, 545, 556–557, 561
    LZW, 153
contours, 381–382
Contract command, 80
contrast
    adjusting, 170, 262
    curves and, 205–207
    decreasing, 206–207
    described, 215

evaluating, 170
increasing, 205–206
Control setting, 35
Copy Color As HTML option, 22
copying
    Copy Color As HTML option, 22
    between documents, 104–105
    layers, 116
    Via Copy option, 116
Crop tool, 64–66, 104
cropping
    described, 91
    images, 64–66
    layers and, 104
    perspective, 65–66
curves, 189–216
    adjusting brightness, 205, 213
    adjusting color images, 201–203, 212
    adjusting grayscale images, 201, 212, 213
    adjusting image contrast/detail, 205–207
    adjusting images with Input/Output numbers,
      211–215
    changing direction, 362
    converting to points, 210
    creating with Pen tool, 361–363
    defining with Pencil tool, 209–211
    detail and, 205–207
    ending, 363
    flattening, 207–208
    freeform, 209–211
    ghosting images, 203–205
    gradients and, 197–199, 201, 208, 212–213
    grids, 197–198, 200
    Input/Output numbers, 211–215
    keyboard shortcuts, 216
    layers and, 202
    modifying, 362
    posterizing, 210
    previewing changes, 201
    S curves, 208, 215
    smoothing, 210
    using histograms with, 207–208
    working with, 200–211
Curves adjustment layer, 258
Curves dialog box, 185, 190, 193–213
Custom Color Picker, 21
Custom Shape tool, 502–503
customization
    colors, 21
    gradients, 46
    ICC profiles, 228, 232–236
    shapes, 502–503

D

Darken mode, 376–377, 438, 448
DCS (Desktop Color Separation), 284–285, 303
DCS format, 284–286, 294
deleting
    backgrounds, 300–301, 316, 334

channels, 273, 288
layer masks, 358–359
vector masks, 365
Deselect command, 75
Desktop Color Separation. *See* DCS
device profiles, 227–239
Difference mode, 399–400
Diffuse filter, 316
digital cameras
    noise and, 278–279
    resolution, 141–142
display. *See* monitor
Dissolve mode, 375
Distort transformation, 81–84
distortion
    layers, 106
    photograph edges, 351
    selections, 81–84
Dither setting, 553
dithered transparency, 555
dithering
    colors, 496–498
    described, 52, 511
    gradients, 45
    Web-safe colors and, 19, 20, 497, 556
Divide Slice feature, 521
documents. See files
Dodge tool, 159, 160, 440–443
dodging
    Color Dodge mode, 389–390
    Dodge tool, 159, 160, 440–443
    highlights, 441
    images, 440–443
    Linear Dodge mode, 391
    photographs, 440–443
    retouching with, 440–443
    shadows, 441
dot-gain settings, 175
dots per inch (dpi), 147
download times, 544, 547, 548, 550–551
dpi (dots per inch), 147
drivers, printer, 233–234, 274
drop shadows, 311, 312–313, 383
Dual Brush setting, 36, 37

E

Edge Contrast setting, 69
Edge Touchup tool, 300
edges
    beveled, 473, 504–505, 511
    contrast, 69
    crisp, 300
    distorted, 351
    fading, 382, 383
    finding, 382, 383
    glowing, 387
    indented, 510–511
    layer masks, 350–352
    photographs, 351

shadows, 317, 320–321
touching up, 300
Wet Edges setting, 39
editing
channels, 277–278, 289, 291
layer masks, 343–344
text, 458–469
tools for, 26–56
effects
fireworks, 388
glow, 351–352, 386–391
Layer Mask Hides Effects checkbox, 356–357
lightning, 336–337, 342, 388, 399
Elliptical Marquee tool, 61–63, 72, 334
Emboss filter, 392, 393–394, 396, 480
embossing items, 393–394
Encapsulated PostScript (EPS), 303
EPS format, 122, 162, 284, 303, 366
Eraser tool, 29, 101, 102, 107–108
erasing
with Background Eraser tool, 29–31
with Eraser tool, 29
Exclusion mode, 400
Expand command, 80
Extract command, 295–301, 302
eyeballs, 100, 101, 272, 292
Eyedropper tool, 23, 78, 253–255, 260

F

Fade settings, 35
fading items, 35, 318, 322, 382, 383
Feather command, 78–79
Feather option, 62
feathered selections, 59, 87, 289–290
feathering, 91
File Browser, 49–51
file formats
BMP, 163
DCS, 284–286, 294
EPS, 122, 162, 284, 303, 366
GIF, 122, 162, 553–555, 559, 561
image maps and, 516
JPEG, 122, 285, 286, 551, 559, 561
line art, 162
PDF, 366
PSD, 122
slices and, 515, 516
TIFF, 122, 162, 285, 294, 366
File Transfer Protocol (ftp), 532
files
ASCII, 286
binary, 286
cloning between, 439
copying between, 104–105
GIF, 534, 549, 556–557
HTML, 531, 560
layered, 122
PDF, 48, 366, 457
Photoshop. *See* Photoshop files

reducing size of, 161
selecting everything in, 75
size of, 142
TIFF, 121
fill layers, 114
fills
layer masks, 348
Paint Bucket tool, 297–298
filters
applying to channels, 278–279
Clouds, 399–400
Color Halftone, 480
Diffuse, 316
Emboss, 392, 393–394, 396, 480
Find Edges, 382, 383
Gaussian Blur. *See* Gaussian Blur filter
Glowing Edges, 387
layer masks, 349–350
Lighting Effects, 387, 388
Offset, 482
Pattern Maker, 483–484
Plaster, 407
Pointillize, 377
Sharpen, 377
tileable, 480–482
Unsharp Mask. *See* Unsharp Mask filter
Find Edges filter, 382, 383
finding
edges, 382, 383
text, 469
fireworks effects, 388
Fit On Screen option, 18
Fixed Aspect Ratio option, 62–63
Fixed Size option, 63
flattening curves, 207–208
flattening images, 122, 161, 341
Flow setting, 28, 38, 39
Font field, 458
fonts, 458, 467, 507–508. *See also* text
Force Foreground checkbox, 300, 301
Foreground/Background setting, 37
Foreground To Transparent preset, 314, 315, 348
foregrounds
color, 18–19, 27, 46
Force Foreground checkbox, 300–301
gradients, 46
transparent, 314, 315, 348
formats. *See* file formats
frames, 531
freeform curves, 209–211
Freeform Pen tool, 317, 360
Freeze tool, 415
ftp (File Transfer Protocol), 532
Fuzziness setting, 76, 78

G

Gamma setting, 174, 229
gamut, 224, 225, 246, 264, 303
gamut warnings, 19, 263, 271, 275

Gaussian Blur filter
    grayscale and, 162
    layer masks, 350
    removing noise, 279
    retouching with, 448
    shadows, 315, 317, 318, 323
ghosting images, 203–205
GIF compression, 546, 552, 556
GIF files, 534, 549, 556–557
GIF format, 122, 162, 553–555, 559, 561
GIF images, 553
glow effects, 351–352, 386–391
Glowing Edges filter, 387
GoLive, 560
gradient bar, 22
Gradient Editor dialog box, 46
gradient layers, 114
Gradient tool, 43–47
gradients
    applying, 43–44
    color, 22, 45, 46
    curves and, 197–199, 201, 208, 212–213
    customizing, 46
    dithered, 45
    foreground color, 46
    layer masks, 348–349
    layers, 108
    presets, 44
    settings, 44
    shadows, 314
    simulating lighting with, 510
    transparency, 45, 47–48
graphics. See also images
    object-based vs. pixel-based, 456–457
    optimizing, 552–557
    Web. See Web graphics
graphics tablet, 415
grayscale, 165–188
    choosing, 22
    color correction and, 249–259
    Levels dialog box, 167–172
    neutral gray, 264
    posterization, 181–182
    Quick Mask mode and, 88–90
    resolution, 132–142
    in shadows, 321
grayscale channels, 290–292
grayscale images
    adjusting with curves, 201, 212, 213
    colorizing, 405, 409–410
    forcing to black and white, 279–280
    layer masks and, 347–348
    optimizing, 164–188
    printing, 174–179
    sharpening, 182–185
grayscale mode, 151
grids, 197–198, 200
grouping layers, 329–330, 332–335
grouping shadows, 333–334
Grow command, 81

H
halftone dots, 187
halftone screen, 154, 155
halftones, 134
halos, 263–264, 377, 406
Hand tool, 16
handles, 361–362
Hard Light mode, 393–394, 398–399
Healing Brush tool, 428–431
hiding
    with layer masks, 345
    palettes, 12
    selections, 345
Highlighter tool, 295–297, 298, 299
highlights, 255–257
    color correction and, 253–259
    dodging and, 441
    maximum settings, 177
    reflected, 450, 451
    Smart Highlighting checkbox, 296–297
    specular, 264, 450, 451
Highlights setting, 441, 443, 444
histograms, 168–169, 173–174, 180
History brush, 159, 160
horizontal scale, 461
HSB color, 53
HTML (HyperText Markup Language), 532
HTML files, 531, 560
HTML links, 517–520, 523, 531
http (HyperText Transfer Protocol), 532
hue
    brushes, 37
    described, 53, 401
    selecting colors by, 20–21
Hue mode, 401–402
hue/saturation/brightness blending modes,
    400–412
Hue/Saturation dialog box, 407–412
Hue setting, 37
Hue slider, 408, 411, 412
HyperText Markup Language (HTML), 532
HyperText Transfer Protocol (http), 532
hyphenation, 466

I
ICC profiles
    assigning, 239–240, 241
    canned, 227, 228, 234, 238
    converting to, 240, 241
    creating, 228–232
    custom, 228, 232–236
    described, 223–224, 246
    ICC, 223–224, 226, 246
    missing, 226–227
    monitor, 228, 229–232, 233
    obtaining, 227–228, 234–235
    printer, 233–237, 243
    printing press, 237–238, 241–242
    scanner, 238–241

standard publication types, 238
tagging images with, 226
visual adjustment, 227–228
Web browsers and, 551
Illustrator, 456, 457
Image Map palette, 523–524
Image Map tools, 523–530
image maps, 515–516, 523–524, 531. *See also* slices
Image Size dialog box, 131, 137
ImageReady, 522–523
   animation, 533–541
   described, 522–523
   GIF compression, 552
   image maps, 522–530
   image resolution and, 138–141
   layer styles, 528
   optimizing in, 549–550
   rollovers, 516, 524–530
   Rollovers palette, 516
   saving items, 559–560
   slices and, 523
   Styles palette, 528, 529
   tool palette, 528
images. *See also* graphics; Photoshop files
   16-bit, 181–182
   adjusting with curves. *See* curves
   background, 99–100, 335, 345
   black-and-white. *See* black-and-white images
   blending. *See* blending modes; collage
   blurring. *See* blurring
   cleaning up, 299
   cloning, 431–439
   colorizing, 293, 405, 409–410
   complex, 295–301
   converting to bitmap, 154
   cropping, 64–66
   fine tuning, 298–299
   flattening, 122, 161, 341
   ghosting, 203–205
   grayscale. *See* grayscale images
   information about, 50
   inverting, 209
   line art. *See* line art
   linking Web pages to, 519, 523
   locking, 109, 110
   optimizing. *See* optimization
   previewing, 49–50, 146
   refining, 159–160
   renaming, 51
   resizing, 43, 65
   retouching. *See* retouching process
   rotating, 64–65
   scanned. *See* scanned images
   scrolling around, 16
   selecting in File Browser, 50–51
   sharpening. *See* sharpening images
   slicing. *See* slices
   stock, 259
   straightening, 42, 154
   vector, 359, 365–366

imagesetters, 147
importing, 30
indexed color, 546
Info palette
   color samples, 25–26
   Curves and, 196, 214
   Measure tool and, 42–43
   measuring colors, 25
   overview, 25–26
ink ranges, 208
Inner Glow effect, 351–352
interface design, 489–511
Interlaced checkbox, 553
interlacing GIF images, 553
Internet, 138–141. *See also* Web
Inverse command, 76
IT8 targets, 238, 239

J

jaggies
   line art, 152–153
   printers, 366
   selections, 62
   text, 451, 456–457
   vector images, 359
   vector masks, 331
JavaScript, 519, 526, 531
Jelly type, 473–474
Jitter settings, 34–35, 36
JPEG compression, 544–546, 550
JPEG format, 122, 285, 286, 551, 559, 561

K

kerning, 460, 485, 507
keyboard shortcuts
   blending modes, 418
   channels, 304
   collage, 347, 368
   curves, 216
   layers, 117, 123
   optimizing images, 187
   palettes, 54
   retouching, 451
   selections, 75, 92
   shadows, 326
   tools, 54
   vs. screen mode shortcuts, 13
keyframes, 536, 542

L

Lab channels, 275
Lab color, 54
Lab mode, 203, 274–275
Lasso tool, 67, 74
layer clipping paths. *See* vector masks
Layer Mask Hides Effects checkbox, 356–357
layer masks
   Add Layer Mask command, 345

adjusting, 343–344, 352
blurring, 350
collage and, 330–331, 343–359
converting blending sliders into, 357–358
creating, 343–344
disabling, 346
edges, 350–352
fills, 348
filters, 349–350
gradients, 348–349
hiding information with, 345
link symbol, 354, 355, 364
moving, 354, 355
opacity, 347–348
pasting items into, 352–353
removing, 358–359
selections, 356
styles and, 356–357
switching between image and, 347
thumbnails, 347, 348, 356
transparent, 350
viewing, 347
layer sets, 117–118
Layer Style dialog box, 336, 472–473, 504–506
Layer Style menu, 110–112
layer styles
ImageReady, 528
layer masks, 356–357
Layer Style menu, 110–112
shape layers, 41–42
Web graphics, 504–506
Layer Styles dialog box, 471–475
layered files, 122
layers, 95–125. *See also specific layers*
activating, 98, 116, 117
adjustment, 112–113, 156–158, 333
alignment, 504
areas outside physical document, 91
background, 99–100
basics, 97–106
blurring and, 449
channels and, 275
cloning, 435
color, 120
copying, 116
creating, 97–98, 111
curves and, 202
described, 96–97
distorting, 106
duplicating, 106
eyeballs, 100, 101
fill, 114
gradient, 108, 114
grouping, 329–330, 332–335
keyboard shortcuts, 117, 123
linking, 107, 117
locking, 107–110
merging, 116, 120–121
moving, 103, 118

opacity of, 101–103, 123, 318
pattern, 114
properties, 120
repositioning, 364, 365
rotating, 42, 106, 539
scaling, 106
selecting, 115
shadows, 315
shape, 41–42, 500–504
solid color, 114
spot color and, 281–282
stacking order, 98–99
styles. *See* layer styles
switching between, 117
text styles, 471–475
Threshold, 155, 156
thumbnails, 119
transforming, 106
transparent areas of, 100, 103
trimming, 103–104
type, 470–471
Layers palette, 96–106, 117–119
leading, 459, 485
Levels dialog box
mask layer adjustment, 352–353
optimizing grayscale, 167–182, 185
Levels sliders, 167–186, 352
ligatures, 467
Lighten mode, 160, 386–388, 438, 448
Lighting Effects filter, 387, 388
Lightness slider, 409
lightning effects, 336–337, 342, 388, 399
line art
converting images to, 155–160
described, 132, 163
file formats, 162
jaggies, 152–153
resolution, 132, 152–153
scanning, 149–164
Linear Burn mode, 385
Linear Dodge mode, 391
Linear Light mode, 396–397, 399
lines
angles between, 43
drawing, 29
straight, 29, 68, 210, 434
lines per inch (lpi), 135–137, 147
Link Slices command, 558
link symbol, 354, 355, 364
linking layers, 107, 117
links, HTML, 517–520, 523, 531
Liquify command, 413
Liquify dialog box, 413–416
liquify tools, 413–416
Load Selection command, 84–85
Lock Transparency option, 107–109, 123
locking layers, 107–110
lossless compression, 561
lossy compression, 545, 556–557, 561

lpi (lines per inch), 135–137, 147
Luminosity mode, 202, 406–407
LZW compression, 153

M

Mac OS X
    CMYK settings and, 238
    profile creation, 228–232
Mac OS–based systems
    profiles, 228–232, 234
    RGB settings, 499
    vs. Windows, xii
Magic Wand tool, 70–71, 74, 76, 181
Magnetic Lasso tool, 68–70
magnifying glass trick, 334–335
marching ants, 87, 91, 290–291
Marquee tool, 334
marquees, 91
masks
    described, 303
    layer. *See* layer masks
    Quick Mask mode, 85–91
    type, 168
    Type Mask tool, 71
    Unsharp Mask. *See* Unsharp Mask filter
    vector. *See* vector masks
Matte color, 554–555
maximum shadow dot, 187
Measure tool, 42–43, 154
measurement system, 43
megapixels, 141
memory, 121, 417, 495–496
menu bars, 12
Midtones setting, 441, 443, 444
millimeters option, 459
minimum highlight dot, 187
Minimum settings, 34–35
Modify menu, 79–80
monitor
    browser dither and, 556
    calibration, 229–232
    color accuracy, 495
    color limitations of, 491–492, 556
    print size and, 17
    profiles, 228, 229–232, 233
    resolution, 494
    screen size, 15, 492–493
    settings for, 494
Monitor RGB working space, 226
Move tool
    accessing, 117
    arranging collages, 354–355
    layer masks, 354–355
    layers, 102–105, 354, 364
    moving layers, 118
    vector masks and, 364
multimedia, 138–141
Multiply mode, 324–325, 378–383

N

natural shadows, 311, 318–325
navigation, 15–18
Navigator palette, 15, 140–141, 146
noise
    brushes, 39
    color channels, 271
    described, 52–53
    digital cameras, 278–279
    GIF files, 556
    histogram and, 171, 173
    removing, 279
Noise setting, 39
Notes tool, 47–48

O

Offset filter, 482
Only Web Colors checkbox, 497
opacity
    brushes, 39
    cloning and, 433
    Eraser tool, 101, 102
    layer masks, 347–348
    layers, 101–103, 123, 318
    shadows, 316
    vs. transparency, 27–28
Opacity setting
    brushes, 39
    channels, 292
    layer masks, 347–348
    layers, 123
    Layers palette, 101–103
    Paintbrush tool, 27–28, 101–102
    painting tools, 38
    shadows, 316
optimization
    animations, 559
    combo images, 558
    graphics, 552–557
    grayscale images, 164–188
    ImageReady, 549–550
    keyboard shortcuts, 187
    photographs, 550–551
    Photoshop, 547–549
    rollovers, 559
    saturation, 262–263
    Web graphics, 543–561
    weighted, 544, 557, 558
Options bar, 14–15
Overlay mode, 391–392, 398
overprinting, 323

P

Paint Bucket tool, 41, 297–298
Paintbrush tool, 27–29, 101–102, 442
painting
    with Paintbrush tool, 27–29
    with Pencil tool, 27–29

retouching, 428–431
with spot colors, 283
tools for, 14–15, 27–29
palette alley, 6
Palette well, 8, 9
palettes
    Actions, 538–539, 540
    Animation, 535
    Brushes, 31, 32–40
    Brushes Presets, 31, 32
    Channels, 272–273
    Character, 458, 462–464, 469
    collapsing, 5–6
    Color, 21–22, 196, 497
    controlling, 4–7
    expanding, 8
    hiding, 12
    Image Map, 523–524
    Info. *See* Info palette
    keyboard shortcuts, 54
    Layers. *See* Layers palette
    Navigator, 15, 140–141, 146
    Paragraph, 458, 464–468, 469
    regrouping, 6–7
    repositioning, 5, 6, 9
    resetting defaults, 7
    Rollovers, 516, 524–527, 530
    showing, 12
    Slices, 523
    stacking, 8–9
    Styles. *See* Styles palette
    Swatches. *See* Swatches palette
    Tool, 13–14, 48–49
PANTONE colors, 21, 281–282, 304
PANTONE inks, 281, 282, 304
Paragraph palette, 458, 464–468, 469
Paste After Selection command, 537
Paste Into command, 346
Patch tool, 425–428
paths, clipping, 366–367
pattern layers, 114
Pattern Maker filter, 483–484
patterns, 480–484. *See also* textures
PDF annotations, 48
PDF files, 48, 366, 457
PDF format, 366
Pen tool, 361–363
Pencil tool
    defining curves with, 209–211
    painting with, 27–29
Perceptual option, 244
perspective cropping, 65–66
photographs
    adding text to, 203–204
    applying textures to, 392
    black-and-white, 409–410
    burning, 440, 443–446
    colorizing, 405, 409–410
    creating contour drawings from, 381–382
    distorting edge of, 351

dodging, 440–443
optimizing, 550–551
Photoshop
    new features, xiii–xvi
    optimization in, 547–549
Photoshop files. *See also* files; images
    File Browser, 49–51
    moving, 50–51
    opening, 49, 50
    previewing, 49–50
    renaming, 51
    selecting, 50–51
    straightening crooked, 42
    thumbnails. *See* thumbnails
Photoshop Tip of the Week, xiii
Pin Light mode, 398, 399
pixel-based text, 456–457, 507–508
pixels
    described, 130
    resolution, 130–131, 152, 359
    selecting, 79–80
    size of, 130–131, 152
    Web browsers and, 494, 495
    zooming to pixel size, 18
pixels option, 458–459
pixels per inch (ppi), 139, 145–146, 148
Plaster filter, 407
Pointillize filter, 377
points
    converting curves to, 210
    creating shapes from, 361–363
    described, 485
    measuring text in, 459–460
points option, 459
Polygonal Lasso tool, 68, 69
posterization. *See also* dithering
    curves, 210
    described, 52
    eliminating, 181–182
PostScript, 366
PostScript printers, 457
ppi (pixels per inch), 139, 145–146, 148
presets
    brushes, 31, 32, 39, 40
    Foreground To Transparent, 314, 315, 348
    gradients, 44
    rollovers, 528
    saving, 48
    swatches, 24–25
    Tool palette, 48–49
    tools, 48–49
    workspace, 9–10
previewing
    browser dither, 556, 559
    color, 19–20
    curves, 201
    images, 49–50, 146
    Photoshop files, 49–50
    printed images, 146
    rollovers, 559

print preview, 146
Print Size command, 146
Print Size option, 17, 18
printers
    desktop, 283–284
    drivers, 233–234, 274
    dye-sub, 132, 137, 147
    imagesetters, 147
    inkjet, 132–134, 147, 175, 366, 457
    jaggies, 366
    laser, 132, 134–137
    non-PostScript, 274
    PostScript, 457
    profiles, 233–237, 243
    resolution, 132-137, 152
    thermal-wax, 148
printers, professional. See printing presses
printing
    accuracy, 242–243
    grayscale images, 174–179
    resolution, 131–146
printing presses
    CMYK mode and, 243
    grayscale images, 175–179
    preparing for, 175–179
    profiles, 237–238, 241–242
    resolution and, 132, 152
    saturated colors and, 409
    simulating, 242, 243
profiles. See ICC profiles
Progressive option, 550–551
Proof Colors command, 19, 20, 499
Proof Setup option, 499
Propagate Frame 1 Changes feature, 530, 535
ProPhotoRGB working space, 226
PSD format, 122
Pucker tool, 413–414
Purity setting, 38

Q

Quick Mask mode, 85–91
quote characters, 465

R

Radius setting, 155, 156, 182, 183–186
RAM, 121, 417, 495–496
Range menu, 440–442
raster data, 365
Reconstruct tool, 416
reconstructed shadows, 311, 316–318
Rectangular Marquee tool, 60–61
Reflection tool, 414
reflections, 393, 450
Relative Colorimetric, 245
Render Clouds filter, 399–400
resampling, 142–145, 163
Reselect command, 75
resolution, 129–148

35mm slides, 138
color images, 132–142
described, 130
digital cameras, 141–142
dye-sub printers, 137
file size and, 142, 152, 153
grayscale images, 132–142
image quality and, 152, 153
increasing, 153
inkjet printers, 132–134
Internet and, 138–141
laser printers, 134–137
line art, 132, 152–153
monitor, 494
multimedia, 138–141
pixels, 130–131, 152, 359
printers, 132-137, 152
printing and, 131–146
printing press, 134–137
resampling, 142–145
scanned images, 132, 136–137, 494–495
scanners, 145, 153, 494
sharpening images, 145
vs. ppi, 145–146
Web browsers, 138–141, 494–495
Web graphics, 138–139, 494–495
Windows systems, 493
retouching process, 423–454
    Blur tool, 447–449
    Burn tool, 440, 443–446
    Clone Stamp tool, 431–439
    Dodge tool, 440–443
    Healing Brush tool, 428–431
    intensifying colors, 447
    keyboard shortcuts, 451
    overview, 424–425
    Patch tool, 425–428
    Sharpen tool, 449–450
    Sponge tool, 447
    toning down colors, 447
    wrinkle reduction, 448–449
RGB channels, 274
RGB color
    color management and, 220–224
    described, 53
    Mac OS systems, 499
    multimedia and, 19, 25
    Windows systems, 499
RGB color correction, 249–252
RGB mode
    curves and, 203, 212
    non-PostScript printers and, 274
    RGB Spectrum option, 22
    shadows and, 324–325
    uses for, 274
    vs. CMYK mode, 275
RGB working spaces, 225–227
rollover states, 525–527
rollovers
    complex, 529–530

creating, 524–530
described, 514, 531
image maps and, 516
ImageReady, 524–530
optimizing, 559
previewing, 559
simple, 528
triggering animations, 541
Rollovers palette, 516, 524–527, 530
Rotate transformation, 81–83
rotation
    images, 64–65
    layers, 42, 106, 539
    selections, 81–83
    thumbnails, 49
Rubber Stamp tool, 482–483

S

S curves, 208, 215
Sample Size option, 23
samples per inch (spi), 148
saturation
    brushes, 37, 38
    color, 20–21, 37, 38, 447
    described, 53, 402
    optimizing, 262–263
    selecting colors by, 20–21
Saturation mode, 402–404
Saturation settings, 37, 244, 447
Save For Web dialog box, 547–549, 559–560
Save Selection command, 84–85
saving
    alpha channels, 287–288, 294
    animations, 560
    brushes, 39
    in ImageReady, 559–560
    Input/Output settings, 211
    optimized images, 559–560
    presets, 48
    selections, 84–85, 287–288
    slices, 530–531, 560
    spot color images, 284–286
    swatches, 24
    vector data, 365–366
    for Web, 547–549, 559–560
Scale transformation, 81–83
scaling
    layers, 106
    selections, 81–83
scanned images
    jaggies, 152–153
    line art, 149–164
    resolution, 132, 136–138, 494–495
    sharpening, 154–155, 182
    straightening, 154
scanners
    24-bit, 180, 187
    30-bit, 180, 187
    D-max specs, 171

line art mode, 150
profiles, 238–241
resolution, 145, 153, 494
Scatter setting, 36
scratch disks, 417
screen, 492–493. *See also* monitor
Screen mode, 388–389
screen modes, 10–13
Select All command, 75
Select menu, 74–85
selections, 57–92
    adding to, 72
    alpha channels, 287–288
    basic tools, 60–71
    with Border command, 79
    color, 81, 90–91
    color ranges, 76–78
    complex images, 295–301
    complex objects, 72–74
    described, 58–59
    deselecting, 75
    distorting, 81–84
    enlarging, 80
    entire document, 75
    with Feather command, 78–79
    feathered, 59, 87, 289–290
    hiding, 345
    intersecting, 74
    inverse, 76
    isolating, 64–66, 90
    jaggies, 62
    keyboard shortcuts, 75, 92
    with Lasso tools, 67–70, 74
    layer masks, 356
    layers, 115
    loading, 85, 287–288
    with Magic Wand tool, 70–71, 74
    with Marquee tools, 60–63
    multiple objects, 72
    normal, 59, 87
    pixels, 79–80
    Quick Mask mode and, 90
    reducing size of, 80
    refining, 72–74
    reloading, 287–288
    removing part of, 73
    reselecting, 75
    rotating, 81–83
    rounding corners of, 80
    saving, 84–85, 287–288
    scaling, 81–83
    text, 71, 459
    with Type tool, 71
    "unfeathering," 89, 291–292
shadows, 309–326
    adjusting position, 312
    blurring, 315, 316, 318, 323
    brightness, 316, 322
    cast, 311, 313–316
    color, 322–323

Color Burn mode, 384
color correction and, 253–259
dodging and, 441
drop, 311, 312–313, 383
edges of, 317, 320–321
fading out, 318, 322
grouping and, 333–334
keyboard shortcuts, 326
light source and, 310–311
Linear Burn mode, 385
maximum settings, 177
natural, 311, 318–325
overprinting, 323
overview, 310–311
reconstructed, 311, 316–318
RGB vs. CMYK, 324–325
Threshold command, 255–257
transparent, 323, 324–325
types of, 311–325
Shadows setting, 441, 443
shape layers, 41–42, 500–504
shape tools
overview, 41–42
Web graphics, 500–504
shapes
brushes, 33–36
converting text into, 475–476
creating, 361–363, 502
custom, 502–503
for navigational elements, 500–504
Sharpen filters, 377
Sharpen tool, 449–450. *See also* sharpening images
sharpening channels, 278–279
sharpening images
automatic sharpening function, 438–439
cloned images, 438–439
color correction and, 263–264
grayscale, 182–185
resolution and, 145
scanned images, 154–155, 182
selectively, 447, 449–450
Shift Pixels tool, 414
shortcuts
keyboard. *See* keyboard shortcuts
screen mode, 13
Similar command, 81
Single Column Marquee tool, 63
Single Row Marquee tool, 63
skin tones, adjusting, 259–262
Slice Options dialog box, 518–520
Slice Select tool, 517, 518
Slice tool, 516–523
slices, 514–523. *See also* image maps
creating, 516, 521
described, 514, 531
layer-based, 521
moving, 517
names, 519
optimization and, 558
resizing, 517

saving, 530–531, 560
turning into HTML links, 517–520
types of, 516–517
vs. image maps, 515–516
Slices palette, 523
sliders
blending, 330, 336–343, 357–358
Hue, 408, 411, 412
Levels, 167–186, 352
Lightness, 409
resetting defaults, 167
Saturation, 408, 411, 412
Unsharp Mask, 183–186
Web Color, 21, 22, 497–498
slides, 138
Smart Highlighting checkbox, 296–297
smart quotes, 465
Smooth command, 80
Smooth setting, 505
snapshots, 154–155, 417
Soft Light mode, 392–393, 398–399
specular highlights, 264, 450, 451
spell checker, 469
spi (samples per inch), 148
Sponge tool, 447
spot channels, 270, 271, 280–286
spot color, 280–286
sRGB working space, 226
stair-stepping, 52, 181. *See also* dithering
stock images, 259
stripes, horizontal, 508
Style menu, 62, 458
styles
layers. *See* layer styles
text, 458, 463–464, 467, 471–475
Styles palette
ImageReady, 528, 529
Photoshop, 475–476
swatch books, 21
swatches
color, 46, 47
presets, 24–25
saving, 24
transparency, 47
viewing, 24
Swatches palette, 24–25
system palette, 493, 511

T

text
adding to buttons, 507–508
adding to photos, 203–204
alignment, 464
anti-aliased, 461–462, 507
baseline shift, 461
beveled edge type, 473
capitalization, 461, 462–463
character options, 462–464
Character palette, 458, 462–464, 469

color, 461
converting into shapes, 475–476
editing, 458–469
entering, 457
finding, 469
fonts, 458, 467, 507–508
hyphenation, 466
indenting, 464–466
intertwining, 475–476
jaggies, 451, 456–457
Jelly type, 473–474
kerning, 460, 485, 507
ligatures, 467
line breaks, 467
object-based, 456–457
Options bar, 468–469
Paragraphs palette, 458, 464–468, 469
pixel-based, 456–457, 507–508
replacing, 469
selecting, 71, 459
size, 459–460
spacing, 466
spell checker, 469
styles, 458, 463–464, 467, 471–475
textured type, 473
typographical controls, 458–469
vector-based, 456–457
vertical, 468
warped, 468–469, 471, 538
Web and, 507–508
Wild type, 474
text annotations, 47, 48
textures. *See also* patterns
applying to photos, 392
backgrounds, 476–479
brushes, 36–37
Linear Light mode and, 396
retouching and, 427
types of, 477–479
Thaw tool, 415
thermal wax, 148
Threshold command, 156–158, 255–257
Threshold layers, 155, 156
Threshold mode, 170–172, 179, 180
Threshold setting, 155–158, 183, 185, 186
threshold value, 163
thumbnails
File Browser, 49–51
layer masks, 347, 348, 356
layers, 119
resizing, 49
rotating, 49
sorting, 50–51
swatches, 24
vector masks, 363
TIFF files, 121
TIFF format, 122, 162, 285, 294, 366
tileable filters, 480–482
Tolerance setting, 70–71

Tool palette
illustrated, 13–14
presets, 48–49
Tool Presets palette, 48–49
tools. *See also specific tools*
keyboard shortcuts, 54
overview, 13–15
presets, 48–49
selection, 60–71. *See also* selections
Trace Contour feature, 381–382
tracking, 460, 485
Transform commands, 364–365
Transform Selection command, 81–84
transformations
layers, 106
vector masks, 364–365
Web graphics, 538–541
transparency
backgrounds, 30, 155
dithered, 555
foregrounds, 314, 315, 348
GIF format and, 553–555
gradients, 45, 47–48
importing and, 30
JPEG format and, 551
layer masks, 350
layers, 100, 103
locking, 107–109, 110
shadows, 323, 324–325
vs. opacity, 27–28
transparency swatches, 47
triggers, 527
Trim command, 161
trimming, 161
TruMatch colors, 21
Turbulence tool, 413, 414
Tween command, 536
tweening, 536–537
Twirl tool, 413, 414
type. *See* text
type layers, 470–471
Type Mask tool, 71
Type tool, 71, 457, 468
typographical controls, 458–469

U

Uniform Resource Locators (URLs), 532
Unify icons, 530
Units & Rulers command, 458–459
Unsharp Mask filter
color correction, 263–264
grayscale images, 183–185
line art, 155
Unsharp Mask process, 182, 187
URL field, 519
URLs (Uniform Resource Locators), 532
Use Unified Color Table option, 559
user slices, 517

V

vector-based text, 456–457
vector data, 365, 366
vector images, 359, 365–366
vector masks
    adding, 359–360
    collage and, 331–332, 359–367
    creating with Pen tool, 360–363
    deleting, 365
    described, 359
    disabling, 363
    modifying, 360
    Shape layer option, 42
    thumbnails, 363
    transforming, 364–365
vertical scale, 461
Via Copy option, 116
View menu, 16–18
virtual memory, 417
Vivid Light mode, 394–395

W

Warp tool, 413
warped text, 468–469, 471, 538
Web
    resolution and, 138–141
    saving images for, 547–549, 559–560
    text for, 507–508
Web browsers
    color and, 498–499
    downloads and, 550–551
    ICC profiles and, 551
    JavaScript support, 519
    memory and, 495–496
    pixels and, 494, 495
    resolution and, 138–141, 494–495
    text-only, 519–520
Web Color Sliders option, 21, 22, 497–498
Web graphics, 487–581
    animation, 533–541
    color, 495–498
    creating interface elements, 500–506
    design principles, 491–499
    design solutions, 506–511
    drill holes, 509–511
    image maps, 523–530, 531
    interface design, 489–511
    layer styles, 504–506
    navigational elements, 490, 503–506
    optimization, 543–561
    resolution, 138–139, 494–495
    rollovers, 524–530, 541
    screw heads, 508–509
    shape tools, 500–504
    slices. *See* slices
    sRGB working space, 226
    stripes in, 508
    transformations, 538–541
Web Graphics Defaults option, 499
Web pages
    animation and, 534, 541
    download times, 544, 547, 548
    linking to images, 519, 523
Web-safe colors
    choosing, 19, 20
    described, 496, 511
    dithering and, 19, 20, 497, 556
Web site, companion, xii–xiii
Wet Edges setting, 39
white, choosing, 20
Window menu, 9
Windows-based systems
    profile creation, 228
    profile location, 234
    resolution, 493
    RGB settings, 499
    vs. Mac, xii
workspaces
    preparing, 4–10
    presets, 9–10
    switching between, 10

Z

Zoom In option, 17
Zoom Out option, 16, 17
Zoom tool, 9, 16, 298–299
zooming
    fitting images to screen, 18
    in/out, 16, 17
    with Navigator palette, 15
    percentage settings, 18
    to pixel size, 18
    to print size, 18
    with View menu, 16–18
    with Zoom tool, 16

THINKER

RESOURCEKIT SIX / SIXTH SENSE / THINKER

stockbyte®
RESOURCEKIT SIX

RESOURCEKIT SIX is Stockbyte's newest collection of royalty-free stock photography. Twenty-one stunning titles are available for licensing as single images or CD collections.

To order your free copy of RK6, call Stockbyte today toll free at 1800 660 9262 or register at www.stockbyte.com.

Take a free test drive of some RK6 HIGH RESOLUTION images. Over $500 worth of FREE images are waiting to be downloaded when you register at www.stockbyte.com. Existing registrants simply need to log on and click on Free Images.

www.**stockbyte**.com/RK6
Toll Free 1 800 660 9262

HUNGRY FOR MORE?

SATISFY YOUR APPETITE

Join Ben in the never ending quest for Photoshop enlightenment!

Free Tip of the Week

Over 20,000 Photoshop users from all over the world enjoy Ben's free email tips. You can too. Sign up for Ben's FREE Tip of the Week at *www.digitalmastery.com/tips*

In-Depth Seminars

Over 12,000 design professionals have attended the most in-depth, comprehensive Photoshop seminar ever offered. Find out if Ben is coming to a location near you by visiting *www.digitalmastery.com/mainsite*

Can't Pry Yourself Away from your Desk? Get the Videos!

Learn from Ben at your own pace, on your own time with the Master Series videos that sold out at Photoshop World. Order the videos online now at *www.digitalmastery.com/videos*

WWW. DIGITALMASTERY .COM

Licensing Agreement

By opening this package, you are agreeing to be bound by the following:

This software product is copyrighted, and all rights are reserved by the publisher and author(s). You are licensed to use this software on a single computer. You may copy and/or modify this software as needed to facilitate your use of it on a single computer. Making copies of this software for any other purpose is a violation of the United States copyright laws.

Please remember that existing artwork or images that you may want to include in your project may be protected under copyright law. The unauthorized incorporation of such material into your new work could be a violation of the rights of the copyright owner. Please be sure to obtain any permission required from the copyright owner.

This software is sold as is without warranty of any kind, either expressed or implied, including but not limited to the implied warranties of merchantability and fitness for a particular purpose. Neither the publisher nor its dealers or distributors assumes any liability for any alleged or actual damages arising from the use of this program. (Some states do not allow for the exclusion of implied warranties, so the exclusion may not apply to you.)

WARNING! The Stockbyte low resolution (comping) images contained on the accompanying CD may not be used for any item which will be printed or published in any medium. Please carefully read the full text of your License Agreement, contained in the CD folder titled "Image Use Restrictions." By using the images you are consenting to the full terms of the license.